Prog Rock
FAQ

Prog Rock FAQ

All That's Left to Know About Rock's Most Progressive Music

Will Romano

Backbeat
Books

An Imprint of Hal Leonard Corporation

Published in 2014 by Backbeat Books
An Imprint of Hal Leonard Corporation
7777 West Bluemound Road
Milwaukee, WI 53213

Trade Book Division Editorial Offices
33 Plymouth St., Montclair, NJ 07042

Except where otherwise noted, all images in this book are from the author's personal collection.

The FAQ series was conceived by Robert Rodriguez and developed with Stuart Shea.

Printed in the United States of America

Book design by Snow Creative Services

Library of Congress Cataloging-in-Publication Data

Romano, Will, 1970–
   Prog rock FAQ : all that's left to know about rock's most progressive music / Will Romano.
      pages cm
   Includes bibliographical references and index.
   ISBN 978-1-61713-587-3
1. Progressive rock music—Miscellanea. I. Title.
   ML3534.R676 2014
   781.66—dc23

                                                                2014027918

www.backbeatbooks.com

For Sharon, Molly, Maggie, and Gilligan

Contents

Acknowledgments

I'd like to express my gratitude to those who have either participated in this project or given me the opportunity, time, assistance, support, inspiration, and encouragement to complete it. I'd like to express my gratitude to those who have either participated in this project or given me the opportunity, time, assistance, support, inspiration, and encouragement to complete it. Many thanks to the following (and to anyone I may have inadvertently omitted): Mick Abrahams, Lee Abrams, Jan Akkerman, Roye Albrighton, Dave Anderson, Ian Anderson, Jon Anderson, Jody Ashworth, Brian Auger, Julian Bahula, George and Judy Bailey, Benton-C Bainbridge, Dave Bainbridge, Carl Baldassarre, Peter Banks, Hugh Banton, Martin Barre, Nick Barrett, Michael Beck, David Bedford, Ray Bennett, Ronald S. Bienstock, Robin Black, John Bradley, Johan Brand, Ann Barbara Brenells, Jon Brewer, Adam Budofsky, Jessica Burr, Christopher Buzby, Debi Byrd, Nic Caciappo, Dik Cadbury, Fred Callan, Phil Carson, Michael Cartellone, Colin Carter, Bob Catania, John Cerullo, Roger Chapman, Ryche Chlanda, André Cholmondeley, Andy Clark, David Clemmons, Lindsey Clennell, Simon Collins, Marian Conaty, Nicolae Covaci, Chris Cutler, Frank Davies, Daniel Denis, Dave Doig, Tom Doncourt, Dwight Douglas, Geoff Downes, Terry Draper, André Duchesne, Francis Dunnery, Rod Edwards, Phil Ehart, Colin Elgie, Terry Ellis, Keith Emerson, Kim Estlund, Guy Evans, Richard Evans, Thomas Ewerhard, Franco Fabbri, Walter Bella "Wally" Farkas, Jesús Filardi, David First, Paul Fishman, Dave Flett, Kim Fowley, Fred Frith, Simon Frodsham, Peter Gee, Gregg Geller, Randy George, Jeff Glixman, Nigel Glockler, Mick Glossop, Ed Goodgold, Chip Gremillion, Patrick Gullo, Michelle Gutenstein, Jo Hackett, John Hackett, Steve Hackett, Randy Haecker, Roger Hand, Christopher Hansell, Michael "Thor" Harris, Annie Haslam, John Hawken, David Hentschel, Simon Heyworth, Rupert Hine, Mark Hitt, Steve Howe, Leslie Hunt, Tom Hyatt, David Jackson, Randy Jackson, Jakko Jakszyk, Gary Jansen, Eddie Jobson, Nat Johnson, Jessica Jones, Sidonie Jordan, Tim Kane, Dave Kean, Conrad Keely, Rick Kennell, Dave Kerzner, John Kosh, Bill Kotapish, Sonja Kristina, Brett Kull, Jean-Yves Labat de Rossi (M. Frog), Greg Lake, Justin Lang, Gary Langan, Jérôme Langlois, Dave Lawson, Geddy Lee, Anne Leighton, Collin Leijenaar, Chris Letchford, Martin Levac, Ron Levine, Jessica Linker, Steve Luongo, René Lussier, Chris Macleod, Patrick MacDougall, Nick Magnus, Bernadette Malavarca, David Mallet, Brian Malouf, Mark Mancina, Gered Mankowitz, Ed Mann, Manfred Mann, Sue Marcus, Toby Marks, Lee Marshall, Ryan Martin, Ian McDonald, Dave McMacken, Bruce Meek, Lesley Minnear, John Mitchell, Paddy Moloney, Patrick Moraz,

Alberto Moreno, Alan Morse, Neal Morse, Peter Morticelli, William Neal, Christiana Nielson, Per Nordin, Gerald O'Brien, Eddie Offord, Martin Orford, Christopher O'Riley, Dee Palmer, John Payne, Anthony Phillips, Gretchen Phillips, Shawn Phillips, Michael Phipps, Bruce Pilato, dUg Pinnick, Chris Poland, Peter Princiotto, Roger Quested, Paul Ramsey, Hossam Ramzy, Phillip Rauls, Luciano Regoli, Steve Reich, Keith Reid, Ron Riddle, Billy Ritchie, Robert Rodriguez, Mick Rogers, Michael Romano, Sharon Romano, Tony Romano, Glenn Rosenstein, Michael Rother, Steve Rothery, Coco Roussel, Paolo Rustichelli, Mike Sadler, David Sancious, Jonathan Schang, Paul Sears, Sandy Serge, Wil Sharpe, John Shearer, Peter Sinfield, Graham Smith, Martin Smith, Ray Smith, Sterling Smith, Chris Squire, Travis Stever, Gary Sunshine, David Surkamp, Kevin Sutter, Ty Tabor, Michael Tait, Stephen Takacsy, Jim Tashjian, Geoff Tate, Stephen W. Tayler, Sam Taylor, Rod Thear, David Thomas, Andy Tillison, Eric Troyer, Mick Underwood, Jim Vallance, Mark Volman (a.k.a. "Flo"), Virginia "Gini" Wade, Kevin Wall, Kelly Walsh, Darryl Way, Helmut Wenske, Paul Wertico, Ray Weston, John Wetton, Stanley Whitaker, Tony Williams, Steven Wilson, Bruce Wolfe, Frank Wyatt, Phideaux Xavier, and Carise Yatter.

Introduction
Signs of the
Aprogalypse

T hroughout the process of putting this book together, what has struck the author time and time again were stories of progressive rock artists who have demonstrated continued perseverance, innovativeness, and resiliency, under some of the most adverse conditions of this post-punk music world.

Prog has come a long way since its perceived implosion in the late 1970s and early 1980s. For decades, prog rock had been largely relegated to fringe status, and today, the music continues to surprise and thrive in what can only be categorized as a hostile mainstream musical environment. Prog rock has returned—and with a certain amount of credibility and respectability that wasn't always afforded the pioneers of this style who were making music in the 1960s and 1970s.

Several historical, cultural, technological, and social factors have helped to pave the way for prog's return, including the presence of the Internet in nearly every aspect of our lives, the formation of numerous record labels willing to claim and disseminate esoteric recordings (be they original or reissued), a loyal fan base with a long memory and attention span, artists' commitment to musical excellence, and the affordability and accessibility of recording technology—audio recording software—making it possible for aspiring prog rockers to cut their very own masterwork in the privacy of their own home studio.

Labels

Knowing that mainstream culture did not reflect their musical values, enterprising individuals established avant-garde, avant-prog, and progressive rock labels, from the mid-1980s through to today, helping to rescue the genre from near obscurity.

Spurred on by the ubiquity of the Internet, labels such as Musea, Cuneiform, Cyclops, Magna Carta, Laser's Edge, Inside Out Music, One Way Records, Repertoire, Esoteric Recordings, Syn-Phonic, ProgRock Records, ProgQuébec, ReR (Recommended Records, established in 1978), MoonJune Records, Vinyl Magic (and www.btf.it), Mellow Records, Japanese distributor Marquee, Kinesis retail site (www.kinesiscd.com), Kscope, Archie Patterson's Eurock (established as a radio program in the 1970s and eventually evolving into a mail-order company and retail website), and others have either discovered, promoted, or rehabilitated the reputations of artists in the progressive rock field. This is to say nothing of independent labels established by individual artists.

Media outlets continue to hold our attention: *Prog* magazine, *Progression* (published by John Collinge), *Exposé*, www.allaboutjazz.com, www.progressiveears .org, www.seaoftranquility.org, www.gepr.net (the Gibraltar Encyclopedia of Progressive Rock), www.Progarchives.com, www.DeliciousAgony.com, etc.

Important Signings

Despite the mainstream music industry largely ignoring progressive music, there have been a few significant major-label signings in the last two decades, including British band Porcupine Tree contracting with Lava/Atlantic in the early 2000s, and, previous to this, Pennsylvania-based prog rock band Echolyn joining Sony 550 Music's roster.

Formed in 1989, Echolyn released their Sony debut, *As the World*, smack-dab in the middle of the alt.rock revolution of the 1990s. Prior to this the band had been selling out three-hundred-seat theaters in the Philadelphia area and penning a twenty-eight-minute composition, "A Suite for the Everyman," which appears on their 1992 EP, *Suffocating the Bloom* (Velveteen), a song born out of the band's "struggles in trying to be ourselves," says guitarist/vocalist Brett Kull. "We were trying to do something different and still be in a rock band. That's it in a nutshell."

The band would eventually garner the attention of Michael Caplan, senior A&R executive at Sony Music, who was alerted to the band's growing following and intricate compositions through their manager William "Biff" Kennedy. "Michael was a fan of progressive rock and was looking to see if he could put the band U.K. back together," says Kull. "He was talking with Eddie Jobson and John Wetton and neither of those guys were interested in being in a band together at the time. At that point Michael said, 'Why am I wasting my time on these guys? There's got to be someone younger.' So, Michael and [industry veteran] Alan Mintz checked us out in the studio and said they would sign us. It was like we won the lottery."

The hope of some at the label was that Echolyn could drag prog rock kicking and screaming into the mainstream arena, again. Echolyn's music was so wide of the general public's tastes that it was being identified as "true alternative" music—more so than what was being labeled as such at the time.

"That was the billing: we were the alternative to the alternative," says keyboardist Chris Buzby.

"Not very many people were making this kind of music," says producer Glenn Rosenstein, a closet prog rock fan, who took a gig engineering for

Cinderella simply because Derek Shulman, formerly of Gentle Giant, signed the band to Mercury/Polygram.

Echolyn's highly orchestrated, Stravinsky-influenced, counterpoint-heavy prog rock was a shock to the mid-1990s music industry system. *As the World*, recorded in Nashville, Tennessee, boasted tracks that ran the gamut from the five-minute, autobiographical "The Cheese Stands Alone," to "Never the Same," written for a friend who lost his brother in a car crash, and the less-than-one-minute twelve-tone-inspired "The Wiblet."

"The recording process was intense for that record," says Rosenstein, who explained that the band did pre-production in their studio, a converted barn in West Point, Pennsylvania. "We were as meticulous as we could be in creating something that, if it was going to be competitive, it would be competitive with our favorite progressive rock records. Whether we accomplished that is not for me to say. But that's what we strived for."

Despite building a following in the Midwest and Canada, and going down a storm as the opening act for Dream Theater in 1995, Echolyn quickly became another music industry casualty when they were dropped by Sony in December 1995. "We wanted to try a number of things to keep up momentum," says Kull. "We wanted to have a website and the label said, 'What's a website?'"

"Their game plan was: make album, put the band on road, album sells, make money," says Buzby. "It wasn't meant to be. [The record] cost somewhere around three hundred eighty-five thousand dollars and they just wrote it off."

"Sony didn't want to sink a dime into promoting the record, in my opinion," says Rosenstein. "On a certain level, I can't blame them because there really wasn't a market for it. The guys really got swallowed up by the system, and it was pretty damaging to them individually. They went through some serious shit afterwards."

However, the fact that the band did not find commercial success with Sony—and briefly split up after the devastating incident—doesn't discount their experience. With the hindsight of two decades, what Echolyn accomplished was the near impossible. After all, this was a band from the outskirts of Philadelphia, who won a major-label deal, at a time when even the giants of the style couldn't, still suffering from residual effects of the punk revolution.

Today the band is playing better than ever and continues to develop their music and record independently, stressing a different focus for each of their releases, such as 2000's *Cowboy Poems Free* (a musical tapestry of true-to-life American stories, respective of the band members' individual family histories); *mei* (a Japanese word translated as dark and intangible, pronounced "may") from 2002, boasting one fifty-minute symphonic suite linked with the theme of reincarnation and containing lyrical concepts of love and redemption; and 2013's delectable, self-titled double album.

Other bands such as Spock's Beard, Glass Hammer, the Flower Kings, and Dream Theater—all of whom are said to be members of prog rock's third wave (the second involved European bands who were established or breaking in the late 1970s and 1980s, such as Pallas, Marillion, It Bites, Galadriel, Twelfth Night, Pendragon, Nuova Era, etc.)—were gaining, or would gain, fans by the thousands on both sides of the Atlantic.

Dream Theater, in particular, became the model for progressive metal bands everywhere (i.e., get out there, flash your chops, and you'll put asses in the seats). Although founding member Mike Portnoy has been booted from the band (the sordid details of which were described to the author off the record by a source close to the band), DT have consistently charted on *Billboard*'s Top 200 Albums chart since their earliest days, and continue to tour the globe based nearly solely on their virtuosity.

Festivals

Walking virtually hand-in-hand with the growth of labels was the evolution of prog rock festivals around the globe. ProgFest, Baja Prog, ProgDay, NEARfest, CalProg, RIO, Le Festival des Musiques Progressives de Montréal (FMPM), RoSfest, and ProgPower events in Europe all were established in the 1990s or later.

The Spanish band Galadriel, formed in 1986, solidified its resolve in the 1990s by releasing two studio records, *Chasing the Dragonfly* in 1992, which featured a distinct Spanish-music influence (a tradition Galadriel had sidestepped over the years), and five years later, *Mindscapers*. In 1996, the band was invited to appear at the nascent prog rock festival ProgDay in North Carolina.

"That show brought us to the U.S., and gave us the opportunity to play before folks in the U.S.," says Jesús Filardi, keyboardist and lead singer. "We met a lot of people who, we're sure, supported us for our next record, *Mindscapers*. Making music is good for the soul. Take it on the road, meet new people, visit different countries, share the experience with others and then you've got the makings of something special."

As codirector of ProgFest, held at UCLA's Royce Hall in 1993, Greg Walker, along with Gary Whitman and David Overstreet, helped to procure bands such as Änglagård, Kalaban, Citadel, Giraffe, and others. (Walker is also the founder of Syn-Phonic mail-order company, established in the 1980s, which evolved into a record label.)

Giraffe, which featured the late Kevin Gilbert, staged a performance of Genesis' *The Lamb Lies Down on Broadway* at the 1994 ProgFest in L.A., commemorating the twentieth anniversary of the monumental work. Gilbert assumed the role of Rael.

The band, composed of drummer Nick D'Virgilio, later of Spock's Beard and Genesis, guitarist Dan Hancock, bassist Stan Cotey, and keyboardist Dave Kerzner, had two weeks to learn the songs. "It was something insane where we had to learn two songs a day and we rehearsed it all the way through just once," says Kerzner, who relates that the band rehearsed in Gilbert's Lawn Mower and Garden Supplies Studio in Pasadena. "Then we just did it. It was the hardest gig I ever had to do, at the time. It was an amazing experience, but one of the things I learned is that is how you grow: you have to throw yourself into the fire."

Sadly, Gilbert died too young, but Giraffe's staging of *The Lamb* was a 1990s prog milestone, and the establishment of the festival ProgFest foretold of other events to come.

Paying Tribute

The establishment of tribute bands has also been an important part of prog rock's revival. Montréal's The Musical Box, for instance, is one of the leaders of this trend, recreating vintage Genesis performances for a worldwide audience hungry to witness the band's early productions replicated to a T.

It's perhaps no accident that The Musical Box was formed in the largest city in Quebec. Montréal, and Quebec, in general, is one of the prog rock capitals of North America, having given birth to acts such as Harmonium, Octobre, Maneige, Pollen (keyboardist/multi-instrumentalist Claude "Mégo" Lemay later became Celine Dion's musical director), Dionne-Brégent, Et Cetera, Morse Code, fusion bands Sloche and UZEB, chamber rock band Conventum, and others.

"Quebec, in terms of almost anything involved in the arts, is by far and away the leader in Canada," Stephen Takacsy, founder of the nonprofit Musique ProgresSon Music/ProgQuebec label in 2004, which promotes bands such as Conventum and Maneige among others. (Takacsy also put a stop to much of the illegal bootlegging of Quebec's prog recordings and helped to raise consciousness about little-known artists such as Jérôme Langlois, formerly the pianist/guitarist/wind player of the instrumental band Maneige. Langlois now performs classical avant-garde/progressive rock crossover music as evidenced by his 2005 release, *Molignak*.)

"There's something in the European blood here that is conducive to the arts and music, in particular," Takacsy continues. "I think, there were so many different influences in Quebec, whether it was American jazz and blues, or Quebec folk music, that Quebec became a kind of melting pot. When Peter Gabriel and those guys stepped off the 'boat,' they were welcomed with open arms. My belief is that had Genesis not caught on in Quebec, I'm not sure they would have caught on anywhere in North America. Those guys know that. When you speak with Peter or Phil Collins: they will tell you, 'Thank God for Quebec.'"

As if lending credence to this assertion, Greg Lake had always maintained that Montréal is a European island in the middle of the North America continent. "Greg Lake was right, I think," says Martin Levac, formerly the drummer of The Musical Box and currently leading the Phil Collins tribute act Dance into the Light. "Montréal has, indeed, a particular character, that's quite different from any other cities in North America. The Latin-European cultural influences of Montréal might be a possible explanation as to why prog music, and especially a band like Genesis, was so popular here."

In the 1970s, unconventional music was being composed and recorded by Quebec artists such as (clockwise from top left) Conventum, Pollen, and Jérôme Langlois (cofounder of Maneige), among others.

Some maintain that Quebec's amalgamated pop culture is due, in part, to artists' fierce independent spirit walking hand-in-hand with the politically charged environment of the province in the late 1960s and early 1970s. "I think the impact of the separatist movement in Quebec had an effect on me—and a lot of people in Quebec," says André Duchesne, one of the founding members of Conventum who, in the mid-1980s, formed Les 4 Guitaristes de l'Apocalypso-Bar, which also featured Conventum guitarist René Lussier. "The army was here and everyone was 'frozen.' It was frightening. We were not sure if our phones were being tapped. At that moment, it was a political decision for me to develop my music in an unconventional way."

Exactly why progressive rock found a foothold in certain regions in North America or Europe, such as Quebec or the Northeast or the Midwest of the United States, might be difficult to pinpoint. Some speculate that it was simply due to the playlists of radio stations in proximity to certain large cultural centers. Others subscribe to the theory that it was a mysterious alignment of time, place, and opportunity. Whatever the arrangement or ingredients, Quebec had a big part to play in the early development of the careers of British progressive rock bands—and a tastemaker like Takacsy is doing a great job preserving the province's progressive rock legacy.

Subgenre

One of the many subgenres, or subsects, of prog rock has been the development of Christian Progressive Rock (CPR), which claims Ajalon, Iona, Syzygy, Glass Hammer, Neal Morse, and Unitopia among its major proponents.

Prog rock and spirituality, or even Christianity, are not mutually exclusive concepts. Numerous prog rockers over the years have dealt in religious or spiritual themes, from Genesis to Yes to Kansas to Geoff Mann of Twelfth Night, but there never appeared to be a unified movement—a kind of Rock in Opposition (RIO) for the Christian crowd—connecting artists of faith, who feel the need to praise God through their music and support one another's endeavors.[1]

In 2004, bassist Randy George (Neal Morse, Ajalon), along with Gene Crout, co-produced the first CPR CD compilation as a two-disc set, and included names such as Kerry Livgren, Rick Wakeman of Yes, and Morse. (There are four compilations available via www.cprog.com.) Fittingly enough, it was Wakeman who gave George's band, Ajalon, its first big break. "Rick had started his Christian record label [Hope Records] and was looking for talent," says George. "I thought we sounded a lot like Yes so we sent a copy of our first record, a cassette of *Light at the End of the Tunnel*, to Rick. He liked it and, to our surprise, he released it on CD for us."

Perhaps the most visible supporter of the CPR cause is former Spock's Beard frontman/keyboardist/guitarist/songwriter Neal Morse, whose music can often be autobiographical, even testimonial, but rarely strays from Christian-based themes.

Morse told the author that he had grieved over his decision to leave Spock's Beard in the early 2000s, just at the point when the band appeared to be on the cusp of a major breakthrough with the release of their concept double album, *Snow*.[2] Morse claimed God called him to do so, but in the immediate aftermath of his exit, Morse was still filled with uncertainty in his life.

"While I was grieving and going through this decision process, I remembered when Jesus was in the Garden of Gethsemane, and he is praying, and [the Bible] says that he sweat drops of blood," Morse said, who explained that right around the time of the record's release his daughter, Jayda, was diagnosed with a heart condition. (After surgery and much prayer, Jayda's health improved.) "That's how grievous it was for him to face the cross. I don't mean to be overly dramatic, but I think of that time as being my Gethsemane. To [leave the band] was so hard for me, mainly because of the guys and because my own brother [Alan, guitarist] was in the band. It was a hard thing to do, but I knew it was right. The more I prayed about it I knew that God would take care of them and it would be okay, ultimately. And, anyway, I became afraid to stay. If God is not 'in' something, I believed, then it can become dangerous to stay in it."

Putting it all on the line—his music, his career—Morse took the biggest leap of faith of his life. "My wife and I put our house on the altar," Morse said. "We didn't know if all the fans and people at the record company would disown us. I didn't even know if God was going to call me into some other line of work or if he wanted me to continue in music."

Before long, a dramatic turn of events, what J. R. R. Tolkien would have called the "eucatastrophe," changed Morse's life forever—and for the better. "Then the *Testimony* album exploded in my mind," Morse said. "But before that it was a matter of months not knowing what was coming."

Neal Morse (left) in Wolverhampton, England, with Luca, David Bainbridge's son, subject of the *Songs for Luca* releases.   *Photo by David Bainbridge*

Testimony, released in 2003, is still one of Morse's most popular solo records. "There's something about a first-person testimony," Morse said. "That was the first time I had written from the first-person perspective and told the whole truth. I wasn't hiding behind a character. It was pretty interesting to write an album from the perspective of everything being true and not needing to construct a work of fiction to get my point across."

Confessional lyrical themes aren't the norm in progressive rock. "A lot of times in prog, you're writing words that make you feel something, but you're not sure what they mean," Morse said. "There isn't a whole lot of imagery on *Testimony*. I tried to tell my story in the most direct way possible."

Testimony is, essentially, Morse's search for God, his leaving the party life of rock and roll, experiencing a spiritual awakening. "I had written a couple of ideas I thought I could put into a concept album about how God has dealt with me and how Jesus entered into my life," Morse said. "Once I did, it just poured out. . . . *Snow* took two years and *Testimony* took about a month. It rolled out. Quite a gift from God."

"Neal's autobiographical approach certainly connects to his listeners and many can relate to his openness and honesty, and his recurring theme of the prodigal returning to the Father," says guitarist/keyboardist Dave Bainbridge of Irish Celtic/prog band Iona. "With Iona's music our focus has generally been on our connections to the ancient roots of our faith and also the joy and exuberance in knowing 'The Great Other' in our lives. Less specifically autobiographical than Neal's lyrics, but I think what people really respond to in both is the honesty and passion we both share. We have listeners of many faiths and of no faith but get incredible responses from all."

"People who could not stand Neal's Christian message stopped coming to the gigs," says drummer Collin Leijenaar. "But, somehow, that's always a small number of people. In the years I played with Neal, from February 2005 until August 2011, I saw his audience grow and more and more people digging his music. And, also, because of his Christian message, a lot more Christians are coming to his shows."

The author spoke with some men of the cloth who had questioned whether Christians should become entangled in rock music and, more specifically, the rock lifestyle, thus taking their focus away from praising God and putting their energies into, shall we say, distracting extracurricular activities. By contrast, nearly every progressive rocker that I'd contacted who is Christian rebuked such sentiments.

"[M]usic was originally meant to be a means by which our spirits could connect to the Great Creator and be in awe at his glory rather than ours," says Bainbridge.

"If there's the element of joy in the process and production and in the way the people are being affected by the art, then I think that's a great thing," says Peter Princiotto (However).

"Some people would say that any music apart from Christian music is self-centered and could be worship of self or idolatry, but I would say that the same dangers of pride and selfishness exist in playing Christian music, too," says Peter Gee (Pendragon). "Ultimately it all comes back to your heart. Do you desire in your heart to worship God when you're playing music, whether secular or Christian? If the answer is yes, then I believe that God is pleased with this worship and honors and receives it."

The Grunge Connection

As prog was gathering force, preparing for a comeback, innovative artists from all corners of the musical underground were surfacing.

While King's X may not fit within the parameters of some listeners' definition of progressive rock, elements of their music, such as rich multipart harmonies, soulful and personal lyrical concepts, alternate tunings, mammoth distorted bass tones, studio experimentation, and orchestral flourishes (the latter, in large part, due to classically trained musician and one-time band producer/manager Sam Taylor), had put them on the cutting edge of soul-metal in the late 1980s and early 1990s.

Alternative rock, or "grunge" as it would become known, revolutionized an industry, killing off "dinosaur" bands that were surviving (even thriving) in the George H. W. Bush era. Yet, many of the proponents of the so-called Seattle sound, from Alice in Chains to Pearl Jam, had been influenced by King's X, a band formed in 1980 and evolved from bands such as The Edge and Sneak Preview, which covered bands such as Yes in their early concerts.

Although rock artists had performed in alternate or drop tunings for years, few had claimed such maneuvers as a musical style. King's X, with the help of Sam Taylor, did just that, creating a heavy, melodic, even mystical sound that, despite followers and admirers, has yet to be matched.

"In a place like Seattle, as it was, major bands didn't always come through in the '70s and '80s," says bassist/vocalist Doug (a.k.a. dUg) Pinnick. "So, when we came through, most of the major artists who were in Seattle would come to see us. People like Jerry Cantrell from Alice in Chains and the Pearl Jam guys. We were on the cover of *Kerrang!* magazine with the cover line that read something like 'ushering in a new kind of metal.' I mean Ty [Tabor, guitarist/vocalist] put his guitar in drop D. He grew up on bluegrass and he wrote a song that was more or less in that style of tuning, which was 'Pleiades' [co-written by Dale Richardson]. He really wanted to play his own version of the Beatles' 'I Want You (She's So Heavy)'—and this was two years before we recorded it. So, when I heard this, I went home and tuned down my bass. You have to understand that people like Van Halen and Black Sabbath tuned down, too. We weren't the first. But most people played in 440 standard tuning. Metallica played drop tuning, but we went two steps down from there. What we had was the funk grooves with a more structured prog thing."[3]

The author had witnessed a show in the early 1990s at New York City's Limelight, a converted church that felt as though it was harboring ghosts of past parishioners and sinners alike. King's X was the headliner this night and Alice in Chains, a band largely unknown outside of Seattle at that point, was the support act. It was a study in contrasts—and a lesson about history and how it's written.

Aside from the bizarre after-set stage antics of Alice drummer Sean Kinney, who rushed from behind his kit to take the forefront of the stage and appeared to mock-masturbate his drum sticks (or with them), Alice's set was well played but not particularly outstanding.

The main course was, of course, the trio from Katy, Texas, who delivered in a big way, even though two-thirds of the band was fighting the flu. Although we may not have been aware of it at the time, this slightly covert prog rock band, with Christian ideals, was directing the entire music-listening world to the next big thing in rock—from deep inside a secularized, once sanctified, building.

"Basically Jerry Cantrell [Alice in Chains guitarist] came up to Jerry [Gaskill, King's X drummer] and said, 'I can't wait for your next record, so that we'll have something to steal,'" says Tabor. "That was his exact phrase. It was meant to be a compliment. Doug wrote the song 'Faith Hope Love' on a twelve-string bass. Put on Pearl Jam's 'Jeremy' and you will hear exactly where it came from. All our friends are famous and they borrowed heavily."

Alice had released their Columbia Records' debut, *Facelift*, in August 1990, but King's X's 1988 debut, *Out of the Silent Planet*, and its seminal follow-up, 1989's *Gretchen Goes to Nebraska*, were instant classics and studied by up-and-coming metal acts on both sides of the Atlantic. (In case you missed King's X live at the time, check out Molken Music's limited edition concert DVD, *Gretchen Goes to London: Live at the Astoria*, recorded in May 1990.)

"At first it freaked me out when I heard Alice in Chains," says Pinnick. "I just went, 'Oh, my God. They sound like us ... but better.' They stripped it down to what I love about King's X. Take all our muse away and all the frills and all the stuff that we pile on top of [the composition] and that little piece of meat there is Alice in Chains. They admitted it to us. They said that we were a big inspiration to them. I admired them because they were inspired by our sound that created something that changed the world. I used to want to sit back and take credit for it, but I realize that nobody can take credit for anything. We're all copying each other all the time and everything I do even to this day is copied from someone."

King's X: The true fathers of grunge?

After the band's relationship with Taylor disintegrated, King's X doubled down on guitar-heavy grunge, releasing 1994's *Dogman*, produced by Brendan O'Brien. (*Dogman Demos*, an MP3 download release, issued via Molken Music, www.molkenmusic.com, recorded in 1993, demonstrates just how little the songs were altered from their initial state.)

"That was in your face," says Tabor. "We split from Sam Taylor and by the fourth album [self-titled] we felt like we were repeating ourselves. We were parodying ourselves. I think we were asking ourselves, 'What are we now?' I bought new equipment to make me play differently. We laid down that stuff and it was raw and brutal. We were dropping to C and B and even dropping down to low A. We were inventing tunings in low registers."

Widespread mainstream success would prove elusive for King's X, but the band's greatest work, *Gretchen Goes to Nebraska*, a title dreamt up by a roadie as a joke, remains a classic of the progressive metal genre.

"When I was discussing the cover art with illustrator Jim McDermott," says Taylor, "I told him that I wanted the cover to depict a chunk of space being ripped from infinity and Ty's, Jerry's, and Doug's faces carved into the trees. The idea of the record was to take someone on a journey: take them out of space and time."

King's X and Taylor succeeded: the band may never go multiplatinum, but its radical material and approach remains timeless.

From Small Beginnings

I view this work as a kind of alternative history of progressive rock that will, hopefully, shine a light on some of the more underappreciated artists of the genre. The deeds and music of people such as Echolyn, Billy Ritchie, and even Peter Banks, who sadly died in March 2013, have filled my head for years. Banks, in particular, has been a much-misunderstood figure, who, in the times I'd spoken with him, was still confused, decades on, as to why he was asked to leave the band Yes.

Banks' electric guitar playing, of which The Who's Pete Townshend was a fan, was simply visionary and, arguably, just as inventive as that of his legendary and versatile replacement. It's commonly accepted as fact that it was Banks who had thought up the name Yes, and that he was a focal point of the band's live performances.

"Peter was a tortured genius, like so many people born with incredible gifts," says ex-wife Sidonie Jordan (a.k.a. Sydney Foxx), co-founder of Banks' post-Yes/post-Flash band Empire. "Sometimes we rise above the cruelties in our life and sometimes I think they take us down."

The entire Yes episode plagued Banks with questions. It was these questions, seemingly, that dogged him even as he formed his next band, Flash, with singer Colin Carter, bassist Ray Bennett, and drummer Mike Hough.

The history and trajectory of Flash is a messy one. At different moments members were either walking out or nearly axed in some half-baked scheme. Talk of replacing Banks had surfaced during the sessions for the band's second album, 1972's *In the Can*, when Derek Lawrence had suggested the band dump Banks and get someone like Eric Clapton or Ritchie Blackmore, both friends of the producer. To their credit, the band declined to take Lawrence up on his invitation. Subsequently, and ironically, Peter was plotting to replace Carter with a female singer, his future wife (and ex-wife) Sidonie Jordan. The band broke up, in Albuquerque, New Mexico, before this could come to pass, and today Jordan takes issue with the notion that she's responsible for the irreparable damage suffered by Flash. (Carter, who claims he was being courted by the band Captain Beyond at the time, simply acknowledges, "Mistakes were made.")

The original Flash lineup was full of potential, a potential that was sullied by irrational motives, impossible expectations, numerous communication breakdowns, *Spinal Tap*-esque mishaps, seemingly deliberate acts of sabotage, and Banks' personal prescription for self-medication—a cocktail of foreign substances.

In later years, Banks acknowledged that his erratic behavior was a band stressor and took responsibility for some of the problems arising among the members. "Certainly with Flash there was a self-destructive element within myself," Banks told me. "If you'd asked other people they would agree with that. Certainly with other projects of mine there was a point, not necessarily when things were going well, but there was always a point where I would get frustrated because it wasn't quite going the way I thought it would. I would take most of the blame, not for the disastrous things that happened to [Flash], but for being very impulsive and saying, 'That's it. No more.' I quit the band while we were on tour in America. After I quit, in the

The Empire material, some of which includes Phil Collins on drums, went unreleased for years. The above image was the "projected album cover," says Sidonie Jordan (a.k.a. Sydney Foxx), for recordings done at Cherokee Studios in Los Angeles in the late 1970s, and was intended for release through Tattoo Records/Warner Bros. Music. In the 1990s Banks inked a three-record deal with One Way Records. At press time Gonzo Music was set to reissue Empire tracks on CD. *Courtesy of Sidonie Jordan*

middle of night, I realized [laughs], 'Oh, God. What have I done?' . . . I think I knocked on everybody's door and, of course, nobody wanted to speak with me. I said, 'I am really sorry. This is ridiculous. We have to finish the tour. We've got four more gigs to go. I'm sorry . . . Let's go back to England and talk about it . . . I'm an idiot. . . .' I was still probably extremely drunk."

"Flash broke up in 1974, and we all continued to be friends for a few years and worked together in different combinations," says Bennett. "Colin and I had a short-term band that started and stopped fast. I did some recordings with Peter and his wife and played on some sessions with them and briefly with their band Empire. When Peter and his wife [Jordan] split up, I got involved with her for a while, and did some recordings with her. This was in late 1970s into the early 1980s. The final episode was in L.A. in the early '80s when I got into a fistfight with Pete in a bar. That was the last time I saw him. We spoke on the phone and I sent him my solo album, *Whatever Falls*, and Peter loved it. He was very complimentary. This was right around the time we were talking about doing a Flash reunion."

"I happened to have the misfortune of being boyfriend and girlfriend with Ray," says Jordan. "I do regret that. Not because of Peter. It was because Ray was married and separated and had a daughter, and it was wrong."

What sometimes gets lost in all of the behind-the-scenes drama is Flash's initial optimism and the successes it tasted. Flash achieved a Top 30 U.S. hit with the edited version of "Small Beginnings," a kind of electric guitar symphony that's part "Pinball Wizard" and part Mahavishnu Orchestra's "Meeting of the Spirits," featuring former Yes organist Tony Kaye on keyboards, who declined the opportunity to join Flash full-time to devote his energies to his own projects, which would soon include his own band, Badger.[4] In fact, the entire first album is brilliant and the band was going to release Bennett's "Children of the Universe," a song informed by Max Ehrmann's inspirational poem "Desiderata" as the second single, when Capitol Records asked for a second album, instead.

Over the years there had been talk and overtures to reunite Flash. But, apparently, too much time and too much bad blood had passed, and too many unforgivable personal transgressions had eroded whatever trust existed between the former bandmates. One of the last times the original Flash attempted to make it work—in the early 2000s—they couldn't even agree on a location for rehearsals.

"I suggested we get together in Ohio and let my friend George Mizer arrange a rehearsal place," Banks told me. "My whole idea was to get together for three or four days and see if anything worked. If it didn't, then we would just knock it on the head and not do it anymore. I just wanted to see if we could all be together for twenty-four hours without arguing."

Banks told the author he simply could not bear to see his beloved Flash playing two-hundred-seat (or less) theaters in secondary cities across the U.S. and Europe. It's a tough pill to swallow, perhaps, to know that material you consider classic must be resold to a new generation of fans. The reality is, of course, that any rock act, and this is particularly true of bands trying to survive and make it in the music biz in the early twenty-first century, has to get on the road and promote themselves.

"I think [Peter] had the same thing wrong with him that Michael Jackson had," says Jordan. "He wanted to hit the high notes, again. Can you imagine watching your friends, the people for whom you helped develop a sound, getting rich while you're struggling? I don't know how one overcomes that without becoming bitter and angry and having it destroy your life. The same thing happened to my mother: she couldn't cope with life and her anger, so she drank. She gave up."

In recent years, Bennett and Carter had stayed in contact with each other, and have since resurrected Flash, performed at Baja Prog in 2005, and recorded and released a studio record, *Flash Featuring Ray Bennett & Colin Carter* in 2013, boasting original material as well covers of Nine Inch Nails and Flash. (In addition, and concurrently, Banks was working on releasing a vintage live recording of Flash from 1973 at the time of his death. *Flash—In Public* surfaced in 2013. See www.peterbanks.net.)

Before Banks died, friend and booking agent, Nic Caciappo, threw the guitarist a lifeline and was in the process of setting up a tour for him with American band Ambrosia, a quasi prog outfit, as his backing band. "The drummer, Burleigh [Drummond], was friends with Peter and lived with him for a while when Peter was living in Los Angeles," says Caciappo. "Peter said that Ambrosia was one of his favorite bands when he was living in L.A. The plan was for Peter to play some Yes and Flash material. I started pouring money into it, and then Peter got sick, and that caused doubts. I called the guys in Ambrosia and said, 'I think we'll have to do this at another time.' If Peter had remained healthy it would have been a great tour and a great thing to see. At that time I was talking to Jon Anderson about it and was close to having Jon perform a couple of songs with them in L.A., maybe 'Sweet Dreams.' At that time Peter had in his mind that it would be great if we could record a version of 'Sweet Dreams' with Trevor Rabin. Trevor was a big fan of Peter's. Big supporter.

"When Peter was sick in the hospital the last time [2012], I called Jon [Anderson] to tell him about it, and Jon said, 'Get me the number where he is at,'" Caciappo continues. "Jon called Peter on the phone and the conversation wasn't too easy for Peter, but Jon said, 'This is another path you have to take. Get well, and when you do get well, let's make some music together, Pete. Let's make some songs together.' Jon said he did that to give him some motivation and some happiness. Jon still cared about Pete a lot. Jon told me that Peter never called him back once he did get out of the hospital."

It's sheer speculation as to why Banks never phoned Anderson, but perhaps Banks knew his health was in irreversible decline and decided not to commit to anything. Perhaps he was still snakebit about Yes past or the infamous *Union* tour fiasco in which he was invited to perform on stage with the band in L.A., only to be turned away and humiliated. Perhaps Banks simply decided to let sleeping dogs lie. It's difficult to discern—and we'll never know for certain.

Regardless of the past, bruised egos, or failed reunions, when all the smoke clears, what's left is Peter's incredible command of the fretboard and those crazy triplets spider-crawling all over the optimistic and exuberant nine-minute album version of "Small Beginnings."

Some had tagged Flash a Yes copy band and for years Banks was in denial about his work with his former band, and would go to great lengths to distance himself from that juggernaut. In many ways Flash *did* resemble Yes, but in retrospect this was unavoidable. Banks was a member of Yes and organist Kaye was guesting on the band's first album. And, for cryin' out loud, it was Yes' former drummer, Bill Bruford, who directed bassist Bennett, a childhood friend, to Flash when the band was still in its embryonic stages.

"Since I was from Yes, people thought Flash sounded somewhat like Yes, which used to annoy the hell out of me," Banks said. "I used to say, 'Of course it doesn't. Of course it doesn't.' Well, of course, *it did*, because I had been the guitar player in Yes and that never really occurred to me until . . . probably three years after Flash had broken up."

"Being compared to Yes was probably a mixed bag," adds Colin Carter. "The first album, two out of the five guys who were in Yes at one point were recording this material, so what do you expect it to sound like? Truly, the last thing we wanted to do was something that sounded like Yes."

"Peter always claimed to have written that main riff of 'Roundabout' [a Top 20 U.S. hit]," adds Caciappo. "He eventually recorded that riff on the *Two Sides of Peter Banks* album [recorded simultaneously with Flash's third album, *Out of Our Hands*], for the song 'The White Horse Vale,' but it was more swingin' . . . A couple notes are different, but it was largely the same. I asked Peter about that, and he said 'Oh, yeah, that's the riff. I was playing that a lot during the gigs in the last year with the band. I would play that during soundcheck, and think about that riff.'"[5]

To what extent Banks contributed to Yes' material, even in his absence, is unknowable. And just how far Flash could have gone had the guitarist been more centered and stable remains to be seen. Whatever his contributions, and regardless of his personal proclivities, Banks was, to steal a phrase from his old bandmate Bruford, "One of a kind."

This book is, in part, dedicated to the spirit of Banks and every prog rock artist who never received proper credit and who continues to fight the good fight.

Prog Rock
FAQ

Clockwork Soldiers

Are Proto-Prog Rockers Clouds the True Fathers of a Musical Movement?

usic journalists have done their best to document the rise of progressive rock in the second half of the twentieth century. The basic narrative that rock musicians, particularly in Britain, began taking cues from jazz, folk, classical, and other forms of music to forge a new subgenre is generally accepted as historical fact today.

But so much of prog's history has happened in the margins and in between the pages of countless biographies, guidebooks, and encyclopedias. Opposing and alternative views of history are often dismissed, even ridiculed, while valuable information—and dynamic musical personalities—remain shrouded by decades of pop culture trends.

Such is the story and fate of William Edward "Billy" Ritchie, one of the early lead organists of the British rock scene of the mid- and late 1960s.

Ritchie, along with Procol Harum's Matthew Fisher, Jon Lord (Deep Purple), Vincent Crane (the Crazy World of Arthur Brown and Atomic Rooster), Mike Ratledge (Soft Machine), Brian Auger, South African Manfred Mann, Rod Argent (Zombies, Argent), Don Shinn, and Keith Emerson, was in a select group of superior class of organ players breaking ground in the new psychedelic, proto-prog, jazz-pop, and/or hard rock fields. Yet, Ritchie, and his bands 1-2-3 and Clouds, have largely been filtered out of the mainstream discussion on progressive rock, like water through a kitchen strainer.

"History always depends on who's telling the story," says Ritchie. "When I read autobiographies, biographies, or accounts of bands of that period, I sometimes wonder if I was ever there at all. Rock history is no different to mainstream history in that sense."

Often the downside of being on the cutting edge is experiencing the agony of invention, roaming the wilderness of innovation, and learning painful life lessons, while followers make clearly designed plots to conquer the world.

"A tendency I've noticed in rock musicians is to cite influences, or so-called influences, that are not related to them, i.e., jazz musicians, obscure artists, especially from another genre," says Ritchie, Scottish by birth, living in London at the time of this writing. "This, of course, is to distance themselves from the

1-2-3: The first U.K. progressive rock band?

real influences—their contemporaries and rivals."

It's almost Shakespearian, really: Ritchie's bands 1-2-3 and Clouds created some extraordinary work, but did not achieve much commercial success, and imploded at the exact time when their prog rock contemporaries, such as the Nice (formed in 1967), ELP, King Crimson, and Yes (formed in 1968) were hitting pay dirt. Perhaps it's just this unfortunate timing, at the moment when the machinations of the nascent rock music business were powering up to propel musical talent to the stratosphere—when Britain was effortlessly churning out commercially successful bands—that has made Ritchie's and 1-2-3/Clouds' checkered bio so frustrating and imbued with what one U.K. writer termed a romantic sense of Scottish heroic failure.

To understand how Ritchie and Clouds have been held, for decades, in limbo, we should first provide some background information.

Ritchie, born in April 1944, grew up in the Scottish village of Forth, and was introduced to the harmonica, his first instrument, when he was only six years old.

"I was told one story that when I was just a few years old, some elders of mine were trying to play an accordion, and for a joke, they handed it to me," says Ritchie. "I stunned everyone by playing it. I always thought that story was probably exaggerated, or made up completely. But someone who was there repeated the story back to me several years ago. When I was eight, the people next door threw a piano out, and we gave it a home. I started playing, but no one really knew it. Piano was a kind of secret activity, and I thought nothing of it."

Ritchie's first major band, the Premiers, was originally a six-member group, which was eventually slimmed down to five, featuring two future 1-2-3/Clouds men, vocalist/bassist Ian Ellis and drummer Harry Hughes. But after their demos for Pye Records went nowhere, the band broke up, leaving Ritchie,

Hughes, and Ellis to pick up the pieces. With only three members onboard, the band conveniently became known as 1-2-3. Almost immediately, 1-2-3 began radically dissecting and rearranging hit songs, spiking them with a soul/R&B flavor.

As so many musicians of their generation had done before, and since, 1-2-3 left their native Scotland for Swinging London, England, in 1967, where they quickly won a residency at the Marquee Club, one of the epicenters of progressive music in late mid- and late-1960s Britain.

"We were getting stoned and stonewalled in Scotland," says Ritchie. "We thought it was because we were playing something different. All the other groups were playing Tamla Motown/pseudo-soul, that sort of thing. At that moment in time, I'd say that only 1-2-3 and Pink Floyd, at the UFO club, were doing anything different. Everyone else was conforming to the audience expectations."

Ritchie remembers the Marquee as ground zero for the progressive rock field. "It was a hotbed of trainee superstars," says Ritchie. "The Syn was one of the bands playing there—Chris Squire, Tony Kaye [as a session keyboardist], Peter Banks were all in that group. John Gee [Marquee club manager] was basically a jazz fan promoting pop groups. He was very snooty about it. We got lucky. When he heard us, he thought he'd found the missing link, a pop group that played like a jazz band."

What set 1-2-3 apart from other emerging bands was that there were few, if any, keyboard-led rock trios in the mid- and late 1960s playing in a proto-progressive style.

Life in the Fast Lane

England was a small place, relatively speaking. Unlike in the U.S., where music scenes seemed to be regional phenomena, many of the musicians we today consider stars undoubtedly were influenced by each other, soaking up raw material that they could interpret in their own fashion. "I think because of the Beatles, in London we felt we were *it*," says Ritchie. "There was a real buzz about the place. We were right at the sharp edge of things, we thought."

Around Europe, various bands began making noise in the underground in the late 1960s, and not just in the U.K., such as Pink Floyd, East of Eden, Eyes of Blue, the Nice, Can, Guru Guru, Hansson & Karlsson, an influence on Jimi Hendrix, the American band Touch, which likely influenced Yes (and admittedly Kerry Livgren of Kansas), Ars Nova, Silver Apples, High Tide, It's a Beautiful Day, Panna Fredda in Italy (as well as Il Sistema), Procol Harum, the Collectors from Canada, America's Spirit, Brazil's Os Mutantes (which went from pop to Tropicália and would morph into a full-fledged prog band), Ekseption, Soft Machine, Quintessence, and Poland's Czesław Niemen, who after his psychedelic pop/soul period, ventured into organ-based instrumental progressive music.

Swiping a page from the classical world, Polish keyboardist and multi-instrumentalist Czesław Niemen set the poetry of Wojciech Młynarski to music for 1970's *Enigmatic*.

1-2-3 was in the thick of things, wasting no time pummeling audiences with their cover-tunes-gone-wild approach. Brian Epstein, famous for managing the Beatles, began overseeing the details of 1-2-3's career. Although Epstein wouldn't be the band's manager for long, a fateful business deal put 1-2-3 under the purview of Robert Stigwood, of NEMS Enterprises Ltd., manager of the Bee Gees and Cream.

As early as 1966, Ritchie had rearranged the song "America," a tune written by Paul Simon, a demo for which was recorded in London in 1965. (Simon & Garfunkel's recorded version of the song wouldn't appear until 1968.) Today, most music historians associate the song with prog heavyweights Yes.

"We had picked up 'America' from a tape that Stu Francis—the engineer at Radio Luxembourg—had given us," says Ritchie. "The result of that was that we [1-2-3 and Clouds] did 'America' and 'Sounds of Silence' long before Paul Simon had ever officially released them on record."

Ritchie claims that prior to Emerson, Lake & Palmer and the Nice, even lead organist/keyboardist Keith Emerson had heard 1-2-3's ability to infuse rock with classical references.

1-2-3's iconoclastic rendition of David Bowie's 1966 tune "I Dig Everything," was treated with Bach's Fugue in C Minor from the grand work *The Well-Tempered Clavier*. (This particular Bach piece, as well as Friedrich Gulda's "Prelude and Fugue," influenced Emerson during the writing of the Nice's later "Five Bridges Suite." It's been reported that Emerson had also performed snippets of Bach in the spiritual "Wade in the Water," with his pre-Nice band, Gary Farr & the T-Bones, a band managed briefly by Giorgio Gomelsky. Emerson would also find a way to slot Bach into the song "Rondo," a takeoff of Dave Brubeck's "Blue Rondo à la Turk," from the Nice's debut album, *The Thoughts of Emerlist Davjack*, a mumbo jumbo of the names of the band members, Keith Emerson, Keith "Lee" Jackson, Brian Davison, and Davy O'List.)

Did Ritchie and 1-2-3 help foster Emerson's and the Nice's recorded work? "Keith may have had an idea germinating in there that was triggered when he heard me carry it off," says Ritchie. "For me, it was only an aspect of the music, not the whole thing. ELO did the same thing with 'I Am the Walrus'—they used an aspect of someone else's song to make a style for the band."

Whatever the truth of the matter is, Ritchie and 1-2-3 were well ahead of the pop-rock curve. For years, Ritchie and 1-2-3, and later Clouds, had performed bits of the classical rock ditty "Nut Rocker," a number-one British hit for B. Bumble and the Stingers in 1962, based on the March section of Tchaikovsky's *The Nutcracker* ballet. (Portions of it appeared in the song "Imagine Me" from Clouds' 1970 record, *Up Above Our Heads*, a North American–only release.) Famously, ELP would record the song, too, immortalizing the Tchai-rock version on *Pictures at an Exhibition*, released in late 1971.

In *Circus* magazine, March 1972, Emerson had explained that when his post-Nice band ELP began playing England after forming, Mussorgsky's *Pictures at an Exhibition* was "like a blueprint to get the group's musical direction together." Because the band didn't have a system for writing original music, reworking *Pictures* was the first step, Emerson said.

"Keith . . . used to buttonhole me . . . when I played. [Emerson would say] '[B]ut surely the angle's wrong?,'" says Ritchie. "A year or so later he was diving on the Hammond organ and sticking knives in it."[1]

Some eyewitnesses report that Ritchie similarly abused his Hammond M102 organ in a show of Pete Townshend–like destructive art. Ritchie sets the record straight: "When I got the Hammond M102 organ just before we did the Marquee residency," Ritchie says, "I noticed that when you banged it, it kicked off these reverb bombs. I took to giving it a bang now and again, especially at the end of a number, when I sometimes threw the organ all the way over to the floor. But it wasn't something I made a big thing of, so I can't really claim it preempted Emerson in a giant sense."

The band appeared to be fast-tracked on a path toward stardom, rubbing elbows with the biggest and brightest, supporting the likes of Jimi Hendrix at the Saville Theatre. It was here that a young David Robert Jones [a.k.a. David Bowie], Ritchie's one-time "drinking pal," was in attendance when the band performed an iconoclastic reinterpretation of his "I Dig Everything."

When *Record Mirror* ran a less-than-favorable critique of the band's performance, the future Thin White Duke, whether in an act of self-promotion or genuine passionate outrage, wrote a letter chastising the publication.

"When we played the Saville Theatre, as 1-2-3, in the afternoon rehearsal, David [Bowie] came with us," says Ritchie. "He wanted to get into the show, and to get him in we said he was one of our roadies and had to help carry the equipment into the theatre. At one point, he ended up carrying Jimi Hendrix's guitar, walking behind Hendrix as if he was his personal roadie. None of us thought anything of it at the time, but you can see the irony now. That kind of thing was common in those days. If you wanted [to obtain free admittance] to a club, and knew the band, you pretended you were a roadie. Ian Anderson of Jethro Tull used to do it all the time at the Marquee when we were playing, and we used to do it when other guys we knew, like Cream, were playing there. We were on talking terms with Cream, having the same manager, but they were already big stars, so we never got really close. But the Bee Gees and us were pals, we were both more up-and-coming at that time. . . ."

Despite a raised profile, Ritchie recalls having reservations about working with Epstein and later Stigwood. "Epstein only signed us, because it seemed like we were going to be the next big thing," says Ritchie. "The Marquee performances were so chaotic and revolutionary. He had no idea of the quality of the songs, and he died not knowing. As far as Stigwood, he sent us on cabaret tours up north as if we were a novelty act instead of a genuine rock band. Stigwood really didn't know what to do with us, and in the end, he didn't care either."

Enter Terry Ellis, of the Ellis-Wright Agency, who was taken with 1-2-3's sound and style. Ellis, who would cofound Chrysalis Records (the label branded by a mash-up of the names of cofounders, Chris Wright ["Chrys"] and Terry Ellis ["alis"]), became world famous over the next two decades for handling and/or signing superstar acts such as Jethro Tull, Billy Idol, Blondie, New Order, Huey Lewis & the News, and even 1-2-3/Clouds celebrity fan David Bowie, who'd recruit Ellis and Hughes for demos for his 1972 record, *Hunky Dory*. (Legend has it that Harry also appeared on an early Jethro Tull album, but this remains unconfirmed at press time.)

Ellis was considering managing and booking 1-2-3, but they needed to drop their name and adopt the moniker Clouds. They willingly did so, although Ritchie regrets this today. "I remember there was one poster, a promotional poster for us, that read, 'Get high on the Clouds,'" says Ritchie. "It looks naf now, but it looked naf at the time, too."

And it wouldn't be until March 1969 that the band released a single, through the Island label, "Make No Bones About It" (with organist Ritchie singing lead) b/w "Heritage." Although Clouds finally had a record out in the marketplace, the year or so wait between the band's changing its name and releasing recorded material may have contributed to the lack of recognition Clouds suffers from today.

"1-2-3 alone were about two years ahead of their time," says Ritchie. "Because the records were released when they were, it sounded as though we were copying everyone else, but this wasn't the case. The inspiration of 1-2-3 was never recorded, and that let all the other bands off the hook. They could then say it was all their own idea."

Finally, in August, 1969, the band's LP debut, *The Clouds Scrapbook*, was released, including songs that range from jazzed out soul-rock ("The Carpenter"), American blues/R&B ("Old Man," "I'll Go Girl," which dates to the Premiers days and features a guitar solo by Chrysalis labelmate Alvin Lee of Ten Years After), British military/music hall ("Grandad," "Union Jack"), symphonic pop balladry in the vein of a Sinatra standard ("The Colours Have Run"),

Touch, an influential proto-prog band led by Don Gallucci, formerly the keyboardist of Oregon-based the Kingsmen, released its debut album, *Touch* (pictured), in 1969.

brass-laden orchestral jazz ("Ladies and Gentlemen"), acoustic folk ("Scrapbook Intro"), and Buddy Rich–like Big Band drum-kit bombast ("Humdrum").

Affectionately called *Scrapbook*, the album is remarkably evocative, as if we're witnessing glimpses, moments in time, of an individual's life passing before our, or the songwriter's, eyes. "I think the thing that gives it that ring of truth is that the songs seem to represent different moments in the band's musical history," says Ritchie. "'Humdrum,' 'The Carpenter,' which developed from Harry's beat pattern, and 'Waiter, There's Something in My Soup' are very much 1-2-3 type songs. ["Waiter ... "] was nearest to this muso-prog thing. That was the precursor to King Crimson, in my opinion."

The other songs on *Scrapbook*, Ritchie admits, are very much part of his own personal history. "'Grandad' is a real story, for instance," Ritchie says. "Grandad shows up in the title track of the album *Watercolour Days*. He's the Smoky of the second verse, his colors fading as he 'ran out of time.'

"A song like 'Ladies and Gentlemen,' some of that was changed by [arranger] David Palmer [Jethro Tull]," Ritchie continues. "He changed some of the chord voicings, not drastically, but it was bits at the end of the verses. I don't really agree with it, even now. It's the verse that's important, because that's what's telling the story. But the song was inspired by an experience I had. It was early in the morning, and I had quite a few hard days of parties and gigs, and I looked in the mirror and . . . I didn't really recognize the person staring back at me. As the song says, it was a moment that I realized that things were getting out of hand. Burning the candle at both ends. I thought it would be fun to make it seem as though I was standing at a dinner table and making an actual speech. It was an important song for me, because I had to find a different way to live and survive the process of being a recording and touring musician. I didn't want to burn out. I actually did change my lifestyle, though not drastically, because I was still on the road."

Although the songs on *Scrapbook* weren't conceptualized as pieces of a larger united musical theme, Ritchie acknowledges a Beatles/*Sgt. Pepper's* influence. "The album, as a whole, seems to be unified," Ritchie says. "The short and, probably, sensible answer to all of this is that our manager, Terry Ellis, was influenced by *Sgt. Pepper's*. *Scrapbook* existed as demo tapes initially and from these Terry most probably gleaned the *Scrapbook* idea."

Obscured by Clouds

1970 saw the appearance of the band's second album, *Up Above Our Heads*, a North American release only (at the time) in August of that year. (The U.S. version contained songs appearing on *The Clouds Scrapbook*.)

"Imagine Me," bolstered by Ritchie's stuttering, otherworldly organ effects/ textures, demonstrates why Ritchie was at the forefront of British keyboardists in the late 1960s. "Nothing in there is an 'effect,'" Ritchie corrects. "It's me playing staccato organ with both hands. The speed of it makes it sound like an effect. My two hands are playing ascending diminished chords, each hand playing a different inversion from the other. In fact, in a missing video from 'Beat Club' in Germany, you could hear exactly the same thing . . . I played much the same thing even faster on our version of 'Sing, Sing, Sing' [also from *Up Above Our Heads*]. Listen to the crescendo ending as it builds to a climax, albeit this time masked a bit by the overall power of the band.

"I never considered myself particularly good at sound, though people like keyboardist Tony Kaye, formerly of Yes, seemed to think so," Ritchie continues. "On one occasion he asked if he could pull his Hammond organ next to mine and copy the drawbar settings. He couldn't figure out why mine sounded so much stronger than his, despite being exactly the same model. The answer was simple: I played all the solos in unison, or sometimes in harmony, with both hands. It gave the sound a double strength."

Clouds was nothing if not a thrilling live act. One of the great milestones of the band's career was its North American tour in 1970. "Where the U.S. was different to the U.K. in the late sixties, was that the audiences were so generous, so honest, and so broad-minded," says Ritchie. "Here in the U.K., you could play really well, but you could never surpass the leading acts in the audience's mind. In the States, it was different. That played to our strengths. We had many fine reviews, and great audience reactions. At the Aragon Ballroom in Chicago, *Billboard* magazine had come along to review Jethro Tull, Leon Russell, and Sha Na Na, but we got the headline review—'This band will be a giant.' It was very heartening to work in an atmosphere like that, where your efforts and value were recognized."

Ritchie freely dispenses tales from rock and roll's rough and ready years of the late 1960s and early 1970s; some of these stories are printable, some not so much. One of the more PG-rated anecdotes occurred on Clouds' trip to the U.S. in early fall 1970.

"We were playing at the Fillmore in New York, and we were on stage doing a sound check," says Ritchie. "A guy with a broom was sweeping around near my feet, and he growled at me to move out the way. I said, 'Look, if I want a fucking cleaner, I'll let you know. Meantime, do something really useful and fuck off!' He looked at me quizzically, and turned to the stagehands, shrugging. Then, in a gruff New York accent he said, 'I'm terribly sorry, sir, please excuse my lack of respect.' As soon as I saw the stagehands' reaction I knew that this was Bill Graham, the boss. But I was in it, so I had to go with it, and said, 'That's okay, just don't let it happen again.' That became a running theme between Bill and me. We played the Fillmore twice, with Jethro Tull and John Sebastian [Friday and Saturday, May 22–23], then later with Steve Miller and Pink Floyd later. Nick [Mason] was always saying to me, 'Billy, get Bill Graham to put some Jack Daniels in the dressing-room ice box.' Nick knew the repartee between me and Bill. I would wind Bill up just to get something out of him, like the Jack Daniels. But I got lucky, because Bill loved it. He genuinely thought that I had known who he was and didn't care, and he liked that."

Yet, amid all of this memory making, Ritchie sensed that the cracks were beginning to appear in the foundation of the band. Clouds seemed to be victims of a lack of direction. "The title of the second record didn't do any favors," says Ritchie. "In fact, I hate the title. That was Terry. I absolutely hate that title. When I saw that I said, 'How corny!' It made us look like real nerds."

Still, there were deeper concerns and technical issues revolving around the band. Redesigning what was, first and foremost, a cover band, regardless of how radically creative this cover band was, proved to be increasingly frustrating to Ritchie, who was saddled with the responsibility of having to incorporate original material in Clouds' repertoire.

"Suddenly, it became necessary for bands to do only their own songs, and my writing and the band were forced into marriage," says Ritchie. "Clouds, to me, was a somewhat watered-down 1-2-3, pandering much more to the audience, though still trying to be inventive. I was the arranger in 1-2-3, and I found it difficult to write the songs and then try to rearrange them, too."

Ritchie's creativity was, essentially (excuse the Pink Floyd pun), obscured by Clouds. For this reason, 1971's *Watercolour Days*, released on the Chrysalis

Clouds (left to right): Ian Ellis, Harry Hughes, and Billy Ritchie.

label, is still a point of contention for the groundbreaking organist forty-plus years after it appeared.

"I was still struggling with the Clouds concept at the time of *Watercolour Days* and that's why, perhaps, the album is like a flickering light bulb, with the brilliant and banal, in writing terms, side by side," says Ritchie.

Although some of the band's material from the early 1970s, unreleased at the time, such as "The World Is a Madhouse" (1970), "Why Is There No Magic?" (1971), "A Day of Rain" (1971), "Shadows" (1971), and "Clockwork Soldier" (1971), reveal a distinctive (and not-too-subtle) connection to iconic West Coast psychedelic rockers the Doors, they do show promise. (The rich vocal textures and lyrical symbolism would have made Jim Morrison proud, one thinks.) "Great singers make poor songs—even awful songs—sound good," says Ritchie. "But [the singing] is what spoils a good song like 'Watercolour Days.' It's me singing, but I only sang it because Ian hadn't time to learn it for the recording. That was a mistake. It was even Ian's key, not mine, which made it worse."

Adding fuel to a growing blaze, manager Terry Ellis went all in, promoting rising stars Jethro Tull (Ian Anderson and crew) and perhaps, from Ritchie's perspective, not dividing his time evenly amongst his stable of talent. As Ellis and Tull were rocketed to the upper echelons of the music industry, by 1971, Clouds were locked in a ground war with ever-increasingly competent progressive rockers of the British popular and underground music scenes.

"Ironically, it was because [Ellis] liked us so much, he couldn't bear to delegate us to someone else," says Ritchie. "I remember the Reading Festival [Sunbury Festival, 1968] with some bitterness. It was a lesson in how the press works. That was supposed to be the venue where Jethro became stars, and essentially, that's true, but that stardom was created and decided by the mythmakers in the press. We actually had one of the best ovations of the day, far better than anything Jethro Tull had, yet to the press we had 'created a minor sensation.' The thing was, they [Tull] were interesting to look at, and that gave the press images to write about. We just played."

The rift between Chrysalis and Clouds widened by the day, as the parties couldn't even reach common ground on song selection for *Watercolour Days*. Ritchie still believes some of his best material was left on the cutting-room floor. "Terry made the wrong decision about those songs," says Ritchie. "If they had been on our albums, our legacy wouldn't be so problematic. We would have been clearly seen as being way ahead of our time."

A cynic would say that Clouds simply couldn't settle on a musical direction, contributing to uneasy compromises apparent in the band's later material. It almost seems cruel: as Clouds was vaporizing, literally disappearing from the scene, progressive rock was redefining pop music. Records such as *The Yes Album, Fragile, Pawn Hearts, Tarkus, Aqualung, Acquiring the Taste, Air Conditioning, In the Court of the Crimson King, Nursery Cryme*, and other seminal works were, more or less, the product of original and creative bursts of energy, heralded in their time—and decades since—as groundbreaking, even visionary, which rivaled and perhaps bettered the entirety of Clouds' recorded output.

"I had heard Crimson and you can't duplicate that wonderful sound with just three guys," says Ritchie. "ELP had a certain thing, but I don't think it had that kind of magnificence that Crimson had. Keith using all those sounds was great, and it worked well, but I don't think you could duplicate Ian McDonald's wonderful saxophone and that Mellotron . . . I heard [Crimson] live before I heard their debut album, and when they did ["21st Century Schizoid Man"], I said, 'That's it. They've done it.'"

By 1970, Emerson had jettisoned from the Nice to found the so-called supergroup Emerson, Lake & Palmer, and Yes were well on their way to becoming the most enduring and beloved progressive rock bands on the planet, still touring as of this writing. Emerson was using the Moog as early as the later days of the Nice. Outside the Mellotron, a Moog synth, for example, was the single greatest sonic weapon in a prog rock keyboardist's arsenal. Emerson, himself, has said that his use of the Moog is an extension of the noises he'd create with the Hammond, noises that even the Hammond Organ Company hadn't designed for their instrument. (It's been reported that Emerson was the first to use the modular Moog on stage, and some have credited the psychedelic band Kensington Market with being the first to take the Moog on tour.)

It became apparent, as never before, that Clouds needed to play catch-up. To Ritchie's continued astonishment, somewhere along the line, keyboardists Keith Emerson and Rick Wakeman (Strawbs, Yes) had assumed the position as the new faces of British progressive rock keyboard-playing.

We must also be careful of revisionist history. Pioneering English keyboardist Don Shinn (the Shinn, Dada) has long been accepted as a major influence on Emerson. Given the fact that Shinn was a showman, making a name for himself in Britain years before Emerson (and Ritchie) would attempt similar stage antics, it's conceivable that Keith was just as inspired, if not more, by Shinn and his appearances at the Marquee when he developed his brand of showmanship with the band the V.I.P.s, which featured two future Spooky Tooth members,

EKSEPTION, HOLLAND'S NO.1 GROUP,
HAS MADE BACH, BEETHOVEN,
KHACHATURIAN, AND PEOPLE LIKE THAT
TURN ON IN THEIR GRAVES.
(BUT THAT'S JUST THE START OF
THE UNDERGROUND MOVEMENT)

Mercury Record Corporation Family of Labels / Philips • Mercury • Smash • Fontana • Limelight •
Of Mercury Record Productions, Inc./35 East Wacker Drive, Chicago, Illinois 60601/A North American Philips

After hearing the Nice interpret classical pieces, Ekseption keyboardist Rick van der Linden rearranged Beethoven's Symphony No. 5, rechristening it as "The Fifth." This ad shows Beethoven emerging from his grave, presumably to show appreciation for Ekseption. The Dutch band also covered Bach, Mozart, Tchaikovsky, and even Jethro Tull, reimagining the instrumental "Dharma for One."

vocalist/keyboardist Mike Harrison and drummer Mike Kellie.

Organ trios, or just the concept of a heavy rock band being led by the sounds of a Hammond or Moog, would draw the inevitable comparisons not to Ritchie but Emerson. Bands such as Quatermass, the Trip (from Italy), Ekseption from the Netherlands, and even Le Orme (mainly due to their 1971 album, *Collage*), proved just how vital and ubiquitous Emerson had become on the rock scene.

"I think ... I took my eyes off the ball, and didn't notice others like Emerson and Wakeman expand their sound into synths and the Moog," Ritchie admits. "I was still flogging organ and piano, becoming an anachronism without noticing. People in Cleethorpes were accusing me of copying [Emerson]. I was affronted, but couldn't do anything about it, as he was the famous one. I think the idea of an organist standing there on his own is what's important. [1-2-3 and Clouds] were organ trios, which didn't have a guitar player being the lead instrument."

In an ironic twist, Clouds had entertained bringing in a guitarist, a notion that was anathema to the entire 1-2-3/Clouds saga. The late guitarist Peter Banks once told the author that he had auditioned for the band circa 1971, after he was unceremoniously dumped by his bandmates in Yes, although Ritchie has trouble remembering the incident.

"On the plane trip back from a tour, Harry said he wanted to add guitar and brass to the band," says Ritchie. "We were asking ourselves if we wanted to change the band radically. Maybe have a singer, too. At the same time Ian was being pulled away from our circle by a coterie of hangers-on. We were clutching at straws, and as happens with a lot of bands, the second America tour was the straw that broke the camel's back. The whole thing was fragmenting. I felt alienated even from the guys."

The fact that Ritchie was offered a potentially lucrative business opportunity does little to soothe the sting of the band's experiences in the early 1970s. "At the Chrysalis office in New York I had blown my top and called the guys in the office everything under the sun," says Ritchie. "Harry and Ian thought I had gone nuts. . . . In addition, Terry offered me my own publishing company: I probably should have taken it. But I was so mad at him. I told him to 'stuff it.' We kept going for a while, but a sour taste had set in. I think from that moment on none of us had our hearts in it anymore. In the end the decision was to break up. That seed was in my head when I heard King Crimson the first time. I knew it was not about the quality of what we did: it was about the lack of variation in the sound."

"They had exposure," Terry Ellis told the author in 2008. "They played in a supporting role with Jethro Tull and Ten Years After. Plenty of exposure. I got them released in America. . . . Billy was a talented guy, a songwriter who wrote good songs, but things just didn't gel for them. [Ritchie] probably blames me [for their lack of commercial success] and probably feels that they missed out, because I was spending most of my time with Jethro Tull. . . ."

"The public at the time, and the music press, didn't buy into what we did," says Ritchie, "so it's difficult to change that perception, especially at this late hour in the day. Everywhere we went, there would be a crowd of musicians at the front of the stage with chins hitting the floor, while behind them there were howls of rage and clenched fists. It's just amazing how upset people get if you play music they don't understand. Terry was actually just about the only person in the world, even up till now, who realized I was the real deal in songwriting, and saw *Scrapbook* as a way of bringing that to the fore. I truthfully wrote one-thousand-plus songs in those years, no exaggeration, though only about thirty or forty were recorded. It was a valiant thought by [Ellis] to bring original music to the Clouds or 1-2-3 template, but I think it only added to the confusion between the two styles."

Sphere of Influence

There's no denying that Clouds were an influence on the early progressive rock scene, even if it was for a brief period of time. In the twenty-first century Yes' Jon Anderson has given a nod to Clouds and in 2010 retro rockers Rob Clarke and the Wooltones covered "Mind of a Child" (originally appearing *Watercolour Days*) on a compilation album titled *A Phase We're Going Through* (appropriately enough full of reworked cover tunes). In addition, a recent BGO reissue of Clouds' material, *Up Above Our Heads [Clouds 1966–1971]* (BGOCD966), sheds a light on why Clouds was so innovative. Although Ritchie himself labels the reissue a "deep catalogue" entry, Clouds has managed to claw their way back into the fringes of mainstream consciousness, having let out what Ritchie believes to be his greatest material.

"If you hear past the flashy playing and prog-y stuff, you'll notice the craft and guile in the songs," Ritchie says. "'Clockwork Soldier' is my finest hour, but it should have been done with a vocal and not a spoken piece over it. . . . The piece is actually very poignant. At the time I wrote it, my wife had lost a son, he was stillborn. 'Clockwork Soldier' is partly a reference to him and partly my progress through time. He didn't even have a funeral. Back then a stillborn child was regarded as never having lived. Many years later I found out where he was buried. That sounds strange, because at the time [stillborns] were put in a communal grave. The local council in Scotland couldn't tell me where he was. I made a fuss and pursued them and they eventually found the plot with the thirty children in it. They erected a stone on the plot and within six months of the stone being laid it was covered in flowers and toys for all the people who had children there. That just shows you something of this nature was just waiting to happen. 'Clockwork Soldier' was written about a year and a half after that event. . . . To make that song even more poignant, a year or so after I wrote that, my wife had another boy and he was born severely disabled. When I perform it, it is very personal for me. . . . I think that would have been a great track to have ended the album."

Cruel as it may be, getting a jump on the starting gun doesn't ensure enduring commercial success—or even a lengthy musical career. After all, the Russians were the first to send a satellite into orbit, but we all know who won the Space Race. By the same token, old traditions die hard: Americans have long known the truth about the origins of their country, yet continue to observe Columbus Day.

There's a whiff of fatalism in Ritchie's voice when he speaks of the heady days of prog rock's early years. "When I knew Jon Anderson he was working at the bar [near] the Marquee Club," says Ritchie, referring to the La Chasse Club. "Even when I did see those guys [Yes] sing and play, they were all good. They were all good, yet, only a handful made it to stardom. You couldn't possibly have chosen which one it would be. It was a very random thing. I always liken it to soldiers running through a battlefield in a hail of bullets. Some get killed and some don't. You think that they would all get killed, but they don't. Some get through to the other side, unscathed. And that's the people who are famous."

Ritchie spins one last poignant tale about his musical career as the leader of 1-2-3 and Clouds: "Paul McCartney used to drop in a lot [to the Pheasantry Club in Kings Road, Chelsea], because he was going out with Maggie [McGivern], who was a waitress there, as I remember. She was such a lovely girl in every way. [*Note: Readers may remember that McGivern once expressed regret at not taking seriously Paul's talk of marriage.*] One night I said to Paul, who had just come into the club after we'd finished playing, 'Tough luck, Paul, you've just missed the best band in Britain.' To which Paul said, 'What, again?,' which I thought was a quick answer to a mad Scotsman. As the club began to close, we went for some chips, and drove past the entrance, now dark and empty. Paul and Maggie were standing outside on the pavement, madly thumbing [for a ride] as we drove past honking and shouting, thinking how funny they were, mucking about like that. I remember thinking how ironic it was that Paul never even knew we had shared the same manager. The next night we went to the club, Maggie was mad at us: 'Why didn't you stop?' she said. 'We really wanted a lift; we couldn't get a taxi!' Story of my life, I'd say."

Drum Crazy

As seminal a role model as Ritchie was, he wasn't the only influential member of Clouds. For instance, it's difficult, in retrospect, to hear Harry Hughes' ostinato snare drum patterns in "Humdrum," from *The Clouds Scrapbook*, without thinking of Carl Palmer's solo in ELP's "Tank," from the trio's self-titled 1970 debut record. (It should be noted that Palmer does take the opportunity to perform drum solos in tracks "Decline and Fall," credited solely and incredibly to Vincent Crane, and "Before Tomorrow," both recorded in 1969

As Clouds' fortunes dwindled, prog acts, such as ELP, were achieving massive commercial success. In September 1974, *Cash Box* reported that Atlantic Records' Ahmet Ertegun had awarded ELP its fifth consecutive gold record at a luncheon engagement in New York City.

and appearing on Atomic Rooster's first album.)

Significantly, on Clouds' second album, 1970's *Up Above Our Heads*, Hughes not only recaptures Gene Krupa's syncopated tom pattern for a thirteen-minute-plus rendition of Louis Prima's "Sing, Sing, Sing" (recorded perhaps most notably by Benny Goodman and His Orchestra in the late 1930s), but a dash of Max Roach's drum showpiece in 3/4, "The Drum Also Waltzes," famously recorded by Bill Bruford on the 1985 Moraz/Bruford album *Flags* (EGMC 63) and, later, performed onstage by Rush's Neil Peart, the reigning king of the rock drum solo.

Cracking That Nut: The Clouds Debate Continues

Borrowing and rearranging someone else's compositions is nothing new. In fact, blues artists—and even some rock musicians, influenced by those same blues

A Fillmore West poster for Quatermass, a powerful organ trio featuring musical journeymen keyboardist J. Peter Robinson, drummer Mick Underwood, and bassist/vocalist John Gustafson.

artists—have been doing this for decades, legally and not-so legally.

1-2-3 and Clouds made a run at stardom by interpreting other people's music, from the Zombies' "She's Not There" to Louis Prima's "Sing, Sing, Sing." As mentioned above, Ritchie quoted classical music, Bach and Tchaikovsky, intersplicing European art music with organ-based rock.

The American hard rock band Vanilla Fudge (formerly the Electric Pigeons), formed on Long Island, was reinterpreting popular and even classical music, certainly recording it, years before the term *progressive rock* was in popular parlance, playing clubs such as the Action House in Island Park. Fellow New York–based band Rat Race Choir, which had roots in the early 1960s band the Continentals, largely worked as a cover band in the 1970s.

"We got old Dvořák recordings and tried to use those as a basis for material," says drummer and cofounder of Rat Race Choir Steve Luongo (John Entwistle). "We did covers, but they were ambitious covers. We weren't doing the typical hits. Our playlists were what was fun to play rather than what was popular to play."

Keith Emerson, with the Nice and ELP, would interpret classical works, among others, Leoš Janáček's *Sinfonietta* ("Knife Edge") and Béla Bartók's *Allegro Barbaro* ("The Barbarian"), quite controversially since ELP did not initially credit the composers. ("Take a Pebble," from *Welcome Back My Friends to the Show That Never Ends—Ladies and Gentlemen, Emerson, Lake & Palmer*, quotes various classical pieces, and the Nice's *Ars Longa Vita Brevis* references Sibelius' *Karelia Suite* and Bach's Brandenburg Concertos.)

In addition, Birmingham native and ELP drummer Carl Palmer thanks his entertainer father, music-educator uncle, and percussionist grandfather for introducing him to classical music, including Mussorgsky's *Pictures at an Exhibition* at age seven (Carl has indicated in the past), a piece of music that ELP would, of course, famously perform at the Isle of Wight Festival in 1970 and record for Atlantic Records.

But was Ritchie the first classical rocker? Attempting to find the "first" of anything becomes difficult because we can only trace history back to a certain point. Beyond the known chronology, interpretation plays a big role. Perhaps we should look down other avenues and consider another source, such as producer/songwriter/agent provocateur Kim Fowley, who later produced the Runaways.

It was Fowley who took the "March" section of Tchaikovsky's *The Nutcracker* ballet and rearranged it for B. Bumble and the Stingers, an American instrumental band composed of session musicians. This creative move influenced both Ritchie and Emerson. It was released through Rendezvous Records in the States, the Top Rank label in the U.K.

The story begins in 1957, after Fowley had been diagnosed with nonparalytic polio, for the second time, and was convalescing at a Kaiser rehabilitation center in Southern California when a chance meeting helped change his life.

"They had a jukebox," Fowley remembers, "and the jukebox [maintenance worker] came in to fix it. I told him that someday I was going to be in the music business, and asked, 'What's the most popular song you service?' In those days, jukebox companies owned record companies and distributed music for jukeboxes, not radio airplay or retail. He said, 'Any variation of *The Nutcracker* Suite.' So, I said, 'Oh, a cha-cha-cha version, a blues version, a country version . . . ?,' and he said, 'Yeah. Always successful.' I said, 'What about the rock and roll one?' He said, 'There has never been one.' I said, 'There will be someday.' Since there actually *was* a cha-cha-cha version, I had him give it to me. I carried it with me for four years. One day I reopened the idea and I composed my own parts that I put in the public domain melody. I put in my own 'Kim Fowley parts' and linked them all together so that I would own the copyright. 'The Nut Rocker' had various musical parts that Tchaikovsky never wrote, linked together. It was a simple case of understanding copyright law and being creative enough to [work] within the boundaries of copyright law."

Fowley's flirtation with classical rock continued into the mid-1960s. He's credited as a co-songwriter of the Lancasters' 1965 instrumental "Satan's Holiday," a rock-guitar interpretation of Grieg's "In the Hall of the Mountain King."

Story goes that guitarist Ritchie Blackmore, later of Deep Purple and Rainbow, had been playing with the Outlaws, English producer Joe Meek's in-house band for many recordings in the early 1960s, which included the likes of bassist Chas Hodges, and drummer Mick Underwood. The band was backing a girl vocal group, the Murmaids, and had banged out the day's work with a half hour to spare. Rather than let the time go to waste, producer Derek Lawrence

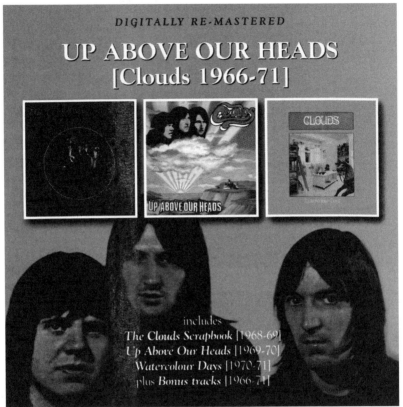

DIGITALLY RE-MASTERED

UP ABOVE OUR HEADS
[Clouds 1966-71]

includes
The Clouds Scrapbook [1968-69]
Up Above Our Heads [1969-70]
Watercolour Days [1970-71]
plus Bonus tracks [1966-71]

Although recordings could not fully capture the fire and innovation Clouds exhibited on stage in the 1960s, this 2010 BGO Records compilation demonstrates just how musically sophisticated the band really was.

wrung two instrumentals out of the band, one of them being "Satan's Holiday," which was released under the name the Lancasters.

"We all knew classical tunes, and it was not anything that was alien to us," says Underwood, who was on the session and later of Quatermass. "The Gladiators had a song with a classical slant and instrumental groups, like the Shadows, were playing good stuff, as were American bands. The thing about music is it all builds on itself and everyone borrows a bit here and there."[2]

The track appears on YouTube but also the CD *Impossible but True: The Kim Fowley Story*, among others. "It's been proven that Elvis wasn't the first white guy to do rockabilly," says Fowley. "I mean, Bill Monroe, right? 'Blue Moon of Kentucky' was one of the earliest songs recorded by Elvis Presley. History is full of loose ends."

2

Of Pawn Hearts and Horn Parts

A Q&A with Former Van der Graaf Generator Saxophonist David Jackson

When labels such as *art-rock* or *progressive rock* were being thrown around in the 1970s, Van der Graaf Generator (VdGG) largely shunned them, not wanting their jolting and highly impressionistic music to be connected to this, or any, movement.

Throughout its career, VdGG, as its name might suggest, has created an electrifying blend of musically violent, emotionally charged, hair-raisingly chilling songs. Buzzing with life, a world apart from other British prog bands of the time, VdGG's music was a combination of the European art music tradition, twentieth-century "atonal" contemporary classical music, jazz, and, of course, rock. These elements were fused to such a fine point that it's often difficult to extract where the jazz and rock ended and the European classical musical influences began.

Having taken their name from Robert Van de Graaff's electrostatic device used to break up atoms, VdGG rocked and shocked with an often disturbing intensity, boasting lyrical narrative threads inspired by mysticism and science-fiction fetishism.

Formed at Manchester University in 1967 by guitarist and vocalist Peter Hammill, a computer programmer for IBM prior to being accepted into the school's Liberal Studies in Science program, songwriter/multi-instrumentalist Chris Judge Smith, and organist Nick Pearne, the band released its first single for Polydor ("People You Were Going To"/"Firebrand," released in December 1968, but which quickly disappeared off the musical map).

By the end of 1968, VdGG had received a facelift: bassist Keith Ellis joined, the lineup added drummer Guy Evans, and, after quitting his job at the BBC, organist Hugh Banton, a classically trained pianist who'd attended Silcoates, the prestigious private school in Wakefield, England established for the children of congregational ministers, won the spot vacated by Pearne. "I bumped into Tony Stratton-Smith who was managing the Nice and Keith Emerson ... and was about to start up a record label," says Banton. "I played him a tape of Peter and Judge and he said, 'Oh, yes. I'd like to meet them.' And that was it. We were signed to him."

VdGG's full-length debut, *The Aerosol Grey Machine*, a U.S.-only release, was originally intended to be a Hammill solo record. *Aerosol* contained many of the ingredients that would make VdGG a cult success: dense lyrics, nihilistic themes, radiant organ tones, and Hammill's harsh, distinctive voice in "Afterwards," "Orthenthian St.," "Aquarian," and "Necromancer."

"Strat used to manage Liverpool bands called the Coobers—and they had just split up—and their bass player had joined us, Keith Ellis, who had been playing for years in highly professional setups," says Banton. "He was exactly what we needed to sort us out, really, and turn us into a proper band. Peter was kind of an acoustic guitarist and Judge was playing spoons and making odd noises. And we also had Guy. We could actually be a proper electric band. The early rehearsals, which were toward the end of 1968, it all happened so fast, within weeks. It takes years nowadays. We just spent day after day after day, inventing numbers [songs] and getting the show on the road, as it were."

Sensing that there was less and less room for him in this music, Judge Smith exited the band to form Heebalob. More personnel changes followed: Nic Potter replaced bassist Ellis, and acoustic/electric saxophonist/flautist David Jackson, who had been in Heebalob with Smith, came into the fold, bringing with him radical horn techniques and musical concepts. (More about this in the interview later in this chapter.)

It was in this configuration that VdGG began hitting their creative stride, releasing albums that featured alternately screeching and soothing sonic patches, such as 1970's *The Least We Can Do Is Wave to Each Other* (what Hammill has referred to as the band's official debut), featuring "Darkness (11/11)"; "Refugees"; "After the Flood"; "Whatever Would Robert Have Said?" (which refers to the inventor of the infamous generator); and the alchemically laced "White Hammer," a song that the Peter Hammill fanzine, *Pilgrims*, interpreted in 1989 as white magic surviving "the beatings of the Grey hammer (= the Inquisition) and is now beginning to triumph over both that and the black hammer (= black magic)."

H to He, Who Am the Only One followed in 1970, featuring the soon-to-be-classic lineup of Hammill/Jackson/Banton/Evans (less Potter, who exited during the album's recording process), an album Jackson once described as "challenging, just about playable."

The band's crowning achievement and most experimental effort of the early '70s was 1971's *Pawn Hearts*, containing "Lemmings (including Cog)," about "extreme political ambivalence," Hammill said; the hell-raising rant on the duality of human beings, "Man-Erg"; and the twenty-three-minute spellbinder, "A Plague of Lighthouse Keepers."

"There were lost tracks to *Pawn Hearts*, which came out a few years ago on reissue [CASCDR 1051], weird solo pieces," drummer Guy Evans once told the author. "Mine ["Angle of Incidents"] involved, at one point, putting all the expensive microphones from Trident Studios down the stairwell and dropping a bunch of neon tubes from the top and hooking up all the effects units and recording the results."

Earlier in 1971, Stratton-Smith, Charisma label owner, organized the now-famous Six Bob Tour, so named because admittance to the shows was officially six shillings ("bob" being slang for "shilling"). Designed to capitalize on the underground credibility and slow-building buzz developing around acts such as Genesis, Van der Graaf, and folk rockers Lindisfarne, the Six Bob tour began in late January and was scheduled to run only nine shows, but the tour was extended well into the spring, apparently due to popularity.

Legend has it the bands stoked a friendly competitive environment and got on famously. Besides the occasional negative review (and some equipment malfunctions) Six Bob was a stroke of genius that's remembered today quite fondly as one of the seminal moments in the early progressive rock movement in Britain.

"It was ahead of its time, I suppose," Banton told the author.

"It was inspired by what Strat had seen Bill Graham do at the Fillmore," drummer Guy Evans told the writer. "The tour began at the Lyceum, in London, which was this old ballroom in town. Van der Graaf and Audience used to play there a lot. When we played the North of England, I remember people up there didn't have much money. It was an impoverished time, the early 1970s. Still, it was like another country. So, for them to get that kind of event to come to a town was something. Everyone used to come out to see these types of shows."

Though *Pawn Hearts* didn't make a dent in the British charts (only *The Least We Can Do Is Wave to Each Other* charted in Britain and even that landed outside the top 40), the record would become an icon of the band's early career. "We had great success in Italy," says Banton. "We did concerts there in February and they had us back in June, playing two gigs a day."

But touring Italy was taking its toll. With their resources (physical, mental, and financial) quickly dwindling, the band was starting to feel trapped. "Promoters asked if we could come back in '72 and I thought, 'Oh, God,'" says Banton. "We were driving around, doing two gigs a day and just going mad. And the drink . . . We just had enough. And it was just so hot, adding to the malaise. It was like, 'Can we get off this train now, please?'

"We never had any money," Banton continues. "We never, ever had any money, because our records never sold. We would sell a few thousand and that would be it. That was the way it went on."

"We were the maddest bunch [Charisma] had on the books," Evans said, "and probably the biggest risk. I think we always thought we would have the big breakthrough."

The band never really did, not in a commercial sense, anyway, and VdGG split. "If we had just been able to take a break, if someone would have had

PETER HAMMILL & 5 VDGG MAGAZINE

A 1989 VdGG and Peter Hammill fanzine.

the vision to say, 'You can stop for two months, have a holiday,' things may have been different," says Banton. "It was sort of nonstop from 1970. Week in and week out."

After calling it quits, Hammill continued with his slightly more accessible solo career, which had officially kicked off with the somewhat pop-y *Fool's Mate*, released when VdGG was still active. Others followed, such as *Chameleon in the Shadow of the Night, In Camera, The Silent Corner and the Empty Stage* and the pre–New Wave shot of adrenaline, *Nadir's Big Chance*, revolving around Hammill's alter ego (of sorts), Rikki Nadir. It would be another two years before the dust settled and the VdGG boys had coalesced around the idea of becoming a cohesive recording and touring unit, again.

Then, in late 1974, the guys reconnected, and began working on new material. The result was music that would appear on 1975's *Godbluff* (cut in legendary Rockfield Studios in Wales) and 1976's *Still Life*, both of which explode with impressionistic bursts of sonic colors (enhanced by Hammill's decision to "plug in" and use an electric guitar). The band sounds like a well-oiled jazz quartet, having gained enough maturity and confidence to use the space between notes to allow a composition to breathe.

Songs such as "The Sleepwalkers," "Arrow," and "Scorched Earth" from the four-track *Godbluff*, and "La Rossa," "Childlike Faith in Childhood's End," "Pilgrims," and "Still Life" from *Still Life* are an odd mixture of stream-of-consciousness mysticism (ruminating on life and rebirth) and personal confession. (Hammill is notorious for often not revealing the inspiration for and meanings of his words.)

World Record emerged in 1976, and Van der Graaf Generator appeared to be on the precipice of breaking through into the mainstream when, after a North American tour, they were once again nearly at financial ruin (despite sell-out crowds in the U.S.). Banton decided that this was a good time to leave to focus on his personal life and a career outside music.

"Suddenly, they were looking for someone to take Hugh's place," says String Driven Thing violinist Graham Smith, who had then just finished working with Hammill on his 1977 solo record, *Over*, a collection of tunes written about the VdGG leader's broken marriage. "The rehearsals went well, but then Dave Jackson decided to leave, too, and hopefully not because of me. We then did a gig at the Roundhouse, Chalk Farm [Road, London] in early 1977. It was a great success and we toured and eventually made the album *The Quiet Zone/ The Pleasure Dome*."

Nic Potter returned as bassist, Charles Dickie was tapped as a cellist (as well as piano and synth player), and the band, which had shortened its name to Van der Graaf, carried on until the late 1970s.

The live effort *Vital*, a massive live document infused with the raw energy of the New Wave and the ambitions of prog rock, followed. Composed of Hammill solo and would-be solo, as well as recent, vintage, and obscure VdGG material, *Vital* was recorded in 1978 at the Marquee in London, featuring Jackson, who'd agreed to take part in the limited engagements.

Vital would prove to be Van der Graaf's last record of the 1970s and, what appeared to be, their swan song. VdGG had folded up shop, once again. "I think the band folded at the end of the '70s, because of money pressures," muses Smith. "It was more practical to let Peter tour as a solo artist. It was so much easier."

Hammill continued to record and perform as a prolific solo artist, while VdGG lay dormant for nearly three decades. Then, at the end of 2004, Hammill, Jackson, Banton, and Evans reunited for the recording of the double album affair, 2005's *Present* and the live album *Real Time*.

Sans Jackson, the trio of Hammill, Banton, and Evans, carries on today, touring and recording, having since released the appropriately titled 2008 record *Trisector*, a digitally tracked, DIY musical affair; 2011's *A Grounding in Numbers*; and *ALT*, which appeared in 2012.

What follows is a Q&A with longtime flutist and saxophonist—and double saxophonist—David Jackson, who discusses alternative views of some aspects of the band's history, the Italian prog outfit Osanna, twelve-tone music, and his surprising collaboration with former King Crimson violinist David Cross.

WR: What was your first introduction to horns and wind instruments?
David Jackson: Well, I had heard an oboe on the radio. I can't remember the piece, now, but that's what got me interested, initially. Of course, I grew up with an elder brother, who's five years older than me, and he used to make wooden flutes out of bamboo in school. He gave me one and taught me how to play it. . . . One Christmas, when I was fourteen, my brother said, "I have a present for you. . . ." It was his original saxophone, but it was broken, and he'd said we would fix it together. By default I became a saxophone player.

WR: What kind of mentor was your brother?

Jackson: My brother would make me learn Charlie Parker tunes when I saw him on the holidays and would hit my fingers with a ruler and things like that. He was . . . very dismissive of my abilities, because he was absolutely brilliant. He had auditions for major orchestras.

WR: When did you develop your double horn technique?

Jackson: When I was sixteen I had a job and managed to get enough money together for a tenor sax. I had an alto, which my brother gave me, and a tenor, and immediately, I just started to play both of them at once.

WR: People like Dick Heckstall-Smith from Colosseum, Wilbur Sweatman (with clarinets) and, the famous example of Roland Kirk and his homemade hybrid instruments, blew two horns at once.

Jackson: I tried to play Roland Kirk–type tunes with two saxophones and I made up a few tunes of my own. But it wasn't serious. Suddenly I was in a rock band . . . and I was writing double horn parts faster than Peter [Hammill] could write songs.

WR: Were you specifically influenced by a player vis a vis your double horns technique?

Jackson: The idea came from Roland Kirk and an old carol called "We Three Kings." I remember hearing that on the radio, and he was playing that on three saxophones. When I was in Van der Graaf, I was able to go into music shops and have my instruments modified. The horns are such that I can play . . . two octaves in each hand. I can't play everything. I can't play "Flight of the Bumblebee" in harmony, but I can play a lot of very clever things now.

WR: Can you switch off between horns, or is it completely insane to be able to blow out one and not another?

Jackson: It's impossible to really switch one "off." You can make one louder than the other, and I have a special harness I use for complete control. The great thing about the saxophone is, there are the seven notes I can play plus the semitones in between. When you press a button on the saxophone it changes the octave. It's as simple as that. You can jump an octave without moving your fingers, just your thumb. If you can imagine you have two thumbs and two sevenths in each hand, fourteen notes, so you basically have two octaves. It means you can jump in any combination of notes you want. You can play the same note [with each horn], you can play semitone intervals between stated notes on one horn, and you can switch which instrument is playing the tune and which is playing the harmony . . . I play four saxophones on stage, now. I have a little baby one, a tiny little sopranino, very much like the oboe I had heard when I was young. But doing this hurts my diaphragm for some reason. It takes a special effort to play. I'm practicing that now . . . and I love doing orchestrations.

David Jackson thinks he knows the real story behind the title of *Pawn Hearts*.

WR: You talked about orchestration. Please give me an example of how you approached orchestration with Van der Graaf Generator?

Jackson: "House with No Door" [from VdGG's *H to He, Who Am the Only One*], there's a melody in the middle of it, and there's sixteen [horn] parts in there. It's a very classical melody that was written by Judge Smith, not Peter Hammill. And, the record *Pawn Hearts*, do you know how it got its name?

WR: Just from what I've heard over the years.

Jackson: I would quite like to hear your idea first.

WR: My understanding is that Peter Hammill was very much into chess, which ties in with Paul Whitehead's cover artwork . . .

Jackson: That's a perfectly reasonable explanation and that's the explanation that people use. Here's my perspective: When we were in Rockfield . . . studio, we would say, "Look, tomorrow, David really needs to get his horn parts sorted out," because I'd always want to do some multitracking on a certain piece. The band was quite happy to allow me to layer horn and flute tracks. They realized that I was quite good at it and it made a special sound. They said, "Okay, David.

Go and do your fuckin' horn parts!," excuse my language. But sometimes they were a bit irritated with me. One day, as I remember, someone said, "Do your fuckin' pawn hearts!" [laughs] You see? The genius of Peter Hammill is his language. Well, he writes beautiful tunes, as well. The moment he made that mistake—or someone made that mistake—Peter realized what he had. Peter was obsessed with chess, so he probably realized it was a hell of a phrase. I haven't told many people that story. Nobody has ever asked.

WR: So, the official story doesn't always give the full picture. . . .
Jackson: Peter is difficult. There's no other word for that. He might easily deny that this was the case. In my view that's how [the title] came about.

WR: To backtrack, producers such as John Acock, John Burns, and John Anthony—the Three Johns, as I refer to them—made a significant impact on the progressive rock bands of the early and mid-1970s. . . .
Jackson: It is a lost chapter.

WR: What's your take on John Anthony?
Jackson: John Anthony was wonderful. He was a house producer [for Charisma]. In those days musicians didn't know anything about recording. John . . . came into the room where we were playing and got excited about the music. When John Anthony produced the records for Van der Graaf they sounded amazing. Now, that's not just John Anthony, but he was working with some brilliant engineers [Robin Cable, David Hentschel, Pat Morahan, Ken Scott, etc.], as well. John's sort of disappeared off the face of the planet. God knows what's happened to him.

WR: Any sort of impropriety?
Jackson: Well, let's call them the dark forces.

WR: The general perception is that there was a dark force in VdGG's music. Maybe it was Peter's lyrics, which have been interpreted as nihilistic.
Jackson: One of my first encounters with the dark side of Peter's writing is with a piece called "Necromancer" [from 1969's *The Aerosol Grey Machine*]. I did not even know what that word meant. I know it refers to something involving the occult, but I always thought it was about people wanting to have sex with the dead. I remember we had just released one song and I was playing it, on record, to a girlfriend at the time. I wasn't married to her, but she had small children, and the children came into the room and I rushed to the record deck. I lifted the needle off the vinyl, because I was so worried that the children would hear this music. I have to tell you that the music seemed so evil—and I had written it! I had written that particular passage. I couldn't bear the thought of someone young hearing that, that it would corrupt. The song is on the second record, *H to He*. The end of the first side . . .

WR: "The Emperor in His War-Room"?

Jackson: Yes. I mean, would you want to turn the record over after that?

WR: The song "Darkness (11/11)," from *The Least We Can Do Is Wave to Each Other*, seems to be symbolic. The number eleven has certain dark connotations. It might represent imbalance and even demonic forces.

Jackson: Over the years Peter has tried a lot of things. He's tried a lot of substances, a lot of relationships, and he's lived life to the full. He wanted to know about all these things. I don't think he was completely obsessed with any one thing. He is an intellectual. I used to live with the guy for a while, sharing a room and writing a lot of music together. That was for a short time and then he went off into his own world, and I went off into my own world, and we met in the band. I remain friends with him and he's a godparent to my daughter. But families didn't exist in [the 1970s]. Nobody had families except for Guy. It was very difficult to be in a band like Van der Graaf and have a family or any permanent relationships, because the band was the most important thing.

WR: You were touring and recording constantly?

Jackson: You could not find anybody to put up with us.

WR: You had lived with Peter and collaborated with him. Would he pick up the acoustic guitar and then you'd play sax or flute and jam?

Jackson: Absolutely.

WR: How did you join Van der Graaf Generator?

Jackson: When I first met Peter, I was actually playing with Judge Smith, a founding member of Van der Graaf. He was trying to form a band. He and Peter Hammill were in the first Van der Graaf, ever, and the band was just not big enough for two writers of that strength. I then joined Judge in his band [Heebalob]. We had just done a demo recording at Polydor, and, as a friend, Peter had come round to listen to what Judge's band was doing. He listened to the recordings and I think one of the first questions he'd asked was, "Who's the sax player?" . . . We were just sitting around the room, kind of like a listening party, and there were quite a few people there. The band was playing the demo to as many people as possible, connections. The singer from Yes, Jon Anderson, was there and he was the most important person there. Someone said, "Jon, would you like to sing?," and I think he grabbed a guitar and started to sing, as I remember. We were introduced and then this other guy, Peter Hammill, sang a song, and it was unbelievable. I was blown away. . . . Later on, in a matter of weeks, my band with Judge collapsed. We didn't get a deal—Polydor didn't want us, and the band broke up. Peter asked if I would like to live in his flat, because he had a spare bed. I moved in with him and we started writing together immediately.

WR: How did writing proceed?
Jackson: We actually played a few songs on the street, like "After the Flood" [*The Least We Can Do . . .*], because Peter at that point was playing only the acoustic guitar. He didn't have a piano then. I had a flute and a sax and . . . I didn't do any double horn parts at the time, because we didn't write material like that. Then, I had an audition with the other guys in [VdGG] and I won the job. It was Hugh, who played a Farfisa; Guy, the drummer; and Nic [Potter], the bassist. I played some of the songs I was doing with Peter, so I knew the material really well. Peter and I were working closely together for a time. But later on, once we got some money and we were gigging, I didn't want to live there anymore, because it was really small and even [Peter] didn't want to live there. He moved somewhere else, much nicer. When we were out of that apartment Peter got a nice place with a big piano. I also moved to another place and I had a piano and wrote lots of music on the piano. I used to see Peter and tell him about what I'd written. Some of the tracks we wrote together, like "Pilgrims" [*Still Life*], "Scorched Earth" [*Godbluff*], things like that. We would sit together on a piano stool, and I would play something, and then Peter would play something and shove me out the way. Then I'd play something and shove him out the way. We were fighting for the keyboard. All I had to do at the end of the session was show Peter how to play the bits that I [wrote] so he knew them. We would meet again and it was a song.

WR: Were the basic bits of " . . . Lighthouse Keepers" written on the piano?
Jackson: Yeah, because I was writing on the piano then. The bits of saxophone parts that became very influential in songs like "Man-Erg" [*Pawn Hearts*], I wrote things like that in band rehearsals. What happened was that skeletons of songs were formed by Peter, or they were formed by Peter and me, and sometimes Hugh would have something. . . . Hugh was a bit private. . . . He would have a piece and he would present it. "Wondering" [*World Record*] was an example of that: Hugh wrote it and it was suddenly a Van der Graaf piece, because Peter had written some words for it. I would have to present my ideas and he would have something that fit with it. Or he would like something and learn it and not necessarily use it at that moment. Peter is a self-taught musician.

WR: You had mentioned the fact that you collaborated on "Pilgrims."
Jackson: That's one of those tunes where I sat down and I played the tune and Peter said he liked it. I think he just took it and learned it. But the seed of the song was mine. Same with " . . . Lighthouse Keepers."

WR: How do you go about writing the parts and deciding that this was going to be a large composition?
Jackson: We were living together, in the country, locked in his house, and the manager would go and get food. We would just rehearse all the time. One of

those passages would be a heavy demonic riff and then over the course of a morning or evening or afternoon the four of us would write a section that was just unbelievable. We said, "Let's change key there and do it this way." When I was living with Peter I introduced Peter to a lot of musical concepts that he didn't know. I'd say, "You can write really unusual music if you use every semitone once, and then use them all again. It's called twelve-tone writing." I had already written pieces like that and played them for Peter, and he said, "That's really weird." He would learn that in the bedsit and go out in the street to develop it.

WR: Where am I hearing those twelve-tone concepts in VdGG's music?
Jackson: This kind of structural stuff, you're hearing that in "After the Flood," the first one he wrote [in this vein]. [Hammill] wrote another one, a piece that was incorporated into " . . . Lighthouse Keepers"—"(Custard's) Last Stand." The other is in "Black Room" ["(In the) Black Room/The Tower" from Hammill's 1973 solo record, *Chameleon in the Shadow of the Night*]. They are so cunningly concealed and developed by inter-rhythmic structures, as well as musical, they just become weird harmonic music. It's not based on normal writing.

WR: Let's discuss the first band breakup in 1972. Was the band exhausted, physically, artistically, and financially?
Jackson: Well, when Peter says, "Go," we go. Peter says, "Stop," and we stop. It's as simple as that. It's always been like that.

WR: Are you're saying it was really Peter's decision in the end . . .
Jackson: I'm not too good on these details. There's an enormous amount of trauma involved in these things. My version of things is that Peter wanted to stop, and so we stopped. He wanted to get on with his solo work. I've always felt like I was public enemy number one and I didn't help what had happened in 1972.

WR: In what way?
Jackson: The Italians thought I was the image of Van der Graaf. Every bloody magazine had me on the cover at that time. That's why I play with six Italian bands now, because Van der Graaf "was" David Jackson in their minds, but that's not what I wanted. By that time I was the only person who actually stood up on stage. Peter used to sit down and play the piano most of the time. I leapt around. I was completely wired up. I didn't have to go anywhere near a microphone. I could play the sax anywhere I wanted to with a big stereo electric sax stack of power and make a hell of a noise. . . . Everybody else was trying to figure out this complicated music and play it. It was no trouble for me to figure it out and run around, a bit like a guitarist would in a guitar band. That got a lot of attention and I'm not sure [Hammill] was happy with that.

WR: Why did you think you were public enemy number one?

Jackson: [laughs] It happens in everything I get involved in. It's like a jinx. I've been too popular for the band. I'm not leading the band, but everyone thinks I am. I pissed off Van der Graaf, I'm sure, in the 1970s.

WR: You'd think the band would have welcomed whatever attention it was paid.

Jackson: Well, it doesn't always work out like that, I'm afraid. It's very complicated—and full of grief. It was tied into stupid deals, and I learned more in recent years than I ever knew at the time.

WR: You'd once said that mixing VdGG records was a nightmare. Why?

Jackson: We didn't need a producer when we were writing the material in the mid-seventies. After *Pawn Hearts* John Anthony was gone. We only had ourselves, and our belief in the music, so we were working with an engineer. . . . Literally it was all four of us, eight hands on the mixing console, with the engineer, trying to make things work and not be distorted. Everything was done live. You couldn't save a mix. If you made a mistake you had to go back and do it again. One mistake might be my fault or Peter's fault or Hugh's or Guy's. They were riding their solo or backing track against something else. Since those days I have lost all faith in my ability to mix anything. I don't trust myself and don't think musicians should mix their music, because I'm never satisfied listening to that music. I can remember thinking, *Bloody hell. We have to do it again.*

WR: I'd like to discuss your exit from Van der Graaf in the 1970s. You'd once said that finances were an issue in your leaving. When I spoke with violinist Graham Smith he wondered if his presence was part of the issue. . . .

Jackson: What happened just before Graham Smith joined is Hugh Banton left the band. Some people say to me, "Van der Graaf is not Van der Graaf now, because you're not in it anymore, David." That's a matter of opinion. Well, for me, in my opinion, Van der Graaf Generator without Hugh Banton is not Van der Graaf Generator.

WR: Why do you say that?

Jackson: Hugh is absolutely crucial to the concept of Van der Graaf Generator. He was there at the beginning and understands Peter's music. I think what I've done has helped make it Van der Graaf music and people have strongly argued that. But when Hugh left Van der Graaf I was having some rehearsals. Suddenly we have a bassist, Nic Potter, who I hadn't played with, at that point, for five years. Then Peter is only playing electric guitar, and he wants to play with an electric violinist. You have an electric violinist, an electric saxophone player, and an electric guitar player, who's playing so loud nobody can hear anything. I *ain't* comfortable. It wasn't really anything to do with Graham Smith. It was to do with the situation.

Although Jackson's sax track had to be built "from the bleed of other micro-phones," says mixing engineer Dave Anderson, *Vital*, VdGG's last album of the 1970s, "was really a triumph."

WR: You talk a lot about your work with Italian musicians. You've worked with Osanna. How did you get that gig?

Jackson: When we went to Italy in 1972, we had a number-one record there. At that time they had a prog rock chart and we had a number-one record for seven-teen weeks. We were absolutely massive. There was so much record corruption and nobody got any royalties or anything. We were all ripped off. I have signed hundreds of vinyl records every time I got to Italy. None of which I had seen before. They're all bootlegs. Van der Graaf were massive and we were headlining festivals and gigs all over the place. One of the bands I met at the festivals was Osanna, a hard rock band playing complicated, slightly Arabic music. They had a sax player and were parallel to us in time. When I was on the front pages of all the magazines, two saxophones blasting away, the band said to their sax player, Elio [D'Anna], "Get to playing two saxes." When Van der Graaf re-formed in 2005, everyone saw I was still alive and out there.

To answer your question, I think it comes down to promoters. You must not rule out the importance of promoters. One promoter was looking after Osanna and he wanted to look after Van der Graaf, too. When I left Van der Graaf in 2005, he had a bright idea of trying to get me to play with Osanna. So, I did loads of research and saw pictures of [D'Anna] playing two horns. I learned bits and pieces that he had done. I went into the sessions knowing what Elio had done, and the band was delighted. I said, "What happened to Elio?" They said, "Oh, he's found God." Elio was, and I think still is, running a shrine on an Italian island where pilgrims go. Knowing my history as persona non grata, I wanted to check out that I wasn't going to get in Elio's way. I did and ever since we've been to Japan and Korea and I've done a lot of gigs with the band. I've written a lot of double horn parts for them. [Jackson was scheduled to play with them again in 2014.] They don't speak a word of English, so it can be quite hard work sometimes.

WR: What about communication?
Jackson: It's virtually nonexistent. We started out playing quite a bit of my music and they've gradually phased it out. They wanted me to be more involved with the band, but after two years, the management company that put the whole thing together decided to drop the whole band.

WR: Osanna has been known for their theatricality.
Jackson: Lino [Vairetti], the director, leader of the band, a wonderful guy, delightful guy, looks incredibly scary, like Mussolini. He's terrifying onstage. But he's the sweetest man you ever met. The face paint—that's the big thing. It's Neapolitan rock. It's all fantastically aggressive rhythms. It's a lot of Neapolitan slang and street language, and the band wears makeup masks—it's like Italian vaudeville. It's the hardest music I've ever played.

WR: Have you played the band's concept album, *Palepoli*, onstage?
Jackson: We are remaking *Palepoli*. *Palepoli* is what Naples used to be called. It's an opera about the origins of the city. Lino changes direction every two years. The group we had, the Prog Family, lasted about four years. I still work with them, but it's only two or three gigs a year and only festivals now. I had a gig in Italy, a festival, 2010, and Trey [Gunn], and I did an album with an Italian band called NYX. Brilliant musicians and brilliant writers, and we were booked to do this festival. However, at the last minute it seemed to fall apart. The festival promoter I know said that he can get a violinist by the name of David Cross to come and play. "Can you do something with this guy David Cross?" I thought, "Okay, King Crimson . . . I'm sure I can play with him." My wife said, "You and violinists. Half an hour. Half an hour I give it." Miracles never cease: we have been firm friends ever since. He comes and works with me with special-needs children [the Twinkle project] and I've lectured at his teaching course in London at the London Metropolitan University. We are going to finish an album together. We have been working together for the last four years.

WR: What details can you give about the project's name and the new recording?

Jackson: Excellent question. In England there's a very important company that makes food, canned food, called Crosse & Blackwell. The slogan on the label used to say, "By appointment to her Majesty the Queen." Crosse & Blackwell— there's no finer food in a tin, right? Now there's also a famous company that makes garden tools and they're called Spear & Jackson and they're equally famous, and they are "By Royal Appointment to Her Majesty the Queen." They both have distinctive logos. So, right now, we are Cross & Jackson—"By Royal Appointment to the Queen." The half an hour that my wife predicted is still going strong.

WR: So, you enjoy working with a violinist at this point?

Jackson: It's a bit like playing with Peter and Van der Graaf in the early days. I go places, musically, I never would have imagined.

3

The Mellotron

Raising the Mammoth

The Mellotron. It is perhaps unlike any other single instrument ever made. Temperamental. Beastly. Overpowering. Majestic. Devastatingly effective.

We can't downplay the importance of other devices, keyboards, or machines used during the progressive rock era of the 1970s, most notably guitar effects and, of course, synthesizers such as Minimoog and ARP Soloist, but few pieces of musical equipment have left such an irrevocable stamp on the psyches of the people who've used and heard it.

Based on a similar machine designed by Harry Chamberlin in the late 1940s, the Mellotron was first commercially available in 1963 and aimed at re-creating the sonic swells of an orchestra through the use of analog tapes. Often called the world's first sampler, the Mellotron became a must-have item for any self-respecting prog rocker—as well as any aspirant progers, who were influenced by the likes of King Crimson, the Moody Blues, the Beatles, and Strawbs.

The instrument, its name derived from the words *melody* and *electronics*, offered users access to a chorus of flute sounds, ballsy brass, and idiosyncratic symphonic strings. It was thought, in the 1960s and 1970s, that the Mellotron was a perfect way to beef up a band's overall sonic impact and save on the hassle and expense of traveling with a multiperson symphony orchestra.

Because of the instrument's touted logistical economy, some in the music industry were nervous. Session musicians began to detest the mechanical beast, not so much for its odd sound, but more on the belief that these machines would replace union musicians on recording dates.

"I remember getting our second Mellotron," says David Surkamp, formerly of the Missouri-based Pavlov's Dog. "The musicians' union—it was bad enough we had one, right?—thought we would put orchestras out of business with these. Because of this the guys from Nektar were coming in from Frankfurt and we had them bootleg a second one in with their equipment, and that was like espionage, underground activity. They didn't have to do that. But what's one more instrument that the guys in customs didn't recognize?"

Ultimately, of course, musicians weren't put out work. In fact, after a few years, pop, rock, and R&B artists knew they couldn't replicate the sound of an orchestra even if they'd tried; they were perhaps more interested in harnessing the holy racket, the sonic oddities, that only the Mellotron could produce. In other words, people sought out the Mellotron ... for the sound of the Mellotron—an unsettling and almost monolithic (if not prehistoric) racket that no other musical tool seemed capable of producing. It became the go-to instrument for many bands. The Moody Blues, formed in Birmingham, whose resident keyboard player, Mike Pinder, had worked for Streetly Electronics, which manufactured the Mellotron in their factory in the middle of England, helped to elevate the drama within the tracks recorded by his band in the 1960s and 1970s. Similarly, Yes used to call it the "doctor." If a track wasn't quite complete, the only sure, and quick, fix was bringing in the Mellotron to smooth out the song.

"You'll hear something like Genesis, and the Mellotron comes in and the hair stands up in the back of your neck," says John Bradley, of Streetly Electronics, which makes, restores, and services Mellotrons in England. "The whole purpose of the Mellotron was to reproduce a certain sound, but it doesn't quite do that. What it does is produce a *Mellotron-ized* version."

How Did It Work?

In layman's terms: When the keys of this strange keyboard/organ were pressed down, analog tapes, containing prerecorded samples of flutes, orchestral strings, brass, etc., were dragged across a playback head and a sound was generated. Each strip of analog tape under the hood contained different samples, which could be selected by the user. Holding down the keys spooled the tape, and once pressure on the keys was released, the tape would return to its original position. (This mechanism has spawned what is called the "seven- . . ." or "eight-second rule": a vintage Mellotron would only hold a note for a short span of time before decaying and going silent.)

Initially a light and sensor system tripped the sounds on the tapes. "They tried optical to start with," says Bradley, "but couldn't get it to be reliable. Chloroform was used on the tape, so a small section of it was see-through, allowing for a lamp-and-sensor operation to occur. But this was scrapped in favor of the tape-sync system, which involves a recorded pulse noise that trips the cycling mechanism in the instrument so that the sound can begin." [*Note: In modern machines a digital system is employed.*]

Ingenious, really, but on the other hand the functional limitations of the instrument impacted the creative process, sometimes for the good (sometimes for the bad), and imprinted in our minds the machine's instantly recognizable signature, what Dave Kean, who resurrected the Mellotron brand in the late twentieth century, called its "sonic archetype."

Mellotrons would go out of tune, largely due to the motors not being powerful enough to handle more than one key being pressed down at once. And since the machine was dealing in analog tapes of actual performances, any slight imperfections in those performances would be magnified when

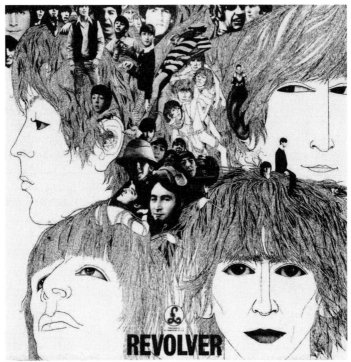

The Beatles (in the song "Tomorrow Never Knows," from 1966's *Revolver*), along with artists such as Graham Bond, the Moody Blues, and King Crimson, were early Mello-maniacs. "From the bootlegs I have, I know [John] Lennon had an Mk II at home in his studio," says John Bradley of Streetly Electronics.

transferred to the Mellotron. In essence, if a recording artist or performer was not achieving perfect octaves, it may not have been the machine's fault. Since sampled notes were recorded one at a time, of course, when chords were played on a Mellotron, it was likely that the resultant chord might contain slight dissonance or be a bit weird. Perhaps more importantly, faulty servomotors affected the pitch. In the M400 machine, for instance, when the motors were run for a while, it would heat up, causing the motor to speed up, impacting the pitch of the notes played.

For some, the very name Mellotron conjures horror stories of being isolated onstage wrestling with a beast that could not be controlled. "They don't like to travel," says John Hawken, formerly of Strawbs. "They don't like heat; they don't like the cold; they don't like erratic power sources; they don't like to be played, basically."

Hawken's lament is the same refrain echoed by musicians around the globe. But, ultimately, most musicians simply didn't care, or if they did, a basic instinctual need to play the instrument overrode their apprehensions. Hawken, himself, admits that despite their trouble, the instrument was very nearly an irreplaceable piece of equipment. "We had a tour when, bless the poor bastards, the roadies had to carry those things in and out," says Hawken. "But on those nights that it did work as advertised you forgave them anything because . . . it would tear the place apart."

Dabbling in a bit of masochistic delight, American bands, in particular, caught a bit of the Mello bug, because it meant they were able to capture the atmospheric sound, at least on some level, of their British prog rock counterparts/heroes. "We had one of the first Mellotrons in the country," says Wil Sharpe, formerly of the Indiana-based band Ethos. "Ralph Nielsen, Rick Nielsen's [Cheap Trick] dad, was importing them through Rockford, Illinois. We knew what was going on in the English scene through *Melody Maker*. We would look at ads for used and new equipment and then I would always contact Manny's Music in New York City to see what new equipment they had. We would drive to New York just to buy the equipment. We had every conceivable keyboard, and we were also able to buy a Chamberlin from Mr. Chamberlin, himself, who was in Upland, California. We went over to his garage where he built them. We always had the latest stuff."

The height of the Mellotron sales, says Bradley, was 1972 through 1973. Demands were so high at one point that parent company Mellotronics could hardly keep machines in their Streetly Electronics factory. It was a great relationship: Streetly Electronics, which began operations in late 1962 as Bradmatic, did the physical labor required to put together Mellotrons and Mellotronics marketed models such as the Mk I; Mk II (basically the same animal with a few improvements); the M300, a home model with fifty-two notes (with pitch control removed to make it more affordable); and then the M400, in 1970, which was designed to be a more transportable and affordable model. (The M400 also came equipped with a removable tape frame to switch in and out different sounds.)

Two thousand of the M400 machines were made, says Bradley, and soon Mellotronics entered in a distribution deal with Dallas Arbiter. Suddenly machines were being shipped all over the world. However, by 1976, Dallas Arbiter went belly up, still owing Mellotronics in London a significant amount of money. "I've heard upwards of sixty thousand or eighty thousand pounds," says Bradley, son of one of the cofounders of Streetly, Les. "That was a bloody huge amount of money."

When a wealthy member of Mellotronics' board passed away, it removed most of the company's financial security. Plus, the advent of more affordable synths with wider sonic capabilities sank Mellotronics for good and, by extension, Dallas Arbiter. When Mellotronics went up for sale, Les Bradley of Streetly wanted first crack at buying the business. Unfortunately, Bradley did not win the day and Streetly was threatened with legal action if they continued to build machines bearing the name Mellotron. As a result they produced the Novatron, although not many were ever made. "A lot of people used to refer to Mellotrons as 'Trons, even people at Streetly," says Bradley. "So, a Novatron is a new 'Tron."

M400s being assembled in Streetly's Birmingham factory.
Photo courtesy of Streetly Electronics

By 1986, interest in the Mellotron had waned among professionals, spelling the end of Streetly, for a time. The company wouldn't be revived until the early 1990s, a process that was kicked off by the appearance of the CD *Rime of the Ancient Sampler*, featuring some of the Mellotron's greatest champions, from Stuart John "Woolly" Wolstenholme of Barclay James Harvest to David Cross of King Crimson and Mike Pinder of the Moody Blues, underscoring the instrument's range and idiosyncratic nature, as well as how each musician had his own approach to playing the instrument.

The CD was compiled by Martin Smith, who had been fascinated with the machine since he was young. "In 1989 I wanted to get a Mellotron," says Smith, "and at that time they were not really popular. I spoke with Les and he said the only person he knew of selling a Mellotron is the Moody Blues. He gave me a number for Ray Thomas [flute, vocals] and I bought his Mark II. Les and John came up to see me to tweak the instrument and get it going. We went down to the pub, like English people do, and the idea of doing a CD came up. I began calling people to ask if they would like to appear on the record. I phoned Robert Fripp and Robert called back, and, in a slightly Wiltshire accent, said, 'I don't want to play Mellotrons anymore, but I still have my Mellotrons. If you want to take them in and service them . . .' So, we took in all six King Crimson Mellotrons: the Mk II from *In the Court of the Crimson King*, the *In the Wake of Poseidon* Mk II, the *Red* machine, *Islands* machine, two or three others."

A mid-1970s promo poster for the Mellotron.

Sensing a rise in popularity of the instrument, Streetly decided to get back into the game by providing instrument service. But as demand grew, so did the Streetly business. In recent years, Streetly, now run by John Bradley (since Les' death in 1997) and Smith, make their own version of the Mellotron and still provide service refurbishing services.

The three big names in the field over the last twenty-five years have been Streetly, Dave Kean at Mellotron, who bought the name in the 1990s, and Swede Markus Resch, who made the scene in 2002 with his modified M400.

There's no doubt that these gentlemen have done nearly the impossible: raising the mammoth, bringing a once-loved mechanical beastie—what was once deemed a fossil of a bygone era—back to life. Many, if not all, of the technical malfunctions, which bogged down the original machine, are gone, and a saner, more predictable instrument is now on the market.

Since returning to the Mellotron game with the M4000 machines, Streetly, among other changes, updated the cycling system so that the Mellotron will hold its pitch for a longer period of time. The playability was increased, and the company also offers twenty-four standard-issue sounds, which could be accessed via a system of buttons. In addition, there's less friction obstructing the pathway of the tapes in the M4000s; the infamous clacking or tapping noise generated by depressing the keys emanating from the original instruments has been virtually eliminated thanks to a leather strap dampening that sound. (Some users actually liked that noise, though, as it was just another odd and distinctive characteristic of the instrument.)

Streetly manufactures the parts for the machines—even the metal—and makes the "sample" tapes. It is, literally, a cottage industry. "We have a garage in the garden—in my garden," says Smith. "I live in a cottage in the center of England and there is a twenty-two-foot-square garage. . . ."

Sure, modern technology can approximate the audio frequencies of a Mellotron via digital modeling and software-powered keyboards (so-called "soft synths")—and at a fraction of the cost. But younger-generation musicians want the tactile experience of pressing down the keys and feeling the excitement of actually creating strange noises through organic means. Names ranging from Radiohead to Sigur Rós, Foo Fighters, and Kanye West have grown up listening to the beast, and want to claim some measure of satisfaction by actually playing the damn thing. In fact, when we were speaking with Streetly, Steven Wilson of Porcupine Tree had called into the office, hoping to order a new machine.

Vintage Mellotrons are so treasured that some can fetch well over five thousand dollars on eBay.com. It seems the myth and aura surrounding this brilliantly idiosyncratic musical device have grown exponentially in the last couple of decades. "As human beings we like chaos," Kean says. "I think the Mellotron is chaotic enough in its mechanical vagaries that it's different every time you play it. So, it sort of has an organic quality, like other instruments. In addition, I think we like the Mellotron for some of the same reasons we like horror films: it resembles enough of the real thing but we're not actually experiencing the real thing. So that, in and of itself, becomes creepy to us."

A Sampling of "Mello" Tracks

In alphabetical order, here's a short list of some key progressive rock tracks featuring Mellotron. This is only a partial list. Not every track featuring the Mellotron on the albums listed below was highlighted.

Anekdoten (Mellotronists: Anna Sofi Dahlberg, Nicklas Barker) "Sad Rain" (Barker, Dahlberg, Japanese bonus track on *Vemod*, 1993), "When I Turn" (Barker, *Chapters*, 2009), "In for a Ride" (*A Time of Day*, 2007, Dahlberg), "Monolith" (Dahlberg), "Ricochet," "The War Is Over" (Peter Nordins, Dahlberg, *Gravity*, 2003)

Barclay James Harvest (keyboardist: Woolly Wolstenholme) "After the Day," "Ursula (the Swansea Song)" (. . . *And Other Short Stories*, 1971), "She Said" (*Once Again*, 1971), "Summer Soldier" (*Baby James Harvest*, 1972)

Ekseption (keyboardist: Rick van der Linden) "Air" (*Ekseption*, 1969)

Genesis (keyboardist: Tony Banks) "The Fountain of Salmacis" (*Nursery Cryme,* 1971), "Watcher of the Skies" (*Foxtrot,* 1972), "Fly on a Windshield," "The Chamber of 32 Doors" (*The Lamb Lies Down on Broadway,* 1974), "Eleventh Earl of Mar" (*Wind & Wuthering,* 1976)

Peter Hammill (Mellotronist: Peter Hammill) "Easy to Slip Away" (*Chameleon in the Shadow of the Night,* 1973)

Harmonium (keyboardist: Serge Locat) "Depuis l'automne," "Histoires sans paroles" (*Si on avait besoin d'une cinquième saison,* 1975), "Comme un fou," "Chanson noire," "Comme un sage" (*L'Heptade,* 1976)

Heldon (Mellotronist: Richard Pinhas) "Perspective I," "Perspective III," "Perspective V" (*Heldon IV: Agneta Nilsson,* 1976)

Hoelderlin (keyboardist: Joachim von Grumbkow) "Schwebebahn" (*Hoelderlin,* 1975)

Il Balletto di Bronzo (keyboardist: Gianni Leone) "Introduzione," "Secondo incontro," "Epilogo" (*Ys,* 1972)

Jethro Tull (keyboardist: John Evan) "Cross Eyed Mary" (*Aqualung,* 1971)

King Crimson (keyboardists: Ian McDonald, Robert Fripp, David Cross) "The Court of the Crimson King" (*In the Court of the Crimson King,* 1969,

(k)scope

STEVEN WILSON
The Raven That Refused To Sing (And Other Stories)

FOR PROMO USE ONLY

1. Luminol (12.10)
2. Drive Home (7.37)
3. The Holy Drinker (10.13)
4. The Pin Drop (5.03)
5. The Watchmaker (11.43)
6. The Raven that Refused to Sing (7.57)

www.kscopemusic.com/stevenwilson

Steven Wilson, of Porcupine Tree, is one of many modern rockers using a real, honest-to-goodness Mellotron for his studio recordings, including *The Raven That Refused to Sing (and Other Stories).*

McDonald), "The Devil's Triangle" (*In the Wake of Poseidon*, 1970, Fripp), "Cirkus," "Lizard" (*Lizard*, 1970, Fripp), "Easy Money" (*Larks' Tongues in Aspic*, 1973, Cross), "Lament," "The Mincer" (*Starless and Bible Black*, 1973, Fripp, Cross), "Exiles" (*USA*, 1975, Cross, Fripp), "Mars" (*Epitaph* box set, 1997, McDonald)

Lift (keyboardist: Chip Gremillion) "Simplicity," "Caverns," "Tripping Over the Rainbow" (*Caverns of Your Brain*, 1977, reissued in 1990 by Syn-Phonic)

The Moody Blues (keyboardist: Mike Pinder) "Nights in White Satin" (*Days of Future Passed*, 1967)

Pavlov's Dog (keyboardist: Douglas Rayburn) "She Came Shining," "Valkerie," "Did You See Him Cry" (*At the Sound of the Bell*, 1976)

Pulsar (keyboardist: Jacques Roman) "Halloween" Parts I and II (*Halloween*, 1977)

Radiohead (Mellotronist: Jonny Greenwood) "Airbag," "Exit Music (for a Film)" (*OK Computer*, 1997)

Rush (keyboardist: Geddy Lee) "Faithless" (*Snakes & Arrows*, 2007)

Spring (keyboardists: Pat Moran, Ray Martinez, Kips Brown) "The Prisoner (Eight By Ten)," "Gazing" (*Spring*, 1971)

Strawbs (keyboardists: Blue Weaver, John Hawken) "Benedictus," "New World" (*Grave New World*, 1972, Weaver), "Autumn," "Hero and Heroine" (*Hero and Heroine*, 1974, Hawken), "Ghosts," "The Life Auction" (*Ghosts*, 1975, Hawken)

Tomita (keyboardist: Isao Tomita) "Mars, the Bringer of War," "Neptune, the Mystic" (*The Planets*, 1976)

The Trip (keyboardist: Joe Vescovi) "Little Janie" (*Caronte*, 1971)

Steven Wilson (Mellotronist: Steven Wilson) "Luminol" (*The Raven That Refused to Sing (and Other Stories)*, 2013)

Wobbler (keyboardist: Lars Fredrik Frøislie) "La Bealtaine," "The River" (*Rites at Dawn*, 2011)

Yes (keyboardist: Rick Wakeman) "Heart of the Sunrise" (*Fragile*, 1971), "And You and I" (*Close to the Edge*, 1972), "The Revealing Science of God (Dance of the Dawn)" (*Tales from Topographic Oceans*, 1973)

Mindcrimes and Misconceptions

Concept Albums (That Are and Aren't)

C oncept albums and, perhaps, innovative rock in general, presented
the naked ambition of the artist and offered escape to young listeners,
who were faced with the everyday and sometimes catastrophic issues
of the late 1960s and early 1970s, such as the draft (i.e., the lottery), quickly
shifting societal mores, the fallout from political scandal, economic recession,
environmental concerns, and the craziness of their own personal lives.[1] Rock
musicians may have perfected the theme, or concept, album, but it is not the
exclusive cultural property of rockers. The interconnection of words and music
dates back millennia.

The Ancients

Ancient Greek musicians, West African griots, and Eastern European bards
with lyre in lap spun epic tales of myth involving heroes, monsters, gods, and
great floods. It's not much of a stretch to suggest that the story-song form
likely predates our academically accepted concept of Western civilization. One
philosopher even suggests that smoke signals are a form of story and perhaps
the very basis of music. The fact is, no one really knows for sure how far back
story songs go, except to say that they might date to thousands, maybe tens of
thousands of years.

Fast-forward several millennia and the Western world comes to a work
like *The Song of Roland,* one of the most popular story songs in the history of
mankind. It's likely that *Roland* is not the first story song, and it's often analyzed
as a piece of straight-up literature, but *Roland* is one of the best and earliest
documented examples of the French song-poem, or chansons de geste ("songs
of deeds"), a recitative form with musical accompaniment enjoyed by the French
ruling class. The identity of the creator of *Roland* is unknown, though it's been
said that the story is based on historical events involving King Charlemagne in
the eighth century.

A manuscript (MS Digby 23), which likely dates to the twelfth century,
resides in a library at Oxford University, and contains nearly four thousand

verses. It's thought that this song was performed with a stringed instrument by a jongleur (which can be translated into English to "roving minstrel," someone who, it's believed, performed music and other such acts as juggling).

"We have virtually no knowledge of the music which accompanied the chanson de geste," wrote translator Glyn Burgess in the 1990 Penguin edition of *The Song of Roland*. "It was probably a simple monotonous tune repeated unchanged line after line."

Although the story is based on the 778 defeat and annihilation of Charlemagne's rear guard in Spain, scholars don't know exactly when *The Song of Roland* was written; many believe it dates to the time of the First Crusade. And with the coming of the Crusades, great French troubadours—usually a caste (or two) above traveling minstrels—sang poetic and romantic tales of love and chivalry in the native language of the people of southern France.

"The crusades were the real cause for the origin of the art of the troubadours," wrote Karl Nef in his scholarly *An Outline of the History of Music*. It was the troubadour's northern France counterpart, the trouvère (dubbed "minnesingers" in Germany in the thirteenth century), that more closely resembles the modern conceptual rocker, however. A thirteenth-century trouvère, Adam de la Halle, is credited with writing France's first secular musical play, *Robin and Marion*, and, as Nef wrote, "entered upon the field of polyphonic music" with his motets (unaccompanied vocal compositions sung in two different languages at once, usually Latin and French) and rondeaux (a popular musical form of the Late Middle Ages—the thirteenth and fourteenth centuries) that combined poetry and music in a set structure featuring rhyming and repeated lines. Musicologist and author Timothy Smolko, in his 2013 book *Jethro Tull's Thick as a Brick and A Passion Play—Inside Two Long Songs* (Indiana University Press), notes the connection between the medieval French laisse or lai (a "form of music and poetry of the thirteenth century," according to *The Oxford Dictionary of Music*) and the expanded song structures of epic rock works, such as Jethro Tull's "Thick as a Brick" and "A Passion Play."

Smolko also points out Guillaume de Machaut's importance in developing the form. According to Nef's *An Outline of the History of Music*, Machaut was a master of the fourteenth-century musical movement in Europe, a renewal of art, dubbed "ars nova," which encompassed such developments as polyphony—two or more melodies performed simultaneously—and the inclusion of secular lyrical concepts and musical forms.

Funnily enough, the tag "ars nova" could be applied (albeit loosely) to the explosion of progressive rock in the late 1960s and early 1970s—perhaps most notably the mixing of musical styles—resulting from an expansion of pop's parochial (or limited) musical horizons. Just as prog rock challenged and expanded the scope of popular music marketed by the record industry establishment, so, too, the developments of ars nova enriched medieval church music—the standard of the day.

The next two centuries saw the rise, continuance, and improvement of art forms and structural elements important to conceptualized music—the Italian madrigal, the French chanson, the use of motifs in church music for unity in the Mass, and opera.

"The Battle Between David and Goliath," composed on harpsichord by the baroque, pre-Bach Bohemian master Johann Kuhnau, attempted to capture the passion and fury of the Biblical story through instrumental music. Later, J. S. Bach's St. John Passion and St. Matthew Passion would appear and echo in thematic sympathy. (Interestingly, we hear fragments of these works and Bach's famous Mass in B Minor dimly recalled centuries later by diverse and unlikely rock artists, such as the Electric Prunes with their ambitious 1968 undertaking *Mass in F Minor*, Spooky Tooth and Pierre Henry in their collaborative effort, 1970's *Ceremony*, and the Italian progressive rock band Latte e Miele, with 1974's *Passio Secundum Mattheum*.)

Other classical composers worked at similar ends. Hector Berlioz, whom some refer to as the father of the modern large-scale symphony orchestra, composed the programmatic and dynamic five-movement *Symphonie fantastique*, which tells the tale of a young musician's vain pursuit of an idealized woman.

As the story goes, our artist/antihero attempts to commit suicide via an overdose of opium, but instead experiences phantasmagoric, frightening dreams—something like a mid-twentieth-century "bad trip." "*Symphonie fantastique* by Hector Berlioz is the seminal work in terms of the symphonic poem or the dramatically, thematically derived from work which inspired Wagner and Liszt and all those composers," says classical pianist Christopher O'Riley, who recorded instrumental versions of Radiohead and Pink Floyd songs.

Iconic American conductor Leonard Bernstein called the Berlioz work the first piece of orchestral psychedelia. "You take a 'trip,' you end up screaming at your own funeral," Bernstein said, referring to the programmatic work. (The main character/artist in Berlioz's piece is beheaded in the fourth movement, which is followed by the final section, "The Witches' Sabbath.") This theme is echoed throughout the decades, from Rush's sidelong masterwork, *2112*, to the Mars Volta's psychological nightmare *De-Loused in the Comatorium*, a concept album centered on the images a coma patient envisions while in an incapacitated state, and even *The Lamb Lies Down on Broadway* with its characters the Lamia and Lilith.

A recurring musical theme, called *idée fixe*, or fixed idea, represents the appearance (and reappearance) of the hero's beloved, which mutates each time it is reintroduced in order to meet the thematic needs of a particular movement. Wagner was infusing his operas, or, as the composer was fond of calling them, "dramas," with *leitmotifs*, similar to the idée fixe. Running the risk of offending opera and classical music purists everywhere (probably too late for that), we could conclude that it was Wagner alone who unwittingly provided the raison d'être for rock concept albums, which would appear nearly a hundred years after his death. Concept albums were the music of the future or, in the language of the land, *Zukunftsmusik*.

"With leitmotifs you have a seminal . . . musical idea that would be associated with a feeling or a character," says O'Riley. "You also have the intermingling of those motifs that, even if nobody is singing on stage, you feel like you are hearing the thoughts of the character as they are standing there, waiting for their next line. It's an amazing new design of musical architecture and discourse and that really did come from Berlioz."

From the programmatic came one of classical music's experimental (and cerebral) spheres: the *tone* or *symphonic poem*—one long piece of music that's meant to tell a story. Liszt, who's sometimes credited with inventing the form, Strauss, Elgar, Debussy, Tchaikovsky, Franz Schubert, and later Gustav Holst, among others, were all guided by overriding themes when constructing their symphonic poems, sometimes seeking to reflect and replicate sounds appearing in the natural world or simply to tell a story through music, using pitch, volume, rhythm, and instrumental timbre.

The rock equivalent of these symphonic poems can be found in the extravagant efforts of bands in the progressive rock and progressive hard rock or metal categories, such as Yes, Genesis, Jethro Tull, Pink Floyd, Manfred Mann's Earth Band, Rush, Henry Cow, Emerson, Lake and Palmer, Aphrodite's Child, French bands such as Ange and Pulsar, South America's Espiritu, Germany's Triumvirat, Frank Zappa, Planet P Project, Marillion, Gentle Giant (*The Power and the Glory*, on how power corrupts), and even prog metalers like Voivod and Queensrÿche, most notably for its 1988 entry, *Operation: Mindcrime* (a play on words of sorts: speaking both to the nature of psychological brainwashing and psychotic delusion), and many others.

Vangelis Papathanassiou's *Fais que ton rêve soit plus long que la nuit*, written on the student riots in France in 1968, was subtitled "Poème symphonique." (Vangelis and his band, Aphrodite's Child, were recording their debut album in Paris during the riots.)

As we move into the twentieth century, other influential composers and musical figures pushed the boundaries of musical drama, such as Kurt Weill with his idea of a "song play" and *The Threepenny Opera*, and Rodgers and Hammerstein's stage and screen work. The connection between visuals, or theatrics, and music is just as crucial to the integrity of the entire work of art as it was in opera. Due to the technological advances of audio reproduction and recording, as well as the economics of mass production, a shift in the retail marketplace occurred. No longer was the epic song the only way to communicate the subtleties of a complicated story or musical theme. Though the LP had made an appearance in the late 1940s, by the latter part of the 1950s and throughout the 1960s, the phonograph—the 12″ vinyl album—becomes every bit as important a marketing tool as the then-commercially-viable 78 rpm disc format commonly manufactured by record companies.

If one plays loose with the definition of the concept album, Depression Era folk icon Woody Guthrie was attached to thematic efforts as early as 1942, when he appeared on the Library of Congress' first folk compilation, *Folk Music of the United States: Anglo-American Ballads*. For our focus and needs, however, Guthrie's later releases are more cohesive examples of thematic works, such as the seminal 1956 collection of children's songs, *Songs to Grow On for Mother and Child*, 1958's *Songs to Grow On: Nursery Days* and the 1960 release *Ballads of Sacco & Vanzetti*. It goes without saying, perhaps, that concept albums, in general, were birthed via the emergence of the 12″ long-playing platter. The 12″ record offered many possibilities to creative minds—and a much larger canvas on which to sketch.

Music icons of all stripes were going conceptual: *Sing and Dance with Frank Sinatra*, from 1950, was vaguely thematic, as the songs appearing on the album supposedly emphasized such amorphous concepts as swing and rhythm; nevertheless Sinatra's first recording issued on a 33⅓ 12″ LP. It was really Sinatra's 1954 LP, *Songs for Young Lovers*, a 10″ disc, and his first record for Capitol, that was a true expression of focused musical forethought that contained original music organized around a well-defined romantic theme conceptualized prior to the recording of the project.

Others took advantage of the long-playing record, including country, blues, and jazz artists. Musicians such as Duke Ellington, Charles Mingus, and saxophonist John Coltrane all created thematic efforts during the middle years of the twentieth century. (Coltrane achieved what might be his career-defining work with the four-part metaphysical masterpiece *A Love Supreme*, from 1965, dedicated to the Almighty's omnipotence and infinite mercy.)

Wouldn't You Like to Be a Pepper, Too?

By the mid- and late 1960s, rock commanded the pop music field; superstar quartet the Beatles were producing "rock" music and had revolutionized the idea of the themed, or, what was quickly being dubbed, the "concept," album with the release of 1967's *Sgt. Pepper's Lonely Hearts Club Band*. New York Times writer Paul Nelson observed in a June 1968 article that *Sgt. Pepper's* could very well be blamed for making "the themeless rock LP all but obsolete."

"I suppose the madmen took over the asylum," Procol Harum lyricist Keith Reid told the author once. "The musicians grabbed hold of the reins. In the old days you went into a recording studio and made a record and if your guitar was too loud they told you to turn it down. Then here come the Beatles. All of a sudden you thought, 'I'm going to make [the guitar] twice as distorted.' The business said, 'Shit, these guys know what they are doing.' Suddenly the guys who control the purse strings . . . let the hordes in and let them have their way."

Despite the misconceptions surrounding the record, or perhaps because of them, *Sgt. Pepper's* is often perceived as ground zero for the rock concept record and, as I've argued in the past, the entire progressive rock movement, which took hold in Britain in the mid-and late 1960s. Fact is, *Pepper's* isn't really a concept album in the strictest sense. The variety show aspect of Paul McCartney's initial idea doesn't seem to follow through to the end, or even throughout the work.

Yet, high-profile and underground artists alike followed the Beatles' artistic lead, such as Nirvana (*The Story of Simon Simopath* released in October 1967 on Chris Blackwell's Island Records), the Family Tree (*Miss Butters*), the Seeds (*Future*), Traffic (*Mr. Fantasy*), the Moody Blues (*Days of Future Passed*), the Kinks (with *Arthur (Or the Decline and Fall of the British Empire)* and others), the Who (*Tommy* and *The Who Sell Out*), the Small Faces (semi-conceptual *Ogdens' Nut Gone Flake*)[2], and Vanilla Fudge (with their pop history of the world, *The Beat Goes On*). The Beatles, themselves, further contributed to this overload of musical overindulgence by offering a quirky and catchy string of tunes—a suite, really—appearing on the second side of 1969's *Abbey Road*.

Although most of the abovementioned records are not story-form albums, they do hint at a conceptual plot or overriding concept.

Similar to the classic Tony Clarke–produced Moody Blues records of the era, Family's long-playing debut from 1968, *Music in a Doll's House*, co-produced by Traffic's Dave Mason, benefits from clever crossfading techniques, which created the illusion of an intentional lyrical narrative.

Family, which evolved from the Farinas, and were named by their early producer Kim Fowley (who apparently thought the band's stage dress gave them the appearance of being in the Mafia) were creating their own vocabulary, somewhere between blues, ethnic music, and art-rock.

Music in a Doll's House is one of the best examples of the band's melting pot of musical ideas. Minor interludes, including "Variation on a Theme of Hey Mr. Policeman," "Variation on a Theme of the Breeze," and "Variation on a Theme of Me My Friend" further imprinted the notion that each song is an individual section of a larger suite.

Rolling Stone writer David Ascher, in a 1968 review of *Music in a Doll's House*, mused that Family had been heavily influenced by the *Sgt. Pepper's* "strategy of rock" and compares the song "3 X Time" with "Lucy in the Sky with Diamonds," and "Mellowing Grey" with an earlier Beatles tune, "Eleanor Rigby."

"We must have been influenced by *Sgt. Pepper's*," says iconic lead singer Roger Chapman, whose onstage bodily convulsions and intense vocal vibrato has been an inspiration to generations of British progressive rock singers, "because we were all in the same company. I assume we were all listening to each other's records, to be honest. We were moved to London as Family and put in the same company [as some of these bands]. . . . We were using some of the same studios, because our management at the time really knew how to get its foot in the door. They put us in a house in Chelsea, which was seriously happening then, and so Family had its own house, a big house, just off Kings Road, and mingled with all the people, who were ruling the music world then."

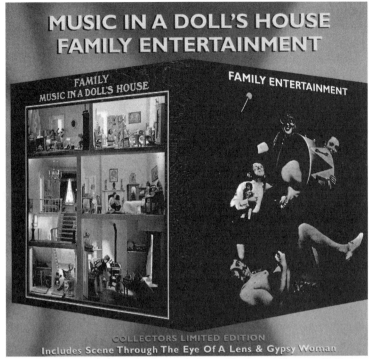

Family's mélange of musical styles was bolstered by Roger Chapman's distinctive and influential vocal vibrato. Surely names such as Peter Gabriel and Fish (Marillion) owe him a debt. "Most of the time I hate the sound of my fucking voice," says Chapman, with a laugh. "But I can't stop doing it [the vibrato], because I love doing it."

Even if the early and mid-1970s Family records aren't concept albums in the conventional sense; the individual songs featured on them act as pieces of a larger puzzle—sonic Rorschach tests, coaxing us to find repetitive musical and lyrical patterns. For instance, the sonic qualities of songs found on 1970's *A Song for Me*, such as "Drowned in Wine," "Wheels," "Love Is a Sleeper," "Stop for the Traffic—Through the Heart of Me," "Song for Sinking Lovers," "93's OK J," and the title tune, seem to suggest that the music itself tells a dark unfolding story.

The record is a kind of thematic symphony or oratorio: musical themes, and variations on those themes, appear throughout the song cycle. An individual can read seemingly endless possible meanings in Chapman's penetrating, repetitive vocal trills, John Weider's disturbing violin sawing (which, sonically, falls somewhere between Appalachian bluegrass and Eastern European gypsy) and John "Poli" Palmer's surprisingly arresting flute playing. All of this, of course, is to say nothing of the band's collective technical proficiency and synchronicity, which only add to the hypnotic and fantastical nature of the music.

"We were a real buzz, a serious buzz at that time," Chapman says.

This Is for Rael

Perhaps one of the greatest story-form concept records of the 1970s was Genesis' double studio album from 1974, *The Lamb Lies Down on Broadway*. The most notable aspect of *The Lamb*, aside from its sheer audacity, is the music's schizophrenia, a by-product (no doubt) of the record's thematic concept. (Interestingly enough, the band operated on a schizophrenic level during the production process, dividing the workload fairly evenly: for the most part Gabriel wrote the words, the band the music.)

Gabriel explained the basic premise of the plot to an audience at the Shrine Auditorium in Los Angeles in 1975: "It tells of how a large black cloud descends into Times Square, straddles out across Forty-second Street, turns into wool, and sucks in Manhattan island. Our hero, named Rael, crawls out of the subways of New York and is sucked into the wool to regain consciousness underground. This is the story of Rael."

Gabriel chose New York City as the story setting, not only for its pace and excitement, but for its mid-1970s grittiness. Presenting an urban youth, prone to violence, seems to reflect Gabriel and Genesis' curiosity about and fascination with working classes (i.e., "The Battle of Epping Forest").

If *The Lamb* is the apotheosis of Genesis' Gabriel-era progressive and conceptual output, then "Looking for Someone" could be viewed as the spiritual entry point for this incredible journey. It's fitting that this psychedelic trip through spiritual transformation leading to enlightenment, this kind of *West Side Story* meets a "punk" version of *The Pilgrim's Progress*, was Gabriel's final album with Genesis, and something he has not successfully redone or revisited.[3]

In Carl Jung's *Man and His Symbols* M. L. von Franz wrote that the only worthwhile adventure left for man was the exploration of his own subconscious. The opening line of "The Grand Parade of Lifeless Packaging" reads, "It's the last great adventure left to mankind," which is spoken by a merchant, a "drooping lady," hawking dreamdolls. It's doubtful Gabriel picked his imagery by chance. (It's doubtful, as well, in the post–*The Who Sell Out/Tommy* world that Gabriel chose the lead character's name at random. In addition, much has been made of the Gabriel surname and its possible link to the main character's name.) A spiral staircase, for instance, in "Carpet Crawlers" is symbolic of either madness or rebirth (and, in the era of DNA testing, it could be interpreted as speaking to the very core of what makes us human—the double helix). Other timeless, sometimes ominous and evocative images such as the raven, water rapids, caves, dark chambers, doorways, tunnels, and blinding white lights tap our deepseated subconscious minds. It's this use, this conga line, of Jungian archetypal imagery and its symbolism, not a logical narrative flow, at least not one that is readily apparent, that drives the record.

The Lamb works as an allegory as well as a fantasy tale—a kind of Jungian slideshow that taps into levels of human consciousness that we may not fully comprehend. *The Lamb* is an instrument, as much as a reflection, of the idea of the universal consciousness and how we interpret symbols. By dabbling in discussion about the work, and even listening to it, in writing and performing it, we are connected to a universal consciousness.

Gabriel once described Genesis' music as inducing or motivating listeners to create an atmosphere that mimics (if only vaguely) the kind of sensory deprivation typical of isolation experiments conducted by Jack Vernon and John C. Lilly. "We find that people like listening to our albums alone, with candles on," Gabriel said to *Circus* magazine in 1974. "It's very escapist. I personally think it's a more satisfying way to hear music—being isolated."[4]

In 1974 *Circus* magazine once asked Gabriel what his favorite fairy tale was and he replied *Lilith* by George MacDonald, a Scottish Victorian author of fantasy literature whose work was an influence on J. R. R. Tolkien and C. S. Lewis, among others. "Peter understood the world of fairy tales and mythology and those fairy tales are very important on a psychological basis," says Francis Dunnery, formerly of It Bites and confirmed Genesis fan. "There's always a hidden story inside the fairy tale."

A Lilith-type character (i.e., "Lilywhite Lilith") crops up in the story of *The Lamb*. Lilith is a Queen of the Night figure, the anima—the feminine aspect of the male psyche, someone in touch with the supernatural realm, as C. G. Jung observed—who guides Rael. *The Lamb* begs us to pose questions of ourselves: Are archetypes a by-product of some learned instinctual process, something that has developed over hundreds of thousands of years of evolution? Fact is, we'll never know and we may never be able to peel back enough psychological layers to peer into the work to ascertain how these symbols originated.

At the least, we can say that Gabriel was clever enough to include and juxtapose symbolic, or some might say Jungian, archetypes into his writing to keep us guessing forever that there are profound hidden meanings inherent to his lyrics.

The author also sees *The Lamb* as one big loop. Flip to the bottom of your old LP record sleeve and you'll notice something intriguing. Gabriel customizes a line from the famous Rolling Stones hit "It's Only Rock 'n' Roll (But I Like It)," which appeared on the record of the same title also in 1974, and the lyrics don't so much end as trail off with an ellipsis. In addition, the text—the libretto for this kind of rock opera—wraps around the inside of the LP gatefold and begins with the line: "Keep your fingers out of my eye . . . "

Once the tale of Rael is presented, and we read the line, "Copyright Peter Gabriel 1974," the text picks up, again, from the beginning with the line "Keep your fingers out of my eye. . . ." It's likely, not certain by any means, however, that this was done on purpose for effect. However, if this was intentional, in the sense that the flow of the text has meaning in its current state, then the story is, indeed, cyclical. Once we put on the record (or CD) or click our mouse pad on a certain track, we, too, are caught into this circle, or loop. It's possible that *The Lamb* text and conceptual narrative thread is an elaborate Möbius strip— the story is folded over on itself. So then, Rael, too, is caught in a repeating pattern, experiencing clarity—satori—over and over again. In essence, Rael gains insight, then loses it, and repeats the process.

In Douglas R. Hofstadter's book *Gödel, Escher, Bach: An Eternal Golden Braid*, the author points to twentieth-century Dutch illustrator M. C. Escher's *Waterfall* lithograph as an example of a "strange loop" and paradoxes. Interestingly, the abstract geometric designs featured on the sleeves for the original LPs are very similar to Escher's art by tessellation. They seem to hint at Escher's 1940 woodcut *Metamorphosis*, in which shape and form meld to reveal infinite evolutionary processes, returning us to an earlier developmental stage.

The track "Broadway Melody of 1974" is, essentially, a parade of paradoxes: the contents of a mind, with all of its mixed messaging, impulses and thoughts, on display: the Ku Klux Klan serving soul food as a band plays Glenn Miller's "In the Mood"; children playing with needles and pins, etc. Whether there's such a thing as "musical tessellation," either in reality or on *The Lamb*, may be difficult to tell at this point and would require further study. However, there are certain slight variations on basic themes that are repeated throughout *The Lamb*, and certain rhythmic loops also occur. (Although, admittedly, this device is used more effectively and with more frequency for 1976's *Wind & Wuthering*.)

"Our brains are wired in such a way that we recognize patterns, even as infants, and we gravitate toward patterns as a survival skill," says Carl Baldassarre of the Ohio-based progressive rock band Syzygy. "It is not a surprise to me that maybe Gabriel doesn't know a thing about Gödel or strange loops or a Möbius strip or recursive logic or meta-language, but that doesn't mean that he's not able to create them incidentally."

Genesis
GASP Archive

LIVE AT GRONINGEN

Jung punk: A series of archetypal images helped shape *The Lamb Lies Down on Broadway*'s surrealistic storyline, centered on a seemingly schizophrenic street tough named Rael. Pictured: a GASP (Genesis Authentic Soundboard Project) recording of Genesis in the Netherlands, April 1975.

Symbolism

The mere appearance of four sides is also significant. The number four has always held humanity's fascination. There are four cardinal points of a compass, four gospels, four seasons, etc. Just as importantly, there are four cycles of the hero myth (as noted by Dr. Paul Radin). With further developmental research, we could interpret each side of the original LP as (very roughly) coinciding with the four cycles of the hero myth (i.e., "Trickster," "Hare," "Red Horn," and "Twins").

The packaging for the original record—an LP slipped inside a liner bag or record sleeve—constitutes a circle inside a square—the image of the perfect union as defined by the purveyors of ancient alchemy. In addition, the actual product, the object—the vinyl LP etched full of grooves—presents a physical labyrinth, which we enter each time the needle drops. The ancient image of the labyrinth is a symbol for the self. To follow this logic one step further, the stylus scratches the V-shaped microgrooves of the record, evoking physical consummation.

Interestingly enough, *The Lamb* takes us back to nearly the beginning of Gabriel's professional career. Gabriel sings of being lost in a subway, losing time, and finding himself "a name" in the track "Looking for Someone," the first song to appear on the band's Charisma Records debut, *Trespass*, released in October 1970. *Trespass*, a transitional album, seems to shed light on the spiritual pathway and growth Gabriel would undertake over the next few years as an artist and individual. Amid references in the lyrics to Buddha and Damascus (alluding to the Apostle Saul's/Paul's acceptance of Christ recounted in the New Testament?), the song could be interpreted as a revelation—a satori—and an ardent, if confusing, search for the self—or a higher consciousness.

Catapulted by Gabriel's soulful vocals, harking back to the singer's love of 1960s R&B and soul (i.e., Otis Redding, Wilson Pickett, etc.), "Looking for Someone" is an early example of the band presenting a lengthy, dynamic piece pockmarked by peaks of sonic upheavals and moments of pastoral passages and overtures to European art music—masculine and feminine sonic qualities that, when wed, would later be identified as "progressive rock" by music scholars.

Looking for someone? Maybe that person was Gabriel, himself. If this is the case, this search for the self resonated with so many listeners. "When I came to England in 1975," says Egyptian percussionist Hossam Ramzy, who later recorded with Peter Gabriel, "I heard *The Lamb Lies Down on Broadway*. 'The Chamber of 32 Doors.' The song is about choices in life. I remember my father saying to me that I have to become a doctor or an architect, engineer, lawyer. Have a respectable life. But another part was saying, 'Don't sacrifice your dream for anything.' I said, 'This song is going to be my motto.'"

"I would listen to it again and again," says Nick Barrett of Pendragon, "because I had to find out what this guy [Gabriel] was on about. Finally after hearing it so many times, the penny dropped. I got it. If I had just written it off, like so many younger people do when they download a song from iTunes, then I never would have gotten into this kind of music and never discovered Genesis."

When Genesis toured *The Lamb* it confused audiences initially, who were expecting to hear the band's old "hits," and instead got a recital of new material complete with stage costumes (so elaborate it became difficult at certain points in the show for Gabriel to even sing in front of a microphone), pyrotechnics,

Visuals for the cover of *The Lamb* were captured in a number of different locations, including the waterfalls of south Wales, Hipgnosis' design studios in London, vaults underneath the legendary music venue the Roundhouse, and the interior of the building (now the Renaissance London Hotel) above St. Pancras railway station. "The mirror image logo links up with the whole idea of self reflection," says former Hipgnosis in-house layout man Richard Evans.

and slide shows. It was a multimedia event, with moving parts that never quite worked correctly. But perhaps this didn't matter.

Martin Levac, of Dance into the Light, and a former drummer of The Musical Box—a Genesis-sanctioned tribute band that re-created the band's classic performances—can attest to how difficult those times were for Genesis to stage a multimedia presentation.

"I can recall many times where the old Elmo slide projectors were not working properly in The Musical Box's restaging of *The Lamb*," says Levac. "I used to turn my back to the crowd to play the vibes parts in many songs especially 'The Lamia,' and many times the projection that I was looking at was not what it should have been. Visually, we religiously reproduced the whole thing without any technological improvement to it. I guess that was not the ideal thing to do."

Over the Wall?

Often the late 1960s and 1970s concept albums evolved into multimedia events, echoing dramatic theories Wagner had put into practice a century earlier. David

Bowie's *The Rise and Fall of Ziggy Stardust and the Spiders from Mars*, Jethro Tull's *A Passion Play*, Genesis' *The Lamb Lies Down on Broadway*, Pink Floyd's *The Wall*, and Frank Zappa's *Joe's Garage* all contained a theatrical flair that begged for elaborate stage productions.

The temptation is to conclude that after *The Lamb* was staged and its natural predecessor, Pink Floyd's *The Wall*, had been staged that the golden age of the concept record had crumbled with it. Undoubtedly, the decade of the 1970s was the golden age of conceptual rock efforts, having produced numerous staples of the classic rock FM radio format. Certainly, on one level this was true, but the concept record was very much alive, especially in metal circles. The dream of rock musicians expressing themselves so lavishly did not die at the dawning of the Reagan era.

It's not generally discussed, often kept hush-hush by the powers that be, but the decades that followed the 1970s produced intricate tales and personal narratives out of character with the times. History tells us that concept albums had become passé in the 1980s and beyond: they were ignored and ridiculed by critics and even some fans. Yet, an alternative reading of events leads us to quite a different conclusion. Within a fifteen-year period, pop, jam-band, neo-prog, and metal acts alike, as diverse as Queensrÿche, Weezer, Iron Maiden, Phish, and Marilyn Manson, defied the so-called trends and conceived of, wrote, and recorded popular and enduring conceptual releases such as *Operation: Mindcrime*, *Antichrist Superstar*, and many others.

"Bands that you've mentioned, like Pink Floyd and Jethro Tull and others, were the bands that I grew up with and been very inspired by," says Queensrÿche vocalist/keyboardist Geoff Tate. "All of us in the band pulled a lot from those artists and bands who told a story. That was very interesting to us."

Resurgence?

Because the relevance and validity of concept albums had dropped considerably in the 1980s (in the mainstream, anyway), it's a small miracle that any concept albums were being produced at all after the 1970s. In particular, the late 1980s/early 1990s was a time of great transition and seismic shifts in popular rock music: the grunge and alternative genres ruled the clubs, airwaves, and record stores. Heartache, dysfunction, and broken lives—the so-called "real" emotional deal—monopolized the rock field. (That some in the alternative and grunge scenes were not immune to the lure of the almighty dollar, much like their 1970s punk rocker predecessors, is perhaps a discussion for another time.)

By the year 2000, the atmosphere in and surrounding the music business was undergoing radical change, even as it experienced its greatest financial uptick in recent memory. The digital revolution democratized the process of making, producing, absorbing, selling, and disseminating music. Technology, though opening a veritable Pandora's box in other respects, put bargaining power back in the hands of the artist: a circumstance reminiscent of the mid- and late 1960s when, as Keith Reid had pointed out, the "madmen took over the asylum."

With a newfound liberation, artists cut out the middleman and went directly to the consumer/listener. Continually artists are free to explore their personal and sometimes extravagant musical visions, perhaps for the first time in nearly twenty years. The record business and label executives seem more open to taking chances, as well, and visionary rock has made a full-fledged comeback, helping to spur the growth of underground or so-called "prog" rock, and legitimizing, once again, the concept album as a form of musical expression.

One might argue that these groundbreaking modern-day rock acts, having been encouraged to continue to experiment by the very culture of the music business that had once shunned this kind of artistic activity in the past, have succeeded in the virtually impossible: *decriminalizing* a once-taboo approach. Many serious and critically lauded modern rockers realize the importance of the concept record as a creative vehicle. They also understand its power to communicate basic ideas of the human condition. Artists, from Trans-Siberian Orchestra to Radiohead to Coheed and Cambria, Spock's Beard (and Neal Morse solo), Porcupine Tree (and Steven Wilson solo), Mastodon, and the Mars Volta have written and/or continue to write and record extravagant (if not convoluted) story-based records, with little fear of reprisals from the recording industry.

Coheed, for instance, wrote an extended story line that spanned three records and spawned a comic book series, *The Amory Wars*. "What we hope is that the music takes you on a journey and fans can look deeper into the story," says Travis Stever, guitarist for Coheed and Cambria. "Claudio [Sanchez, bandleader] and I grew up together. A lot of the lyrics hint of things that I know he's gone through. He fictionalizes his personal experiences. For instance, the name of the comic book series, *The Amory Wars*, is a reference to the street he grew up on in Valley Cottage, called Amory Drive."

Ghostly Concept, Show

Steven Wilson, the driving force and mastermind of Porcupine Tree (which began life as a recording project Wilson created for himself), released the conceptual *The Raven That Refused to Sing (and Other Stories)* in 2013.

Although Porcupine Tree started as a solo project for Wilson, over the years other musicians would join the ranks, and PT developed into something resembling a band with some (if limited) creative input from a few of the members. In recent years, however, Wilson has increasingly cultivated his solo brand apart from the influential Grammy-nominated band he established, and some of the bandleader's nascent professional instincts have resurfaced.

Since 2011, having written and recorded ever-increasingly complex, knotty, and jazz-influenced solo studio albums, not to mention carving out a niche for himself as a 5.1 mixing/remixing engineer extraordinaire, working with such heavyweights as Jethro Tull and King Crimson, Steven has stepped out as a solo artist.

Wilson's 2013 solo record, *The Raven That Refused to Sing . . .* boasts such tracks as the title song (about a man approaching death who looks for comfort from the spirit of a dead relative), "Luminol" (a busker who returns to the same street corner even in death), "The Watchmaker" (husband murders his wife of fifty years, and she comes back to haunt him), and others. These songs have been inspired, in part, by classic supernatural fiction, Gothic literature penned by British authors from the late nineteenth and early twentieth centuries, such as M. R. James ("Oh, Whistle and I'll Come to You, My Lad") and Algernon Blackwood.

Despite the origin or inspiration, these ghost stories are about us—the living—our regrets, guilt, and fear of our own mortality. "We are a unique species on this earth, because we know that we will cease to exist," Wilson told me in 2013. "What an extraordinary burden to carry around, isn't it? You wonder why we invent these things like the myth of religion and the myth of ghosts, if it is, indeed, a myth, and that's the answer: we are terrified of our own mortality. For me, the whole kind of concept of this record started out with the idea of it being a book or a set of supernatural/ghost stories. As soon as you have that basic principle, it is like a gift in terms of visuals and lyrical content. Of course as soon as I came up with this idea, I said the special edition is going to be a book, similar to the kind you'd find at the back of the antique store, a hundred years old, covered with dust with these kind of beautiful Gothic fairy tales."

Previously, when I spoke with Wilson on the eve of his 2011 tour, he seemed genuinely happy to break free of the Porcupine Tree orbital pull, saying: "[W]e are trying to do something bigger and better than I've ever done before. I don't want . . . people to perceive this as some little side project."

It is this form of "paranoia," says Wilson, that may have caused him to overcompensate in his solo tour's productions and present bigger stage shows than Porcupine Tree could have staged. "I have always been fascinated by the combination of music and visuals," Wilson said to the author in 2013. "I've always thought of my music in terms of cinema and visuals. This is a continuation of that, but I think [the production] has stepped up another level."

It's one hell of a haunting show. Wilson uses a dazzling (near psychedelic) lighting show, an intro film, and a transparent gauze/kabuki screen on which video imagery—some of it featuring good old-fashioned analog animation (not CGI) created by South African Jess Cope—related to music appearing on *The Raven* is projected.

"The thing is it's much easier to do these things these days," said Wilson. "It's amazing what you can do with a couple of laptops and imagination. Thirty years ago, when Pink Floyd was trying to put on *The Wall*, it was really expensive. Now with a couple of laptops you can do something pretty equivalent. That's why Roger Waters is doing something beyond. More creative. More bizarre.

You're talking about a surface to project upon and having a couple of extra speakers at the back of the room and having some thought as to how you could use those resources."

There's no denying that theme and concept albums helped to shape the personalities, artistic tastes, and worldviews of roughly three generations (and counting) of musicians, rock enthusiasts. and general listeners, and progressive rock artists have had a large part to do with why this is the case.

Misconceptions

Due to the number of progressive rock concept albums released during the 1970s, listeners were looking for patterns everywhere. It's no wonder. The human mind searches for patterns in art, even where none exists or had been consciously intended by the artist. So, when we think we discern a dozen different broad ideas being explored throughout a song cycle, the likelihood that these concepts are connected is simply in the mind (and perhaps nowhere else) of each individual listener.

An album such as ELP's 1973 breakthrough, *Brain Salad Surgery*, for instance, appears to be held together by slender threads, if any. Still, what ELP's interpretation of "Jerusalem," England's unofficial national anthem, has to do with "Karn Evil 9: Third Impression," a nightmare sci-fi world where computers rule, is open for interpretation. (We should point out that the record is not entirely composed of the Impressions.)

Beyond that, of course, each of the three sections, or Impressions, of "Karn Evil 9" literally creates an impression—an emotional reaction. Says Emerson, there really wasn't much thought put into even using the phrase *Impression*.

"No real reason for [using *Impression*], really," Emerson told me. "[It was] a bit like Mozart labeling his music 'K something' or other. I don't put myself in his category, by the way. There was no logical form to my writing back then. It flowed and found a harbor."

In actual fact, the Impressions of "Karn Evil 9" were meant to be, at least initially, works in counterpoint. Lake and Palmer were not sold on the idea, but bits of Emerson's counterpoint concept do survive in "Karn Evil 9: First Impression, Part One," however.

"The use of counterpoint was a starting point to open up ideas for Greg and Carl," Emerson said. "If I'd have written the same piece today I probably would have gone more in depth as to its continuing structure, but back then I felt the idea may be too intimidating for the band. Now I'm more inclined to take a motif, however simple, and follow it to its ultimate conclusion. Put it through all sorts of chord changes and arrangements until I'm satisfied."

Without the expressed intent of the artist it becomes difficult to find evidence of all-encompassing musical statements. Any perception of cohesiveness or overarching narrative from song to song could simply be attributed to the time and emotional space in which a batch of songs were written.

ELP's *Brain Salad Surgery* (1973) left great Impressions.

This final section attempts to highlight popular releases that have been habitually and incorrectly identified as concept records. Perhaps we can sometimes read a bit too much into an artist's intent? You decide. Are the following concept records . . . or not?

King Crimson: *In the Court of the Crimson King* (October 10, 1969)

Why It's Great, Just Not a Concept Album: We Could Be on the Fence with This One

Crimson's direct predecessor was the Bournemouth-area band Giles, Giles & Fripp (featuring bassist/vocalist Peter Giles, brother drummer Michael Giles, and guitarist/piano player Fripp), which recorded *The Cheerful Insanity of . . .* for Decca's Deram sub-label in 1968.

After a false start with Judy Dyble as lead singer, the fated and legendary Crimson lineup, Fripp, singer/guitarist Greg Lake, who had switched to bass guitar at the request of his friend Fripp (the band needed a singer who could play bass), drummer Michael Giles, multi-instrumentalist Ian McDonald

Vroom
Frame By Frame
Dinosaur
One Time
Red
Fripptronics/Soundscapes
B'boom
Thrak
Elephant Talk
Matte Kudasi
Sex Sleep Eat Drink Dream
Vroom Vroom
People
Indiscipline
The Talking Drum
Lark's Tongue in Aspic
Vroom Vroom Coda
Walk On Air

RECORDED LIVE JUNE 3rd, 1995

TOWN HALL, NYC

105 MINUTES

KING CRIMSON IN COURT 95

Nearly thirty years after its appearance, Barry Godber's shocking album cover illustration was still being linked with King Crimson. Pictured: a 1995 bootleg concert video of Crim, then a double trio featuring two guitarists, two bassists/Stick players, and two drummers.

(Dyble's then-boyfriend) and his pal, lyricist Pete Sinfield, had its first rehearsal in January 1969.

Their first show, at the Speakeasy in April 1969, was practically ground zero for modern progressive rock. This meteoric rise and good fortune (something Fripp and the band attributed to the mysterious idea of a "Good Fairy") led to their now-famous Hyde Park gig opening for the Rolling Stones and a residency at the Marquee Club that same year. Their popularity was building on itself until they were packing in every venue they were playing.

Packed crowds thrilled to see Crimson's now-legendary shows, which were punctuated by improvisational pieces, informed by jazz, and the slow-building, Mellotron-soaked "Mars, the Bringer of War" from Holst's *Planets* suite. Attendees, many from rival bands in and around London, were simply floored. Crimson had put the London progressive underground on notice: there was a new act in town and it was obliterating any preconceived notions of what a rock band should be.

Even events that could, to some, be misconstrued as major setbacks, such as the now-infamous failed sessions with Moody Blues producer Tony Clarke, led to something bigger and better (with the help of the financial backing of David Enthoven and John Gaydon, the band's management, EG Records, of course). Crimson was forced to scrap those tapes only to begin work on what is often seen as the beginning for the entire British progressive rock movement of the late 1960s and early 1970s. (Maybe Fripp was onto something with his idea of the Good Fairy. . . .)

The band's debut, *In the Court of the Crimson King: An Observation By . . .* , cut at London's Wessex Sound Studios, would have a profound impact on the band and a bourgeoning genre. Bands from Genesis to Yes, even those who predated Crimson, were threatened, flattened, deflated, inspired, snookered, or utterly smitten by Crimson. Whichever one you were, it was a virtual certainty that you'd react radically to the band's music.

Was the "first"—and perhaps most influential—progressive rock record in history also a concept album? Sounds nice. But what do we really know about the record?

Sinfield has told the author that the album was political in its lyrical dimension and, indeed, some of the underlying reasons for 1960s societal upheaval seemed to be reflected in songs about war, injustices, lack of faith in traditional institutions, even sexual freedom. *In the Court* seemed to encapsulate the era: it's fitting that this "observation" should be unleashed on the public at the tail end of the decade.

Much like *The Dark Side of the Moon* released four years later, *In the Court . . .* is a microcosm of the progressive rock movement. The record encompasses the sounds of jazz ("21st Century Schizoid Man") and classical ("The Court of the Crimson King" contains an actual quote from Rimsky-Korsakov's *Scheherazade* in Ian McDonald's flute solo); the music is of a fairly technical nature (i.e., Michael Giles' off-the-wall, over-the-bar line fills, for instance); medieval lyrical imagery abounds (funneling into the romanticism of the past manifesting itself in many ways, including Carnaby Street fashions so trendy then); and a healthy dose of dreamy escapism smack-dab in the middle of the record (i.e., "Moonchild," the first song on the second side of the original LP).

Hints of concurrent themes run through the work. Songs expound on war, disillusion, unveiling true power behind the throne (i.e., "I Talk to the Wind," "Epitaph" [including "March for No Reason" and "Tomorrow and Tomorrow"]), while, at the same time, a strange sort of lyrical symbolism seems to be embedded into these tunes. References to the moon and sun crop up (perhaps more than one would expect by chance) in tracks such as "Moonchild," "Epitaph," and "The Court of the Crimson King." This imagery suggests a kind of balance, in an almost supernatural (or Masonic) way.

Maybe listeners attuned to Sinfield's use of polar opposites, even at a nearly subliminal level, instinctually and understandably believe all these songs are tied together. That's difficult to ascertain. On the surface, at least, a song such as "Moonchild" seems to have very little to do with Crimson's anthem to paranoia, "21st Century Schizoid Man." (Fripp once said the song was inspired by Sprio Agnew.) Likewise, what does "I Talk to the Wind" really mean relative to "The Court of the Crimson King"? These are vignettes, scenes, of a moment in history, captured by a talented band and its visionary lyricist. It's possible what we're witnessing is the product of an extraordinary creative thrust, which operates by its own idiosyncratic set of laws, causing music lovers to bunch these songs together.

Barry Godber's watercolor artwork also contributed to the perceived cohesiveness of the work. The screaming face, or paranoid man (i.e., the "schizoid man"), is supposedly Godber as seen through a mirror.

Undoubtedly, this face speaks directly to one song, if not more, appearing on the album. (The inner gatefold of the original LP shows a vampiric ghoul, whom Robert Fripp called the "Crimson King." His facial muscles seem to exhibit a smile, but his saddened eyes tell another story. What we're left with is a weary, melancholy sage of sorts, beckoning us, with his finger gestures and his open palm, to listen to the wisdom he's presenting to us in the record. The ogre's devilish countenance is so unusual, and so ambiguous, that it could be considered the closest prog rock ever came to the *Mona Lisa*.)

Retail record stores in London, equipped with large-scale posters of the front cover, were only too happy to imprint the gigantic screaming head in the minds of walkersby and potential consumers, thereby further underscoring the perceived subliminal nature (universality?) of the work.

Jethro Tull: *Aqualung* (1971)

Why It's Great, Just Not a Concept Album: Because Ian Says So ...

We know that the Tull head honcho himself has said that *Aqualung* is not a concept record; in fact, Ian Anderson has long maintained that it was the public's interpretation, or misinterpretation, of the origins of this record that inspired him to write the concept album spoof *Thick as a Brick*.

So, why the debate and discussion about whether *Aqualung* is a concept record? For one thing, there are still lingering doubts as to whether we should be taking Anderson's word for it, or making up our minds. Anderson has said that the making of *Aqualung* was the first time he undertook a conscious effort to write material with serious subject matters, a fact that seemingly has offered conspiracy theorists plenty of fodder for the rumor mill.

What has largely fed this belief that there are plenty of conceptual breadcrumbs to snatch up is the simple fact that the original LP was divided into two parts: Side One was dubbed "Aqualung" and Side Two "My God," implying that, at least, each half of the album operates via its own thematic rules. So, *Aqualung*, it would appear, is really two concept records, or one half of two different concept records coexisting on one album. Proving there's a connection presents a double hurdle.

There does seem to be some links connecting songs from Side One with those on Side Two, but the author thinks these are only surface connections. Firstly, there's the decorative lettering, the detailed calligraphy, on the back cover, as found in centuries-old Bibles, which seems to join the ideas of the character of Aqualung with, at least, some surface aspects of religion or spirituality.

Secondly, Anderson's obsession with trains runs along a few tracks, from "Cheap Day Return" to, of course, "Locomotive Breath." The musicologist will likely find all sorts of musical styles wrapped up in the piano intro to the song "Locomotive Breath," from blues and jazz to classical. John Evan slides through all three, it seems, with this opening, transporting us through time and space, really. That's what trains have symbolized forever. Whether it was Howlin' Wolf's "Smokestack Lightnin'" or covers of Alan Lomax's "Rock Island Line" by the likes of Lead Belly, Lonnie Donegan, and Johnny Cash, trains were symbols of freedom.

"The first sessions [Cash] did at Sun, you know, included 'Hey, Porter,'" says Gregg Geller, Columbia Records consultant. "'Folsom Prison Blues,' while a prison song, strictly speaking, was also a train song. There's 'Old 97' and 'The City of New Orleans.' He loved train songs and sang about them constantly, but never put them together on an album. I grew up on Long Island and when I was a kid I remember the train whistle. I heard [Cash] talk about this, too. You could hear the train whistle but . . . the train didn't pass within five miles of my house and yet you could hear the train go by and off to somewhere else. When you're Johnny Cash and you're a kid and it's the Depression, there's maybe a whole lot of hope that you can escape where you are. The train implied adventure and discovery and all of that good stuff. I think he tended to romanticize the train. Incidentally, it wasn't until the mid-1970s that Cash put together a concept record about trains—*Destination Victoria Station*, which wasn't generally commercially released and was only all of his train songs re-recorded and put on one album."

However, the train in "Locomotive Breath" is menacing, speeding out of control, even meant to induce dizziness in the speaker, who is obviously off the rails of sanity and spinning with rage and depression. (We can hardly refrain from mentioning that the Spanish word for "crazy," *loco*, of course, appears in the word *locomotive*. . . .) Maybe Anderson's thought here is that the train, when not controlled, is a loose cannon, unstoppable. So, "Locomotive Breath" stresses the darker side of the train's symbolic power. Simply put, "Locomotive Breath" is one of the meanest, dirtiest songs on the album. It chugs along so deliberately that it unnerves the listener, a sensation heightened by the fact that Anderson sings in a quite matter-of-fact fatalistic voice, reflecting the inevitability of a crash somewhere down the line.

Legendary blues piano man Sunnyland Slim, who moved to Memphis (from Mississippi) in the mid-1920s, took his stage name from the Sunnyland train, which ran from Memphis to Missouri. Slim told the story that he'd watched people attempting to cross the tracks and not quite making it, being, instead, crashed by the speeding bullet. In addition, a painting by protosurrealist Giorgio de Chirico, *The Anxious Journey*, presents a steaming locomotive (or a smokestack lighting, to steal a phrase from Wolf) as brooding brick clock towers loom in the distance. Darkened archways, recessed entryways, and something as seemingly harmless as a billowing cloud suggest that these ominous oddities arranged precisely to catch the eye, shuttling the artist's ideas from the surreal to the slightly threatening.

Incredibly, Anderson, in the liner notes to the fortieth anniversary special edition of *Aqualung*, admits the song was aimed at criticizing our reckless growth as a race. Essentially, Anderson was tackling overpopulation and our competition for limited natural resources. Although the author does not interpret the lyrics this way—and certainly not within the context of the piece appearing on the "My God" side of the equation, Anderson could be dabbling in a bit of rehabilitation, bending the concept of the song to suit his current political and environmental stances, positions that have gained increasing attention over the last forty-plus years thanks to the extraordinary popularity and longevity of Tull and its music.

As some others have already noted, including author/professor Allan Moore, the lyrical lines seem ambiguous and difficult to follow. There appears to be a plot, but it's difficult to discern exactly who is doing what—and with whom? Is "Locomotive Breath" a metaphor for God, who keeps the Earth spinning, regardless of the fate of certain hapless victims? That might be a bit of a stretch. And is the "all-time loser" a hapless victim?

The image of the loser being on his hands and knees in a kneeling or praying pose recalls the religious theme implied by the "My God" banner heading. But does Anderson invoke God as a tease, a mere lyrical expression the narrator would utter in his sheer exasperation, or something more substantive? The author thinks it is little more than a cunning word game, and a well-placed one.

The last song, "Wind Up," a final fuck you to organized religion, helps to bookend the side, but doesn't truly tie in with the image of Aqualung the character or its theme.

What, after all, does knowing God, and accepting God on our own terms without the need of an intermediary, have anything to do with a vagrant ("Aqualung")? Philosophical arguments and Biblical references aside, not much. The substance simply isn't there. Indeed. The character of Aqualung was based on a photograph of a homeless man, taken by Anderson's first wife, Jenny, who had been studying photography at the time, and her description of the man. These observations were incorporated into the opening song, "Aqualung."

"The mixture of guilt and compassion, embarrassment and sadness, all of these things are slightly more feminine emotions," Anderson told me. They found their way into this record, anyway; one that's dirty, heavy, complicated, mean, and, at times, bordering on sexually perverse (i.e., "Cross Eyed Mary," "Mother Goose," the latter being a combination of absurd humor and double entendre).

While "Hymn 43" and the ghoulish "My God," well known as Anderson's personal attack on organized religion, appear to hang together as songs that take the piss out of dogmatic thought, and "Slipstream" seems to evoke an image of the soul slipping into the afterlife, it's difficult to connect these spiritually based songs with the first half of the record.

Even more importantly, the first side of the record feels disjointed to the author. Despite a reference to Aqualung in the second track, "Cross Eyed Mary" (i.e., Mary, who prostitutes herself and visits the "jack-knife barber"—an abortion doctor?), the hapless vagrant does not return to the scene of the crime. He's virtually invisible in the lyrics.

The last point to consider is the actual process of putting together the record. The band was stressed for time to complete the record and Anderson has said that the band was not even all in the studio at the same time for the recording of "Locomotive Breath," for instance. (Evan's piano part was tacked onto the opening of the song.) Tull recorded *Aqualung* at Basing Street Studios (Island Studios) in late 1970, with sessions spilling over into winter of 1971. (More sessions at Sound Techniques occurred in the spring of 1971 but were completed two months after *Aqualung* had been released, and resulted in "Life Is a Long Song," "Nursie," "Up the Pool," "Dr. Bogenbroom" and "From Later," which were released as an EP with new drummer, Barriemore Barlow.)

Although cohesion in recording practices doesn't denote the presence of a concept record, it does seem as though the songs chosen for *Aqualung* were done so because Tull felt they best represented the band at that point in time.

Another interesting note is the fact that the song "Lick Your Fingers Clean," which was earmarked for *Aqualung*, formed the basis of "Two Fingers" from 1974's *War Child*, a record that is, itself, vaguely conceptual (due to its relation to a failed movie and 1973's *A Passion Play*). Fascinatingly, "Two Fingers" drops references to a locomotive, and seems to have something to do with making a deal to enter paradise. ("Lick Your Fingers Clean" was featured on Tull's twentieth-anniversary boxed set in 1988.)

What we're left with, then, is the possibility that we might—might—be able to link songs that appear on each side with an overall theme, but when attempting to glue the two halves together we fail to produce a round object.

We'll have to stick with Ian on this one a call it an almost-, but not quite, concept record.

Pink Floyd: *The Dark Side of the Moon* (1973)

Why It's Great, Just Not a Concept Album: The Jury Is Still Out

Is *The Dark Side of the Moon* a concept album? Not in the strictest of senses, no. It doesn't really follow a chronological path, regardless of how synchronous *The Wizard of Oz* seems to be with the song cycle's various accents and crescendos. Yet, since the record deals with some overwhelming issues that continue to plague our species and its time on Earth, coupled with the fact that the Floyd drops tantalizing clues that there is, indeed, more than meets the eye (ear?) here, the record seems to overcome its perceived disjointedness.

Continuity is maintained, in part, through the studio technique of *crossfading*. The only real break, either on the original LP or standard CD releases, is before the start of "Money" (which opens the original Side B). Other than that, songs appearing on Side A flow into one another, as they do for Side B. Also important is the idea that tracks "Breathe," "On the Run," "Breathe (Reprise)," "Time," and "The Great Gig in the Sky" approximate a cradle-to-grave story line—which spans the entire first side of the original album.

The record really opens with "Speak to Me," a maelstrom of sights and sounds previewing for the listener all that he'll/she'll experience throughout the course of the long player (i.e., a looped kick-drum pattern approximating a heartbeat, which is repeated near the end of the record; random voices speaking about madness; the ticking sounds of clocks at various speeds; the cries of singer Clare Torry; hair-raising laughter; and the rhythmic pulses of two EMS VCS-3 Synthi-AKS synths, etc.).

The second side opens with "Money," written in 7/4, which rattles with the ringing of cash registers, ripped paper, the clicking noises of an analog telephonic call-switching system, and the jingle-jangle of coin bags (all of those noises were featured on separate pieces of tape, which were eventually evenly cut, pieced together, and made into sequence). This is followed by "Us and Them," originally written for Italian director Michelangelo Antonioni's 1970 movie, *Zabriskie Point*, which focuses on war and racism. "Brain Damage," inspired, in part, by cofounder Syd Barrett, is next and expounds on the theory that we all are insane in our own ways. Finally, "Eclipse" closes the record, indicating that all we ever knew and will know will come to an end. (Or will it?)

Dark Side, despite being one of the most commercially successful records in rock history, took a stand against modern society's march toward materialism with its implicit protests against our culture's constant degradation of spirituality. The very phrase "the dark side of the moon" is said to be occult jargon for the subconscious. As we've seen with Crimson's *In the Court of the Crimson King*, the moon is a very powerful symbol of the female, the soul, and suggests an alchemical process at work. (It's impossible to think of the moon without the sun, and vice versa.)

As some observers have already pointed out, *Dark Side* seems to be a combination of opposites, employing keyboard and recording technology, yet also ringing every ounce of emotion, or soul, from the sessions' participants. (Look no further than Clare Torry's improvised, passionate, albeit edited together, performance.) Again, like Crimson's debut, not only does *Dark Side* embody the very essence of prog rock and its timeless qualities (i.e., the recurring fusion of the masculine and feminine occurring in the music of the genre), but the scope of the record's very broad themes might make them difficult to fully grasp or come to terms with.

Just as in the end of the song "Time," the speaker tells us that he believed he had more to tell the listener—more insight into, presumably, what his life (or any life) means—we, too, grapple with the concepts that Waters and the band present to us in such a stark and naked way. Undoubtedly, listeners are hit by the music and the lyrics on a number of levels of which we are not consciously aware.

I've written in the past that *The Dark Side of the Moon* is as much an examination of the twentieth-century British psyche and the temporal nature of time and space and the everyday stresses applied to that psyche, as it is a descent into madness. But in retrospect, this explanation seems inadequate.

Perhaps to get closer to the mark we should consider the moon itself, which has come to symbolize femininity. The celestial world can be interpreted as the *anima*—the female aspects of a male personality related to unconscious, "the soul." Perhaps the overarching concept was speaking to the dark side of the soul, of life.

Later in this work I refer to the images seen in the film *Pink Floyd: Live at Pompeii* as a portrait of a band chasing the sun. In retrospect, what we were witnessing with *Pompeii* are Floyd's last days in the sun: right around the *Meddle* time frame, 1971–1972, inner disharmony was becoming the norm, not the exception, shaping the band's internal dynamics and writing infrastructure. The lyrics of "Breathe," although in the context of putting one's head down and working hard, even beckon us to "forget the sun."

Bassist/lyricist/vocalist Roger Waters began asserting himself in the leadership position, steering Floyd's lyrical content toward the darkness and the more isolationist. The sun was, indeed, eclipsed by *The Moon*—a seismic event that changed the band, personally and professionally forever. (With *The Dark Side of the Moon*, the other shoe dropped. The rumination on the archetypal opposites—the sun and the moon—was complete with *Dark Side* and the band, interestingly enough, seemed to embody this duality.)

As with so many progressive rock records of the 1970s, the album is given further cohesiveness and significance via the cover artwork, in this case created by design firm Hipgnosis, founded by Aubrey "Po" Powell and Storm Thorgerson, friends of the band since their early Cambridge days.

Storm and Po were mates from film school, studying to be directors, and so it's no accident that Hipgnosis' covers were enigmatic and cinematic in their scope.

The inner gatefold shows a heartbeat pulsing through the bands of refracted light, which was Waters' idea, and one that links the music with the iconic cover artwork (more about this in a moment). The now-famous heartbeat motif heard at the opening and conclusion of the record, dare we say, symbolizes the endless cycle of life, death, and cosmic rebirth. When discussing the record, Waters has talked about the cycles of life. Despite Waters' claim that he does not believe in life after death, the inner gatefold and the arc of the record seems to be belie this fact.

In hoping to link the cover illustration with the recorded music, Floyd keyboardist Rick Wright dealt with Hipgnosis, some reports say, and asked for a "simple, clinical, and precise" image. Although many proposed ideas were shown to the band, including a mark-up of superhero Silver Surfer gliding out of a cosmic background, Floyd unanimously chose the sleek and slightly scientific image of a prism splitting white light into its invisible-to-the-naked-eye

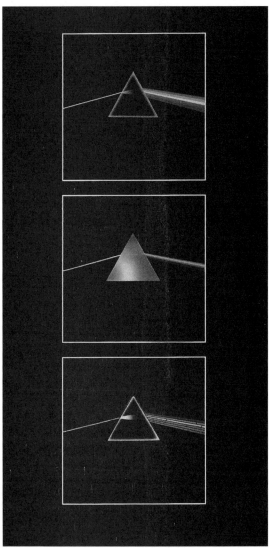

The many phases (of the faces) of *The Dark Side of the Moon*, from the *Classic Albums* series DVD booklet.

components, or ROYGBIV. (Well, actually, the original LP release featured only six bands of light. The so-called spectrum appeared less indigo: so, it became ROYGBV. In later CD versions of the record this was changed to include the seventh band.)

Drawn by George Hardie (and airbrushed by Bob Lawrie), the opaque triangle centered on the front cover, supposedly a reference to Floyd's live light show at the time, was inspired by a photo, "Po" once said, he found in a book on great twentieth-century photographs, depicting a prism resting on top of sheet music, refracting white light. The prism practically branded Pink Floyd in the minds of classic-rock listeners, and when we flip the record over to its back cover, we notice that the white light is actually a reconstituted beam that has passed through a second, inverted prism. (Recalling the concept of life cycles?)

"How *Dark Side* came about," says Richard Evans, layout designer for Hipgnosis in the 1970s, "was there were several ideas that were put to the band and Rick Wright said to Storm, 'I don't want anything arty-farty. We don't want weird photographs. We want something clean and classy.' . . . In the studio Hipgnosis had lots and lots of reference books of this and also a physics schoolbook that showed how light goes through a prism. That is where it came from. The whole thing about Pink Floyd was not just the light; it was *son et lumière*—sound and light, and the heartbeat. The reason we did it on a black background is because it looked cooler than the white. Very simple idea. The actual album artwork is nothing really to look at. It's . . . what you call a mechanical. Basically it's instructions [for the printer], a mark-up, done on various layers of tracing paper, saying, 'Drop black into this area . . . drop yellow into this area and drop red into this area.' When people look at the artwork, expecting to see the wonderful full-color image, there's no illustration as such. The cover, as you see it, was really made at the printers."

Is *Dark Side* a concept record? Perhaps this would be the case if each song had been meant to represent a pivotal scene in a larger musical tapestry. Less likely is the idea that *Dark Side*'s plot unfolds in a pre–*Pulp Fiction* nonlinear way. Compare and contrast it with 1977's five-song, Orwellian *Animals*, for instance, which does not boast a story line, either, but does seem to trace Waters' increasing misanthropy and cynical view of modern society and our culture's headlong flight into vapid materialism (i.e., the three variants of "Pigs" represent the rich and greedy; "Dogs," symbolizing the aggressive, overachieving alpha dogs; and "Sheep," the mindless, hapless followers). Band disputes over writing credits and royalties during the sessions for *Animals* only underscored just how wickedly insightful and incisive Waters' lyrics really were.

Further contrast *Dark Side* with the double studio album *The Wall*. If *The Dark Side of the Moon* examined existential angst and madness, then *The Wall* was a blow-by-blow depiction and psychoanalytical dissection of a despondent rock star's growing paranoia and isolation.

"Is there anybody out there?" Perhaps the question the album is conveying is more like, "Is there anybody in there?" *The Wall* is all about the internal landscape, the psychological peaks and valleys of a damaged psyche sheltering itself from the outside world. In fact, rock star Pink's situation becomes more and more dire as the record progresses, leading some to question the meaning of the last song on the album, "Outside the Wall." There's a debate over whether Pink decides to shake off his psychic lethargy and rejoin the world at large or remain hidden.

Much like Genesis' dramatic interpretation of *The Lamb* a few years earlier, no idea was too extravagant for staging *The Wall* on tour. Throughout the 1970s Floyd's live concerts were legendary for their outrageous stage props, and *The Wall* tour didn't disappoint. A construction crew was called upon to erect a 35' × 160' wall of white made of nearly 350 cardboard bricks, a design created by illustrator Gerald Scarfe, which separated the band from the audience. The wall featured built-in gaps through which concertgoers could see the band performing. By show's end, the wall would topple over, revealing the musicians passionately interpreting the climactic moments of the concept album. Other visual attractions included a virtually life-size bomber plane, huge puppets designed in the manner of Scarfe's slightly grotesque characters, and a decoy Floyd band wearing creepy expressionless masks (think: the Captain Kirk mask used for *Halloween*'s Michael Myers). Floyd thoroughly redefined the rock-concert experience. Although it's been reported that initially Waters wanted the wall to remain, blocking off the audience, thus changing the complexion of the entire production.

Producer Bob Ezrin (Alice Cooper) initially organized Waters' demos in a logical story line to help create what would be a double album of material.

The Wall was recorded, mixed, and completed in three countries and was like a survey of all the musical territory the band had traveled for the decade before: from symphonic rock ("Vera," "Nobody Home," "Bring the Boys Back Home") to blues-based licks ("Comfortably Numb"). New influences also crept into the proceedings. With the benefit of hindsight, it is slightly amusing and perverse that one of prog's early protagonists had hijacked a four-on-the-floor disco beat for *The Wall*'s best material (i.e., "Run Like Hell," "Another Brick in the Wall—Part II").

Growing tensions behind the scenes (which was old hat in the Pink Floyd camp by 1979) led to keyboardist Rick Wright's exit from the recording sessions. (He'd turn up for the tour of *The Wall*.) Ezrin would eventually have a falling out with the band (perhaps only just Waters), and the producer, who was supposed to be involved in the stage show, was either held back by personal issues or from a decision made from within the band's ranks—or both.

There were some distinguishable parallels between *The Wall* and *The Dark Side of the Moon*. Aside from the recorded, swirling voices appearing in interesting places in the stereo mix, and Waters' obvious issues regarding isolation, many of the musical ideas were Waters'. (Guitarist/vocalist David Gilmour, of course, contributed mightily to one of the band's greatest songs on *The Wall*, and ever—"Comfortably Numb.") Back in 1973, Waters saw his opening to streamline the band's penchant for cosmic messaging and speak to listeners on a more cellular level.

Syd Barrett's seeming descent into madness provided one inspiration for Waters, and certainly Waters distills Barrett's LSD-induced trips into insights about subjects ranging from isolation and death, to conflict, existential angst, love, and dementia. In so doing, Waters' lyrics are often unnerving, clearly defining subjects we often suppress to protect our own sanity. They represent the first of Waters' cohesive statements on the subject of emotional retreat, a theme he would develop throughout the course of the 1970s, which would reach its apogee with Floyd's *The Wall*.

Largely due to the universal quality of the observations made by Waters on *Dark Side*, undoubtedly we will divine some form of narrative thread upon repeatedly ruminating over the track sequence. It's an achievement Floyd had accomplished with the indirect assistance of Barrett, whose very presence had helped *Dark Side* (and its successor, *Wish You Were Here*) retain its psychological potency four decades on.

"Pink Floyd kept it fairly abstract," says Ray Bennett, who developed the story line for the concept album *Out of Our Hands* for his band Flash, featuring former Yes guitar player Peter Banks, which appeared the same year as *Dark Side*. "If you allude to some overarching mood, without getting too specific, or being tied to a story line, that's the way to go. Anytime you have a set story line, music suffers from having to be slave to a narrative."

Dark Side holds the record for most consecutive weeks (a whopping 724) appearing on the U.S. *Billboard* Top 200 Albums chart. Counting reentries, the album charted a combined total of 740 weeks in the time frame between 1973 and July 13, 1988, after which it dropped off the charts. Simply put, it's the Joe DiMaggio hitting streak of prog rock (and rock, period, really), a record that's likely never to be broken. Although it didn't remain there for long, *Dark Side* did hit the No. 1 album slot in America, when it first appeared in '73 and several times afterward as a reissued release, even as recently as 2013.

Saga: *Saga* (1978), *Images at Twilight* (1979), *Silent Knight* (1980), *Worlds Apart* (1981), *Full Circle* (1999), *House of Cards* (2001), *Marathon* (2003)

Why It's Great, Just Not a Concept Album: A Narrative Thread Spanning Several Albums . . . but Has Anyone Truly Figured Out What It All Means?

The brainchild of keyboardist Jim Gilmore, the Saga "Chapters" story line spans several records, and was originally meant to break off after eight installments. (The Canadian band revisited the story and added chapters to it, making a total of sixteen.)

Supposedly based on science fact rather than fiction, Saga's conceptual chapters were written and recorded in a jigsaw fashion and concern a central character. Rather than present a full concept record, Saga decided that it would be best to tease the audience with one or two what they called "Chapters," or entries, of the larger story, with each successive record.

"We spread it out purposely and out of sequence, as well, to arouse some interest and pique people's curiosities and creative abilities because we left the lyrics somewhat ambiguous," Saga lead vocalist Mike Sadler told the author in 2009.

Since the meaning of the overall concept is cryptic, the songs were, by design, written to be stand-alone tracks. "It is weird because I see them more as stand-alone songs than as part of a larger concept," said Sadler.

By the time the band reached the final chapter, which ended with the 2003 album *Marathon*, Saga took a break from the conceptual thread. "It was amazing," said Sadler. "People would write in to the forum and say, 'I've listened to all of the chapters back to back' and they had it all figured out. They would give two-, three-page synopses of what the story is about. They understood certain elements, but on the grand scheme of things, no, they didn't quite get it. But they went through the trouble of using their heads and saying, 'This is what it is about. . . . ' It was such a great compliment. It was done not as a marketing tool—I always joke about that—but more to make it interesting.

"The other thing was, we got through the third album and . . . we would have all the music written and most of the lyrics and then, and actually before we got to the lyrics, Jim and I would look at the songs that we had chosen for the album and say, 'Which ones sound like Chapter songs?' Then next question: 'Which part of the puzzle do we want to fill in?' . . . 'We need a ballad-y thing to link up with the story, and we're writing a ballad, so we'll call it "Chapter 5"....' It was fun in a way."

But what is the story about? Some have speculated that it is about Einstein (specifically his brain), but Sadler wouldn't reveal many details when I spoke with him. "There are all kinds of stories and you can keep me on the phone for days. Still not to be revealed for future animated film or video game, but for the sake of that [future projects] we don't give it away yet. In other words, not do a conceptual record right off the bat. We decided to do two each time, at least for the first four records. This was a way to, at least, guarantee that we do four records with eight Chapters."

Few bands were willing, let alone able, to create in this fashion. (The band would produce an indisputable, proper concept album, *Generation 13*, released in 1995. Some people consider 2004's *Network* a concept album as they do 2009's *The Human Condition*.)

"I don't know of anyone else crazy enough to try this," said Sadler, who had intended his final album with the band to be 2007's *10,000 Days*, but has since returned to Saga. "If it started seeming pretentious, we didn't have to continue it, because it could have wrapped up logically after eight chapters, [which was] another smart thing we did, I guess. As you said, the songs pretty much can stand alone, with the exception of a few words here and there. We play them live, but we don't make a big deal about the fact that they are 'Chapters.' Although we did do a Chapters Tour . . ."

Pallas: *The Sentinel* (1984)

Why It's Great, Just Not a Concept Album: Blame the Powers That Be!

Well, okay, to be fair this album started life as a concept record—a rumination on the ancient myth of Atlantis and that fictional culture's decline (filtered through the lens of our modern-day, technologically advanced society spiraling out of control). The Scottish band's label, Harvest, directed the quintet to deep-six the long conceptual pieces in favor of incorporating songs that were more commercially viable. The band obeyed, undoubtedly in a compromised position, and received advice they thought would help their career (and possibly catapult them to a place in which they could record and release a concept record based on Atlantis in the not-too-distant future).

Remnants of the band's original intent remained, but the damage was done. Pallas acknowledged that whatever story line existed had been obliterated and was nearly impossible for fans to follow.

Although Pallas was formed in the mid-1970s (originally under the name Rainbow) and went on to record an EP in 1978, their music is most closely identified with the so-called *neo-prog* movement that had come to the attention of mainstream audiences in the early and mid-1980s. Neo-prog bands, although opposed to the neo-prog tag often affixed to them, played in a musical style that drew unabashedly from the genre's heyday. (Other perpetrators of the style included Marillion, Pendragon, IQ, Solstice, etc.) Musical comparisons to the likes of Yes (Eddie Offord produced Pallas' *The Sentinel* in Atlanta, Georgia), Floyd, ELP, and Genesis were self-evident. (Indeed. Pallas made a name for itself in Scotland by performing Floyd's "Echoes" and Genesis' epic twenty-three-minute song, "Supper's Ready.")

Though prog was generally perceived as only a British phenomenon, in fact, bands from around the globe, from Spain and Italy, to South America and Eastern Europe, had glommed on to the classic prog style and generated music that owed much to the genre's heyday. Pallas, and other neo bands, including Marillion and IQ, employed theatrics, such as elaborate masks and costumes, which recalled the stage antics of Genesis (circa 1972–1975).

"[Marillion] approached me to produce their first album and [I] turned them down," says producer Mick Glossop. "I actually found Pallas more refreshing in a sense. Marillion was so Genesis-orientated. In fact, funnily enough, Marillion was one of Pallas' big competitors, because they both had members from Scotland. Pallas was always in the shadow of Marillion because Marillion made it first. They were even [both] signed to the same label, EMI. But Pallas didn't quite take off. Maybe at the time there was only room for one successful [retro] prog band, and that was Marillion. In retrospect, maybe I shouldn't have worked with the band, from a career point of view."

Yet, Pallas, and also Marillion, took a bit from New Wave and punk, injecting their music with an intensity that was not always present in the more pastoral wing of the progressive rock field. (For proof, look no further than Pallas' live favorite "The Ripper," written about Peter Sutcliffe, the infamous Yorkshire Ripper, which appeared on *Arrive Alive*, their independently released cassette from 1981.)

By the early 1980s, the band had developed their concept for the *Atlantis Suite* and performed it in its entirety prior to the release of their debut. The immense excitement among members of their fan base led to confusion and even anger when the actual song cycle of *The Sentinel* appeared. Since the mid-1980s the band has released demos and live versions of the material from *The Sentinel* sessions on their *The Sentinel Demos* album.

Rush: *2112* (1976)

Why It's Great, Just Not a Concept Album: A Simple Explanation

The conceptual conundrum surrounding this record stems from the misidentification of a story line hidden (somewhere) in the nooks and crannies of the spacious title suite, which spanned the first side of the original LP release. The poor public reception of the Canadian power-prog trio's 1975 album, *Caress of Steel*, one of the most musically adventurous statements the band has ever made, and *Steel*'s lack of commercial success, elicited calls for Rush to return to their blues-rock roots. Unconvinced that scaling back their artistic approach was the proper direction, Rush (singer/bassist Geddy Lee, guitarist Alex Lifeson, and drummer/lyricist Neil Peart) refused to heed the panicked cries of record-label executives and, instead, risked their professional careers by developing the nineteen-minute, Ayn Rand–influenced, *Symphonie fantastique*–flavored sci-fi-based title track. (Elements of Rand's novella *Anthem*, as well as bits of her other novels, such as *The Fountainhead* and *Atlas Shrugged*, seem to shape Peart's story involving an individual fighting for creative freedom in the face of an overbearing Nanny State. Although unlike the main character of Berlioz's masterwork, Rush's dreamer/musician protagonist succeeds at the deed.)

The gamble paid off. Air-drumming-inducing anthems, such as "2112: Overture" and "The Temples of Syrinx," and lyrical themes of individual freedom helped the record to achieve gold-certified status within six months of its release. (In addition, in 1981, *2112* became Rush's first platinum-selling album.)

Geddy Lee once told the author: "*2112* saved us." Indeed, it did. But the mere existence of the album's epic title-track has compelled some listeners to overstate the gravity of the sidelong cosmic opus. *Attention All Planets of the Solar Federation*: none of the other tracks on *2112* relate to the plot of the sidelong suite.

Ironically, as Rush crept further into the mainstream, their releases gradually became more conceptual or, more precisely, thematic. For instance, each song on 1981's breakthrough, *Moving Pictures*, was meant to be a tiny film. "Tom Sawyer"; "Limelight" (an observation on the subject of the isolation of fame), which could be viewed as Rush's/Peart's mini *Wall*; "The Camera Eye" (one can be forgiven for thinking that Peart has a little bit of contempt for "the rat race"; the lyrics are cinematic in their scope and train their focus on ambitious citygoers filing (mindlessly?) through the streets on their way to work. They are purposeful but what do they miss by being so focused?).

"Red Barchetta" (inspired by Richard Foster's short story "A Nice Morning Drive"), using a Ferrari Barchetta as its protagonist, is a sci-fi tale of individual freedom versus an overreaching and overregulating government; fear is personified in "Witch Hunt," an epic theater-of-the-mind tune, which clearly denounces the evils, and ignorance, of mob thought (part of Peart's "Fear" trilogy, which included "The Weapon" and "The Enemy Within"). Even the album's instrumental and technically muscular "YYZ" conjures visuals and garners a visceral reaction from listeners (this slightly jazz-rock workout was meant to capture the transience of airports).

The closer, "Vital Signs," chosen in favor of a song based on Thomas Hardy's *Wessex Tales*, dives further into the band's interest in minimalism and reggae, traces of which appeared in the breakdown sections of "The Spirit of Radio," from 1980's *Permanent Waves*. (The cut-to-the-quick anthem of individuality foretold the coming of New Wave-ish and Police-like tracks, such as "The Weapon" and "New World Man," both from 1982's *Signals*.)

Five years after *Signals, Hold Your Fire* (released in September 1987) boasted tracks such as "Mission," "Second Nature," "High Water," "Time Stand Still," and "Lock and Key," which are connected by the theme of primal

RECAPTURE THE BEGINNINGS OF RUSH

RUSH
ARCHIVES

"ARCHIVES"
A specially-priced, limited edition set containing
three legendary Rush albums: "Rush," "Fly by Night" and
"Caress of Steel." Over two solid hours of very solid Rush.

Produced by Rush and Terry Brown.
Rush appears on Anthem Records, in Canada.

mercury

2112 symbolism: The individual confronting oppressive authority.
By the late 1970s, Rush had branded this image.

drives. As Lee put it, "a burning desire to do something, and how important it is to keep your fire lit . . ."

Each song may tell a personal tale or wrap allegory or political commentary inside easily decipherable lyrics, but taken as a whole, the track listing does not advance character development or form the basis of a plotline. This does not diminish the power of the record, or its "concept," however.

Hold Your Fire is perhaps the most successful theme album in the band's career—a career that, for nearly a quarter of a century, has produced a slew of themed efforts, including 1985's *Power Windows*, 1989's *Presto*, 1991's *Roll the Bones*, 1993's *Counterparts* and 2007's *Snakes & Arrows*. In 2012, Rush released a full-fledged, steampunk/sci-fi influenced concept album, *Clockwork Angels*.

Hold Your Fire might also represent the pinnacle of Geddy Lee's keyboard explorations, which can be traced back to earlier works, such as *A Farewell to Kings*, *Permanent Waves*, *Moving Pictures*, *Grace Under Pressure*, and *Power Windows*.

Other prog rock artists worked within extended thematic formats. Gong's Daevid Allen devised a mystical storyline that spanned three albums, culminating in 1974's *You* (and continued with 2009's *2032*), and Rush concluded their sci-fi tale, "Cygnus X-1" (from 1977's *A Farewell to Kings*), with the sidelong epic, "Cygnus X-1 Book II: Hemispheres" (1978's *Hemispheres*). Pictured: the cover of an early 1990s Allen solo tour program.

The band largely abandoned their guitar-driven progressive hard rock/R&B sound in the 1980s and immersed themselves in synth and early Mac computer programming technology; this cutting-edge tech played a prominent role in the writing and pre-production stages of *Hold Your Fire*. (Reportedly, even Peart began composing his thoughts and lyrics on a Mac word processor.)

Peart once remarked that freedom and responsibility are preferable to reliance on a machine. If this is the case, how could Rush have roamed so far from their roots, allowing the very structure and architecture of their music to be shaped by programmable machines? Does the material on *Hold Your Fire* reflect musicians becoming slaves to technology, or artists employing state-of-the-art tools to rise above the purely robotic? Perhaps, impossibly, both are true, as Rush discovered interesting musical hybrids along the path of creating this album.

One of the criticisms of Rush's recordings over the years has been the "squashed" sound of the tracks and the application of layers upon layers of overdubs, choking the mix. With 1985's *Power Windows*, Rush began working entirely in the digital realm (i.e., the record was recorded, mixed, and mastered in the digital environment), further compressing their sound. How did the band manage to escape making a cold and bloodless album? Somehow, and with the distance of nearly thirty years, it's apparent that Rush did. Credit should be given to producer Peter Collins, affectionately dubbed Mr. Big due to his uncanny resemblance to Edward G. Robinson, and engineer Jim "Jimbo" Barton, for thinking outside the "boxed sound." Bob

Ludwig, mastering engineer, may have had a hand in why the record sounds so powerful, punchy, and full, as well.

Lyrically, things appear to be a bit more personal this time around. Peart writes often in the first person here—a rare occurrence outside the scientific and science fiction realms explored in the band's earlier music. There were exceptions, of course (i.e., "Freewill," "Distant Early Warning"). Prior to 1987, Peart's lyrical vantage point was that of a largely objective voice (i.e., a camera's eye). Peart's softer, more personal touch paints him as sympathetic observer. It's a stylistic approach that serves this thematic effort well and foreshadows his greater lyrical achievements of the 1990s and beyond.

Ever making overtures toward a more balanced, objective view, Peart confessed that, although the songs for *Hold Your Fire* were written in the first person, they aren't necessarily autobiographical. Ironically, Peart once explained that he thinks it's "immoral" to write introspective lyrics; that "there's something wrong with looking inside and writing about myself. . . ." Yet, these words are—to coin a phrase—a simple kind of mirror for Peart's mind and soul circa 1986.

Despite the high-tech equipment used to create *Hold Your Fire*, the album boasts moving "pictures" centered on the themes of primal drives and instincts.

Procol Harum: *Grand Hotel* (1973)

Why It's Great, Just Not a Concept Album: Not Enough Decadence . . .

The record-buying public has long connected the elegant decadence depicted on the album cover of *Grand Hotel* with the undercurrent of crushing sadness found within the music. The album's track listing appears to pull back the curtain on a world of privilege and scandal, suggesting that each song is a small but significant piece of a larger thematic puzzle. In fact, these musical vignettes operate independent of one another. Consider this: the title track seems to express a need to cling to traditions; "A Souvenir of London" was inspired, in part, by street musicians; and "For Liquorice John" was dedicated to a friend of the band, who committed suicide during the making of the record. Not even PH, masters of the long-form rock song, could tie together such disparate concepts. In actuality, they didn't. "[*Grand Hotel*] was very European," reflects lyricist Keith Reid. "It was kind of ballrooms and chandeliers, I suppose. Decadence just seemed to be the order of the day. The Eagles got it right. *Hotel California* is where it is at. . . ."

Asia: *Alpha* (July 26, 1983)

Why It's Great, Just Not a Concept Album: The Eyes Have It

Asia is one of the great paradoxes of pop-progressive rock. Its music is eminently catchy yet not without moments of showy musicianship. The band's output was often transparently commercial, yet also boasted some of the same sonic ingredients that made progressive rock so influential.

Whether Asia made great art can be debated. One thing is clear, however: Asia brought muso-friendly rock to an ever-increasingly commercial pop world.

After touring in support of their sole release, the band's self-titled debut, Asia appeared poised for even bigger things to come. Some music writers thought that Asia would begin composing complex songs more in line with fan expectations. Instead, the boys seemed to further alienate listeners.

Bassist/vocalist/lyricist John Wetton and keyboardist Geoff Downes emerged as the main songwriting team for the band's sophomore album, *Alpha*, leaving Steve Howe without one writing credit on the entire record. The differences between the material on Asia's debut and *Alpha* were readily apparent: *Alpha* was chock-full of pop-rock ballads aimed at the top of the charts.

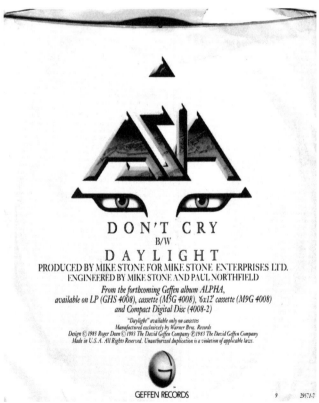

D O N ' T   C R Y
B/W
D A Y L I G H T
PRODUCED BY MIKE STONE FOR MIKE STONE ENTERPRISES LTD.
ENGINEERED BY MIKE STONE AND PAUL NORTHFIELD

From the forthcoming Geffen album ALPHA,
available on LP (GHS 4008), cassette (M5G 4008), 6x12' cassette (M9G 4008)
and Compact Digital Disc (4008-2)

"Daylight" available only on cassettes
Manufactured exclusively by Warner Bros. Records
Design © 1983 Roger Dean © 1983 The David Geffen Company ℗1983 The David Geffen Company
Made in U.S.A. All Rights Reserved. Unauthorized duplication is a violation of applicable laws.

GEFFEN RECORDS   9   29571-7

Alpha: Underappreciated gem or flop? Some of the best material of the period, such as "Daylight" and "Lying to Yourself"—the latter song co-penned by guitarist Steve Howe—was omitted from the CD and LP versions the album. Howe's signature sound, via his big-bodied Gibson ES-175, the same guitar he'd used on *The Yes Album* and *Fragile*, was largely neutralized in the mix.

"We had tremendous belief in it until it got mixed and then we had to mess with [the mix], which never got as good as it should have," says Howe. The second album wasn't such a happy-go-lucky album."

Unsurprisingly, when hardcore prog fans heard the record, jabs such as "flop," "disappointment," and "letdown" littered conversations held in the backs of cars, bedrooms, and basements across the U.S. The *Raiders of the Lost Ark*–themed video for the record's notoriously vocal-rich first single, "Don't Cry," was seen and heard by millions on MTV—a circumstance that did little to convince diehard prog-rock fans that the band was willing to shed its pop aspirations.

Yet, in retrospect, Alpha may have been given a bad rap. Asia was a pop band first and foremost. Although the record is largely buoyed by its original second side (i.e., tracks six through ten on the CD version), *Alpha* is also not nearly as disappointing as some critics would have us believe.

It has been suggested over the years, by at least one member of Asia, that Wetton was blamed, perhaps unfairly, for the "failure" of *Alpha*. Wetton was so much the musical focus of the band—the face of Asia—that he absorbed most of the criticism for the album's relative lack of success. In addition, the pressures of the business—Asia's record-release timetable and the isolation of the recording sessions in the Canadian wilderness—exacerbated Wetton's alcohol dependence. It's no secret that Wetton's addiction helped contribute to his abrupt exit from Asia.

Because of a chain of unfortunate events, *Alpha* was seen, for decades, as a dark chapter in the band's career. A closer examination of the album, however, reveals far more nuance and songwriting craft than had been previously believed.

Because Wetton had used the phrase "eyes" quite a bit in his lyrics, it was once rumored that *Alpha*'s song cycle was grounded by a central theme of seeing life from another perspective, or having the ability to see into someone else's soul. Although the record does seem cohesive—in no small part thanks to Roger Dean's surreal, pan-cultural cover illustration—*Alpha* isn't a concept album.[5]

On some levels, *Alpha* resembles *Aqualung*, a divided work that makes overtures to the thematic. The musical pacing of the original LP's Side Two, titled "Beta," is a ray of hope for prog fans. The leadoff track, "Eye to Eye" (a song Wetton first offered French prog band Atoll), "The Last to Know," "True Colors," "Midnight Sun," and the six-and-a-half-minute closer "Open Your Eyes" hung together very well, as if the band had taken its time to tinker with unexpected compositional transitions and sonic timbre. "Midnight Sun," one of the album's most successful tracks, and one that was performed as early as the band's first-ever tour, is a rare example of Asia invoking '70s prog mysticism while exploring the mysteries and intricacies of physical attraction.

Although the song was written in a 7/4 rhythm, it seems somewhat surreal and dreamlike, and the sonic texture sort of wafts out of your speakers. In simplest terms, "Midnight Sun" refers to Norway, and the breathtaking natural vistas Wetton soaked up during Scandinavia's twenty-four-hour daylight cycle while writing music with Downes at the keyboardist's home in Norway. Downes' cinematic keyboard lines capture the infinite possibilities and distant horizons spoken of in the lyrics. This kind of sonic haze blankets the track and adds to the music's mystery.

Through a haze of layered synth tones Wetton turns in what might be one of his most transcendent vocal performances; Carl Palmer's kick-drum patterns resemble a heartbeat, pumping and circulating rhythmic lifeblood through the tune; and Howe's angular guitar solo twists time, seemingly switching rhythmic flow at the drop of a dime. The song is rich, dare we even say complex, but subtle: a prog rock anthem for a new decade.

Despite fan reaction, *Alpha* garnered platinum status in the U.S. in October 1983 and was a Top 5 hit in Britain (Top 6 in the U.S.), largely on the strength of the band's exceedingly popular debut. But, because *Alpha* didn't perform as well as its predecessor, it was labeled a failure by nearly everyone, including some of the band members. However, in retrospect, even if *Alpha* isn't a concept album, labeling it horrifyingly flat and hopelessly lame might be one of pop music's minor injustices.

Move On Alone

A Q&A with Mick Abrahams

Guitarist Mick Abrahams, whose passionate riffs had earned him comparisons to Eric Clapton, was a strong musical presence in Jethro Tull's early developmental stages. Some might say a little too strong.

In late 1968 it became increasingly apparent that Tull was frontman Ian Anderson's band (a situation that has not changed in well over four decades).

Tull was transitioning quickly, flinging themselves headlong into a more progressive artistic direction at odds with Abrahams' guitar-based blues-rock, which was slowly being edged out in favor of more classical-, folk-, and ethnic-based rock music.

Had Mick Abrahams continued with the band, Tull may have looked and sounded radically different through the 1970s—and into today. Mick himself points to a later Tull album, 1987's *Crest of a Knave*, as one possible musical path Tull could have taken had he stayed as a member, "and we would have gotten there a damn sight sooner," he says with a laugh.

One observer, a contemporary of Tull, who will remain nameless, once told the author that he thought the soul and lifeblood had been drained out of the band when Abrahams exited. He also went on to say the condition was compounded by the exit of drummer Clive Bunker and bassist Glenn Cornick. This position/opinion can be debated, of course, but there's no denying that the band's first studio album, *This Was*, occupies a strange and wonderful place in progressive-rock lore—and in the history of the band.

Dissimilar to much of Tull's later catalogue, *This Was* presents a snapshot of a nascent art-rock group with plenty to offer the world. While chief songwriter Anderson wouldn't totally abandon guitar-based blues-influenced rock, once Tull split with Abrahams, the wild-eyed Pan-like flute player was free to pursue whatever creative development struck his fancy.

Abrahams' story, intertwined with Tull's behind-the-scenes power struggles, stands as one of prog rock's most intriguing "What Ifs?"

WR: You were in a band called McGregor's Engine prior to joining Jethro Tull. How did you join the band?

Mick Abrahams: With McGregor's Engine I was playing guitar and singing, Clive Bunker was on drums, Andy Pyle was playing bass, and Pete Fensome was the singer. All of these guys had played in various bands I had after I left Tull. We did soul and blues material and we performed in a few clubs for a few shows and then went up and down the country. We were playing a local gig in Luton, and most of the band at that time was from Luton, at the Beach Karma Discoteque. It was over the top of a big nightclub called Caesar's. Well, the British version of it, anyway. There were two stages there, one on either end of the hall. We were playing at one end and at the other, the John Evan Smash was playing, with Ian Anderson, Glenn Cornick, and Evan.

WR: What was happening with your band at the time?

Abrahams: Well, we had just come off the stage and the bass player, Andy, told us that he was leaving for the Sea of Gibraltar, to live. Just like that. No warning. And by that point our singer, Pete, had just left for some other work. So we were now down to a trio. I said to Clive, "I can't believe Andy just quit." As we were discussing this Andy had gone off for a drink or something. Then, I kid you not, three or four minutes later, Clive left to go to the loo and I was in the dressing room alone when Ian [Anderson] and Glenn [Cornick] walked in and said, "We've listened to you play and our band needs a kind of guitar player like you. Our guitar player is leaving and we have an affiliation with a London-based booking agency, Ellis-Wright." I knew this was Terry Ellis and Chris Wright, who were based out of Regency Street. "Would you be interested in joining us?" I said, "My band has just folded, so, yeah." They left and Clive came back and I told him what had happened. I just said, "Go ahead, mate. Knock yourself out."

WR: Did you perform rehearsals with the John Evan Smash?

Abrahams: The story follows that I went to [a town] just outside Blackpool in northwest England, and we rehearsed in some old convent or church or something for a couple of days. I know the band all moved down to Luton to be closer to London. We did a couple of gigs, and soon people started falling away, including future Jethro Tull drummer Barrie Barlowe. So, after this happened I rang up Clive and asked if he wanted to join this band and, of course, he did, which left us a five-piece. Then [keyboardist] John [Evan] left and we were a quartet: Clive, myself, Ian, and Glenn. We went under a variance of names after that.

WR: Is it true that the name Jethro Tull was suggested by someone working at the Ellis-Wright booking agency?

Abrahams: Yes. Someone was working on some thesis in history or agricultural history, and had come across the name Jethro Tull. It seemed to work, because people thought we were a little wacky and Ian's image at that time was a bit wild. The thing is everyone thought we were a bunch of druggies, but it was the furthest thing removed from that. But we must have given that impression.

WR: Was the first band you were ever in called the Crusaders?

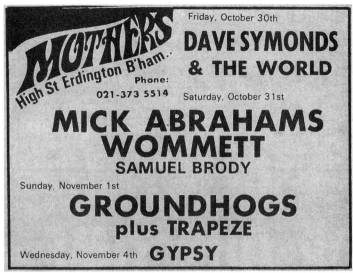

After recording and performing with Jethro Tull, guitarist Mick Abrahams formed Blodwyn Pig, Wommett, and the Mick Abrahams Band. Pictured: *Melody Maker* ad for Abrahams and Wommett, October 31, 1970.

Abrahams: Well, the first known band I was in was the Crusaders. I was also in the Toggery Five, when I lived in Manchester. The first band I was ever in was called the Jesters, which became the Hustlers and that evolved into something else that I forget. It was after my experience with this band that I went up to Manchester and joined the Toggery Five, which was followed by Jensen's Moods, which had Andy Pyle and Clive Bunker. In between the Toggery Five and Jensen's Moods I joined Neil Christian and the Crusaders. I took over for Jimmy Page twice. I took his job when he left Screaming Lord Sutch and when he left Neil Christian and the Crusaders. I was also asked to join John Mayall three times, but every time I was not in a position to do so. I'm not sure that is a good thing or a bad thing, given the turnover in his bands. Yet, a lot of people who played with him had gone on to the heady heights of stardom.

WR: Interesting you should say this because some have compared your guitar playing with Eric Clapton's.
Abrahams: I don't think there's a comparison, to be honest with you, and I don't think there should be. I've always been a fan of Eric Clapton, his playing and his singing. He's matured beyond recognition. I've only just met him, you know, passing each other in the studio.

WR: How did the first Jethro Tull record, *This Was*, come about?
Abrahams: Terry got some money together, I think, which he borrowed from his father, and that financed the recording of *This Was*.

WR: What can you tell me about the recording of *This Was*?

Abrahams: I think it took about a week and a half. I wasn't there when it was mixed, and I don't think I was even asked. It was done by Ian [Anderson] and Victor Gamm, which, in English slang is an unfortunate name. I don't think it means the same thing in America. You'll have to look that one up!

WR: You recorded *This Was* at Sound Techniques in London for something like 1200 pounds Sterling....

Abrahams: As I recall the control room was upstairs and there was an old eight-track analog tape machine in there. A Studer, I think. I remember I did one song on there, which I wrote with me own brain, me own talent, called "Move On Alone," which I also sang. The band decided to put brass on it. People would come up to me and ask, "What did they do to your song?" Everyone wanted to make such a big deal of it, more than it actually was. You know, "Did you approve of having brass on your number?" I simply said, "Fuck, yes. It's good. Why wouldn't I?" It's a good album and there are those who say that it might be the best album Jethro Tull ever recorded.

WR: What do you say?

Abrahams: I have to bite my tongue when this comes up and be careful, because people will think I'm being a dickhead for saying that *This Was* is the best Tull album. But, fact is, it captured the heart of what Jethro Tull was. And when they brought out "Steel Monkey," well . . .

WR: You're talking about the song from Tull's 1987 studio album, *Crest of a Knave*.

Abrahams: When I heard that I thought, "If I were in the band that's where it would have gotten to, and it would have gotten there a damn sight sooner." [laughs] I don't mean for that to sound bigheaded. It's just that "Steel Monkey" and some other songs were more in line with my vision of Jethro Tull. But they didn't want that: band and management. I think I—and that style of music I wanted to play—presented a threat to them. What's threatening about me? My underpants, maybe. [laughs]

WR: Why did you start performing "Cat's Squirrel" with Tull?

Abrahams: I first heard it when Eric Clapton played it with Cream, to be honest. I just liked the lead riff. The riff, about the first twelve bars of it anyway, is the only recognizable part of the song that's remained in my version. Some people say that Doctor Ross [Charles Isaiah Ross] wrote it, but that's not true. It's a traditional song and we're allowed to perform it. I'm still playing it in various guises, actually. I'm getting to the point where I will get strung up if I don't perform it. It's a good song that keeps my chops up.

WR: Can you talk about the drum solo in the instrumental "Dharma for One"?

Abrahams: That's not really a drum solo: we beat Clive and threw his drums down the stairs and recorded that sound. [laughs] No. It was a song that Ian came up with. The song was after a book Ian was reading at the time, *The Dharma Bums* by Jack Kerouac. Ian used this claghorn thing, something he created, that, to be honest with you, I always wanted to shit in. As far as Clive, well, he just hits anything that moves. He's ferocious. He's also a pain in the ass. I don't know why I love the bloke, but I do.

WR: The inevitable question: Why did you leave Jethro Tull?
Abrahams: After being in the band for eighteen months I got pissed off about the whole thing, really. I got pissed off about the way the music was progressing; I didn't particularly like it. I also did not particularly care for Terry Ellis, an attitude that was reciprocated, I think. No love lost there. I just said, "I've had enough." But no one left that band without Terry Ellis' say-so. There is a bone of contention as to whether I jumped or was pushed [out of the band]. The truth is, as I was about to jump I was pushed. Different people will tell different things, but I know the truth.

WR: Was there tension between you and Terry?
Abrahams: Well, he is just not my kind of guy. I'll say that. But don't forget that Terry helped the band get off the ground. His way of doing things got the band to where it was.

WR: What are your thoughts about Ian?
Abrahams: Ian is a smart cookie. I saw the way things were going and I can only speculate that he bided his time. That's all I'm going to say about that. When I left Tull, I had a falling out with Ian. It was an emotional time for me, but I've moved on. To be honest, it was absolutely right [for me to have left]. The direction the band went in was successful. It was proven correct, but that doesn't mean I needed to go down that road. . . . However, in later years, we have played together and we get on well. People have asked what the difference is between Ian and me, and I always say, "I work to live and he lives to work." I enjoy working, mind you, but not 24-7.

WR: How are the two of you similar?
Abrahams: Well, first let me say that Ian is an incredible musical talent. He and I shared a love of Big Bill Broonzy, Brownie McPhee and Sonny Terry, people like that. The thing is he is more along the olde English folk tradition, which is why Jethro Tull went the musical route it did.

WR: The shame of your time with Tull is that there's always going to be that question of, "What if . . . ?"
Abrahams: It doesn't really matter. What if? I mean, I'm here now and I'm perfectly happy with my life. I'm playing better than ever—and playing exactly

what I want. People take joy in my music as I do when I'm playing it, so . . . I'm not a rich person, not physically or financially, anyway. But I've got plenty, you know? It wasn't such a bad deal. I think there are other people that have had a worse deal in life.

WR: After Tull you formed Blodwyn Pig. How did this come about?
Abrahams: Simple: I left Tull in December 1968 and I spent about three weeks ringing up and getting a few guys together. Andy Pyle was one of them. I also got in touch with an old friend who was in Manchester, Jack Lancaster. We agreed on the direction we wanted to take as a band and I had a load of songs already written. We went through those and auditioned a few guys for the drummer's position. We would have liked Clive to join, had he been inclined to do so, but he wanted to stay where he was [in Jethro Tull]. Fair enough. [*Note: Abrahams would link up with Bunker again in the 1970s when the guitarist resurrected McGregor's Engine.*] Ron Berg became the drummer, instead.

WR: How did the name of the band originate?
Abrahams: A friend of ours, Graham Waller, piano player who appears on a couple of tracks on some of the Blodwyn Pig albums, came up with that. He was a very humorous guy.

WR: What was life like in Blackpool?
Abrahams: Nothing going on in Blackpool, but, oddly enough, Luton has spawned a few musos. No idea why. There's a saying, though: the best view of the town you live in is in your rearview mirror as you're driving away.

WR: Why do you say that?
Abrahams: Maybe it's because familiarity breeds contempt. I now live in Milton Keynes, and I've been here for nearly twenty-five years. I love it. I wouldn't live anywhere else. I have a house by the sea and can go there anytime I want. Luton? You should go and try it, then tell me what your opinion of it is after living there for a week. [laughs]

The Gates of Delirium

Top 20 BIG Compositions

The following is an overview of some of prog rock's most massive compositions. The author attempted to take into account the many strains of prog in order to present a diversity of artists. Hopefully, readers will find these entries useful.

1. Pink Floyd: "Echoes" (23:27), *Meddle*, 1971

Contraction and expansion. These two opposing forces helped to shape *Meddle*, one of the major milestones on Floyd's path to excellence (i.e., the monolithic—1973's *The Dark Side of the Moon*).

At EMI's Studios, Abbey Road, members of Floyd separately recorded bits and pieces of sonic ideas known as "Nothing Parts 1–36" (or "Son of Nothing"). From these recordings the kernel of "Echoes"—Richard Wright's piano sent through a Leslie rotating horn cabinet—was born. Lyricist/bassist/vocalist Roger Waters described "Echoes" as a kind of tone poem, an artistic approach that clearly expanded and improved upon the near twenty-four-minute title track of *Atom Heart Mother*.

"Echoes" is Floyd reaching the pinnacle of its psychedelic and progressive rock past while pushing forward into the melodic/commercial rock territory, what *Q* magazine called "the halfway house between *A Saucerful of Secrets* and *The Dark Side of the Moon*." Indeed. "The Dark Side of the Moon" was the abandoned title of a song Waters wrote during the recording sessions for *Meddle*.

After a funky jam, in the mold of what we would later hear in *Dark Side*'s "Time" (i.e., the stratospheric guitar solo section), the musical proceedings fade until we hear guitar squeals, or what sound like "whale" calls, along with layers of ominous keyboard tones, recalling the aquatic life alluded to in the lyrics.

A few minutes later, Wright's opening piano "dinks" crop up, again, around the fifteen-minute mark. Approximately a minute later (15:57), a riff reminiscent of the opening of "One of These Days" ascends to the top of the murky sonic soup. Near the end of the epic tune (22:34) Wright's evocative piano notes are dimly recalled. These distant echoes—the song's namesake—run concurrently with Ligeti-style vocal clusters closing out the record and reinforcing the cohesiveness of the composition, while underscoring concepts ranging from timelessness to universal connectivity.

The use of the Ligeti vocal motif is interesting. It might be evidence of a Kubrick influence, traces of which seem to crop up in other sections of the song. Much in the same way that *2001* skips eons of time, cutting from the image of a floating white bone (in the "Dawn of Man" sequence) to a hovering spacecraft, "Echoes" instantly fast-forwards from primordial creatures scurrying around in underwater caves (and eventually breaking the surface) to strangers passing on the street.

The combined effect of the music and lyrical visuals seems to speak to the idea of birth (or rebirth) and the dawning of a new day. It's absolutely Darwinian.

Some listeners have drawn a connection between the tenets of '60s flower power and the concept of the connectedness we all feel as human beings. Although the author detects an undercurrent of despair and the specter of death even among passages that seem to carry the most hope (the "One of These Days" riff, or just something that sounds like it, serves to emphasize this), this kind of unadulterated optimism would be rendered nearly extinct from Floyd's music by the end of the 1970s.[1]

Other tracks on *Meddle*, "San Tropez," "Fearless," "Seamus," heavily effected dual-bass rocker "One of These Days" (a kind of sister track to "Careful with That Axe, Eugene," which developed from a snippet of an idea called "Murderistic Woman," made available only as a "B" side of a single at first and marked by the same fixation on criminally insane behavior), were inspired by topics ranging from axe murder to mah-jongg. It's the massive composition "Echoes," however, that embodies Floyd's musical development and, perhaps, best speaks to Floyd past, present, and future. What we witness with "Echoes" is a nothing short of the dawning of new Pink Floyd species.

2. Yes: "The Revealing Science of God (Dance of the Dawn)," "The Remembering: High the Memory," "The Ancient: Giants Under the Sun," "Ritual: Nous sommes du soleil" (total time: 80:14), *Tales from Topographic Oceans*, 1973

London's Morgan Studios was buzzing. Vocalist Jon Anderson invited all able-bodied musicians and willing bystanders in nearby rehearsal rooms to hear a playback of Yes' 1973/4 grand work, *Tales from Topographic Oceans*. Written during candlelight sessions conducted by Anderson and Yes guitarist Steve Howe while the band was on tour, *Tales* is a large-as-life work that centers on the search for lost knowledge and self-awareness. Each of the four pieces appearing on the double album, one per "side," had been inspired by a footnote appearing in *Autobiography of a Yogi* by Paramahansa Yogananda.

Tales Side Four: "Ritual: Nous sommes du soleil" recalls musical ideas explored earlier in the record. (Guitarist Steve Howe even sneaks in a snippet of "Close to the Edge" around the 4:23 mark.) The climactic percussion jam, performed by Alan White on kit drums and the other band members on timpani, represents the struggle of life's opposing forces "out of which comes a positive source," read the original LP liner notes. "We are the sun."

After months of shuffling in and out of, and to and from, Morgan Studios, Yes were ready to unveil this four-song double album to a receptive, if not curious, audience. Said former Morgan Studios manager Roger Quested, who was an attendee of the listening session, as people filed into the main listening room to hear Yes' masterwork, some were stunned or simply bored. "They set up speakers in the studio and rows of seats and played it," Quested once told the author. "All but the diehard had drifted away before it had finished."

Forty years later, *Tales from Topographic Oceans* garners nearly the same divisive reactions from listeners as it did when it appeared. Depending on one's perspective, the double album is either the creative pinnacle of the band's career—and the entire prog rock movement—or the proverbial millstone around the neck of Yes (and, by extension, prog).

"It was a kind of intense time and Jon and I were holding the gauntlet in front of the band," says longtime Yes guitarist Steve Howe. "There was some resistance and [they] didn't like the idea that the record was going to be big and so abstract. There were doubts. Jon and I had to push the project forward within some of those doubts and prove to the band that the music had direction; there was a clear creative vision."

Close to the Edge was a commercial success, but Yes was threatening to push their music even further into esotericism with *Tales*. Seen through the prism of *CTTE*, *Tales* is not a regression, but a leap in evolutionary musical development.

It would be months before everyone was convinced, however. In the meantime, Yes worked, tirelessly, logging grueling sixteen-hour days for months. This, after spending some time rehearsing some of the material at ELP's Manticore rehearsal/recording studios in Fulham.

The album credits place the recording sessions between late summer and early fall 1973, although some other estimates say it may have taken as much as six months to complete.

It's well known that there was a difference in opinion within the band and with management about how and where to record the record. When the idea of going out to the country was rejected, the band decorated the studio with images of country life, such as cutouts of cows, barns, etc. The motivation for keeping the band in the city may have been as much to help control the personalities in the band as to ensure that Yes completed the ambitious recording project in a somewhat timely manner.

Given the massive scope of the project, it didn't appear as though the record would ever be completed. The songs were so humongous and the band had to record each track in sections. In fact, the first track was too long to fit on one side of a vinyl record and had to be cut by six minutes.

"But I have to say that we did record and play together and we worked up arrangements, which would then be organized through overdubs," Howe said. "We had isolation/separation in the recording studio, too, so we could take a keyboard part on or off a particular track if so desired. Similarly, we could take away a guitar track and I could record a different one, if we so wished. But we didn't want to do that all the time. Really, we got as far as we could one day and then we edited it the next day."

"We never had enough tracks," says producer/recording engineer Eddie Offord. "We might do a vocal part with six or nine tracks and mix that down to two. Having enough tracks was hard for that kind of music."

"Whilst Yes were doing that, I did an album with an American sax player named Eddie Harris," says Quested, a recording engineer who was managing Morgan Studios at the time *Tales* was being recorded. "He was a mate of Ahmet Ertegun, so he had all his session guys from Atlantic, but he had a very small budget. Chris Squire and Alan White played on that. I had to work quickly . . . I just chucked the drum mikes up, in a smaller studio, and Alan, who's an excellent drummer with a fantastic-sounding kit, said, 'Ah, jeez. We should have worked in *this* studio. The drums are so much better. We've spent months [recording with Yes] and in that time we've recorded most of this album.'"

Arguably, the years from 1972 to 1974, starting with releases such as Jethro Tull's *Thick as a Brick* through *A Passion Play* and Genesis' *The Lamb Lies Down on*

Broadway, would act as templates for thematic rock records for years to come. The irony of all of this is, of course, that *Tales* has often been perceived as the beginning of the end of prog rock's grand musical statements. *Tales* comments on and reflects the zeitgeist of the era, even as it pushed the band to new directions and artistic heights. It was a metaphor for the state of the genre in the mid-1970s, a genre on the precipice between self-indulgence and glorious self-empowerment; teetering on the edge of wild popularity and extinction.

Granted the recording industry of the early and mid-1970s was different from what it would become, even ten years later, but Yes was riding high from the success of a suite of albums, *The Yes Album*, *Fragile*, and *Close to the Edge*, itself containing the massive nineteen-minute title track. Yes certainly didn't need to put themselves behind the eight ball with eighty minutes of music spanning four sides of two LPs.

"It was very risky and it was really hard to play on radio," says Lee Abrams, legendary radio programmer and industry consultant. "It was mainly 'The Revealing Science of God' that we did play, and primarily at night."

Some, however, have questioned the whole endeavor. Atlantic Records executive Phil Carson was skeptical from the get-go and one incident helped to facilitate this feeling.

" ... [Jon] had announced that he had come up with this great name for the concept of this album and he had this word," says Carson, "and we were all sitting at a dinner with Nesuhi Ertegun, who ran Atlantic Worldwide. Jon said, 'I invented this word that has to do with Professor Hoyle's theory of the tubulation of space. 'It's going to be *Tales from Tubographic Oceans*.' Nesuhi said, 'That's a very interesting word you've come up with, Jon, but it is similar to another word that refers to the study of maps.' Jon said, 'Okay, then, we will call it *Topographic*.' Jon was so trite about how everything matters and then in the twinkling of an eye, he changed the title. It said a lot to me at the time."

The initial germ for these songs was birthed while Yes was on tour at a Japanese hotel and the lyrical concept was jumpstarted by an unlikely and unwitting coconspirator. King Crimson percussionist Jamie Muir, who was in attendance for the now-famous wedding reception of the former Yes and then-current Crimson kit drummer, Bill Bruford, had hipped Anderson to the *Autobiography of a Yogi*, which had sent Jon leafing through the book. Anderson was struck by one of the book's footnotes referencing four disciplines, or areas of study, known as the sacred shastras, codified by the ancient Hindu lawmaker Manu, that speak of many aspects of Indian culture, history, and society and involve caste, customs, commerce, and convention. In essence, the shastras are based on the supposed science of one's origins and how an individual should conduct his life. (Interestingly, the shastras name music as one of life's ten great vices.)

There are four classes of scripture: the shruti (revealed scriptures), smriti (the "remembered" folk tales such as the *Mahabharata*), purana (ancient allegories), and tantra (symbolic rituals).

Some Western scholars now believe that the period that gave birth to the documentation of the shastras, written from a Brahmin perspective, was one of multiculturalism and political turmoil. As author Wendy Doniger wrote in *The Hindus: An Alternative History*, ancient Indian Hindu scholars were "inspired" to "bring together all their knowledge, as into a fortified city, to preserve it for whatever posterity there might be."

Perhaps fittingly, *Tales*, much like its cousin (Yes' next studio album, *Relayer*), is prog rock's "fortified city"—at times impenetrable, preserving for posterity some knowledge and some musical treasure; a shining example of a band operating carefree of, and perhaps even oblivious to, the trends of the music world.

Interestingly, Roger Dean, who created the cover for both albums, has referred to the cave dominating the illustration for *Relayer* as a "fortified city for military monks; a secret stronghold for a fantasy Knights Templar." (Caves and oval cavities of all sizes must have had some kind of mystical draw on Dean, because they crop up in many of his paintings, including in the cover artwork for Greenslade's debut. "The cave represents the darkness and seclusion of the unconscious," Jung said, places that Dean's art often explored.)

Tales has one foot in the past, one in the present. It secures prog's link to nineteenth-century romanticism while partaking of 1970s-style artistic and musical self-indulgences, which is undoubtedly a sonic artifact of a hedonistic '70s culture.

At the time, it did seem that most people couldn't really appreciate the work. While the reviews were not nearly as bad as urban legend would have us believe, in random rock magazines, *Topographic* was critics' favorite whipping boy. *Circus* magazine, in a surprisingly favorable review of *Tormato*, mentions the album as a by-the-way, as if it were a given that "*Topographic* had threatened a future course of unmanageable blobbiness. . . ." Such foregone references were frequent and par for the course.

"It never got much audience reaction," says Abrams. "I don't think it was marketed correctly. It should have been, you know, 'An experiment in recording: *Tales from Topographic Oceans*.' We played all of it when it came out—all four sides and once after the buzz wore off we just isolated 'Revealing Science of God.' It sold well early, because it was the new Yes. We used to do a little survey called Call Back Cards. Someone would buy a record, fill out a card with their name and phone number, and explain what record they bought. We would call them back a week later, to help us to determine what the most popular song or tracks were on the album. I remember calling people back and asking, 'You bought *Tales from Topographic Oceans*. Why did you buy it?' 'Oh, yeah, it's the new Yes.' 'What do you think?' Well . . . 'It's weird.' Some others would say, 'It's the greatest thing I ever heard.'"

Based on initial reactions, it would have been difficult to predict that *Tales* would be both an artistic and commercial success: the album charted in Britain in December 1973 and was officially released in the U.S. in January 1974. Despite reservations and strong opposition from outside (and inside) the band,

Tales went to number one on the U.K. charts in December 1973, and peaked at number six in America.

"The most clever thing Yes ever did was to not be predictable and do something that was controversial," Howe told the author. "It was an experimental record that eventually became, sales-wise and in terms of popularity, as strong as all of our other records. So, we didn't really do the wrong thing."

Tales has been the object of ridicule, idolatry, and of satire for years. The cover of the late 1980s record *L'Océan*, from French prog band Atoll, is practically a takeoff of Roger Dean's artwork; and Neutron's *Tales from the Blue Cocoons*, recorded between June and November 1974 at Rockfield Studios, poked fun at both B-sci-fi/horror movies and the grandiosity of albums such as *Tales*. Neither record, however, was as inventive or influential as Yes' masterwork.

Perhaps the most important legacy of *Tales* is the exit of Wakeman from Yes after the 1974 tour, precisely because he could not stand another day performing the music. (He famously called the record *Tales from Toby's Graphic Go-Kart*.) Wakeman would, of course, return to Yes, but the core and dynamics of the classic lineup had shifted once Wakeman had exited and with the eventual recruitment of Patrick Moraz.

Relayer

"There was a bit of a strange time, in a way," says Carson. "*Tales* was a major piece of work and to go out and play four previously unheard songs was a challenge for the group playing it—it was an awful lot of music to learn, and very complex music—and was a challenge for the audience to assimilate. To be honest I kind of agree with Rick at the time. It was a point where they were shooting themselves in the foot, to a large extent, and Rick said, 'Why are we doing this? We have this great career here. . . . Why don't we play one side of it, like we did with *Close to the Edge*, and then give the audience what they want to hear?' But that was an era when bands didn't do that, they were introverted and completely concentrated on what they were doing, and it was self-indulgent. Rick saw that and . . . really chose not to be a part of it."

Once Rick left, the band were looking over their options to replace him. One name, Nick Glennie-Smith, now a film composer, was a contender. Reportedly Eddie Jobson and Keith Emerson were asked to join as keyboardist (the latter at the height of ELP's commercial success).

Anderson rethought things and had other ideas. "Jon came up with the idea of Vangelis [Evangelos Odysseas Papathanassiou]," says Carson. "He and I went to Paris to meet Vangelis. I like him a lot, and we went to his magnificent apartment he has in Paris. He had this enormous sitting room and his father was present, sitting there watching television. Vangelis was sitting in his chair and he had a bow and arrow beside his chair and . . . there's a target on the wall and every once in a while he would loose off an arrow, which would rocket past his father's left ear and land square on the target he was aiming for. It was amusing."

Jon Anderson, during his live solo acoustic concerts, has told a variation of this story in which Vangelis answers the door with a bow in his hand and a quiver basket, full of arrows, strapped around his body. "We had a meeting and he decided he wanted to join Yes but he had a fear of flying," says Carson. "And we were thinking of all kinds of ways to overcome that: one of them was we would get his gear shipped to London and then he would drive to Paris with his chauffeurs ... and it was all set up. But I don't recall if the rehearsal ever happened. I think he had decided that, inevitably, flying would be involved and that is when Patrick Moraz showed up. That's when rehearsals started and that's when he joined the band."

One report the author stumbled across revealed that the pairing of Yes with Vangelis did not occur due to contractual disputes. If Carson is correct (or even partially correct), Vangelis may not have made the journey to the U.K. to rehearse with Yes, but his gear could have. Rick's eventually replacement, Patrick Moraz, has explained in the past (and also to the author) that Vangelis' keyboards were set up for him to play.

"I can't speak to the keyboard thing, but I do know that we did arrange for Vangelis to come to England, which he eventually did," Carson says. "After Rick left it took several months before we really focused on what we were going to do with the band, however."

The group would have to move on, which they did by recruiting a classically trained Swiss keyboardist, Patrick Moraz, who was in the band Refugee with Nice drummer and bassist/vocalist Brian Davison and Keith "Lee" Jackson.

"When I was brought to an audition, at the very beginning of August 1974, I was still going to be doing some concerts with Refugee," says Moraz. "The motivation behind the whole thing was that they had invited me to see one of their rehearsals. It was not supposed to be an audition. Of course, later on, they made me an offer I couldn't refuse ... I still had some dates with Refugee in the months of July and August 1974. I had just finished a movie soundtrack for a movie a Swiss-French movie with Gérard Depardieu. I conducted a chamber orchestra for that. The recording of that was done in Geneva and we finished on a Sunday and I came back to London on Monday afternoon. When I came back, the phone rang and it was Brian Lane, inviting me to see a rehearsal by Yes on that Wednesday.

"When I came to the rehearsal, Vangelis' keyboards were there and it took about twenty minutes for me to tune them up because they had been staying there for a couple of weeks," Moraz continues. "I tuned the keyboards and I improvised some counterpoint and did even some variations on their tunes. They started to play the first few bars of, what was it, 'Soundchaser.' Jon came up and Chris as well said, 'Why don't you come up with an introduction,' and that's where and when I came up with what is the beginning of 'Soundchaser' with that [hums rapid-fire ascending melody]. I just did it and invented it there and then and that was the take. I believe that my keyboard section of that very specific introduction is the one that is on the record. There was a mobile recording studio that was completely new at that point. Eddie Offord had designed an unbelievable array of technology. [Reportedly, in bassist Chris Squire's home studio.] They had written most of the song part but the rest of the tune and all of the arrangements came up during those hours and, of course, later because the song had to be revisited a few days later when they told me I had the gig."

One of the early pieces of music Moraz became acquainted with was the sidelong composition "The Gates of Delirium." "The backbone of the song was kind of in place and, of course it changed somewhat, you know?" Moraz says. "I remember I contributed quite substantially [to it], given the time when I arrived into the band and the logistics. We had a lot of discussion and I was always included in the discussions and we all found the material for what would become the *Relayer* album—we were all composers. The vocals generally always come from Jon and the backbone structures came mainly from Steve and Chris, you know, their guitar parts. . . . Jon gave me some very interesting counterparts to do and I came up with some interesting lines, which I had developed as well. Chris, as well, was very helpful. We had complete interactivity together and that was a very creative time."

It's often been reported that "The Gates . . ." was inspired by Tolstoy's *War and Peace*. It's a piece of music with many shifting moods and a fight scene involving the drums and keys. By his own admission, drummer Alan White introduced percussive objects found in junkyards for the battle. The piece was capped off by Anderson's cathartic "Soon" section of the song, which was released as a single b/w "Sound Chaser."

"What I wanted to do was to find a connection with the divine," Anderson once said. "I sang, 'Soon/Oh, soon the light/Pass within and soothe this endless night. . . .'"

Moraz explains, from his perspective, the title was inspired by an unlikely literary source. "I remember that even the title was not chosen at the time," says Moraz. "'The Gates of Delirium,' that came from a cartoon. . . . It was a sci-fi cartoon, a comic book . . . that was precisely the imagery of that song. When I showed [the comic] to Jon he came up with the title 'Gates of Delirium.' The name of that [graphic comic] book was [*Lone Sloane*] *Delirius* by Philippe Druillet. It's still in the libraries and so on . . . I had a very strong interaction with Jon. I used to come and see him every day. It was really with him that I started to know the material and work with, and get to know the material for *Relayer* and especially 'Gates of Delirium,' he explained to me all of the thing with it, and I was taking notes and [he went through parts]. He explained to me the different kind of movements."

"It was like *Close to the Edge* in the sense that it had one long song and two small tracks on the second side of the original record," Howe once told the author. "*Relayer* proved to ourselves that we were continuing on a musical journey and not going into a stalemate. . . . It was a very angular record and I exclusively played Fender guitars, for a change, and I really, really enjoyed it. It was a tough record."

"It didn't take that long to record," says Moraz. "I think the whole of *Relayer* took about three to four weeks."

There was a time when *Relayer* always seemed to be the oddest record Yes ever made, never truly receiving the attention it probably deserved, perhaps because of the band's shift to the left. In addition, Anderson had his mind on creating something much more European and electronic (a vision that was partially realized with "Gates . . ." and "Sound Chaser").

Moraz fondly remembers playing the massive compositions from *Tales* and *Relayer* on stage. "We really played *Topographic Oceans* with a more structured approach than the record," he says. "If you listen to the whole record, you think it is a little bit limp here and there. I think we gave it a little more life. Having recorded 'The Gates of Delirium,' and the whole of *Relayer*, gave us maybe more of an impetus to attack *Tales*—the way it should be. We were not playing the four sides all at once. We played maybe one side or two sides during the same concert. The strongest part of *Topographic Oceans* onstage was 'Ritual.' I remember with Yes, when we played the twelfth of June 1976, in Philadelphia at JFK Stadium, and one concert in Anaheim in the summer of 1976 where there were 85,000 people. In Philly we had 125,000 people. To play that kind of material in front of all those people [laughs] was quite a challenge. . . . As far as progressive rock is concerned I think Yes is the epitome of all of this, you know."

Moraz worked with Yes on new studio material in Switzerland, in 1976, even providing creative input into the infamous mid-1970s Yes solo albums era. His work on Chris' solo album, *Fish Out of Water*, introduced him to his future collaborator Bill Bruford. But, as everything must, Moraz's stint with Yes came to an end. A rather abrupt one in fact, the details of which haven't all fully surfaced.

Moraz, for the most part, has reserved judgment until such time as he'll reveal what really happened in 1976, and how Yes reclaimed Rick Wakeman as one of their own.

"I discovered years later that Rick was already in town [Geneva] when I was still there," says Moraz. "It was purely a political thing. I've never understood why I was asked to leave, and then I realized that there were other interests at stake."

3. Jethro Tull: "Thick as a Brick" (one song, spanning two LP sides; total time: 43:50), *Thick as a Brick*, 1972

Still one of the most over-the-top album packages in rock music history, *Thick as a Brick* (*TAAB*) was Jethro Tull's jab at the concept album as an artistic vehicle for so-called progressive rockers in the early 1970s.

The concept for *TAAB*, created by Jethro Tull leader Ian Anderson, evolved around the creation of the fictional character, literary prodigy, nine-year-old Gerald "Little Milton" Bostock, winner of a local poetry competition, who was later disqualified due to the "unwholesome" nature of his work. (It was, of course, Anderson who actually wrote the words.)

This entire sordid tale was reported in the fictional weekly newspaper, the *St. Cleve Chronicle*, a mock, physical copy of which served as *TAAB*'s original LP packaging. This newspaper was complete with inside pages and local stories, written by band members, the kind you'd find in any parochial paper. "Bostock's" poem, "Thick as a Brick," was reprinted in these funny papers and conveniently served as the album's lyrics. (For effect, Bostock receives cowriting credit for the music, along with Anderson, on the album.)

"Thick as a Brick" is social commentary, which Anderson has never shied away from, whether it was "Aqualung," "My God," "Farm on the Freeway" (from 1987's *Crest of a Knave*) or "Working John, Working Joe." Like those songs, "Brick" is sufficiently engrossing that the listener is almost numb to the messages being transmitted. One could call the music insidious in this way: the theme and impact of the piece creeps up on the listener until it hits him/her like a ton of bricks.

Elements of Anderson's lyrics for "Brick" can certainly be interpreted as a chilling portrait of a government-engineered society and its crushing impact on the individual, his/her lifestyle, wants, fears, and ambitions. "Thick as a Brick" seems to be a fight against homogeneity and the educational system's mission to weed out the free thinkers (all in service to creating a conditioned, obedient populace).

Anderson began the original composition when he was on the road with Tull. He'd started writing a piece he thought could be turned into a ten-minute number. As he added parts he realized he could fill an entire side of an LP with one continuous song. Then, the next step in the process was easy: extend the track to span both sides of the record.

Anderson has also said that he would get to the studio, hours before anyone else, and work out the material and present it to the band as though he had been laboring over it for weeks. As the story goes, the band had worked out the finer points of the one-song LP in nearly two weeks' time, and recorded it, in sections, in a week or so.

"The recording was done by dropping in on different tracks for different sections of the music," longtime Tull recording engineer Robin Black says. "Always a bit scary since, unlike digital, if you made a mistake the band would have to re-record the previous piece of music. The mixing of the album incorporated lots of editing, hopefully, not where the audible decay of cymbals was present."

Mike Downs, recording engineer for *TAAB* sequel, 2012's *Thick as a Brick 2*, told the author that the second installment was recorded without many effects, similar to the way *Brick* was. (Apparently Ian Anderson wanted to capture a relatively "clean" vibe.) Yet, there are some very effective panning techniques and ghostly sort of echoes (especially as regards the organ on the first "side" of the original *TAAB*).

A Leslie speaker cabinet with rotating horn no doubt leaves a ghostly leakage in some of the microphones used for the mix. Also, there's a kind of "sizzle out" near the end of the first side of *Thick as a Brick* (probably to help facilitate a smooth transition from Side One to Side Two). This might be produced by synth, but it's unclear. The second side begins with a kind of wind sound, which, again, might be synth. There's also a kind of "beeping" or pulsing sound, that appears to be flute, on the second side, around the 29:04 mark on the CD and shows up again at around 30:33 and also after this mark. How was this pulsating- or mechanical-flute sound effect achieved?

"We were quite limited in those days," says Black, "so subtle changes of reverb panning and delays worked well and we just did what we thought fitted the music. The sizzle was achieved by feeding the delay back hard on itself just at the last strike. I think the pulsing sound was a keyboard, but I'm not sure 100 percent."

Brick was important in many ways for Tull, not the least of which being the kickoff point for a band lineup that stayed intact for nearly half a decade. "*Brick* was an important album in the sense of the performances of the individuals who played on that original album," Anderson told me. "The guys who preceded them certainly couldn't have played that music. I'm sure they would admit that. Or if they didn't, more fool they. It did require some really hard work and some development of skills and improvement of skills and they rose to the occasion."

Thick as a Brick hit number one on the *Billboard* album charts, and Tull, mainly through the success of *Aqualung* and subsequent U.S. dates, was a major arena draw. Tull performed at the prestigious Carnegie Hall in November 1972, and to 20,000 screamers at the Madison Square Garden in December, a show for which arty glam-rock up-and-comers Roxy Music opened.

The then–recently constructed, $28 million facility the Nassau Coliseum, in New York, booked the biggest names in entertainment business of the early 1970s—from Led Zeppelin to Ringling Bros.—and rolled out the red carpet for what was surely a three-ringed circus of activity surrounding Tull's shows in May 1972.

When tickets were finally made available, those who had been waiting on line for hours mysteriously rioted. Some fans were literally crushed by a wall of ticket-seekers pushing the crowd farther toward the box office. Some fans fainted in the confusion, were trampled on, or sustained cuts due to broken glass windows. (The New York melee wasn't the only violent incident involving Tull fanatics. The previous summer, in Denver, tear gas was used to control an unruly crowd.)

Despite the negative press, and downright animal display, thirty thousand tickets were sold, selling out both nights, May 13 and 14, 1972. Tull would return in late summer 1973 for their tour to support *A Passion Play*.

Nearly forty years later, Anderson would revisit the world of St. Cleve with a new conceptual album and theatrical world tour. With both *TAAB* and *TAAB2*, we get the sense that Anderson is speaking from experience, that Gerald is, in many ways, actually Anderson, fighting a corrosive system. Most of what appears in the sequel, which was written under the banner of Jethro Tull's Ian Anderson, was penned from personal experiences, or from real-life occurrences of people "close enough to use as discreet sources," Anderson said to me.

"I know actors who really live out the roles they are playing," Anderson told the author in 2012. "I made my son-in-law [Andrew Lincoln] sleep with a submachine gun in order to acquaint himself with the firearms skills to spend, what looks like, the rest of his life being the lead character in *The Walking Dead*, cause he's always shooting things. When I first met him he didn't have any experience at all with guns, and so we got him relaxed with firearms pretty quickly, when he knew he was getting the role. Actors have to absorb the character before they can re-create that person. . . ."

Anderson has done a superlative job branding Tull—and, thereby, himself. The image of a flamingo with a flute is difficult to shake, and even in the twenty-first century Anderson's identity is inseparable from Tull. So interchangeable are the names, the identities of Ian and Jethro Tull, in the public's mind, that the author interacted with industry people who made the excusable and understandable slip of employing the pronoun "he" when discussing their dealings with "Jethro Tull."

"The thing with Ian is, each day you try on a different person," says former bassist Tony Williams, who toured with Tull in 1978. "When Tull were making the money, they were living in Switzerland because of tax reasons, which everybody hated; Barrie [Barlow] hated. He couldn't get TV, and times were different. They eventually came back to London and when they did, Barrie thought, 'I'm going to live by the river, by the Thames.' Martin said that was a good idea and he went to live out in the country somewhere. And John [Glascock] did the same. Ian liked to wear black leather at that point and wanted to stay in the city. That was his bag. He looked like Tony Iommi for a while: much the city heavy rocker. Then he swapped and changed over night. All of a sudden he was a farmer, and he was going to farm fish and he was going to wear deerstalkers [hats] and dress like a farmer."

However, in discussing his 2014 solo album, *Homo Erraticus*, which, ironically enough, was "cowritten" by Bostock, Ian appears to distance himself from the perception that he is Jethro Tull, perhaps, in more ways than one.

4. The Mothers of Invention: "Billy the Mountain" (24:47), *Just Another Band from L.A.*, 1971 . . . and the "Project/Object"

One of Frank Zappa's more theatrical pieces, "Billy the Mountain" was earmarked for film treatment as an animated feature. When it appeared that this was not a viable option, it was up to two very animated ex-Turtles, Flo and Eddie (Mark Volman and Howard Kaylan), to bring the story to life every night on stage.

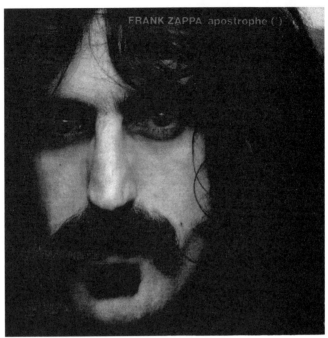

FRANK ZAPPA apostrophe ( )

Conceptual continuity: Is Zappa's output one large musical puzzle?

"I think in Frank's mind, he was creating something that could have been handled by Pixar today," says Volman ("Flo"), who fronted the Mothers as a vocalist with his musical partner, Kaylan ("Eddie"). "I would have to say that about 60 to 70 percent of the piece was very much scripted."

Says Volman, some of the material would vary depending on the town the Mothers were scheduled to play. "We would add personalized things that took place in the town based on what we were able to discover about it," says Volman. "If there was something specific in town that had taken place in the last three to six months, if there was a certain person or group or situation that was personally identified with the community, we would do our best to search that out. Tattoo parlors, places where drugs would be sold, where kids hung out, all kinds of different personalized events and concepts would take place. That gave it fresh approach almost every night."

Volman and Kaylan canvassed neighborhoods in search of fodder. "It was mine and Howard's duty to sort of bring to the stage, every night, something that would make Frank laugh, and to do that you would have to dig pretty deeply into the communities to see if we could discover things that would shock him."

The plotline of "Billy the Mountain" is bizarre even for Zappa. Billy, our hero, and his wife, Ethel, a tree growing on Billy's side, decide to take a vacation, courtesy of the royalty checks Billy's earned by "posing for postcards" and such. When the mountain travels it, of course, leaves a trail of destruction in its wake, and must be stopped. Studebacher Hoch, once described alternately as a "quasi-religious hero" and "hero of the current economic times," accepts the mission to bring down Billy and Ethel, a plot development that no doubt played into Zappa's love of low-budget science fiction movies from the mid-twentieth century.

We don't have the space to tear the lyrics apart line by line, but like so many other Zappa pieces, comic absurdity and self-referential clues litter the work. It's Project/Object Magnified, really. This encompassed everything from cardboard boxes[2] to military bases (Zappa's father was a U.S. Army engineer and a metallurgist, a fact that undoubtedly had an impact on how the younger Zappa viewed life and death, the military defense complex, and perhaps even the nature of scientific research), which appear to hint at something greater and meaningful. Zubin Mehta is referenced in the work and Mehta, of course, conducted the Los Angeles Philharmonic Orchestra in May 1970, when the symphony accompanied Zappa and the Mothers of Invention for a performance of the music from the Zappa film *200 Motels.*

"What is on *Just Another Band from L.A.* wasn't even standard," says Volman. "That was sort of edited down to become what the record company would allow to be released. There were other versions that would be released, such as the *Playground Psychotics* version, which was about thirty-five minutes long or so. There was always instrumental music that Frank would drop in from night to night depending on the length of the show and how much Frank wanted to play, and how much he wanted the musicians to improvise. 'Billy the Mountain' could go, easily, forty minutes. That was the context of an evening. It was generally, maybe a second-half of a show. [*Note: In some reports of the time, "Billy the Mountain" might encompass the first set or half of the show. . . .*]

"I think after *200 Motels* [in which Volman and Kaylan appear], 'Billy the Mountain' was intended to be a full theatrical piece, including visuals. But we never really got to finish. I think Frank was adding to it all the time. It was not something that was written out and done. It was something of a project in motion, constantly, due to the kind of riffing it brought."

The author doesn't want to lose sight of the fact that Zappa was not a prog rocker in the sense that Yes or ELP were. Zappa was a twentieth-century composer who happened to write and record albums that overlapped in time, and perhaps general musical direction, with some of the best efforts of British and European (even American) bands of a certain musical persuasion. Zappa's entire career could be seen as one long progressive movement, developing styles as far-ranging as straight-up classical to comedy rock. (Indeed. The term *Project/Object* was a phrase Zappa used for his entire body of music.)

"I've dedicated a chunk of my life to presenting Zappa's music and getting his alumni out on the road," says André Cholmondeley, who performs in a Zappa tribute band, Project/Object. "Zappa said every note, every song, every concert, every piece of tape, it's all the Project/Object. There's no beginning or end to it. My whole statement is my Project/Object. The second little phrase that is well known with Zappa fans is *conceptual continuity*, which refers to how you can find references in Frank's songs, like in the middle of 'Billy the Mountain,' that suddenly you'll find cropping up in a later work, twenty years later. I love that aspect of Zappa. To this day, as a Zappa freak with hundreds of bootlegs, I love that I can still be listening to something and say, 'I never noticed that.' There is some tie-in or riff that goes back to some other record."

We could write entire book on all the self-referential riffs and musical concepts in Zappa's music. One could say that Zappa delighted in dropping references to, and playing in the style of, other artists he'd admired, from Gustav Holst and Igor Stravinsky to Devo and the late 1960s band the Seeds.

For instance, Zappa recasts Stravinsky's *The Soldier's Tale* as "Titties and Beer" and quotes Stravinsky in "Soft-Sell Conclusion" from *Absolutely Free* (and also the posthumous release *Joe's Camouflage*). Of course, in some cases, such as *We're Only in It for the Money* (the *Sgt. Pepper's* spoof), *Lumpy Gravy*, and *Cruising with Ruben & the Jets*—these works were actually intended to be part of a larger conceptual work, tentatively called *No Commercial Potential*.

Some listeners have even observed an "arctic" theme injected into Zappa's music, based on Lionel Hampton's jazz standard from 1947, "Midnight Sun," which can be heard in songs such as "Keep It Greasy" (1979's *Joe's Garage*) and "Don't Eat the Yellow Snow"/"Nanook Rubs It."

Animal themes run through Zappa's music for both 1974's *Apostrophe (')* and 1973's *Over-nite Sensation*. In fact, they seem similar to Ian Anderson's fixation with animals at roughly the same time. Again, much like what Anderson of Jethro Tull had done with *A Passion Play*, Zappa engaged in a kind of word play, (at least) as far back as the track "Big Leg Emma" (from *Absolutely Free*), in which Zappa gets playful with the title, entangling "big leg emma" with "big dilemma."

The lyrics of "Don't Eat the Yellow Snow"/"Nanook Rubs It," "St. Alfonzo's Pancake Breakfast," "Father O'Blivion," through to and including the final track, "Stink-Foot," are tied lyrically by, at the very least, a phonetic game of mumbo jumbo, involving the use of "o," or multiple "ooos." Words were also typically misspelled on the lyric sheet (i.e., guru appears as "geroo," nirvana as "nervonna"). Even *Over-nite Sensation* dabbles in this a bit with tracks such as "Montana" (i.e., "tycoon").

Before he died in 1993, Zappa released the orchestral *The Yellow Shark* and completed *Civilization Phase III* (which was released posthumously in 1995). Zappa was a creative dynamo whose voluminous output didn't cease even in the final months of his life. He spent untold hours in his private studio, envisioning and creating music with state-of-the-art musical and recording equipment he had on hand. In the years following his death, Zappa's stature has only grown. Spearheaded by Zappa's widow, Gail, the Zappa Family Trust, the going concern controlling Frank's music with the help of vaultmeister Joe Travers have dug into the composer's vast vault of tapes to release material that would have been lost, forgotten, or otherwise irretrievable by issuing CDs such as *Joe's Corsage, Joe's Domage, Trance-Fusion, Imaginary Diseases*, and *The MOFO Project/Object* through Zappa Records. It is a daunting task and fraught with unforeseeable obstacles, such as finding the suitable material to release for public consumption. Zappa's output, in life and posthumously, is climbing upward of nearly one hundred releases.

Percussionist Ed Mann, on his second day in the band, was given a glimpse of the overarching conceptualism in Zappa's work. "We were up at Frank's house and he said, 'Let me show you this . . . ,'" says Mann. "His father was a hugely talented mathematician and used to tutor Frank. He'd died not too long before I joined the band and Frank showed me all of these mathematical equations, and explained that when he was younger his father told him, 'If you always follow a certain set of equations, or ratios, and make sure these fit into the music or make sure the music is constructed around them, the music will be successful. It will have a certain thread of consistency that will be unusual but cohesive.' He said, 'For example, this is why I very rarely play any major chord with any extensions,'" continues Mann. "'I play a II chord where there is no III. There's only I–II–V, instead of I–III–V, which would be major. I–II–V carries a tension that needs to be resolved, that wants to be resolved, and yet, I don't resolve it. I just use it.' As the music moves through different chords within a progression, that II chord would remain so prominent as part of his vocabulary as a composer. You realize why his music has such a tension. It's magnetic and keeps the listener glued to it. I went on to read a lot of his music and within a few months I understood his vocabulary as a composer."

Mann concludes: "I'm sure once it is all added up, Frank Zappa will certainly be thought of as the most prolific composer of the twentieth century."

5. ELP: "Pirates" (13:20), *Works Volume 1*, 1977

When ELP took a break in the mid-1970s (Emerson once said that the band had actually broken up), it was to complete solo records. Chief rivals Yes had split for the same reason at nearly the same time.

Reasons for the split may have been fatigue, the spoils of success, not wanting to repeat themselves, the desire to record solo projects, and/or, frankly, not knowing what to do next as a unit.

By late 1974, Carl Palmer was recording the track "L.A. '74," which developed into the song, "L.A. Nights," originally featuring not only Eagles guitarist Joe Walsh on electric six-string, but also King Crimson's Ian McDonald on sax.

Although each member of the band had been working on his own solo material, Lake eventually reached out to Emerson and inquired about culling all of this material. Emerson was resistant at first, because he had, for years, wanted to do a full-fledged solo record. Eventually Emerson agreed but only if the band changed direction. The result was, of course, *Works Volume 1*.

It was agreed that if ELP were to re-form, each member of the band would be given half a record—a full side—to express himself. The fourth side would be for band collaboration.

The back cover of the program for ELP's 1977 North American tour, which was a logistical nightmare.

One of the most distinctive sounds on the record is Lake's bass tone. That heavy, rumbling clacking sound he achieved from his Alembic bass, a custom-made guitar that has become legendary in its own right. "I've played that exact bass, the 'Pirates' bass. The fret markers were treasure chest, parrot, skull and cross bones," says Steve Luongo (John Entwistle, Rat Race Choir). "The opportunity came to me because John Entwistle bought that bass. He bought it for his collection and took it out on tour with us. It had a graphite neck. I remember John trying to screw a straplock into the back of the neck and the screwdriver was skipping all over the place. I said, 'I'm thinking you're not going to be able to drill into graphite without a pilot hole.' He said, 'Good idea.' That was an incredible instrument.

What attracted Entwistle to that bass, the founder of that lead bass sound, was when you hit that bass it sounded the way it did coming through that huge rig not even plugged. You could hear wood resonating and you could hear that twang edge of the strings. I can't speak to the electronics but I know it had an XLR connector and a quarter-inch jack connector. There was some kind of bi-amping."

"It would go direct into the PA as well as the guitar amp," adds Mark Hitt, Luongo's bandmate in Rat Race Choir and the Robin Zander Band. "Early on he was playing through Hiwatt 400s, which were impossible to find. He had them made for him special. He also used Rotosound strings and put horns in his rig with his speaker, so he was playing through a hi-fidelity stereo system with thousands of watts."

The other sonically booming factor in Lake's corner was his voice, which seemed tailor-made for the orchestrated ballads, for which lyrics were cowritten by former Crimson wordsmith Pete Sinfield. Songs such as "C'est La Vie" and "Closer to Believing," which took two years to finish, were some of the period's strongest tunes, with the former being recorded in June 1973 during the era of *Brain Salad Surgery*. ("I Believe in Father Christmas," a song cowritten by Lake and Sinfield, hit number two on the British charts on December 24, 1975. It does not, however, appear on *Works Volume 1*, but *Volume 2*.)

Palmer's side reflects his growing knowledge of classical percussion techniques, his lessons with James Blades. In the same way that the band was heavily into electronics and Carl used Nick Rose's electronic trigger devices for the drum kit, Palmer's need to explore orchestral and tuned percussion perfectly suited the then-new symphonic version of ELP on *Works Volume 1*.

"Pirates," recorded in three separate studios, features the Orchestre de l'Opéra de Paris, conducted by Godfrey Salmon, and holds the same swashbuckling sense of adventure as anything in the Gilbert and Sullivan canon. Like Yes' "Awaken," "Pirates" is ELP's last masterpiece of the band's glory days of the progressive decade of the 1970s. (In a lateral move, one that would have made former ELP and Yes co-producer Eddie Offord proud, producer John Timperley worked on two pivotal 1977 releases by two rival, gigantic prog bands: Yes' *Going for the One* and ELP's *Works Volume 1*. And both bands had done recording, around the same time, in Montreux. Studio work for *Works* was done in both Paris and Switzerland.)

Emerson's original composition was initially written, but never used, for the Frederick Forsyth film titled *The Dogs of War*, starring Christopher Walken as a mercenary hired by British mining bigwigs. Greg Lake and former King Crimson lyricist Peter Sinfield both objected to the subject matter and suggested the band substitute the concept of pirates for mercenaries.

Lake once recounted to the author his version of how the epic song of treasure, plunder, hedonism, and the search for paradise evolved: "When I heard the opening sequence, it reminded me of the sea, I don't know why," says Lake. "Then I thought, 'Wait a minute. Mercenaries. Oceans. Pirates.' That was a fantastic moment. From that moment forward that became the subject matter."

"I'm very proud of 'Pirates,'" Sinfield told the author. "In my Hollywood head it was fun to write about pirates, and when I actually investigated them they were quite disgusting, bloodthirsty people. The irony was, the more bloodthirsty and real I tried to make them . . . the more Walt Disney they became."

"We were working up a mountain in Switzerland, in a chalet," added Lake. "We bought every book known to man about pirates, historic books, as well as Robert Louis Stevenson's *Treasure Island* and so forth. We immersed ourselves in piracy for about six weeks. There were pirate flags on the walls."

"Pirates" is one of the very best examples of ELP's fusion of rock, orchestral elements, keyboard technology, and drummer Carl Palmer's bombastic and witty playing. Yet, it's one of the more underappreciated pieces of music ELP has ever recorded, and is greatly overshadowed by the nearly ten-minute "Fanfare."

Emerson said he had always envisioned the band's epics as being augmented with an orchestra. Indeed. The Nice recorded the "Five Bridges" suite and

Keith composed the neoclassical piece Piano Concerto No. 1 with the London Philharmonic, which appears as the first side—Emerson's side—on *Works*.

Emerson was proud of Piano Concerto No. 1, as it reflected a progression from rock to classical music. It also reflected the range of emotions Emerson experienced in the period prior to and after his house in the Sussex countryside burned due to faulty wiring. Emerson, who lost work and valuable possessions, was both shocked and angered by this turn of events, and these mishaps and emotions were encapsulated by the three movements of the concerto.

"... I didn't care about anything for months—just stayed drunk most of the time," Emerson told *Rolling Stone* in 1977. (It's a seminal moment that is, perhaps, a bit underreported: one wonders the true cost of the fire and what toll it took on Emerson, his life, his future outlook, and his career.)

One funny anecdote, told and retold slightly different each time, involved famous conductor Leonard Bernstein and the recording of "Pirates."

"We were in a studio in Paris [EMI Studios]," then-lyricist Peter Sinfield recounted for the author, "and ELP and I were there—and I was trying to finish the words. I had a couple of lines left for 'Pirates,' and [the band] wanted to get Leonard Bernstein to conduct the orchestra on the record [the Orchestre de l'Opéra de Paris]. Anyway, Bernstein showed up and swept into the studio with his camel-hair coat across his shoulders and his entourage. He said, 'Commence. Play me the music.' He listened, looked around, and said, 'Stop. Stop. How can you be so primitive?' And then he waltzed out. . . ." [*Note: Godfrey Salmon received the call.*]

In the intervening years, people have flocked to Johnny Depp's *Pirates of the Caribbean* movie series. Perhaps ELP's "Pirates" was twenty-five years too early.

"You listen back to [the song], and I think it's one of the finest pieces of writing we'd done then," says Lake. "It may someday be seen as an unrealized, undiscovered piece of quality writing. The time wasn't right, that's all. How was that going to sell? How was that going to be played on the radio? How was that going to be appreciated? It was neither a piece of classical music or a rock song. In a way it was both. It was brilliant writing from Keith and it was fantastic."

Once the band had completed recording, the plan was to tour North America with a nearly seventy-person orchestra/choir stuffed into three buses. (Fifteen hundred musicians answered ads calling for classical musicians for the tour.) The orchestral instruments were amplified via custom pickups (Arnie Lazarus' FRAP—flat response audio pickups), a team of sound engineer technicians were onboard, and the sound was blasted out to the audience via the same JBL PA system and seventy-two ten-speaker cabinets, a configuration similar to that used for the Olympics in Montreal in 1976, bringing the sounds of the orchestra to the audience with sparkling clarity and booming volume. The band moved twenty-five tons of gear with seven forty-five-foot trucks (ten trucks in total when playing outdoor gigs). According to a July 14, 1977, article in *Newsday*, the road crew was costing the band over $200,000 a week.

The band rehearsed with the orchestra for a month, according to reports, before the tour. To get up to speed physically and mentally Carl Palmer jogged for miles, Emerson swam thirty or more laps a days, and Lake conditioned himself for the rigors of the road via daily training.

But the American tour was doomed from the start. Lake blamed a broken lighting rig, which caused some unfortunate (and quite expensive) rescheduling. It set the band back three days and three outdoor shows needed to be canceled. At hundred of thousands of dollars in expenses for a 120-paid-person rock and roll caravan (according to one source), and the unrecoverable revenue from the canceled shows (estimated at over $2 million), ELP was bleeding cash. (Each of the sixty or so orchestral musicians demanded American Federation of Musicians wages—$40,000 a week. The entire tour had a reported budget of $4 million.)

"One day, I got a call from an agent friend of mine in New York and said, 'Hey, you have a rehearsal studio there that one of my acts can use?'" says Wil Sharpe, who was running a studio in Fort Wayne, Indiana, at the time. "I said, 'We can probably block some time for you.' We had this one large room that you could fit an orchestra, a small orchestra, in. I asked, 'What do you need it for?' He said, 'Well, ELP, they're losing their ass on the road carrying the symphony with them and they need to rehearse as a three-piece.' I said, 'They are more than happy to block out some time for them.' So, we did and they came in to rehearse for three or four days."

As it turned out, ELP nixed the orchestra concept except for a few key major gigs, such as NYC's Madison Square Garden for a three-night stand. As it turns out, ELP set the record for the most number of tickets sold at a concert held in Olympic Stadium, Montreal, and gave what some have called the performance of a lifetime, complete with cannon fire during "Pirates."

Works claimed the number-two spot on the British charts in June 1977.

6. Vangelis: "Heaven and Hell: Parts I and II" (total time: 48:12), *Heaven and Hell*, 1975

Ironically, for all the attention paid to the construction of Vangelis' compositions via layered electronic keyboard tracks, so often here it is the vocalists (Jon Anderson and Vana Verouti) who perfectly capture the mood—and concept—of the piece: a journey of the soul.

Recorded in 1975 in London, at Vangelis' own Nemo Studios, formerly Hampden Gurney Studios, *Heaven and Hell* is Vangelis' masterwork—a classical/orchestral New Age prog hybrid work.

The closing section of Part I, "So Long, So Clear," sung by Anderson, offers a tantalizing peek at the kind of atmospheric and symphonic sounds a Vangelis-Yes collaboration would have produced in the mid-1970s. This record is perhaps significant because a portion of Part I, "Movement III," was used in the Carl Sagan multipart documentary in the 1970s, *Cosmos*.

7. Neu!: "Hallogallo" (10:07), Neu!, 1972

The so-called German Krautrock scene, of which Neu! was a major early participant, ran parallel to the British progressive rock movement. Some of the progenitors of the Krautrock sound (i.e., Faust, Kraftwerk, Can, and Neu!) were perhaps just as influential as their British prog rock counterparts, but not as groups of virtuoso players. Where the U.K. proggers valued individual excellence, the Krautrockers, on the whole, and especially Neu!, one of many influential bands to have appeared on the German label Brain during the 1970s, seemed more entranced by a clash of musical styles, studio experimentation, and exploration of sonic textures.

After splitting from Florian Schneider's Kraftwerk due to creative differences, the duo of guitarist/bassist Michael Rother and drummer Klaus Dinger formed Neu! to create music rife with sonic washes and splashes of *musique concrète* that would encompass all of the fresh ideas that their band name—the German word for "new"—seemed to imply.

"It was a matter of using instruments to create sound," Rother told the author in 2010. "It wasn't about being impressive as a soloist, but the sum of everything at our disposal to create sound."

The trance-like qualities of this famous eighth-note-heavy, common-time "Apache beat" frames the ten-minute opening track, "Hallogallo" (from the band's self-titled 1972 debut). The incessant rhythm was ground zero, the launch point, for all of Neu!'s experimentation, yet to come.

"I've always loved backwards sounds and slowed down sounds," said Rother. "Not sure what inspired it initially, but it was Conny's idea. Because of the tape manipulation in 'Hallogallo,' Conny [Plank, producer] organized this orchestra of guitar melodies. They float above this machine—the driving beat of the drums—that's barreling down that straight, musical highway of 'Hallogallo.'"

Dinger, now deceased, had spent most of his career chasing a certain longing, and some have surmised that the famous Neu! beat was an expression of the drummer's longing for the object of his desire, his Swedish former girlfriend, Anita.

The unwavering Neu! beat, what Brian Eno dubbed one of the top three beats of the 1970s (Fela Kuti and James Brown fathering the other two), has been used in Hollywood movies and influenced numerous artists (including David Bowie, Hawkwind, Brian Eno, Ultravox, and Radiohead). However, Dinger's timekeeping was far from metronomic. Unlike Can's tape-edited grooves and steady-handed beat machine, Jaki Liebezeit, Dinger's style was much more organic, an approach Sonic Youth skinsbeater and Neu! fanboy Steve Shelley once told the author wasn't always perfect; but "a technically perfect drummer is not always what the music needed."

Dinger's playing provided the rhythmic foundation for Rother to explore music that was rooted in European folk and classical music styles. "There was a kind of stability, I suppose, in Klaus' playing," said Rother. "When playing live with Kraftwerk or the times we went out as Neu!, Klaus would sometimes change tempo and this may have been done on purpose."

Konrad "Conny" Plank, who worked with a number of innovative, experimental and electronic German bands such as Organisation, Kluster/Cluster, Moebius, Guru Guru, Kraan, and Kraftwerk throughout the 1970s, demonstrated a willingness to experiment with the structure and sound of recorded material (sometimes through trial and error) and had an uncanny ability to memorize disparate elements of a piece, not to mention inspire frenetic performances.

The album cover for the debut album *Neu!* Klaus Dinger's "Apache" beat helped to propel Neu!'s sonic experiments.

Plank, like George Martin, was more than a man behind the console: he transformed the traditional role of record producer into (what he called) a kind of musical "midwife," affording musicians a setting in which to birth their most creative ideas and deliver artistic statements.

Plank's impact can be felt—and heard—throughout classic Krautrock releases, but especially on "Hallogallo" from Neu!'s debut, a production that Rother estimated cost in the neighborhood of $5,000. "Conny was interested in sound creation," Rother said. "Conny had experience at the mixing board, which I did not, at the time. He had the ability to find the musical 'nuggets,' which were scattered all over the recording tapes, and bring them out."

For the first album, for the most part, Rother and Dinger cut the basic tracks and then embarked on the overdubbing process. But Rother admitted that the band did not have a fully prepared repertoire when heading into the studio to record their debut, in part due to the fact that a small cassette recorder was all he could afford to jot down his musical ideas. As time passed, specifically in the run-up to the band's third studio offering, *Neu! '75*, Rother did invest in a four-track recorder to capture basic concepts, most notably for heavenly songs such as "Isi."

Raising comparisons to the great drone and electronic experiments of La Monte Young, Stockhausen, as well as Lou Reed's *Metal Machine Music, Neu! 2* was a triumph in the face of time constraints. Lack of time—and money—seemed only to open creative avenues for the duo to experiment (i.e., tracks "Neuschnee" and "Super" played at various speeds).

Although Rother and Dinger didn't always see eye to eye, in retrospect, they composed one of the more perfect musical marriages in all of Krautrock-dom, operating via unspoken communication; like "two painters working on one canvas," Rother said. In fact, Klaus' drumbeat pattern had such an effect on Rother that it served as an inspiration for some of the songs appearing on

1975's *Deluxe*, the second album by the ambient rock/Krautrock supergroup Harmonia, formed by Rother and keyboardist/vocalist Hans-Joachim Roedelius and keyboardist/harpist/vocalist Dieter Moebius of Cluster.

Perhaps Rother returned the favor when Neu! reconvened. Dare we say that Rother's experience with the synth-based Harmonia helped to shape the lovely sounds heard on *Neu! '75*?

8. Focus: "Eruption" (23:04), *Moving Waves*, 1971 (release date varies by source and territory)

Focus, formed in Amsterdam in 1969, gave the British progressive rock and classical rock acts a run for their money in the early 1970s. Guitarist Jan Akkerman was just as versatile as his British counterparts, Steve Hackett and Steve Howe (his classically tinged and Mellotron-soaked acoustic number "Le Clochard," from *Moving Waves*, foretells Hackett's "Hackett to Bits"); drummer Pierre van der Linden balanced hard-rock fire with jazz-like precision in his controlled percussive assault; and lead singer/keyboardist/flutist Thijs van Leer nurtured the most bizarre vocal acrobatics this side of the Zeuhl crew in Magma. Putting it simply, Focus rocked just as hard, if not harder, than your average progressive rock band from the 1970s, but could also compose a beautiful pastoral piece of prog rock.

Focus were, of course, no stranger to long-form composition. One look at the band's catalog attests to this assumption. The final track of their debut, *In and Out of Focus*, originally titled *Focus Plays Focus*, spans ten minutes. The band's other noteworthy compositions include "Anonymous Two," which clocks at a whopping twenty-six-and-a-half minutes, and "Hamburger Concerto." Still, "Eruption," largely because of its breeziness and purity, might be the band's greatest entry in this category.

"I arranged the whole thing and played bass on the whole thing," Jan Akkerman told the author in 2008. "I never got a credit for it though, but that doesn't matter. The song was composed of patches and I glued them all together and the tape looked like a . . . [trails off] It was recorded on a twenty-four-track and it was sort of patched-up church-y ideas, sacral stuff. I enjoyed it, but it was like a flea market, musically. It was little quotations from the past. [Keyboardist/vocalist/wind instrumentalist Thijs van Leer] was from the cabaret scene. But, I took great pride in trying to make [the music] sound like a garbage can or a rock band, for that matter. You see? There was more edge to it and . . . it was more up to date. To make blues out of those neoclassical church-like harmonies, that's actually what I did. . . . If it was up to other members of the band it probably would have stayed sacral. Van Leer was heavily influenced by a band from Canada, the Collectors, and their song, 'What Is Love?'"

Despite criticisms that the song is merely a jam, a closer listen reveals some interesting themes floating through the entire piece, as well as a majestic liturgical bent, one that Akkerman, for one, would explore with a release such as his solo record from 1974, *Tabernakel*. (Akkerman even pointed out that the photograph of his face on the cover of 1973's *Profile* and the drawing on *Tabernakel* resemble "the Turin shroud. . . . I can't help that, man," he says.)

"Coming from Europe there's always a greater awareness that we will be molded by the church," says Akkerman. "I think the idea was to make blues out of neoclassical church-like harmonies; that's actually what we did. The song 'Answers? Questions! Questions? Answers!' [from *Focus 3*] was like being in church. The singer is out front and the choir answers."

Of course, Focus is best known, at least in the States, for its whistle-crazy, yodel-icious Top 10 hit (Top 20 in the U.K.), "Hocus Pocus," also from *Moving Waves* (a.k.a. *Focus II*). The song wouldn't appear on the charts until 1973.

"A friend of mine later described to me that there's a certain expression in the Anglo-Saxon world, 'yodeling in the canyon,' which probably helped to make 'Hocus Pocus' a hit," Akkerman says. "I do have this suspicion that that has something to do with it. Maybe people interpreted it as a kind of song of freedom. I don't think Thijs, who yodeled, had any idea that the freedom was one of the meanings behind it. It was more of the mystery. I mean, the phrase 'hocus pocus' is a Catholic expression—it comes from the Catholic Church. Something like, 'a light has come into the world.'"

9. Yes: "Awaken" (15:38), *Going for the One*, 1977

It's all about Eastern Numbers. Seven and eleven, to be exact. We'll come to that.

Jon Anderson had once indicated, in a Yes tour book from the tour to support the band's *Big Generator* album (1987), that "Awaken" is a kind of continuation of "Yours Is No Disgrace" from 1971's *The Yes Album*. "Disgrace" was supposedly about soldiers fighting in Vietnam, showing support for their service.

"I was in a hotel room and I was walking through the halls and I heard Steve playing [sings/hums the main guitar riff of 'Awaken'] in his room," Anderson told me. "I had breakfast and he was still playing the same phrase. I said, 'Hey, Steve, why don't you change key.' He changed key and I said, 'Quick, I'll start singing.' I started singing this phrase and we left it at that."

Months later, three or four by Anderson's estimations, the band was in the studio and Anderson brought up the idea that Steve and he had jammed on.

"I said, 'Let's try that same phrase with three or four key changes,'" said Anderson. "I'm singing but I could hear a full choir [in my head]. It's like a hymn and . . . it had lots of bells. It was very Indonesian, or very Indian, Pakistanian. It had an Asian energy, you know? But there's a choir and everything."

It may have been Anderson's idea to string a number of chords together, over a dozen, which formed the basis for the song. "Steve would play . . . nine chords or something," Anderson said. "And I could hear this melody on top in the 'Workings of Man' section of the song. I started to put it together lyrically, then, about how man has turned his back on himself and doesn't really have his act together."

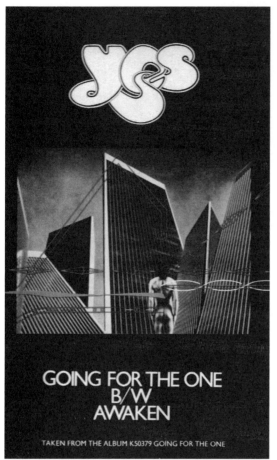

GOING FOR THE ONE
B/W
AWAKEN

TAKEN FROM THE ALBUM K50379 GOING FOR THE ONE

A special limited edition 12″ single, including an edited version of "Awaken."

It wasn't until Wakeman returned that the song could truly be finished. "I think I talked to Rick about finding a church organ," Anderson said. "We found this place near Vevey, Switzerland, which was near Montreux."

Wakeman explained that he lived not far from the church and was granted permission to record there. Wakeman stayed in the church as the band cut "Awaken" and "Parallels," which was earmarked for Chris Squire's 1975 solo album, *Fish Out of Water*.

Before Wakeman entered the church, Anderson was playing a Celtic harp in one of the pews in anticipation of the music that would transpire.[3] "We did some sessions, just experiencing what it was like being in a church together," Anderson said. "It was then that I came up with the idea of what you'd call the middle section, and Alan added the crotal bells."

As the pieces were being assembled Yes were unsure on how to bring the song to a conclusion. "I said, 'Just hold that last chord, and Rick if you could just meander around that chord and I'll sing. . . .'" Anderson said. "Then the idea came to me that we should start the piece like that, too."

Howe plays one of the sweetest, most poised electric guitar riffs of his career, and the album closes. This is "Awaken" and this was one of the more highly composed and highly structured pieces in Yes' catalog. However, before Moraz left Yes, he, or so he claims, wrote a number of pieces for the band, which were likely reworked for their 1977 record, *Going for the One*.

At the time, Moraz had been doing what he had called some sonic research and development, creating new concepts in sounds via polyphonic synthesizers in the run-up to the recording for *Going for the One*, which reportedly was slated for release in late 1976. (It wouldn't be released, of course, until Rick Wakeman returned to Yes.) Moraz had told me to check out the first three minutes or so of "Time for a Change," from his solo record, *Out in the Sun*, as the seed of the idea that became "Awaken."

"I wrote a very interesting introduction, in a kind of symphonic approach with the new synthesizer I had asked Oberheim to design for me," says Moraz. "You can find in my own album, just after [I left] Yes [*Out in the Sun*], there's a piece called 'Time for a Change.' The first few bars and the first minute and minute of a half is what I had come up with for 'Awaken.' It was a very beautiful piece based on the harmony of the beginning of the song. It has been replaced by what is there now. I had a piano opening and I had extended it on *Out in the Sun* to make it a full piece.

"We came up . . . with hundreds of ideas that ended up on the *Going for the One* record," Moraz continues. "There certainly were some of my influences there. . . ."

While there may be some truth in this, it is difficult to argue with the fact that the band had plenty of their own ideas. So much energy has been put into understanding the Herman Hesse–inspired "Close to the Edge"—and for good reason—and even masterworks such as "The Gates of Delirium" and the songs on *Tales*. But "Awaken" seems to be a neglected masterpiece.

Some have noted that *Going for the One*, and specifically "Awaken," completes a kind of thematic arc that began with *Close to the Edge* and progressed through the triple-live behemoth *Yessongs*, through to *Tales* and *Relayer*.

As Anderson once explained to me, "Awaken" is a communion and, indeed, the final words of the song (i.e., "Like the time I ran away . . .") seem to represent a longing fulfilled. "You are asking the presence of the divine to be connected as you create the music, as you perform the music," he said. "And that's what you do onstage. You ask for the power of the divine. It has nothing to do with rock and roll or music or the business or politics. It's just wanting that connection. And it works, because the audience wants it as well. . . ."

After he plays the song onstage, Anderson said, he can "breathe after that."

Tim Jones' liner notes to the expanded and remastered edition of *Going for the One*, released in 2003 (coinciding with the thirty-fifth anniversary of Yes), seem to hint in this direction. Jones writes, the "concept of 'The One' is trademark Yes: a mystical quest for utopia juxtaposing Christian deism, gnosticism, and heliocentric paganism with modern Man's materialistic vainglory."

But what does the centerpiece of the album actually mean?

Anderson has admitted in past interviews, during the *Tales* era, that seven is a vital number and important for many artists (and that *Tales* was the band's seventh release). Why is this significant?

A look at the structure of "Awaken" seems to reveal a kind of hidden value or truth in Anderson's words. A partial key to understanding "Awaken" lies in Anderson's interest in spirituality and numerology. In fact, occult elements shape *Going for the One*, especially as relates to the 2003 reissue, which includes such bonus tracks as "Amazing Grace" and "Eastern Numbers," an early version of "Awaken."

We can't ignore the link binding prog to the occult. In a 1972 *Circus* article Chris Squire explains that there is mind music and there is body music. "[Yes] wanted to combine the two," he said. Presumably, by combining the two elements, Yes created a third.

The work of alchemy and its transformative powers or laws of transmutation present a mirror, a minute imitation, of Creation. ("God" is the greatest "alchemist"—a force by any name Anderson had been trying to commune with via the creation and performance of this song.) Medieval alchemy was, of course, a metaphor for the process through which the soul reaches a divine perfection; if we follow the correct procedures and if we are spiritually worthy, we discover our inner Christ. (Anderson's song "We Have Heaven" from 1971's *Fragile* perhaps relates to the gnostic idea of the inner Christ. Or, as Anderson once said, "Heaven is in your body. You're in your vehicle.")

Alchemists cloaked the true meaning of turning base metals into gold when interacting with their financial supporters, mostly royalty, of the time. There are said to be seven components—steps—of the alchemical process.

Music scholar John Palmer counts seven distinct lyrical, or text-laden, sections of the song. Depending on how one counts there are (roughly) seven major compositional divisions: the piano opening/starry, "High vibration" section; "Awaken, gentle, mass, touch" section; "Workings of man" section; Asian instrumental part with sitar-ish guitar and pipe organ; vocal section with "Master of images . . ."; "High vibration go on" section; and ending with a swirl of grand harp.

Sevens abound and surround *Going for the One.* "Wondrous Stories," for instance, reached, of all slots, number seven on the U.K. charts. And *Going for the One* was released on 7/7/77, a date that the press, at the time, had labeled "Lucky Sevens."

Some astrologers, theologians, and numerologists say that the number 777 represents the Holy Trinity. Seven occurs in other spiritual and religious arenas, such as the Islamic idea of seventh heaven or in Judaic philosophy, which considers the number seven to be a perfect number.

The hypnotic and sublime instrumental section of the song "Awaken" is not in seven (or, specifically, 7/4), but 11/4, and the number eleven, itself, is significant. Although often associated with disharmony, eleven has been described as a master number, a representation of the great vibration; of God and spiritual truth. It's also a number that cannot be reduced to a lower form, except to say that it can be thought of as $1 + 1 = 2$. It's a representation of the symbolic union of male and female energies. It is, in essence, everything.

If there's such a thing as an alchemical process in the creation of prog rock, "Awaken" might be its highest result. It may also be why the song feels so uplifting—and why so many listeners—and the song's chief architects—feel transformed after experiencing it.

10. IQ: "Harvest of Souls" (24:29), *Dark Matter*, 2004

The album's musical focal point, the twenty-four-and-a-half-minute closing piece, "Harvest of Souls," is certainly a tune for the ages. It's the yin to neo prog vet Pendragon's "The Voyager" yang. Here, America is not the great hope: it's merely the fortress of great escape; no place for us to recharge our spiritual batteries.

In the second section of the tune, "The Wrong Host," singer Peter Nicholls tangles up personal feelings, world affairs, apocalyptical visions, and the hope in (perhaps the broken hope and promise of) America. "Deciding on the order of tracks and the overall shape of an album, the journey that you take the listener on, is still a very important aspect of any album to me," says Nicholls. "In some ways, that's something of a dying craft now, because in these days of download-ing people tend to select odd tracks to listen to, rather than the whole album, which I think is a real shame. If anything, the end of 'Harvest of Souls' sounds a cautionary note for the future. We're not making a great job of the world we're leaving for our children." Nicholls' lyrics seem to have a cumulative effect on *Dark Matter*. You don't get "it" until you complete a whole listening cycle.

"Originally, *Dark Matter* was intended to be a concept album, not a story as such, but the idea was that the songs would explore different aspects of fear," says Nicholls. "Although that concept was eventually dropped, some vestiges of those lyrical threads remain in the final songs. 'Sacred Sound' is loosely about the end of the world and judgment day, so that's pretty scary. 'You Never Will' could, I think, be interpreted as fear of commitment in a relationship. In 'Born Brilliant,' the protagonist, who, I should point out, isn't me, is scared of all his faults and discrepancies being discovered. 'Harvest of Souls' has a more overt political angle: there's a certain fear of governments making wrong decisions, assuming that military strength gives them the right to do what they want. As a parent, I'm concerned about the world my daughter will grow up in."

11. Van der Graaf Generator: "A Plague of Lighthouse Keepers" (23:05), *Pawn Hearts*, 1971

Unbelievably, this song appeared one year before "Supper's Ready" and bests it in total length by seven seconds (and Focus' "Eruption" by one hot "second").

Snatched up by manager Tony Stratton-Smith and signed to his Charisma label, VdGG hit their creative stride in the early 1970s, releasing albums that featured alternately screeching and soothing sonic patches, as well as Peter Hammill's notoriously cryptic lyrics.

Featuring the soon-to-be classic lineup of Hammill/Jackson/Banton/Evans, *Pawn Hearts* is, in the minds of some fans, VdGG's crowning achievement and their most experimental effort of the early '70s.

"The bands I worked with from Charisma who came through Trident Studios, namely Genesis and Van der Graaf Generator, were extremely ambitious," says producer David Hentschel, who'd worked on the *Pawn Hearts* sessions as an engineer. "Van der Graaf, in particular, approached their sessions with the idea of anything goes. I remember Peter Hammill taking a plastic cup and cutting holes in it and singing through that. We would literally abuse the tape machines and find ways of making them run at the wrong speeds. Or else we were feeding vocals through Leslie cabinets."

"Lighthouse Keepers" took months to compile and contained numerous recorded mono tracks (on two-inch tape) of the band performing the song (on as many as sixteen different mono tracks, Dave Jackson said), which were combined to create a cluster of total sonic chaos.

In contrast to material found on the band's mid-1970s records, *Godbluff*, *Still Life*, and *World Record*—studio releases that were recorded after the band split (for the first time) and then reassembled—*Pawn Hearts* was certainly a studio creation.

"I think because we had a break," says keyboardist Hugh Banton, "we had split up and come back together again, we just decided that we . . . would simplify, really. There is much less overdubs on those records. I mean, *Pawn Hearts* was insane. From that point of view it was complicated. I think with *Still Life* and the others we wanted . . . a jazz approach. That isn't to say we wanted to play jazz. If we did ten takes it was to get the feel of the band rather than thinking . . . 'Well, the structure is correct. Let's overdub all the things we were thinking we want to do.' That would have been the old way of doing it. I think with *Godbluff* onwards, it was more about playing [the song] until it worked. I prefer to try to get the whole song in the one take—everything I want to say— rather than a construction job. Certainly *Pawn Hearts*—'Lighthouse Keepers' is, I should say—the most extreme of those, which has loads and loads of stuff on that. I mean, 'Lighthouse Keepers' was very skeletal, unlike a song like "Still Life," which was presented [to us] complete. [Peter] could have played that straight through."

Mysteriously, the job of assembling the bits for "Lighthouse Keepers" fell to Hugh and producer John Anthony. "I can't remember why," says Banton, whose early interest in electronics helped him to build his own organs, sound effects devices, and pieces of sound equipment. "I think Peter was off doing a gig on his own, actually, and I got the job of putting it together with [producer] John Anthony. We actually did all the crossfades and edits. Part of the reason for that is we hadn't finished the structure of the tune when we were recording it. After doing all the crossfades and edits we finally had the twenty-three-minute piece. We hadn't even heard it before we invited everyone to come into the studio for a playback."

The tape was mixed to a quarter-inch tape "and that's where all the cross-fades and editing are," says Banton. "How did you do it? . . . You had to record onto a third machine. So, I think, you would play one [machine] . . . then you start the second one, start the crossfade, and now you've got to cut that piece of tape and edit it to the point that you have a single piece of tape with a crossfade.

It all had to be lined up—the levels—correctly so you couldn't hear the join. John Anthony worked on Queen a lot and did a lot of their early stuff, and it was incredible the amount of tape chopping that was done. I used to like doing all of that. It is a lost art. But, fact is, we never played 'Lighthouse Keepers' live in those days. We did for a TV performance in Belgium, and that was the only time we did it apart from when we recorded it. Even there it had to be recorded in parts. We just never really learned to . . . because we found it too difficult to play."

"Lighthouse Keepers" is the epitome of the elusive, esoteric progressive rock track. To wit, there's been some debate as to what meaning we can bestow upon "Lighthouse Keepers." On its most basic level, the lyrical content of the song draws an analogy between our everyday attitudes toward life and death (and the life and death of others), and the mind of a lighthouse keeper, who must come to grips with seeing people die and not having the ability to save them.

Hammill himself, in the 1974 book compiling some of the bandleader's short fictional stories and song lyrics, *Killers, Angels, Refugees*, once described the piece as being "a cinematic presentation of 'self' in several possible matrices." It could be a descent into madness, as Hammill suggests, or a transformative process of self-awareness: shutting out the world to preserve some semblance of sanity. Any more explanation or "extrapolation would inevitably destroy," Hammill said.

12. Genesis: "Supper's Ready" (22:58), *Foxtrot*, 1972

Despite the fact that the piece is virtually twenty-three minutes long and different sections of "Supper's Ready" were written at different locations, the music moves rather rapidly. Compare and contrast it with other long-form rock songs and you get a sense of just how breezy "Supper's Ready" really is.

In the song, Gabriel speaks about seeing someone's "face change," which relates to a story he told Armando Gallo in his book *Genesis: I Know What I Like*, about a supernatural experience he had with his then-wife, Jill, at her parents' house in Kensington, over the course of one strange and frightening night. (Or was it a nightmare? It's tough to tell with Gabriel what should be taken as literal fact and what is wrapped in allegory.) According to the story, Gabriel had watched as his wife had transformed into . . . something else. Her physicality and voice were completely alien to Gabriel, and he was scared to death by this sight.

Gabriel later reasoned that, perhaps, they were both possessed, in the Roman Catholic sense, by an outside intelligence. Gabriel did also mention another incident involving producer John Burns, which was perhaps even freakier. The finer details of these creepy accounts found their way into the intro section of the song, "Lover's Leap."

These insidious events also led to the creation of the final section of the song ("As Sure as Eggs Is Eggs (Aching Men's Feet)," Part VII)—a scene of immense spirituality, existential relief. It also speaks to an apocalyptic battle between good and evil, a theme Gabriel would dramatize during the band's live shows with the help of a stage prop—a fluorescent stick he wielded, a kind of "light saber," which appeared years before George Lucas' Joseph Campbell–informed sci-fi *Star Wars* trilogy would come to theaters. (In addition, a big magnesium flash powder explosion would go off, signaling the climax of the piece. It was something that the band would develop and later use to great visual effect—or blinding and deafening effect during the *Lamb* tour.)

Part IV also employs the image of the "river of life," perhaps the same that winds through "Firth of Fifth"? The cathartic ending concludes with Gabriel straining as though his lungs are on fire, singing about the King of Kings returning, and the coming of "a new Jerusalem." (When the band performed the song onstage, Gabriel, secured by harness and cabling, would be elevated into the scaffolding—a physical representation of the spirit having lifted. . . .)

Ed Goodgold, Genesis' Stateside representation for their first American tour in 1972, remembers "Supper's Ready" fondly. "I maintain that, especially when they did 'Supper's Ready,' what they were staging was a rock and roll mass," says Goodgold. "Peter performed the priestly function at that. That's the way I saw it. I called it 'the high point of the Anglican Church.' They were able to pull off twenty-three minutes of a higher calling than a normal rock and roll group.

"I'm Jewish," Goodgold continues. "Who else is going to recognize Christians? I was receptive to them on a spiritual level. It wasn't that I had A&R chops. They moved me on an emotion. The only thing comparable today is Phish's 'Avinu Malkeinu.' That's the only thing that touches me as much as Genesis did."

"There's a redemptive quality to the song," says Hackett, "but I know that Ed [Goodgold] thought there was a religious quality to the band and, certainly, there was the influences of church music. That's true. But I think that was only one of the influences that the band drew on. It drew on classical music, church, and European harmonies, but it also used American syncopation."

Gabriel himself described "Supper's Ready" as "the ultimate cosmic battle for Armageddon between good and evil in which man is destroyed, but the deaths of countless thousands atone for mankind, reborn no longer as Homo sapiens."

The music for one of the more talked-about sections of the song, "Apocalypse in 9/8 (Co-starring the Delicious Talents of Gabble Ratchet)," was written by Tony, Phil, and Mike, foreshadowing their collaborations as a three-piece unit during the later part of the 1970s and 1980s and beyond.

"Apocalypse in 9/8" could be interpreted as a fantasy sequence representing the internal struggle of opposing spiritual forces inside each and every one of us. If this is the case, it sort of works, and sorta doesn't. "I think the surrealistic aspects of the song will probably prevent it from being adopted as an anthem," says Hackett. "I think there are too many contradictory ideas going on in the thing."

"Willow Farm," Part V, became a slab of heavy-handed British absurdity, a blueprint for later progressive rock band and neo-prog outfits who've copied, co-opted, and misconstrued the section. Genesis themselves directly reference the title of one of their other songs in "Willow Farm" (i.e., "The Musical Box").

Perhaps only Genesis could pull off this level of absurdity, but with a kind of a naïve ambition, Marillion, especially, with *Script for a Jester's Tear* from 1983, makes a run at it. The basis for some of the songs on this record is of a serious nature; prog-rock dramatic trappings and escapist language mask deeper meanings. (The band, and then-lead singer and chief lyricist Fish, a.k.a. Derek William Dick, would learn to be more direct in his lyrical approach and achieve a combination of escapism and realism with 1985's semi-conceptual *Misplaced Childhood* and 1987's *Clutching at Straws*.)

"There was a classic time when I went to see Marillion," says Andy Tillison of the Tangent. "I wasn't even there to see Marillion, but the support act, Peter Hammill [of Van der Graaf Generator]. But when Marillion was on stage, they were playing 'Forgotten Sons.' On record, there's a bit in there where [the music] stops and Fish shouts, 'Halt! Who goes there?!' Then there's silence and somebody says, 'Deeeaath!' or something. At the show, Fish yelled out, 'Halt! Who goes there?!,' and everything went quiet. Then some bloke in the balcony shouts out, 'A flower?!' [the ending line of section IV, "How Dare I Be So Beautiful?"]. At which point the audience was laughing and so was the band."

"When you start out, maybe you wear your influences [on your sleeve]," Marillion guitarist Steve Rothery told the author. "It's more blatant. But as you find your own identity and your own voice, [imitating your idols] can become less of a factor."

13. ELP: "Tarkus" (20:35), *Tarkus*, 1971

It's been reported that Frank Zappa may have given keyboardist Keith Emerson an unfinished manuscript, which helped to inspire the music for the "Tarkus" suite. (One version of the story claims that it was keyboardist/woodwind player Ian Underwood, on tour with Zappa, who slipped Emerson a tiny piece of paper with one musical idea jotted down on it.)

Interestingly, Emerson had told the author that he was inspired by Ginastera, a name that was central to the *Brain Salad Surgery* sessions.

Whatever the origin of "Tarkus," the results can hardly be argued with. It stands as one of ELP's greatest compositional and experimental achievements. It's like Bartók meets avant-rock meets Stravinsky at a heavy metal concert.

Emerson wasn't afraid to get dirty with this piece, despite opposition within the band to actually even performing and writing the damn thing. What gave the piece its angularity was the opening section, "Eruption," which was written in 5/4.

It's difficult, if not impossible, to discuss "Tarkus" without mentioning artist William Neal and his pivotal role in the creation of the concept. Tarkus encounters a few biomechanical beasts, from a metal-winged pterodactyl to a rocket-launching great lizard in the open expanses of grand battlefields.

"At CCS [design firm] we were primarily known for producing reggae albums though we had a fantastic design team," says Neal. "Island Records invited us to submit ideas for ELP and they, too, were all rejected. . . ."

Neal scribbled his armadillo/tank, or *Armordillo* (a.k.a. Tarkus), on the cover sheet of CCS design firm's presentation to ELP, and it caught Emerson's attention. "It just so happened that in an idle way, like you do on the phone sometimes, I had doodled this little Armadillo tank on a cover sheet for an LP presentation," says Neal, who recalls Osibisa's winged mammoth as a possible influence. "It shouldn't have even been there. It's just one of those things artists do."

As far as what the epic piece means, "Tarkus" could be viewed as nature trumping the mechanized world, a theme that seems to run through ELP's music and was crystallized with "Karn Evil 9: Third Impression." The Manticore, which has been interpreted as a symbol of ELP's stance against a press hostile to prog rock's iconoclast status, is like the Greek minotaur, a hybrid creature with characteristics of both human and wild animal. (Others have interpreted "Tarkus" to mean imperialist nation or technology gone haywire.)

The Manticore has the body of a lion, the stinger of a scorpion, and the head of a man. (The word *manticore* is said to be of Persian origin, and its direct translation, ironically enough, is "man eater," but the myths of the Manticore aren't necessarily represented by the illustrated narrative found in the album's gatefold.)

"There's a deeper end since Manticore has the face of a man, really, and it could have been seen as man's triumph over evil, but that's never going to happen," says Neal. "Folks put all manner of meanings into things, don't they?"

Spirituality and religion play a significant role in the lyrics Lake wrote for *Tarkus*. Lake muses on organized religion in "Mass" (part IV of the "Tarkus" composition), presenting the scenario of power-hungry clergy ruling through fear and might; the faithful binging on sin.

The album also features such noteworthy songs as the compound track "The Only Way (Hymn)" and its instrumental chaser, "Infinite Space," a scathing indictment of religion, containing a portion of Bach's Toccata in F Major (written as a church organ piece for which Emerson employs a pipe organ from St. Marks Church) and "Prelude VI" (a jaunty little piece that despite its tight counterpoint, and like most preludes, is meant to have a free-floating feel).

The album went to number one on the U.K. charts.

14. Spock's Beard: "The Great Nothing" (27:18), V, 2000

The song begins with a multivoiced sampled Mellotron (composed in a Ligeti-style chorale arrangement), putting us on notice that we've entered some form of musical and spiritual journey. Besides weaving through a string of genres,

"The Great Nothing" tells the tale of a veteran musician who's been built up and knocked down by the music business. Our hero, or antihero, also appears to be his open worst enemy. A&R men are weary of dealing with him, calling him completely undetectable and a gigantic pain in the ass with which to work. (The plan, it seems, is to get him drunk or keep him drugged so that he'll play the corporate game. . . .)

Our hero is on the verge of realizing that his life has added up to nothing, when, out of the blue, he hears a single note of music being played. This note inspires him to write and play music, something he'd lost genuine passion for years earlier. Despite his experiencing a career of fits and starts, music continues to inspire our hero, regardless of its commercial potential.

Most importantly, the music inspires, even in the absence of commercial aspirations. "The Great Nothing" has special significance for former Spock's keyboardist/vocalist/chief songwriter Neal Morse, who was battling the bottle for years, and wrote the song prior to his spiritual awakening.

"What's interesting about 'The Great Nothing' is that I wrote it in 1997," Morse says. "I wrote it a long time before [it was recorded and released]. I somehow thought it wasn't the right time for it, I don't think, until the *V* album. 'The Great Nothing' is really open to music. Music was my God. . . . That's really how, in a sense, I was raised. Music was the closest thing to a spiritual mountaintop that my family for the most part had known. I was going through . . . the phases of life and becoming a miserable partier, a drunk."

"I remember playing that live," Neal's brother Alan (guitarist) once told me. "I always felt that there was a spiritual aspect to the song that really exemplifies a positive outlook. It's not as dark as some [other Spock's Beard] stuff gets. I remember we were sitting on the bus in Oslo, Norway, and some lady came walking by with an acoustic guitar and a gig bag. We struck up a conversation with her and she said, 'Do you play for the Lord?' And we looked at each other and said, 'I guess we kind of do.' Not in the sense that she meant, and, at least, at that time the music was not overtly Christian. To me it was always about making a positive contribution in some way."

"I was a major drinker," says Neal Morse. "The Lord just dealt with me about it. Even after I became a Christian I thought that there was nothing in the Bible that talked specifically about it. Jesus turned water into wine, right? But, for me, when I would drink I would feel a little buzzy, or if I was going to commit any sin I would be more likely to do it feeling this way. I quit altogether."

Morse says he fell into the trap of believing the myth that drugs and alcohol (specifically the latter) are what an artist needs to create exciting material, to have something to write and sing about. "Oh, yeah," says Morse. "It's a total myth and I believed it. I thought I wrote the best when I smoked pot. But I think I've written much better stuff since I stopped smoking pot. Sometimes it's subtle in how it destroys, but it destroys. Sometimes it's not subtle. Sometimes it's very apparent."

15. King Crimson: "Starless" (12:18), Red, 1974

Red opens with the aggressive title track, the band's musical salvo—a greeting from within the *nuovo progressive metal* beast the trio had morphed into after the departure of violinist David Cross.

Other raw and biting songs, "Fallen Angel" and "One More Red Nightmare," are but the appetizer for the twelve-minute-plus "Starless," one of the band's greatest musical achievements, and perhaps the conflagration of everything Crimson was and could have been at the time.

Crimson had been playing a version of "Starless" on the road earlier in the year (some reports say a portion of it was a holdover from the previous album *Starless and Bible Black*), prior to entering the studio in the summer of 1974 to record their final studio album of the 1970s. No doubt the recorded version was more orchestrated, largely due to guest appearances by founding member Ian McDonald on sax, as well as former Crimsonite Mel Collins and oboist Robin Miller, who had recorded with the band on previous Crimson records.

Simply, the song bursts with 13/8 patterns, which provide the platform, the foundation for wild odd-time sax solos. The intensity builds to a cathartic release as the main melody is reprised by Collins on soprano sax near the song's climax.

Rod Thear, former recording engineer at Olympic, remembers the *Red* sessions: "The Crimson sessions were twelve to two," says Thear, who had just gone freelance at the time of the recording. "The Crimson sessions were organized, like the Ten Years After sessions, and understated. But I got the sense that Fripp was in charge. That's my recollection of it. He was a quiet guy who directed, if you like.

"I also remember the packs he brought in—*Oblique Strategies*," Thear continues. "He presented me with a pack one day. I'm not totally certain if Fripp followed the cards, but he did have them on him. I suppose, it forced you into a different perspective on things. Fripp was a calm and quiet type of guy. No histrionics. And I remember [drummer] Bill Bruford being very technical about his drumming and wanting to work out the passages. I think he just wanted to get it right. He wanted it perfect. If it wasn't right he wouldn't be happy with himself. Bill was on the ball, knew exactly what he was doing and, unusually for a drummer, involved in the decision-making process. The drummer wasn't always involved in those things. 'Shall I play it like this?' He'd do it perfectly and they were all ridiculous patterns."

Because of the spiritual journey Fripp had undertaken, his perspective on life and music was changing, and he was re-examining what he wanted from his career. Before the release of *Red* news broke that Fripp had disbanded the group.

Fripp admitted that when he invited Ian McDonald back to tour with Crimson in the fall of 1974—a tour that never actually took place—the plan was for him to leave Crimson in his capable hands. Fripp thought Crimson could find another guitarist to replace him and he'd move on. As if.

McDonald had wanted to invite original drummer Michael Giles back into the fold, in an attempt to keep Fripp in the band, but EG Management saw this as being a very bad idea.

The band's next release, the live record *USA*, was culled from a performance in Asbury Park, New Jersey, in late June 1974 (and features overdubbed tracks by Roxy Music/Curved Air keyboardist/violinist Eddie Jobson), and appeared in 1975. A best-of compilation, *A Young Person's Guide to King Crimson*, was released in 1976. The initials "R.I.P." were printed near the bottom of the back cover of *USA*.

16. Magma: "Köhntark" (31:03), *Live/Hhaï*, 1975

Listed as two tracks on the original record, the compound piece, recorded at La Taverne de L'Olympia in Paris in 1975, cuts in with a roar, and the sawing sounds of Didier Lockwood's violin. It's arresting, frightening, engrossing, and more than a little disturbing. But that's Magma: a conceptual avant-rock/jazz-rock/prog-rock band founded by drummer/bandleader Christian Vander in 1969 that appears to be set out to attack with their powerful music.

Disgusted by the music industry—and the audience members who attended his pre-Magma shows with Carnaby Street Swingers—Vander largely turned his back on our world and created another, a more mythological one, which he called

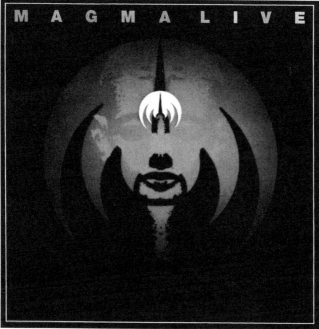

Speaking in tongues: Magma's Kobaïan language lends operatic and otherworldly qualities to the seminal *Live/ Hhaï*, 1975.

Kobaïa. (Magma's self-titled first record was an invitation to join the band in this other dimension.) And because English didn't seem to suit Vander's compositions, and thinking his native French would be a limiting factor in promoting the band, Vander invented his own language, something resembling a Germanic variant, called Kobaïan. (Think: Klingon vocabulary used for a Wagner opera.)

Represented by impresario and Magma producer Giorgio Gomelsky, who'd been instrumental in the careers of bands such as the Rolling Stones and Gong, Vander decided to work with musicians and compositions that were uncompromising.[4] Indeed, Vander's music doesn't soothe, or rarely does, and instead seems to have the effect of attacking the listener. The drummer/bandleader makes good on his threats with this extended work, which is framed by Vander's intense, tight, Elvin-esque, jazz-inflected martial beats and escalated thanks to Bernard Paganotti's rapid-fire bass notes and piercing violin tones from Lockwood, only a teen at the time of this recording. Klaus Blasquiz's and then-wife Stella's wafting vocals possess all the fluidity and density of a romantic opera. Perhaps Magma's rumored connection to Germany's past is better left unexplored, or left unsaid altogether. At the least, no one can accuse Vander of being tame or boring. (In fact, he rarely took the commercial way out, producing what fans consider only two concessions to the mainstream, 1978's *Attahk* and, to a degree, 1976's *Üdü Wüdü*.)

Magma's music is difficult to define. In fact, many consider Magma's approach to be a subgenre of music in and of itself, dubbed *Zeuhl*, which has influenced numerous musicians on both sides of the Atlantic, who play a similar style of music, in part, to honor Magma and Vander's largely uncompromising music.

17. It Bites: "Once Around the World" (14:50), *Once Around the World*, 1988

Let's take the band name, first. It Bites was dreamed up by "one of the guys in my brother's band, Necromandus, the drummer Frank Hall," says former It Bites leader/singer/guitarist Francis Dunnery. "In America it means, 'It sucks.' We used to change our name every other week. We were always called something different. It Bites, that was the one that kept going."

This was an ironic title for a band that appeared to possess the ability to play just about anything it wanted. It Bites has so often been put into the pop category—and many of their songs were just that. But they were so much more and, had the original band not split up, there's no telling what musical horizons they would have crossed.

Formed in the early 1980s as a trio featuring Dunnery, drummer Bob Dalton, and bassist Dick Nolan (they became a quartet with the addition of keyboardist John Beck in 1982), the English crew was one of the few pop bands on the British and American scene with a great command of musical styles. Catch them on the right night and It Bites' live performances were something in the neighborhood of jazz-rock fusion. Even more surprising was the way that this supposed pop band had the ability to slip into hardcore prog, seemingly at whim, each member flexing his technical muscles.

"Once Around the World," produced by Mark Wallis, is a great example of this. It's equal parts pop tune, homage to "Supper's Ready," and balls-to-the-wall prog rock. There's some really great synchronized riffing that begins around the 3:30 mark of the song, involving the guitar and keyboards. It's doubtful this kind of exactitude was created off the cuff, and when pressed on this issue, Dunnery was unclear on the details of the recording.

However, the song holds others treasures. The racing imagery employed in the lyrics, such as the circular track, might be a metaphor for life, people running in circles. "It was all pot-induced," insists Dunnery. "It had something to do with a day being a microcosm for a full life. . . ."

Dunnery would record one more record with It Bites (*Eat Me in St. Louis*) before exiting. Although Dunnery was the bandleader, at least since the release of the band's debut, 1986's *The Big Lad in the Windmill*, the split ruptured a talented lineup with unlimited possibilities. "I wanted to expand the band's musicality and sound, and some of the members didn't," Dunnery says. "I wanted to create something that was timeless and some of the members didn't. I was the bandleader for years and then there was a revolt. It Bites needs a leader."

"It Bites did a reverse Genesis," says the current guitarist/vocalist John Mitchell. "They started out as a pop band and turned into a prog band. Since I've joined it's a different band, again. I think everyone enjoys the 'Once Around the World' period, the second album with Francis, and I keep leading them down that path."

"In those days, if you got involved in the business, with major labels, you had to write three-minute songs that develop in a certain way," says Dunnery. "Once you'd written the three-minute songs, you could do whatever you wanted for the rest of the album. I didn't realize this basic fact back then. So, it was only a matter of time before we were thrown off the label. We sort of plundered the music industry and got out."

18. Michael Oldfield: "Ommadawn" (Parts 1 and 2) (total time: 36:41), *Ommadawn*, 1975

By the mid-1970s, Mike Oldfield, fresh off the global success of *Tubular Bells*, had divorced himself from the world at large, but his music was still very much a part of a larger cultural phenomenon.

The exodus of musicians from South Africa in the late 1960s and early 1970s had a tremendous impact on how music was written, performed, and recorded in Britain. A venue like the 100 Club in London raised awareness of the turmoil of life in South Africa, and hosted musicians who mixed traditional African music forms with political protest. Oldfield had heard *Happiness*, an album by South African drum troupe Jabula led by Julian (Sebothane) Bahula, and immediately knew he could fuse his pastiche/pastoral-rock songwriting approach with African rhythms.

Bahula settled in England in 1973, one of many African émigrés who came to Europe during the height of the era of progressive rock, and later recorded with Oldfield. "Mike was one of the first to bring so many styles together," says Bahula. "Our drums were different from conga drums, for instance, and I know Mike wanted something that was a little out of the ordinary for his recordings. All our drum patterns are indigenous to South Africa and in particular to the Pedi tribe from which I originate. I grew up in townships outside Pretoria and my traditions are Northern Sotho and Pedi, in particular."

Oldfield's 1975 masterwork, *Ommadawn* (one track in two parts), is an ethnocentric New Age art-rock tour de force, featuring Jabula as well as Oldfield on exotic instruments (such as Irish frame drum bodhrán and Greek stringed instrument called a bouzouki), and Uilleann pipes player Paddy Moloney of the Celtic crossover band the Chieftains.

"We went to his studio in [Mike's] home in Gloucestershire and we recorded the drums outside with mikes going up into the studio," says Bahula. "I knew the best sound for the drums would be out of doors and not in the enclosed studio. The drums we used were meant to be played outside. I had a difficult experience trying to get the right sound in a conventional studio. It worked, and I think the sound we achieved was really authentic: the drums sounded as they did live on stage."

Oldfield was crisscrossing genres with abandon and creating his own form of musical communication (i.e., words spoken in Part 1 may be an ancient British dialect—it's never been made clear—and the title could actually be a take on the word *amadan*, the Gaelic phrase for "fool" or "fool and his music," perhaps an autobiographical reference).

Synthesizing folk, rock, and world-music traditions (Oldfield even convinces Irish singer Clodagh Simmonds to perform an African-styled chant) was something Oldfield was doing more effectively than ever. The harshest element of the music is Oldfield's patented bagpipe/bird call/violin-like guitar tone, which is, in any case, balanced by the evocative sounds of Paddy Moloney's Uilleann pipes—an instrument that operates via a system of bellows and chanters/chaunters (i.e., pipes with finger holes).

Moloney, who was whisked away to Oldfield's retreat in between dates on a Chieftains tour in 1975, tapped into memories to elucidate some of the most moving bits of music in *Ommadawn*.

"Mike sent a private plane to bring me down to his mansion and I landed there on the property," says Moloney. "I arrived at twelve o'clock at night, because I had just finished a concert and went up there immediately. We sat down, talked, and Mike played me a tape of what he had done. There was no pressure. Mike set up a microphone and then started to play the guitar along to a taped recording of the song. He asked me to play along to the track, which I did a couple of times, when I realized that he was taping me, you know? [laughs] That was it. That was the session. I got back on the plane and went back to the tour."

After *Ommadawn* was released and went to number four in November 1975 in the U.K., a four-LP boxed set (titled *Boxed*), which contained the first three Oldfield records and alternative versions of "Tubular Bells," was unleashed in 1976.

Life seemed to expand exponentially and dynamically for Oldfield after the success of *Tubular Bells, Hergest Ridge,* and *Ommadawn.* Once a shy recluse, Oldfield appeared in command of a new kind of openness to the world and its possibilities. He began working with a number of other artists, such as Wigwam bass player Pekka Pohjola (for his solo record *The Mathematician's Air Display*), pal David Bedford (on *Instructions for Angels*), sister Sally Oldfield, and Pierre Moerlen's Gong (*Downwind*).

"Mike underwent this strange transformation," says David Bedford, a band member of Kevin Ayers' early 1970s band, with Oldfield. "He participated in these self-help and spiritual seminars, which made him a bit odd. He has gone back to being perfectly normal, thank goodness."

It's no surprise, given his recent spiritual awakening, that his next major studio work was *Incantations*, a kind of meditation on inner and cosmic peace. Inspired by Native American history and mysticism, *Incantations* was composed in four parts, spanning two LPs, featuring recurring themes and variations on those themes. (It's possible that each side represents one of the four winds, or cardinal points of the compass—East, West, North and South, which play a central role in Native American ceremonial cleansing and self-discovery drumming rituals.)

Oldfield also uses Henry Wadsworth Longfellow's poem *The Song of Hiawatha* as a chant in "Incantations (Part Two)." Interestingly, the famous Bohemian composer Antonin Dvořák used *Hiawatha* as an inspiration for the second movement of his "New World Symphony" or Symphony No. 9 in E Minor, "From the New World."

As Dvořák had attempted to do with his "From the New World," Oldfield, too, presents two strains—roots—of American folk music: African and Native American. Oldfield would probably deny it, but *Incantations* is *his* ode to America, its geography, peoples, and ancient past. It also should be noted that Longfellow's poem contains a section—Chapter II—titled "The Four Winds."

"Tubular Bells" may have been more influential, but "Ommadawn," in particular, seemed to open a new world to Oldfield and ranks among his most cogent works.

19. Kansas: "Incomudro—Hymn to the Atman" (12:12), *Song for America*, 1975

The album *Song for America* boasts a number of epic Kansas recordings, from the title track, to the grand haunter "Lamplight Symphony," to this one, "Incomudro—Hymn to the Atman."

"Song for America" (possibly) speaks of the purity of the land later called America, before European settlers traveled across the ocean and colonized it.

Kerry Livgren compares the continent to a virgin maiden, who, by song's end, is (perhaps) exploited, used, in the name of industrial development. (The song skillfully plays with concepts of progress and paradise—and one's definition of such.)

Cuneiform Records' 2002 release *Proto-Kaw: Early Recordings from Kansas 1971–1973* features an eleven-and-a-half minute version of this song, and listeners might detect a vaguely Van der Graaf Generator/Peter Hammill or King Crimson vibe throughout these songs, especially tracks such as "Hegemonium," inspired by Hieronymus Bosch; the fantasy-based "Reunion in the Mountains of Sarne"; and "Nactolos 21," which boasts lyrics recalling Ayn Rand's anti-totalitarian philosophy (which is echoed by "Sparks of the Tempest" from 1977's *Point of Know Return*). Recorded remotely in a cave outside Kansas City in 1971, the abovementioned trio of songs is known collectively, unofficially, and appropriately as "The Caverns Recordings."

The original recorded version of "Incomudro" was cut in the town of Liberal in 1972 by Kansas, but not with the Kansas lineup with which most rock fans are familiar. This band, so-called Kansas II, a tag name retrofitted onto the outfit, featured Lynn Meredith on vocals, two saxophone players, and Zeke Low and Brad Schultz sharing the drum duties on these early recordings, among others.[5]

"Incomudro—Hymn to the Atman" could very well be the most spiritual song of the entire Kansas catalog. The phrase *atman* (or *Atman*) is Hindu (as well as Buddhist), referring to the soul or the divine self. The song speaks of the soul's attainment of nirvana through reincarnation, of connecting to a universal mind.

"Incomudro" illuminates Livgren's interest in Eastern thought and a larger spiritual search for something unattainable, illustrated by songs such as "Miracles Out of Nowhere" (portions of which were likely inspired by Hermann Hesse's *Steppenwolf*), "Carry On Wayward Son" (the opening track on the multi-platinum album *Leftoverture*, which was lyrically tied to "The Pinnacle," the closing track on 1975's *Masque*), the pan-spiritual "Hopelessly Human," "Paradox," "Mysteries and Mayhem," and the ubiquitous "Dust in the Wind."

When Livgren discovered *The Urantia Book* circa 1977, he rejected much of the Eastern philosophy he once found so dear. "A Glimpse of Home," from 1979's *Monolith*, proclaimed as much. The tune plays like one man's account of his path toward "God consciousness." (At fade out, synth lines race at different speeds, evoking the visual image of spiraling universes and far-flung celestial realms....)

However, Livgren's declaration was premature: *Urantia* was a false positive, just another stage in Livgren's spiritual evolution. Ultimately, Christianity passed Livgren's religious litmus test, and Kerry would retrospectively interpret the image of the father figure in his lyrics as Christ of the New Testament. (In the book *Seeds of Change*, which he cowrote with Kenneth Boa, Livgren denounces Urantian philosophy as, largely, amoral "space-age gnosticism.")

In the ensuing years, some fans tracked and analyzed the composer's path back to the Biblical God vis-à-vis Kansas' recorded output throughout the 1970s. "I think Kerry has always been spiritual but he was very much into Buddhism when I first got to know him," says Kansas drummer and bandleader Phil Ehart.

To the surprise of some, both Ehart and co-producer Jeff Glixman maintain that the numerically auspicious twelve-minute-and-twelve-second song was a continuous performance recorded at Wally Heider Studios in L.A. (The number twelve, in numerology circles, represents wholeness, a complete cycle, as if underscoring the cyclical nature of life and death, which was, ironically, referred to in the lyrics of the song.)

"In the early days our songs, and they are so lengthy, even 'Incomudro,' which has a drum solo, was all done from the beginning to the end," says Ehart. "We did it that way into *Leftoverture*. There was never any splicing done."

"That's not cut, at all," says Glixman. "As a matter of fact, I felt bad for Phil because we did two takes of it. One take was an amazing drum solo and the band just wasn't as good. So we had to do another. The one we didn't use was a tremendous solo. But there was no way to put the two together because there was no click, and there are little things going on in the song that would never make combining the two of them sound right. We couldn't cut and then piece them together."

"It was like a live album," says Ehart. "Nobody ever said, 'You can stop in the middle of this and pick it back up and I can splice the tape together.'"

The middle instrumental section of the official Kansas tune from 1975 was played on synth, but the Cuneiform demos demonstrate how heavily the earlier band leaned on the saxophone and jazz elements. More to the point: Kansas II and Kansas III certainly experimented with sonic textures, but the introduction of the synthesizer helped to add dimension to the band's overall sound.

"That gong-y type sound you hear in the middle section of the song?" Ehart says. "That's actually Kerry on his Moog synthesizer. Then I started playing the drum solo."

Interestingly, the phrase "Incomudro" came to Livgren in a dream, much like the title of "Belexes" (versions of which appear on the aforementioned Cuneiform platter and the band's 1974 debut). But its title is complete gibberish: *Incomudro* has no literal definition in the English language (aside from the meaning listeners assign to it).

20. U.K.: "In the Dead of Night"/"By the Light of Day"/"Presto Vivace and Reprise" (13:08), U.K., 1978

This late 1970s prog-rock supergroup, composed of John Wetton, Bill Bruford, Eddie Jobson, and Allan Holdsworth, stressed both a collective and individual virtuosity that reflected the profound impact of jazz, an emerging electronic/ambient field, and classical worlds.

Says Eddie Jobson, the first U.K. album was written in sections. "In the case of the 'In the Dead of Night' suite, I had all three sections—'In the Dead of Night,' 'By the Light of Day,' and 'Presto Vivace'—pretty much completed before rehearsals, although I didn't have them linked conceptually as one long piece. Most of the actual vocal melodies and lyrics were left for John to come up with. Generally, all of the musical ideas would be put on a 'bit list' and Bill and I together would mold them into cohesive pieces. The pieces on the *Danger Money* album were even more completed—'Rendezvous 6:02' was a little piano piece I had written in my apartment in Hollywood when I was still playing with Zappa; John's vocal melody is simply a third harmony to the piano melody."

The first time your stylus scratched the album's pristine vinyl grooves, you likely heard staccato rhythms of "In the Dead of Night," which the recording engineer for the session, Stephen W. Tayler (Brand X, Bruford, Rush, Saga), compared with the staccato rhythm of the opening bars of Yes' "Yours Is No Disgrace" and Rush's "Show Don't Tell." It's all designed to confuse the listener and test his/her ability to find "1." And, indeed, U.K., and drumming master Bill Bruford, did just that by juggling time signatures (i.e., 4/4, 7/8, 9/8, 21/8) in both the first section ("In the Dead of Night") and last ("Presto Vivace and Reprise").

JOHN WETTON
formerly with King Crimson & Uriah Heep
BILL BRUFORD
formerly with Yes & King Crimson
ALLAN HOLDSWORTH
formerly with Soft Machine & Jean-Luc Ponty
EDDIE JOBSON
formerly with Roxy Music & Frank Zappa
ARE

ALL THEIR LIVES, THEY'VE BEEN REHEARSING FOR THIS BAND AND THIS ALBUM.

ON POLYDOR RECORDS & TAPES.

Truth in advertising: A rock supergroup that delivered the goods.

Bruford's flowing, descending roto tom fills and slammin' snare-drum flams are instantly identifiable—as is the sound of his ringing snare. "The thing about drums is that working with Brand X and Bruford at this time, there was this move away from the ultra-dry recorded-in-a-box sound of, say, the early Yes albums," Stephen W. Tayler says. "We're not talking the big-room sound of the classic Phil Collins Townhouse [performances], which came later. What we were doing was recording drums in a room, as opposed to a booth. Both Phil and Bill played together in Genesis, and they were trying out these new kinds of drums called *roto toms*, which had no shell. It was a skin on a rim. That was, I would say, a kind of signature sound. It was a very metallic sound that became part of the percussive palette."

Layered vocal tracks, throaty clangs of roto toms (a timbre that recalls the drummers of Burundi as much as it foreshadowed commercialized, mass-marketed electronic drums, which Bruford pioneered), and emotionally charged and quite sophisticated electric (and acoustic) guitar performances prove that each member of the band was capable of leaving his fingerprints on these tracks without strangling the life out of them.

Allan Holdsworth's legato playing in "In the Dead of Night" seems to share kinship with and is indicative of a jazz horn player rather than a rock guitarist. Holdsworth's beautifully sculpted solo (in 7/4) sizzles with sustain, subtle tremolo-bar action, sweeping picked notes, lightning-fast scalar runs (shades of Holdsworth's hero, John Coltrane, there), pull-offs and hammer-ons (techniques that would be closely identified with Holdsworth fan Eddie Van Halen), and arpeggiated phrases, creating tension via slight melodic dissonances over the song's base chords. (U.K., when Holdsworth and Bruford were still in the band, opened for Van Halen in Reno, Nevada, in 1978, and Eddie, as he told *Guitar World*, "shit [his] pants" upon witnessing Holdsworth's fluidity and, what Van Halen surmised was a style framed by minimal picking.)

"I've spent, basically, my entire musical life trying to make the guitar sound like different instruments," Holdsworth told the author in 1996. "The other thing is that in order to get sustain [from an amplified electric guitar] you have to use distortion, and I don't like distortion. What is appealing to me is getting sustain without the nastiness."

Appearing near the end of the classic progressive rock era, U.K. was, nonetheless, one of the most potent examples of what progressive rock could be if allowed to flourish and ferment.

Honorable Mention

Renaissance: "Song of Scheherazade" (24:37), *Scheherazade and Other Stories*, 1975

The band's music was so fluid one can forget just how complicated and dense the structures of the songs actually were. "Scheherazade" is a nice reminder. Although the band had already written, recorded, and performed their other massive composition, "Ashes Are Burning," "Scheherazade . . ." was the crown jewel in the band's repertoire, a shining moment in time just before the band turned toward more commercial interests (i.e., the lovely hit song about homesickness, "Northern Lights").

Steve Hillage: "Solar Musick Suite" (16:55), *Fish Rising*, 1975

Bookended by two epics (the other being "Aftaglid"), *Fish Rising* was Steve Hillage's solo debut. (*L* was Hillage's first official release after exiting Gong). "Solar Musick Suite" is a lively piece of music with nods to Soft Machine, the Beatles, Pink Floyd, and even Mahavishnu Orchestra.

Pink Floyd: "The Man" and "The Journey" (total approximate time: 40 minutes)

The two epic suites, roughly twenty minutes each, titled "The Man" and "The Journey," premiered at a concert titled "The Massed Gadgets of Auximenes: More Furious Madness from Pink Floyd ('Introducing the Azimuth Co-ordinator')," staged at the Royal Festival Hall on April 14, 1969.

These two classical-inspired compositions were composed of a number of smaller songs that would later appear on releases such as the soundtrack to *More* and Floyd live/studio double album *Ummagumma*. (Sections of "The Man" included "Daybreak," which became "Granchester Meadows" on *Ummagumma*, and "Work" appeared as "Biding My Time" on *Relics*, among others. "The Journey" included "The Beginning," which became "Green Is the Colour" from *More*; "Beset by Creatures of the Deep" was "Careful with That Axe, Eugene" under a different title and saw the light of day on *Ummagumma*; "The Narrow Way" surfaced on *Ummagumma*; and "The End of the Beginning," which became the "Celestial Voices" section of the live version of "A Saucerful of Secrets" from *Ummagumma*.)

During the performance, these compositions were enriched by Bernard Speight's Azimuth Co-ordinator, a joystick-controlled panning device allowing for the user (in this case keyboardist Richard Wright) to send the audio signal to different speakers placed throughout the hall. (The concert was staged in quadraphonic and, reportedly, Floyd was the first to use Speight's device in a live environment.) Performance art was also part of Floyd's multimedia show, as members sawed wood, hammered nails, and sipped tea onstage.

Here's a list of entries for further investigation. The music featured in this list runs the gamut from symphonic folk-prog to avant-jazz rock.

* Nektar: "Remember the Future Part I and Part II" (total time: 35:33), *Remember the Future*, 1974
* Transatlantic: "The Whirlwind" (77:54), *The Whirlwind*, 2009
* Lol Coxhill: "Rasa Moods" (20:09), *Ear of the Beholder*, 1970
* John Cale and Terry Riley: "Church of Anthrax" (9:05), *Church of Anthrax*, 1971
* Big Big Train: "The Underfall Yard" (22:54), *The Underfall Yard*, 2009

- The Tea Club: "Firebears" (17:52), *Quickly Quickly Quickly*, 2012
- Fireballet: "Night on Bald Mountain" (18:55), *Night on Bald Mountain*, 1975
- Caravan: "Nine Feet Underground" (22:40), *In the Land of Grey and Pink*, 1971

7

King Crimson's Lizard

Beyond the Bizarre and Beautiful Album Cover Artwork

King Crimson's personnel had been in constant flux, virtually, since the release of the band's groundbreaking debut record in October 1969. Within a matter of months, three key members—multi-instrumentalist/songwriter Ian McDonald, bassist/vocalist Greg Lake, and drummer extraordinaire Michael Giles—split for duo projects and supergroups.

Undaunted, guitarist Robert Fripp and lyricist/lighting director Pete Sinfield took Crimson by the reins and enlisted a stellar cast of performers to help achieve fresh musical perspectives for 1970's *Lizard*, recorded at London's Wessex Sound Studios.

For decades, *Lizard* has been viewed as one of the most bizarre Crimson albums of the 1970s—a virtual hodgepodge of recycled material (from the pre-Crim Giles, Giles & Fripp days), pretty and gritty vocal performances (courtesy of Yes' Jon Anderson and bassist Gordon Haskell), new musical ideas "weirded up" by Sinfield via his cryptic lyrics and abuse of VCS-3 synthesizer, demonic Mellotron squalls, and one master composition, the jazz-inflected classical-rock title track.

Sinfield has referred to the album as "grotesque in places," alluding to *Gormenghast.* Just as Mervyn Peake's character, the antihero Titus Groan, inherits the semi-decrepit Gormenghast castle, so Sinfield and Fripp were left to guide a once-promising and then-crumbling empire of the Crimson King.

"It's terrible when management tells you, 'Just go make another record,'" Sinfield told the author in 2008. "Once you're given freedom, and being a bit tired, it's quite dangerous."

Liberation, or what some might even term "sinister creative impulse," was visually reinforced by one of the era's most beautifully strange pieces of album cover artwork. Designed by illustrator Virginia "Gini" Barris (now Gini Wade) to resemble an illuminated medieval manuscript, *Lizard*'s wonderfully detailed imagery is rife with geographical oddities and anachronistic peculiarities tucked inside ornate lettering spelling the phrase "Crimson King."

"Not many people know the story of the early Crimson album covers," Sinfield told me. "If you followed the progression of covers from the earliest, it went from one face [*In the Court of the Crimson King*], to twelve faces, the twelve archetypal characters [*In the Wake of Poseidon*], to many faces and characters [*Lizard*], to the origin of it all. That's why there's an amoeba image on *Islands.* Everything does have its vague reason [for being]."

Lizard has mesmerized and perplexed many, in part, due to the juxtaposition of ancient and modern motifs and mixture of surreal and slightly perverted figures, which may (or may not) have any intended meaning.

The following is a Q&A with illustrator Wade.

Artist Gini Wade, illustrator for the *Lizard* album cover, in a self-portrait.   *Courtesy of Gini Wade*

WR: What was your background before you entered the King Crimson universe?

Gini Wade: I was a student in art school in London, at the Central School of Arts and Crafts [Central School of Art and Design]. I studied graphics and finished in 1969. Then, in 1969 to 1970, I traveled with my boyfriend to Indonesia and India. We traveled round for a year . . . I had done a few illustrations before the *Lizard* project, but the *Lizard* cover was one of my first jobs, really.

WR: That's surprising.

Wade: It was a dream job, pretty well paid, and lovely . . . Pete [Sinfield] gave me carte blanche to come up with the idea and to see what they liked. It was my idea to have the cover as a medieval manuscript. [*Note: In 2008, Pete Sinfield told the author: "[The concept] came about because we—I, really—had decided that I wanted it to be sort of like one of those medieval manuscripts. . . ."*]

WR: How did you get the gig?

Wade: I was freelancing at the time and I had heard Pete was looking for an artist to do the cover. I got to know [Sinfield] through a mutual friend, and I remember I went to see him in his house in the Cotswolds, in the country. When

Lizard: One of the most mysterious album covers of the classic prog rock era.

we met we talked specifically about the cover and he commissioned me to do the cover of *Lizard*.

WR: Who was your mutual friend?
Wade: Brian Hart.

WR: The *Lizard* cover artwork is iconic.
Wade: To be honest I really loved Persian miniatures, Indian miniatures, and medieval miniatures, which were my own personal tastes at the time. [Sinfield] went for it. In addition, there was a kind of revival in all things medieval, particularly in fashion and music, in the 1960s in London. There was an attraction to the romantic past.

WR: Why do you think that was?
Wade: God. Well, . . . I was born at the end of the War [World War II] and life was very drab here for fifteen or twenty years for everybody. Everyone was very poor. Then in the sixties things really took off. There was more money around and suddenly everything was in Technicolor. People were looking to all kinds of exotic cultures. The idea of troubadours, knights in shining armor, it was romantic fantasy, really.

WR: Peter Banks of Yes once told me how gray Britain was after the war, and that he grew up playing in bombed-out areas of the country.
Wade: It was unbelievable. I remember sweets were rationed for a long time when I was a kid. I remember having my first lollipop. Also, growing up after [World War II] you heard nothing else but stories about that war. Are you familiar with the scene in *A Hard Day's Night*, which was funny, when the Beatles meet a businessman on a train? The businessman objected to the band messing around and he says, "We fought the war for you . . ." or something. Every time I was naughty when I was kid I would hear that from my dad. You got sick to death of hearing of that bloody war and you just wanted to get on and do your own thing. Now, of course, I can appreciate what they went through, but then I didn't want to hear another word about the war.

WR: I think the U.S. differed a bit because we were ramping up the Vietnam War here . . .
Wade: There were some anti-Vietnam demonstrations here, but [the U.S.] had the draft and people tried to get out of it. Others had to go to Vietnam, of course. The difference here is that London was bombed. It actually happened here, not the other side of the world. Both my uncles were killed in the war. That was the way it was. I did meet Vietnam veterans in the East when we went traveling. It was a whole different experience.

WR: Speaking of the East . . . your detail work on the cover of *Lizard* has an East-meets-West quality.

Wade: I went to the British Museum and looked at the *Lindisfarne Gospels*. I can't remember if I did sketch work first, but I worked it out [before undertaking the actual illustration]. The knotwork is from the *Lindisfarne Gospels*, a sixth-century Celtic book, a fantastically illustrated book. I was like a magpie, randomly picking up bits that I liked and putting it into the album cover. Another source was *Les très riches heures du Duc de Berry*, a French medieval book of hours [prayers]. I had a look at that as well. Some bits I just completely made up and others I nicked from other places. I noticed on websites people have come up with all kinds of weird connections that I never have. That's the thing about images: people are free to interpret them the way they like.

WR: How old were you when you were working on the cover illustration?
Wade: Twenty-four, I think. Twenty-four, twenty-five.

WR: Did you hear any of the recorded material before you began painting?
Wade: Pete gave me the words, but I didn't actually hear the music until much later.

WR: You were working in watercolors?
Wade: I do work in watercolors, but that particular illustration was done in gouache. It's like poster paint . . . It's a bit like watercolor, but it's more opaque. It was on two bits of stretched paper. If you do painting in water you have to wet good watercolor paper and then stretch it with tape on the board, otherwise it will buckle. When it dries it's flat. As far as I remember I painted it in two separate paintings, which were eventually bought by Chris Blackwell of Island Records. The actual paintings were one and a half times the size of the album cover art.

WR: What is the story with the gray background?
Wade: That was watercolor wash, transparent. It was supposed to look like vellum, calfskin, to mimic the look of a medieval manuscript.

WR: What can you tell me about the swirl design of the inside gatefold?
Wade: It's marbling—oil paint floating on water. My then-boyfriend, now husband, ran a company called Koraz [Wallpapers], which made marbling wallpaper at the time.

WR: Let's unpack some of these images, starting with the front cover.
Wade: The Crimson side relates to the songs on the A side of the album. The picture in letter *C* is, of course, "Cirkus." The *R* is "Lady of the Dancing Water." The *I* is "Happy Family," which is about the Beatles breaking up. The *M* I filled with an image of my own fantasy of death, a kind of medieval, fairly common image. The *S* is "Indoor Games." The *O* is medieval musicians. The *N* is my joke: a fantasy supergroup of Jimi Hendrix, my boyfriend Dave Wade [flute player], and Ginger Baker on the drums. I loved Jimi Hendrix, I loved Cream, and that's

my boyfriend. Flying above, waving from inside his airplane, that's Rupert Bear, the children's comic, which was popular then.

WR: Why place Rupert in the painting?
Wade: It was just a little extra bit of fun for me. No particular reason.

WR: How about the reverse side? We see a lizard or a dragon intermingling with, creating, the knotty designs. Within the letter *K* two opposing military forces stampede toward one another, Crusader armies from the West and Mongols or a Samurai army from the East.
Wade: That was my interpretation of "The Battle of Glass Tears" [third movement of the "Lizard" suite]. As for the Mongols, they are really Japanese warriors.

WR: Some of the most disturbing imagery was reserved for the final three letters of the back cover: *I, N, G*. The scene inside the *I* reminds me of nursery rhymes about the Black Plague. This is where it starts to get weird: a man in a gorilla costume or an overgrown monkey plays some form of frame drum.
Wade: It's a bodhrán, actually. In medieval times . . . there was a lot of horrible stuff going, like the Black Death. There was always that dark side, which I think comes out in the words of the album. I like a bit of sinister undercurrent going on.

WR: I remember Peter Sinfield saying that there was something sinister or devilish about the recording and progress of the *Lizard* record.
Wade: If you look at illuminated manuscripts there's lots of little grotesque and humorous touches. That's part of the feel of the art at the time. I picked up on that. I also must have picked up on Pete's—and the others'—state of mind just from reading the text of the songs.

WR: I notice a clash of modern and ancient water vessels (and creatures) in the letter *I* on the front cover.
Wade: The mix of boats and aquatic creatures was purely for fun, and the hot-air balloon [in the letter *R*] was another example of this.

WR: The *N* and *G* on the reverse side might be the most mysterious. *N*, in particular, seems to have been inspired by the lyrics for the "Prince Rupert Awakes" portion of the "Lizard" composition.
Wade: That particular one was taken from the text. I didn't interpret it literally, line by line, but just the general feel of it. And the dragon floating above, as you've referred to it, is actually a lizard. The *I* and *G* are my imaginative medieval people. Above the *K*, that's a pleasure medieval pastoral scene in contrast to the battle going on within the bottom half of the letter *K*. It doesn't have anything particular to do with the lyrics.

WR: But it illustrates the dual nature of medieval life and, maybe, life in general. On the one hand you have agricultural workers in the fields and, some miles away, a battle raging. The *G* contains a scene of ceremonial sacrifice, with a green hobgoblin or alien looking on . . .

Wade: Yeah. Don't ask me what it means. Some of these images, the devil and [the African], they came from medieval manuscripts. Same as the priest you see there.

WR: Do I detect a Taj Mahal–like structure, with a turret at its top, in the background of the letter *N*? What kind of impact did your travels to India have on your designs?

Wade: I don't think my experiences in India directly influenced my imagery, but my visual brain has a tendency to store all glittering objects that may be used at a later date.

8

Escapist Artists

Designing and Creating Prog Rock's Wondrous Visuals

Ever since the 33⅓ 12″vinyl LP had been firmly established as the industry's standard audio recording format, and well in advance of record labels allocating enormous budgets to music video production, album cover illustration was a key component of an artist's public persona—and marketing strategy.

Although the sleeve-art medium was relatively new, the concept of an all-in-one multimedia presentation was not. If anything, it was a modern-rock extension or interpretation of Wagner's dramatic principle *Gesamtkunstwerk*, which sought to combine the text, performance, and symphonic aspects of a dramatic work. This all-encompassing concept was applied by the pop and rock music worlds throughout the second half of the twentieth century.

One of the most public affirmations of this idea occurred in 1967 with Peter Blake and Jann Haworth's iconic design for the Beatles' *Sgt. Pepper's Lonely Hearts Club Band* album cover, which implicitly linked kaleidoscopic pop visuals with the perceived psychedelic sounds heard throughout the album's song cycle. From this point onward, rock artists, and those who marketed them, didn't look back: the bond between cover art and musical material would be continually and extravagantly explored.

In some instances, whether it was the handiwork of Roger Dean, H.R. Giger (i.e., the elaborate packaging that literally wraps ELP's *Brain Salad Surgery* in disturbing, pre-*Alien*, sci-fi imagery), or design firm Hipgnosis, album-cover artwork rivaled the importance of the music it was meant to package. Some fans poured over this imagery and reasoned that every cover, even the most sparse, contained esoteric messages in need of deciphering. Devoid of proverbial tangerine skies and looking-glass ties, so fashionable in the psychedelic era, Bob Dylan's no frills folk/gospel/country-ish 1968 album, *John Wesley Harding*, underscores this point: some observers spotted (or thought they did) the hand of God and faces of all four Beatles in the shapes and shadows of the black-and-white cover photograph—a phenomenon spurred on by the liberal use of recreational substances, an abundance of spare time, and the words of the enigmatic Mr. Dylan himself, who described the record as "the first Biblical rock album. . . ."

As the need for new imagery grew, so independent designers found new opportunities. And as the 1970s wore on, some legends of the field had emerged, each of whom had their own distinct style. Whether it was Roger Dean's strange hybrid fantasy worlds or Hipgnosis' surrealistic, Magritte-influenced montages, prog-rock cover artwork often rivaled the music it was meant to package.

"Great packaging has always been a way to lure, romance, or grab someone's attention and motivate them to buy a product," says Ron Levine, illustrator and designer who worked with labels ranging from Elektra to Columbia Records and perhaps became best known for his work in the Latin and Latin rock music world with photographer Lee Marshall.

Whether it was *The Dark Side of the Moon* or Genesis' *Wind & Wuthering*, the illustrator and graphic artists, as well the recording artists, only presented you with Point A. How one arrived at Points B and C was often left up to the listener's interpretative powers and personal psychology. "*You* have to do it yourself," says illustrator Colin Elgie. "Rather than spelling it all out in a kind of comic book type way."

However, a downgrade from LP to CD format and the shift in record company budgets from album cover art to video production had a massive impact on how music was experienced and marketed in the 1980s. In the 1970s it was the album cover that sold the album. Ten years later, record companies that had once thrown money at elaborately designed covers, from *Catch a Fire* to Alice Cooper's *School's Out*, had to rethink their priorities.

"In those days you didn't think twice about spending thirty thousand dollars on a Pink Floyd or Led Zeppelin album cover," says Richard Evans, who was Hipgnosis' in-house layout person in the 1970s. "People like Hipgnosis would think, 'Where haven't we been? St. Lucia. Right. We'll talk the band into doing something in St. Lucia.' Today you could never get away with that. . . . I wasn't at Hipgnosis then, but [Zeppelin] was going to create the symbols [associated with Led Zeppelin IV] and put them on the Nasca plain, and get in a hot-air balloon and photograph them from above for the cover of *Houses of the Holy*."

"I can say that I feel very strongly about how effective a CD package is versus the old 12″album cover to sell the album," says Levine. "It's not. It's a loss of a great art form. With the digital age so many things have changed. . . ."

While the author admits that there has been some great CD artwork—from Alex Grey's dissectional art inhabiting *Lateralus* for Tool to Hugh Syme (Rush), Silas Toball (the Flower Kings' *Banks of Eden*), and Per Nordin's software-based, blimp-like flying vehicle for Transatlantic—this section is an homage to the prog-rock album covers from the 1970s. The following are visionary words from artists and illustrators alike about select covers from prog's classic era.

Yes: *Tales from Topographic Oceans* (1973)

Illustrator: Roger Dean

Roger Dean deserves a section all his own for the impact his work has had on the once-thriving field of album cover artwork. Dean was one of the few illustrators whose work was viewed on equal footing with the music it packaged. Aside from designing the memorable serpentine lettering for the Yes logo, Dean envisioned the Harvest Records label logo, the slightly risqué "2 Virgins"/mirror image label for a fledgling Virgin Records, and a new Vertigo Records LP label in the early 1970s. (The old version of the Vertigo label was, of course, the iconic eye-teasing Hitchcock-like "swirl.")

Dean toured Japan with Yes in 1973 to formulate ideas for the cover artwork and stage design for the tour to support the then-upcoming *Tales* release. Dean must have been plenty inspired. The result was a strange amalgam of sacred stone circles as well as inspirational input from Anderson (i.e., the Mayan temple at Chichen Itza) and Alan White's Nazca Lines suggestion.

Yes: *Tormato* (1978)

Designers: Hipgnosis

Legend has it that a thoroughly disgusted Rick Wakeman, expressing his hatred of the intended cover image, flung a juicy tomato at it in defiance of what he—and others in the band—saw as subpar work done by icons Hipgnosis. *Voila!* What was once going to be called *Tor*—a Steve Howe suggestion—was now *Tormato*. Or so the story goes . . .

Although we couldn't completely confirm this long-standing prog-rock tale, Richard Evans, Hipgnosis' in-house layout man, remembers working on the cover for the design firm. "What you have there is actually a few different images," says Evans. "The band on the back cover was collaged on. The background was shot in the West Country, in Dartmoor, and [Hipgnosis] wouldn't have gotten the band to go out there. It would have been a matter of getting the surgical scalpel out and gluing down the image. These days you can do it in Photoshop. Back then you cut the photograph out and sanded the back of it so fine that it was like tissue paper. Then you'd glue it down on top of the background print so you don't get any shadows appearing when you copy the artwork.

"I think the photograph of the guy with the divining rods [on the cover] was certainly taken in the studio, because he was one of the photographer's assistants," Evans continues. "Then it was montaged onto the background."

Jethro Tull: *Aqualung* (1971)

Illustrator: Burton Silverman

Most fans recognize this image as the symbolic representation of the band's commercial breakthrough, but Ian Anderson never liked the cover, finding it too "messy" for his tastes.

Silverman's watercolor work perfectly complements and captures the expressive and layered mood of the music (i.e., gothic, urban, yet steeped in European tradition). There's also some confusion about whether the painting actually depicts Anderson or the character of Aqualung or some combination thereof. Either way, the identity of Anderson (who used to wear a shabby overcoat onstage very much like the one seen on the LP cover), Aqualung, and the actual historical figure of Jethro Tull fused in the minds of some confused fans.

Silverman attempted to sue the band and the label for using the cover image for merchandise, and calls to Silverman went unreturned at press time.

Pink Floyd: *Atom Heart Mother* (released October 1970)

Designers: Hipgnosis

The decidedly unhip photo of a cow in a pasture chosen by Hipgnosis to grace the cover of the album may have captured the theme of the album (i.e., "earth mother"), but confused others. The photo simply ticked off EMI, Floyd's label, which became further incensed by the band's refusal to print its name—or the title of the record—on the cover. (Waters reportedly doubled over with laughter when he first saw the photo Aubrey Powell was proposing.)

The title track represents Floyd's major flirtation with symphonic prog. Says Richard Evans, citing logistical nightmares, such as arranging six hundred (or so) government-issued hospital beds—some reports push that number as high as eight hundred—along the shore for the cover shoot for Floyd's twelfth (and first Roger Waters-less) studio album, 1987's *A Momentary Lapse of Reason* (that's the same beach location, Saunton Sands, used for the film *The Wall*), *Atom Heart* was one of the most inexpensive and hassle-free covers Hipgnosis ever created: "The cover of *Atom Heart Mother* cost five dollars for film, plus the additional cost of the petrol to go up the country. Cheapest cover we ever did."

Pink Floyd: *Meddle* (1971)

Designers: Hipgnosis

Hipgnosis' Storm Thorgersen once said that nobody has owned up to designing the cover photo. However, photographer Robert Dowling was hired for the job and snapped droplets of water and the ear of a model from a local agency.

Powell said it was a statement about "pure sound" with the ripples representing sound waves. With a dash of Dali and splashes of Bill Brandt, it's one of the more strangely memorable Floyd covers (even if it wasn't particularly well liked by Hipgnosis), despite the ambiguous nature of the actual image. Undoubtedly, the cloud-like formations—patterns we seem to see in the water ripples and shadows of the earlobe—speak to the amorphous sounds heard in tracks such as "Echoes."

Pink Floyd: *Wish You Were Here* (1975)

Designers: Hipgnosis

Everyone's heard the story of a bald and paunchy Syd Barrett roaming into EMI Abbey Road Studio 3 as the mix of "Shine On You Crazy Diamond," a song dedicated to the Piper himself, was being completed.

Barrett's presence seemed to stir up a multitude of feelings—guilt and regret among them. His dazed demeanor also reinforced the theme of absence, which permeated the band's album *Wish You Were Here.*

Keyboardist Rick Wright went on to say that "to walk in while we were actually doing that particular track . . . Coincidence? Karma? Fate? Who knows? . . ." Barrett was just a "symbol of all the extremes of absence. . . ." Floyd bassist/vocalist Roger Waters said.

For such a simplistic but deep topic, Hipgnosis produced what might be, next to *The Dark Side of the Moon,* their most iconic imagery. The surreal, Magritte-esque visuals speak to universal themes, such as the world's four natural elements, as well as the specific one of absence.

The LP was wrapped in dark plastic, hiding the cover, and the LP label showed two robot hands gripping each other (recalling the cover theme) as the background image of a carved circle recalls the four-elements theme and alludes to the four members of Floyd.

Pink Floyd: *Animals* (1977)

Designers: Hipgnosis

Synopsis: Flying inflatable pig hovers over the dormant Battersea Power Station, an art deco building that would cease operation in the early 1980s. It took three days, supposedly, to actually snap this cover image. After having difficulties blowing up the pig, the Hipgnosis crew got it up in the air only to watch the bloated bovine slip away. The pig was downed in a local farmer's field, making the news. (The farmer was none too pleased.)

With marksmen on hand in case the beast was loosed, again, the crew eventually got the images they needed, but not in the way they had expected. In the end, Hipgnosis' Powell admitted, the job could have been dispensed

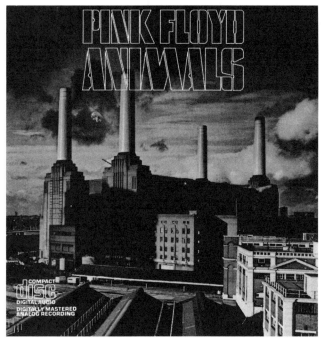

Pink Floyd's *Animals*: Who let the pigs out?

with more efficiently had the firm approached it as the cut-and-paste job it ultimately became.

Genesis: *A Trick of the Tail, Wind & Wuthering* (1976)

Illustrator: Colin Elgie

Genesis' quirkiness—or plain Englishness—was something that set it apart from other progressive rock bands—even those from Britain. From Paul Whitehead's Victorian-influenced hallucinatory dreams/nightmares, to the pastoral scenes of artwork by Betty Swanwick, Genesis album covers spoke to the music perhaps in ways other artwork couldn't.

Selling England by the Pound was one of the Genesis' most beloved and coherent packages, yet its illustrator, Swanwick, was not convinced that she wanted to paint a cover album for a rock group. However, after hearing some of the music she agreed. As Peter Gabriel has stated in the past, "I Know What I Like (in Your Wardrobe)" was written with her and her painting in mind.

One overlooked Genesis cover was 1976's *Wind & Wuthering*. It's a subtle thing, in watercolor and parchment: you either get it or you don't. It appears to be a mist-shrouded ground on the front cover and on the back, we see birds fleeing a tree in early evening. These images are as evocative and just as clued in to the music as any Paul Whitehead painting.

Colin Elgie, who created the illustration for Genesis' previous studio album, *A Trick of the Tail* (a piece of Hogarth-ian/George Cruikshank-esque Dickensian art, reminiscent of a Victorian playbill), was inspired by an unlikely source. "I had gotten this image because I had just seen, on the tele, a movie with Charlton Heston called *The War Lord*," says Elgie. "[Heston's character] just had his evil way with the leading lady in the movie; he was a local warlord and deflowered a local virgin or something. As this was happening you saw this tree and all these birds taking off from it. It's revealed to be a dead tree underneath. That is where that central image came from. This movie."

Family: *Bandstand* (1972)

Designer: John Kosh

Family may have been attempting to streamline their musical approach with *Bandstand*, but their album packaging was as elaborate as ever. Like Family's 1971 album, *Fearless*, which Kosh also designed, the cover was a multilayered, die-cut extravaganza.

"*Bandstand* was a tour de force," says Kosh. "I was playing with retro images—this time an old, British Bakelite TV set. I hand-colored the prints, added the

Bandstand: Designer John Kosh's acetate-window, die-cut tour de force.

decals. . . . The original cover had an acetate window for the screen with the phrase 'Bandstand' silk-screened over it and a die cut featuring the old amp inside. It was very satisfying and won me the Silver Award at the London Design & Art Directors annual show."

The Nice: "America" single (1968)

Photographer: Gered Mankowitz

The Nice were embroiled in controversy in the late 1960s when Keith Emerson burned the American flag at the Royal Albert Hall, an act that got him banned from the building for life. (Lee Jackson, Nice bassist/singer, followed suit and burned a draft card at the Marquee Club.)

Some reports, however, tell us that Keith didn't actually burn the American flag, but a *picture* of the American flag. Whatever the truth of the matter, nearly as controversial was the photo used for the single of the Nice's take on Stephen Sondheim's "America," shot in Mason's Yard, London, by Gered Mankowitz, who was inspired to have the band don masks of famous Americans.

"I believe I came up with the idea of the kids in masks—the kids were models I organized," says Mankowitz. "We were looking for a controversial concept that hopefully said something about the immaturity of America as a nation and the shocking assassination of three great men [JFK, RFK, MLK]. The band painted the U.S. flag background, which was supposed to resemble blood."

King Crimson: *Red* (1974)

Photographer: Gered Mankowitz; designer: John Kosh

This starkly beautiful black-and-white cover, a visual twist on the traditional group portrait, is actually a composite of three separate images. (As photographer Gered Mankowitz remembers, the Crimson boys entered into his Soho, London, studio separately and each spent a couple of hours with him.)

Traveling down the path blazed by Beatles cover album photographer Bob Freeman (i.e., *With the Beatles*), Mankowitz's work perfectly reflected the dark cloud looming over the band's future. "I shot on the large format camera and wanted a very classical look—the lighting is what I call my Rembrandt lighting—very simple and painterly—a classic solution," says Mankowitz.

"It would have been impossible to shoot [the band together] as a group and capture their rather stark and sinister countenance without tripping all over each other's shadows," adds Kosh. "I think the idea for shooting in black and white was Gered's. It worked well to show off the red title, which was me just fiddling with an existing font."

As far as the dial on the back cover? "It was an old sound-balance meter," says Mankowitz, "and it represented going into the red—loudness!"

Manfred Mann's Earth Band: *Solar Fire* (1973)

Designer/Photographer: Fin Costello

"The way that album cover came about is through the photographer shining a lighting through a piece of cardboard with pinprick holes in it to create the illusion of stars. [Fin Costello] took a picture of that," explains Earth Band guitarist Mick Rogers. "Try it at home."

Kansas: *Monolith* (1979)

Illustrator: Bruce Wolfe

In an e-mail sent to me back in 2007, artist Bruce Wolfe explained that he had envisioned an entirely different cover concept for Kansas' 1979 self-produced record, *Monolith*. As Kansas fans may recall, *Monolith*'s postapocalyptic cover features a stoic Native American dressed in buffalo skin, bead necklace, and a space helmet, with two horns protruding out from either "side."

This striking image, a strange visual concoction of ancient astronaut theory, Native American spirituality, and a primordial fascination with the mechanical operation of the heavens, matches the mood of some of the songs of the

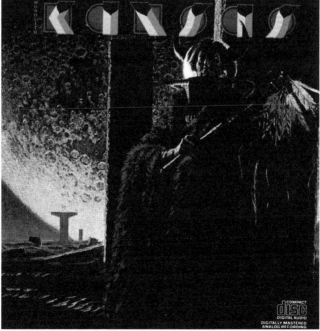

This, the final cover image of *Monolith*, was not the illustrator's first choice.

record. Yet, to hear Wolfe describe it, his original idea was far more involved. Bruce wrote: "Originally, I had done a rough drawing for approval from Kansas that they rejected. On the cover you see the American scene of a motorcycle policeman hiding behind an outdoor signpost that reads, 'Visit Kansas' as a speeding 1963 convertible red Corvette passes by at 100 mph. The inner gatefold had the tunes printed, intermixed, on top of the cop after the Corvette, downview, through verdant Nebraska landscape. On the back cover, forty-three miles above ground, you see the blue ball of Earth beyond. In the foreground the cop is nonchalantly writing the ticket, foot on bumper . . . while car, driver, motorcycle are at zero gravity angles.

"They liked the next idea better."

Procol Harum: *Something Magic* (1977)

Illustrator: Bruce Meek

"I remember Keith [Reid] phoned me about doing the work [*Something Magic*], and read a few of the lyrics to me," says cover artist Bruce Meek, who was involved in the underground music scene in Toronto in the late 1960s and designed posters and fliers for legendary nightclub Rockpile. "I believe he must have sent me the words of 'The Worm & the Tree,' but otherwise we didn't really discuss it. The illustration is set beside the seaside. Nowhere in England is far from the coast. The glorious maritime history drilled into us at school, a mother tongue rich with nautical maxims, and the heavily loaded image of the seashore, representing freedom, probably explains most of the watery elements in Keith's lyrics and this painting. Plus, dismembered ladies were once a very popular magic deception. . . ."

ELP: *Trilogy* (1972)

Illustrator: William Neal

Neal, who had illustrated covers for ELP albums *Tarkus* and *Pictures at an Exhibition*, was tapped, again, to create an original concept for the band's 1972 album, *Trilogy*. It might be one of the most spectacular What-Ifs in the field of rock cover art.

"*Trilogy* was not an all-embracing concept album, and I am fundamentally a large concept artist," Neal says. "The ideas that were put forward and eventually scrapped are too numerous to go into. It was a struggle for us all really, not an easy ride. 'The Endless Enigma,' on *Trilogy*, is a tremendous ELP performance, and it could have brought about a visual of groundbreaking proportions, but it remains written here for the imagination."

Neal explains that he had envisioned the artwork for *Trilogy* as an "artist's still life of gigantic proportions," and planned to employ an aircraft hangar to realize his design.

"I had been involved with BBC set design prior to the music industry, and outlined a massive back projection . . . making a photo montage of the lyrics to 'The Endless Enigma,'" Neal says. "But this was not really the cover. The real cover was revealed by the corners being lifted, showing an another album, and another one, and another . . . An Endless Enigma of its own making."

But the project was too costly and too overwhelming and Neal could never pull it off. Hipgnosis was finally brought in for the cover work everyone is familiar with nowadays: a painting of Emerson, Lake and Palmer looking to a distant horizon.

Nektar: *Recycled* (1975)

Illustrator: Helmut Wenske

The German illustrator makes no bones about his extracurricular activities or the source of many of his artistic inspirations in the late 1960s and 1970s. "I began with smoking pot, almost daily, sometimes psilocybin mushrooms, one time LSD, for a fourteen-hour trip, and overall I smoked opium six or seven times," says Wenske. "Back then most of my friends [took] drugs and almost every picture from this period was painted under the influence of drugs."

Wenske has had quite a history, a symbiotic relationship, with the band Nektar, U.K. natives who transplanted themselves to Germany in the 1970s. Wenske began working with the band for their 1972 lysergic-acid-inspired Utopian dream, *A Tab in the Ocean*. Given Wenske's later, more surrealistic work, the artwork for *Ocean*, which included a back cover that was a cut-and-paste job using old manuals and catalogs (and a dosh of Hieronymus Bosch), appears tame.

Wenske's psychedelic imagery, mostly in watercolor, seems straight out of a vivid acid trip. Shapes and forms spill into one another, creating odd, alogical perspectives.

Remember the Future, from 1974, possibly Nektar's greatest musical work, was a concept album about a winged alien being, Bluebird, who makes telepathic contact with a blind boy from Earth. Not accepted on our planet on the basis of his skin color, Bluebird, who befriends the blind boy, tells him of cosmic events past and future.

"Being blind meant that the boy would have no misconceptions about who he was talking to," says Nektar guitarist Roye Albrighton. "Bluebird tells him of the wonders and the pitfalls that humans will go through before their evolution is complete."

"Drafts for the cover were made without knowing anything about the album concept or lyrics," says Wenske. "I painted the cover . . . while the band was in the studio. Nektar then flew to Germany and visited me at home, looking for the finished part of the picture. The record wasn't finished and I already had painted the blue-winged figures. Sometime after the album was released,

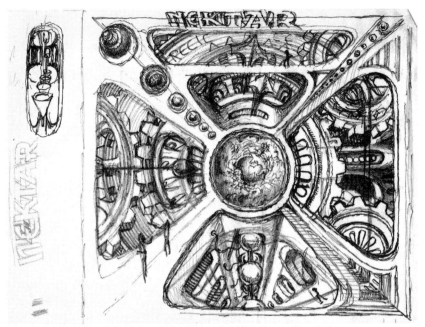

Helmut Wenske's original sketch for Nektar's 1975 album, *Recycled*.

Courtesy of Helmut Wenske

The "completed" crayon-colored artwork for *Recycled*, in a Japanese release.

Mo told me that the song 'Remember the Future (Part I)' was inspired by these shapes."

"It was quite bizarre the way this came together," says Albrighton. "At the time we were on tour and had asked Wenske to design an album cover for our new release. We had the title, but he had never read or discussed the content of it. When he presented the cover to us there, before our eyes, was a blue figure, which was ironically a direct reference to Bluebird. Helmut could not have known about this, but there it was. Very freaky."

Arguably, 1975's *Recycled*, drawn in crayon, was the pinnacle of Wenske's working relationship with Nektar—a perfect fusion of concept and visuals. Yet, says the artist, he wasn't even aware of what the phrase "recycled" meant until the band's bassist, Derek "Mo" Moore, explained it to him.

Incredibly, he also claims he hadn't had time to complete it properly. "As always, the band had no bearing on the cover," says Wenske. "They always trusted me and I painted what'd passed through my mind. For *Recycled* I worked five days and nights, all around the clock, being completely stoned, just breaking to roll another joint and eat something. On the morning of day six . . . I lost my breath, because one of my lungs had collapsed. I was on the ICU for a few days with pneumothorax. In the meantime, Nektar picked up the draft version from my wife and the unfinished picture was what went to the press."

The psychedelic imagery, or "acid geometry" as it was called, carried over into the band's stage production. (The gatefold of *Remember the Future* offers a peek into the kind of slide projection show Nektar used in the mid-1970s.)

Fireballet: *Night on Bald Mountain* (1975)

Illustrator: Ron Levine

A Night on Bald Mountain was a symphonic poem based on a Satanic ritual and composed by Modest Mussorgsky, who described the piece as one that features "appearances of the spirits of darkness, followed by that of Satan himself." Although, ultimately, the light seems to prevail, the composer went as far as to say that the piece was a celebration of the Black Mass.

Fireballet's interpretation of Debussy's "The Engulfed Cathedral" was interspliced with original material and the Mussorgsky piece occupying most of the second side of the New Jersey–based band's 1975 record, *Night on Bald Mountain*, produced by King Crimson's Ian McDonald. "I think [*Bald Mountain*] was a dark enough piece for progressive rock," says Ryche Chlanda (Fireballet, Renaissance, Nektar), "and we could change around a few things in the middle to include other pieces."

The darkness of the music is reinforced by illustrator Ron Levine's water-color- and-ink-based graphics of jagged mountainsides, hooded figures, and reptilian platforms. "I love art nouveau," says Levine, "and I was under the influence of [Czech painter] Alphonse Mucha's work. The dragon face I built into

"The album insert had cutouts of us in tutus," says former Fireballet guitarist Ryche Chlanda, "You have to be careful what you do sometimes."

the platform was taken from one of his paintings from the nineteenth century—part of a chair a woman was sitting in."

For the band's next studio album, *Two, Too*, photographer Lee Marshall shot the band in tutus at the Capitol Theatre [Passaic, New Jersey]. The record company loved it—it gave them an angle from which to market the experimental music—but the cover often is a controversial one, dividing opinion.

"I remember Ron and I discussing the cover with the record company [Passport Records], about how we were going to do the cover," says Marshall. "When the band put these tutus on it was hysterical. Some of the guys got into character. They were dancing around and leaping and all that stuff. So, it was an interesting album shoot."

"It was the result of a bunch of crazy guys having fun and thinking it could be a Mothers of Invention sort of thing," says Chlanda. "Hey, if we could experiment with the music, then the label could with the cover."

Zappa: *Over-nite Sensation* (1973)

Illustrator: Dave McMacken

McMacken's undeniably aberrant, psychological, scatological, and even honest acrylic and water-based oil rendering dissected the deep recesses of Zappa's psyche. The dark foreground, the not-so-still life of a Dali-esque defiled grapefruit, and the intestinal, corn-comb organisms devouring the very frame they form, created a sexually charged version (perversion?) of the seventeenth-century Dutch painter masterworks.

"Frank wanted the painting to be this kind of sexual metaphor," says McMacken. "Everything in the painting had meaning, so we playfully put stuff around the picture that was telling the story of this sexual fantasy of this two-headed roadie . . . of Frank. He wanted me to pile layers upon layers. It was a lot like his music."

Henry Cow: *Legend* (1973)

Artist: Ray Smith

This might be the most unusual and slightly amusing cover featuring a sock. The connection between the image and the band's music is not immediately obvious. Then again, Henry Cow often worked in the gray and subtle areas of popular music, anyway.

The sock, Smith says, is simply that. "It's an independent object,"

Dave McMacken probed the boggy depths of Zappa's mind for *Over-nite Sensation.*

says Ray Smith, "which I made as a painting by weaving dry strands of acrylic paint on the canvas. The color and width of the strands suggest something electrical. I knew that the cover would be striking. The image was strong enough to be developed in future albums."

Cow pounced on the image and used it to brand the band and reflect the mood of the music the band was making at that time. "The image of the sock on the cover of *Legend* is clear, fresh and optimistic," says Smith. "This was the band's first album. The sock on the *Unrest* album is quite different—a movement from subtle gray to black colors with a touch of yellow at the ankle. The surface feels on the move, like a restless sea, reflecting the musical content. Underlying this and pinning it together is the back cover art, for which I've painted diagonal chains in tension, from corner to corner at each side."

The Cinema Show

Prog's Celluloid Heroes

A myth of the progressive rock world is that movie production companies shunned this style of music. This is patently false. From Goblin to Keith Emerson, Gabriel to King Crimson, Moodies to Asia, prog (and its variants) have been featured as either main act—as in a concert film—or as the musical spice to enliven such films as the 2012 reimagining of *Dark Shadows*, Rob Zombie's *Halloween II, Buffalo 66, Children of Men*, and 2005's *The 40-Year-Old Virgin* with Steve Carell.

The entries found here include only theatrical releases (or those intended for theatrical release).

ELP: *Pictures at an Exhibition (a.k.a. Rock 'n' Roll Your Eyes)* (1974)

Distributed by Ohio-based April Fools Films, produced by Lindsey Clennell and directed by Nicholas Ferguson (*Ready, Steady, Go!*), this film promises "a concert performance at movie prices."

Filmed at London's Lyceum Theatre on December 9, 1970, *Eyes* boasts as its centerpiece ELP performing *Pictures at an Exhibition*, Mussorgsky's piano piece, inspired by the death of close friend Victor Hartmann, whose work was exhibited at the Russian Academy of Arts after his death. (*Eyes* also contains performances of "Take a Pebble," "Knife Edge," featuring "Tank" and Aaron Copland's "Hoedown," "Rondo," a rearrangement of the Dave Brubeck tune from the Nice days, and "The Barbarian.") Mussorgsky wrote ten "scenes" steeped in Russian and pre-Christian Slavic myth, which were later orchestrated by Ravel, who supposedly transferred Russian language intonations and inflections to Mussorgsky's musical compositions and, by the same token, ELP infused their version with the language and sounds of their generation (i.e., clacking Hammond organ, avant-garde feedback à la the Nice's sizzling, whirring noises of "Five Bridges Suite," synthesizer sound waves, and gentle vocal performances).

Pictures . . . was one of the first pieces of music the newly formed ELP rehearsed in the summer of 1970, prior to being unveiled to the world, and one they would famously perform at their first major gig, the Isle of Wight Festival, in August 1970, closing their set with cannon fire. No such literal explosive excitement exists in this film, but it seemed only fitting that *Pictures* would figure prominently in the band's first major cinematic project.

Prior to working on the *Pictures* project, Clennell was making "a series of art shorts using the facilities of a television production facility experimenting with video-to-film production using the Technicolor process at that time," says Clennell, who indicates that the film was the brainchild of John House, a friend of Greg Lake, who managed the British psychedelic/prog-rock trio Spontaneous Combustion. (Lake produced the band's 1972 self-titled debut for the Harvest label, which has since been reissued by Esoteric Recordings.)

Although the ninety-five-minute film was rated "G" for general audiences, some scary moments abound. For instance, Keith uses the Moog ribbon controller as some kind of comical sex toy, playing the thing through his legs and by rubbing it on his butt cheeks. (The ribbon controller, a slab of wood with a metal strip, allowed Emerson to remotely operate the Moog. As ELP's stage show progressed, Keith had the ribbon modified to include the ability to shoot off pyrotechnic flashes.) In addition he achieves wild, disturbing elephantine and metallic squeals by abusing his Hammond, and air-raid-siren-like blasts mark "The Gnome" (evoking sound effects-based compositions such as Varèse's *Ionisation*).

"There's different instrumentation all the way through," Emerson said of the film at the time. "There is no way the audience can tire. . . ."

The performances may have been top-notch, but the band—and many fans—disliked the final result. Most gripe about the Richard Preston–created comic book animation, utilizing images of the Fantastic Four, Daredevil, and Spider-Man, as well as the rapidly shifting psychedelic effects—the multicolored geometric shapes and spirals used throughout the film, especially during "The Old Castle," "Blues Variation," and "The Hut of Baba Yaga."

"I think [ELP] were not very keen [about the film]," says Clennell. "I was not too happy with my work, either, as I had so little time to do anything more crafted. But, I think, it helped get the film out and helped distributors promote the concert as a cinema event."

It might be a stretch, but Kubrick's mind-altering cinematic experience of 1968, *2001: A Space Odyssey*, still held sway with audiences. This may have been an attempt to pick up on the expanded scope of the great sci-fi films of the late 1960s and early 1970s. (Kubrick certainly had an impact on the music being made in the late 1960s and early 1970s: tracks such as Pink Floyd's 1968 single "Point Me at the Sky," about a man who rockets off the face of the Earth to make a better life for himself in the cosmos, David Bowie's 1969 single "Space Oddity," born of the same cold isolation depicted in *2001*, and ELP's own nightmarish computer-controlled future of "Karn Evil 9: Third Impression" seem to reveal an indirect, if not a direct, influence on rock songwriting. It's also interesting to note that House's band, Spontaneous Combustion, released their second album in 1972, called *Triad*, which contains tracks with such tantalizing titles as "Spaceship" and "Monolith Parts 1, 2 & 3.")[1]

"Video effects—we are talking 1970—for use in 35mm film was what I was working on at the time," says Clennell. "The production facility's idea was that effects would give the film a chance theatricality. They had become producers of *Pictures at an Exhibition* as finance for the production had fallen through. They paid me to do 'something with it' in a very short time."

Critic Lester Bangs once called ELP robotic, but it's hard to agree with that assessment, at least, upon viewing this concert. Yes, the band was making great use of synthesizer technology, but it never becomes anything other than entertaining. In addition, hearing a three-piece translate portions of Mussorgsky's masterwork to a rock setting is still fairly thrilling, even chilling, viewed from the distance of over four decades' time. The band even throws itself out of time (for a few seconds) in "The Great Gates of Kiev." Can't get more human than that . . .

The Shout (1978)

Strange circumstances led two-thirds of Genesis to being underutilized for this quite bizarre flick, involving the death shrill of an Aborigine, starring Alan Bates, Susannah York, John Hurt, and Tim Curry as English poet Robert Graves.

Producer Rupert Hine, who helped organize the sessions, recounted the events for the author: "David Bowie was booked for the studio, but never showed up. [The filmmakers] called me and asked me if I knew a way to track him down and to see what he's up to. I said, 'You're telling me now?' I knew there would be no way for them to be appeased. I recommended Genesis, but the filmmakers, including Jeremy Thomas, the producer, had never heard of them. . . . I said to them, 'With Genesis I can get something that is instrumental and appropriate. They can lend their name to you and that will help you.' They still said that they had never heard of them, and I gave them a copy of *Billboard* and I pointed to 'Follow You Follow Me,' which was number seven in the U.K. singles charts." I laid it on this chap's lap and said nothing. He looked at the name, looked up at me, looked down again at the magazine, and said, 'Oh, *that* Genesis.'

"Obviously the band said yes," Hine continued, "but I could only work with Mike Rutherford and Tony Banks, because it was short notice, and in the end they couldn't call themselves Genesis, which kind of defeated the purpose. But I got them in and we recorded a couple of pieces in a church. The only bad taste of the story was that they were billed as 'incidental music,' which meant they did one theme, which was repeated throughout the film, and, since most of the sounds I created for the soundtrack were sound effects and electronics, I was billed as 'electronics.' [Rutherford said the music was drowned out by other noises in the film.] It left a rather bad taste . . . in my mouth and, I would find twenty years later, Tony's and Mike's, too. I was at an awards show in England where Tony Smith [Genesis manager] was being honored. In fact, Genesis was being honored. Tony said, 'I've got to get something off my chest, all these years later . . .' I was so embarrassed by that."

Banks couldn't have been too upset: the main theme of the film wound up being the basis for "From the Undertow," which appeared on the keyboard player's solo album, *A Curious Feeling*, a concept record based on the short story "Flowers for Algernon." Surprisingly, the film won a Cannes Film Festival award.

Yessongs (1975)

When we think of the classic era of Yes, it is this, the *Close to the Edge*–era period Yes, with fog rolling over the stage and a flat, faux-disco "ball" beaming piercing white light into the darkness of a concert hall, that most people conjure in their minds. If you were not lucky enough to have seen these shows, then Peter Neal's direction and Richard Ellman's quadraphonic "cinema-sound" for *Yessongs* might be the next best thing to actually being there.

Around the time of the *Close to the Edge* tour many big decision were being made: Bill Bruford had exited the band for King Crimson in July 1972, two months before the *Close to the Edge* (*CTTE*) album was released, and engineer/co-producer Eddie Offord, who'd been the technical guru for the two giants of 1970s mainstream progressive rock, Yes and ELP, was forced to decide which band he wanted to support. History tells us that ELP lost, and Offord worked exclusively with Yes on the prog-rock front, hitting the road with the band. Offord would go on to produce such landmark records as the triple live release *Yessongs*, material for which was largely taken from these shows. (Bruford

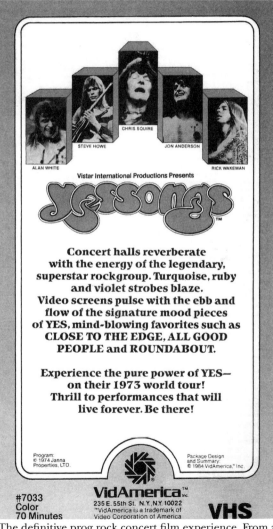

The definitive prog rock concert film experience. From a 1984 VHS copy of *Yessongs*.

appears on three tracks including "Long Distance Runaround," "The Fish" and "Perpetual Change.")

Offord proved useful in the studio and in the concert hall, helping the band recreate its music live, especially the dense nineteen-minute track "Close to the Edge." "I had two tape machines," Offord recalled for the author. "[On the tapes] there were church organs, and there would be vocal parts and even sound effects and a lot of instrumental parts that they just couldn't do live. I would be there cuing in these church organ parts and Rick would actually be kind of miming to some of them, you know? So, it was really a major kind of production."

Michael Tait, the band's lighting designer/director and all-around inventions man, outdid himself for the *CTTE* tour, creating stage elements such as the rotating round mirror (i.e., the flat disco "ball"), but also recalls some of the challenges the production presented.

"The problem with the mirror ball is that it's big, and you have to have mirrors all the way around it, and it has to be transported," says Tait, who provided the lighting design for the film event, assisted by Andrew Barker. "Those were the days when we would drive a van onto the runway and load the passenger planes ourselves, and off we go . . . I thought, 'I'm going to make a flat mirror ball.' So I got some wood, Styrofoam, used a soldering iron to make [the foam] dissolve, so I could stick mirrors on it, one by one. Then when it was rigged, I put all the followspots on it, you know? It was a great effect. It picked up on that twinkle-twinkle sound you hear at either end of the song 'Close to the Edge.' Theater had these types of creations for years, but rock and roll didn't. Then, of course, you need fog, so we needed our own machine. The first ones were like metal trash cans, but we developed them ourselves."

"Michael Tait was the guy who invented the PAR can [lighting fixture], and started to think about washes in terms of light versus focus," says Kevin Wall, a veteran in the live-event industry.

During the song "Close to the Edge" images of water-based molecular organisms scurry across the screen and aquatic flora twist to underwater currents, recalling the natural environments depicted in Floyd's *Pompeii*. In addition, animated illustrations by Roger Dean were used in the opening of the film: the disintegrating planet, the same one gracing the back cover of 1971's *Fragile*, hurls a chunk of its terra firma into the blackness of space—an image central to Dean's illustrative narrative/myth, which began with *Fragile*, continued with *Yessongs*, and expanded upon via Jon Anderson's 1976 solo album *Olias of Sunhillow*. (Influenced by J. R. R. Tolkien, Vera Stanley Alder's book *The Initiation of the World*, and Marvel comics [in particular illustrator Jack Kirby], Anderson created a conceptual world for *Sunhillow*, which reimagined a use for the Moorglade Mover, a name the singer gave to the flying contraption seen in Dean's illustrations for *Yessongs* and *Fragile*.)

Released in 1975, and filmed in London in December 1972 (at the Rainbow Theatre and photographed by Ian McMillan, Anthony Stern, Richard Stanley, and Brian Grainger), *Yessongs* was a snapshot of a band, which would tour North America three times and conquer the stages of Europe, Japan, and Australia from summer 1972 through spring 1973.

Interestingly, amid the sound and fury, *Yessongs* quite unintentionally confirms a story that has been circulating about the possible origins of the title *Fragile*. Bill Bruford told *Circus* magazine (March 1972) that the phrase was a commentary on the band's state of affairs in the wake of Pete Banks' exit and Tony Kaye's abrupt firing during the sessions for what would become the *Fragile* album; it's also a reference to letters stenciled onto the band's tour equipment cases. (During Steve Howe's mad solo in "Yours Is No Disgrace"—*Yessongs*' climax—we clearly glimpse the words "Yes Fragile" illuminated by clear light.)

Jethro Tull—*War Child* movie

At different times Jethro Tull leader Ian Anderson was said to have written a seventy-page treatment for a movie titled *War Child* and, supposedly, had already lined up the director and actors (to play God and the Devil) for this doomed film. (One source reported that Bryan Forbes, who directed *The Stepford Wives*, was tapped to helm the film.)

The plot tackled themes similar to those found on Tull's albums *A Passion Play* and *War Child*, an allegorical tale of a young girl's soul and its journey in the afterlife. However, the project never went beyond the talk/preparation stages, and much of the material earmarked for the movie wound up on Tull's 1974 studio LP *War Child* (orchestral and vocal material meant for the movie soundtrack).

In the ensuing years these orchestral bits were leaked out to the public; a piece that was, in large part, arranged by David/Dee Palmer, which was played over PA speakers at various concert venues prior to the band taking the stage. The actual title of *War Child*, as far as the reports go, was inspired by a Roy Harper song called "Little Lady," from his 1973 album, *Lifemask*. Anderson, a fan of Harper, appears on the prog-folk artist's 1974 record, *Flashes from the Archives of Oblivion*.

The proposed *War Child* flick was not the band's first foray into the world of film. A film shown during Jethro Tull's *A Passion Play* tour—Jeffrey Hammond-Hammond's *The Story of the Hare Who Lost His Spectacles*—was shot by a three-camera crew at a cost twelve thousand pounds. Not a small fee in the early 1970s. In fact, it was a small fortune. Intro and outro films were also shot, and shown, during the band's concerts, but were intended to create an atmosphere prior to the band taking the stage.

Tull had, of course, also appeared in the Rolling Stones' *Rock and Roll Circus*, from December 1968, featuring future Black Sabbath guitarist Tony Iommi, whose brief tenure helped to bridge the gap between Mick Abrahams' stint and that of Martin Barre's.

"Tony was the guitarist for the Rolling Stones' *Rock and Roll Circus*," former Jethro Tull manager Terry Ellis once told the author, "but then was uncomfortable with the whole [concept of] Jethro Tull . . . I was playing golf one day with Steve Van Zandt and Jethro Tull came up. He kind of sneered a little bit and said, 'I could never get into that prog rock.' I think Tony couldn't get into the art-rock, either."

Pink Floyd

Pink Floyd should have a separate category. If ever there was a progressive and psychedelic band tailor-made for cinema it was Floyd. The band recorded their soundtrack to 1969's *More*, the anti-Hippie effort by French critic-turned-director Barbet Schroeder, in just over a week in January and February at Pye Studios, with Roger Waters shouldering most of the writing burden. (Floyd would revisit their relationship with Schroeder for *La Vallée* and the result was 1972's *Obscured by Clouds*, perhaps the most effective use of Floyd's music within the context of a film.)

Of the early films that either feature the band's music or band members, such as Nigel Lesmoir-Gordon's 8mm *Syd Barrett's First Trip* (shows Barrett "experimenting" with a certain mind-altering substance in Gog Magog Downs southeast of Cambridge), the black-and-white art film *The Committee*, Anthony Stern's *San Francisco*, and *Tonite Let's All Make Love in London* (1967), it's perhaps the last that is the most fascinating, boasting footage from, most notably, the Mecca of England's psychedelic underground during the mid- and late 1960s—UFO Club. Some observers have noted that Barrett turns in a surprisingly stable and commanding performance for the camera, essentially leading the band. (A year later he would no longer be a member of Floyd.)

Floyd also found the time to compose for TV programs, such as *The Body*, a documentary by Ron Geesin, who asked Roger Waters to contribute music for the 1970 documentary on the human anatomy, narrated by Vanessa Redgrave and Frank Finlay. The concept was to create music via sounds produced by the human body. Harvest released the soundtrack in the U.K. Although uncredited, Floyd performed on one track, "Give Birth to a Smile."

Bootleg film, photos, and audio of Floyd's performance at the Amougies Pop & Jazz Festival of October 1969 in Belgium have existed for years. One performance is especially significant for prog fans: Frank Zappa jammed with Floyd on a noisy, bluesy version of "Interstellar Overdrive." Audio and stills of the jam—as well as some other moments of the festival—can be found on YouTube.com. Although some doubt whether Zappa ever played with Floyd (saying photos that have emerged merely show Zappa standing onstage with them), one listen to the track and most will agree that this seems unlikely.

Floyd scored Michelangelo Antonioni's 1970 Italian New Wave cinema entry/faux-documentary on the counterculture of the 1960s, *Zabriskie Point*, for which the band reworked "Careful with That Axe, Eugene" (as "Come in Number 51, Your Time Is Up") and played off a racing heartbeat in "Heart Beat, Pig Meat" (shades of *Dark Side?*). Antonioni ended up rejecting much of what Floyd submitted and, indeed, the whole episode is, perhaps, best remembered for music that didn't make the final cut: "Us and Them" (originally titled "Violent Sequence").

Adrian Maben's *Live at Pompeii* (1974), what the French director called an "anti-Woodstock" film, was designed to show Floyd performing in an empty ancient amphitheater, to demonstrate the power of the band's music. Interestingly, it's the combination of the images and music that has the deepest impact.

The director's cut opens with the sound of a heartbeat and human breathing. Next we're rocketed into space for a cosmic trip through the solar system to the opening chirps of "Echoes" (i.e., Rick Wright's Leslie-effected piano notes). The atmospheric music simmers with the same earthy and natural acidity as the volcanic pools percolating in the environs of Mount Vesuvius during the intro sequence. It's made all the more spooky by the appearance of terrified facial expressions frozen in sculpture and mosaic form.

The "A Saucerful of Secrets" sequence is the most iconic scene in the film, showing Mason (viewed from above and behind) pounding out a repetitive tribal beat on his silver-speckled drum set, Wright banging the piano keys, Gilmour, seated on the dirt floor of the empty ancient arena, scratching the strings of his Fender Stratocaster with a metal slide, and Waters, who comes across as a man possessed, abusing a hung gong.

Waters' one-legged whacks at this metallic beastie are silhouetted; a fast-cut technique is applied to the sequence, intersplicing the gong with a filtered photo of the sun and its corona, reminding us that Waters' gigantic noisemaker was forged of the sun. Shooting began for *Pompeii* in October 1971 in Naples, Italy, but technical difficulties prevented the project from being a true concert documentary. To beef up the movie, Maben combined stage performances and interviews shot in Paris and, later, footage of the band working in EMI Abbey Road Studios on *The Dark Side of the Moon. Pompeii* was first shown in Edinburgh in 1972, but this is not the version most people know. *Pompeii* wouldn't see wide distribution until 1974, by which time *Dark Side* had become an instant classic. This is Floyd among the ruins, in many ways, closing the books on a bygone era—their psychedelic- and progressive-rock phase—and ushering in a new one.

That new era was crowned, at least cinematically, with 1982's *The Wall.* When EMI's film department rejected Roger Waters' offer to convert the concept album into a movie tour de force, the Floyd bassist/vocalist reached out to English film director Alan Parker (*Fame, Birdy, Angel Heart*). Parker, Waters, and animator Gerald Scarfe, who created the illustrations for *The Wall* as well as animation for the *Animals* tour (the infamous, so-called "In the Flesh" tour, which featured second guitarist Snowy White, later of Thin Lizzy, for U.S. and

European date) and for the band's elaborate tour production of *The Wall*, produced a treatment for the film that called for animated sequences and live footage of Pink Floyd performances (the latter of which were never included). Although Waters had campaigned for the lead role of Pink—the aging, drug-addled rock star sealing himself off from the outside world—Boomtown Rats' former Floyd-hating frontman Bob Geldof won the role.

Wanting more control of the creative aspects of the film, Waters occasionally clashed with Parker. It's been reported that tensions between the two were so great that the Floyd mastermind was banned from the set before filming began in 1981. Waters' song "When the Tigers Broke Free," which was rejected by the band for inclusion on *The Wall*, was released as a single in August 1982, with Michael Kamen orchestration, reaching the Top 40 on the U.K. charts. The film itself wasn't a smash, but it did gain legs in the then-blossoming video rental market.

Genesis in Concert: A Film of a Rock Band and Their Music (January 1977)

Notorious among Genesis fans, director Tony Maylam's live concert film documents a progressive rock band on the rise, shedding some of its earlier, quirkier material and appearing (albeit only slightly) more the arena rock act, with Phil Collins as the band's frontman. Shot during the band's *A Trick of the Tail* tour (1976), it was screened for HRH Princess Anne and Captain Mark Phillips at Shaftesbury Avenue on January 31, 1977.

White Rock (1977)

We could hardly mention the Genesis concert film without also referencing Maylam's *White Rock*, a documentary of the 1976 Winter Olympics in Innsbruck, Austria, with music scored and produced by Yes' Rick Wakeman. It premiered second on the double bill to the Genesis documentary screened in January 1977. Interestingly, legend has it that Rick's soon-to-be-band Yes had turned down the opportunity to compose music for the film.

All This and World War II (1976)

Quasi-prog band Ambrosia contributed a cover of "Magical Mystery Tour" for this Beatles-themed war film, *All This and World War II*, which ran actual battle footage from the Second World War synched to Fab Four hits covered by a unlikely crew of musical characters, from Peter Gabriel ("Strawberry Fields Forever") to Roxy Music's Bryan Ferry, Tina Turner, and Rod Stewart. The film was released as a single in several countries around the globe, helping to reignite pop culture's obsession with Beatles in the mid-1970s (i.e., Beatlemania revisited).

Deadwing (a.k.a. "Lullaby")—Porcupine Tree

The concepts for Porcupine Tree's early and mid-2000 recordings seemed to grow progressively more disturbing—and epic. 2005's *Deadwing*, based on a script for a planned film (initially titled "Lullaby"), which Steven Wilson wrote in collaboration with art designer Mike Bennion, who'd been working with the band since *On the Sunday of Life*. The phrase "Deadwing," itself, was taken from the script.

Circumstances surrounding this project haven't always been clear or forthcoming, and Bennion wouldn't totally reveal the finer points of the plot (or how it relates to *Deadwing*, the album it inspired) when the author questioned him about it back in 2009. Bennion did say, however, that Wilson drops subtle hints throughout *Deadwing*'s song cycle, and among the music's dark undercurrent and various religious references. (However, Bennion explained that a song like "Mellotron Scratch" bears little overt connection to the film.)

Elements of the story did "out" in other ways, such as the visual elements of Steven Wilson's solo tours supporting releases such as 2011's *Grace for Drowning* and 2013's *The Raven That Refused to Sing (and Other Stories)*.

200 Motels (1971)

Call it celluloid surrealism. Codirected, scored, and scripted by Frank Zappa, whose "role" in this movie is as a kind of puppeteer (as far as the author can surmise), *200 Motels* is beyond bizarre. Try following the plot of this film and expect to get a headache. But that isn't to say you'll regret watching some of the absolutely outrageous and silly scenes of this film.

Zappa once called it "opera for television," when it appeared that the film might have a chance at being broadcast on TV (which didn't happen). The film is supposedly a look at the life of touring musicians, who seem caught in the endless loop, captives of a town called Centerville, U.S. ("a real nice place to raise your kids," reads a town sign). When Zappa does not appear, Ringo Starr (Larry the Dwarf) portrays him (or the puppetmaster/bandleader, or whatever). It just gets weirder (although slightly more coherent) from there. . . . One thing is certain: Zappa's self-referential M.O. is on full display here: we see/hear references to dogs, gurus, religious hypocrisy (Keith Moon as a nun experiencing a nervous breakdown), exaggerated sexual jokes ("Penis Dimension," groupies, etc.), and, doubtless, dozens of other inside jokes.

The *New York Times* called the film "*A Hard Day's Night* in desperate need of the early Beatles" and also proclaimed Zappa as a "McLuhan-age media freak who has mastered the techniques of making music, movies, lightshows, opera, and drama. . . ."

The music of *200 Motels* was performed live in May 1970 by the Los Angeles Philharmonic, conducted by Zubin Mehta and videotaped for Dutch TV. A scheduled performance in London of the program was canceled.

Perhaps the film's greatest strength is the animation (led by Carl Schenkel). The clay animation by Bruce Bickford used in Zappa's next major film production (1979's *Baby Snakes*, a concert film of footage shot on Halloween 1977 with large segments dedicated to Bickford's work), foretold the claymation maneuvers of Aardman Animations, responsible for the success of Peter Gabriel's popular "Sledgehammer" video.

Stamping Ground (1971)

Filmed in June 1970 in Rotterdam, the Netherlands, at the Holland Pop Festival, this West German concert documentary, in the mold of *Woodstock* (from 1970), features Family, Pink Floyd, Holland's own Ekseption, the Flock (featuring future Mahavishnu Orchestra violinist Jerry Goodman) and a pre-paralysis Robert Wyatt with Soft Machine.

Close Encounters of the Third Kind (1977)

American proggers Happy the Man missed their big opportunity to score Spielberg's alien contact film, signaling the end of their relationship with major label Arista. "The producers thought our music competed too much with the visuals of the film," former Happy the Man bassist Rick Kennell reports. "Meanwhile our label, which was wondering what to do with us, thought they could promote us for soundtrack work. Remember: Clive Davis once told us that we needed vocals on some of our songs. So, when the *Close Encounters* thing never happened, and John Williams got the call instead of us, I don't think there was a lot of time between when *Close Encounters* hit and our release [from Arista]."

Of possible interest: The ARP synth, a keyboard used by many progressive rockers in the 1970s, made a vital appearance in the film. Phil Dodds, an audio engineer and ARP tech, plays the iconic and transcendent five-note "alien contact" sequence.

Lizstomania (1975)

Metronomic motorboating, Ringo Starr as the Holy Pontiff, and composer Richard Wagner as a bloodsucking Antichrist ... Welcome to *Lisztomania*, starring Roger Daltrey (as the virtuostic titular character) and featuring Rick Wakeman as Thor.

This is director Ken Russell at his very best, or simply doing what came naturally to him, rivaling Zappa's *200 Motels* for the most sexually charged, phallocentric rock and roll film in history. Russell himself dubbed it his "pop version of the life of the greatest stud in musical history."

Earlier in the film Wagner (Paul Nicholas) appears as a vampire, siphoning off life force and, presumably, musical inspiration and creativity from an unconscious and exhausted Liszt. Wagner attempts to rebuild his nation (Germany) by captivating the imagination of its people through the seductive powers of his electrified and irresistible electronic-based music. (It should be noted that the historical Wagner married Liszt's daughter, played here by Veronica Quilligan. A young, and quite pouty/gorgeous Fiona Lewis is Liszt's love interest.)

Liszt witnesses what can only be called a black mass crossed with an occult Nazi rally, attended by bare-assed babes, who circle a penis-shaped monolith. The cowering coquettish cuties are then violated by a follically challenged, cackling demonic presence. Underscoring and complementing these visuals is Wakeman's Moog sequence, which perfectly captures the majesty, sexual allure, and insidious nature of the scene. (However, Russell said he was never a fan of Wakeman's score.) Surrounded by Wagner Youth, the great composer, dressed in blue suit and red cape, pontificates on the superman, his own self worth, and the master race, among other topics.

In a Frankenstein-esque laboratory scene, Wagner gives life to a silver-skinned (and, evidently, beer-deprived) god Thor, portrayed by Wakeman. Although elements of the plot could have been further explored (i.e., the tension in the relationship between Liszt and Wagner), as with so many other films by the director, including his adaptation of *Tommy* (1975) for the silver screen, which also starred Daltrey, some of the images are hard to erase from your memory.

Smashing Time (1967)

Lynn Redgrave and Rita Tushingham arrive in Swinging London in this light-hearted comedy. Members of Tomorrow (one of many of Steve Howe's pre-Yes bands) are featured on screen as the Snarks. Howe, drummer John Alder (a.k.a. Twink), Keith West, and John Pearce all make appearances in this light comedy.

The Lamb Lies Down on Broadway

It's safe to say that this one has crossed over from the borders of inspiration into myth. No, there has never been a film adaptation of *The Lamb*, but Peter Gabriel had imagined that there could be one, someday.

To occupy the director's chair, Gabriel had tapped Alejandro Jodoroswksy, the director and writer of *El Topo*, a richly symbolic film that had such a heavy influence on Gabriel when he was piecing together lyrics of Genesis' 1974 double concept album. (Gabriel has gone on record as saying he wanted the *Lamb* tour production to "work like a film." Moving slides were, of course, used for the tour, but the Jodorowsky project would be a complete realization of Gabriel's early theatrical vision for the album.)

Gabriel and Jodorowsky had progressed to the point that they had rewritten their screenplay, streamlined it, and discussed which sections of the concept album would work, and which ones wouldn't, on the screen. Gabriel was being considered for the role of the lead character, Rael, and he had hoped that the

税抜¥3.800 | スタンダードサイズ | 125min. | COLOR | MONO
字幕スーパー版 オリジナル予告編収録

900950 017430

発売元：株式会社アミューズビデオ
販売元：アミューズソフト販売株式会社
●このビデオ・プログラムは、一般家庭での私的視聴に用途を限って販売されています。
したがって、最新で複製し、上映、放映、有線送送することは法律によって一切禁止されています。
1967年アメリカ・メキシコ映画 ©ABKCO FILM 1967, ALL RIGHTS RESERVED.

S/R
Sale & Rental

Much like *The Lamb Lies Down on Broadway*, symbolism shapes the
plot of Alejandro Jodorowsky's *El Topo*, a title that translates as "the
mole." The film contains scenes involving castration, a lamb, a rebirth
inside a cave, and a quest that must follow a spiral path. Genesis' *Lamb*
addresses some of these topics in tracks such as "A Visit to the Doktor,"
"Cuckoo Cocoon," and "The Raven," while "Riding the Scree" and
"The Carpet Crawlers" reference spirals, said to be a symbol of the self.

movie would be released as early as 1980. This never happened, of course, for
various financial and creative reasons. (One report even had the film finished,
backed by Charisma Films.) Some still hold out hope, however, that Gabriel will
revisit this project and coordinate with a visionary director who can effectively
match the disturbing imagery of the album with his/her own cinematic tour
de force.

Magma/Christian Vander: *Moi y'en a vouloir des sous* (1973)

The Kobaïan masters make an appearance in one scene of this incisive French
satire on capitalism. A year earlier, Magma founder Christian Vander composed
the music for 1972's *Tristan et Iseult*, a stylized version of the highly influential
medieval romance. Vander also pops up in the 2013 documentary *Jodorowsky's
Dune*, which tracks the director's failed attempt to bring the Frank Herbert
sci-fi novel to the screen. (Legend has it that Jodorowsky hoped to enlist Pink
Floyd and/or Magma for the doomed movie's soundtrack.) The soundtrack was
released as a Magma album titled *Wurdah Ïtah*.

The Devil's Triangle (1974)

Based on a book of the same title, written by director Richard Winer, *The Devil's Triangle* documents the mysterious disappearances of ships and planes in the "otherworldly" vortex known as the Bermuda Triangle. Mr. Suspense himself, Vincent Price, narrates, and none other than King Crimson's song "The Devil's Triangle" (from 1970's *In the Wake of Poseidon*), which includes snippets of the band's interpretation of "Mars, the Bringer of War" from Gustav Holst's *The Planets* suite, a live favorite, can be heard throughout the hour-long doc. (King Crimson's music has been used in other unlikely films, including, without band approval, the French soft-core porn flicks *Emmanuelle* and *Emmanuelle II*.)

Goblin

Did every filmmaker of note in Europe in the early 1970s want Pink Floyd to score his movie? Well, okay, maybe this is an overstatement. But when Italy's undisputed master of horror, Dario Argento, reached out to the Floyd to compose music for his 1975 thriller, *Profondo rosso* (*Deep Red*), but was unsuccessful, he ultimately and perhaps not coincidentally, ended up at the doorstep of Goblin.

Call it vision or fate, but the soundtrack was a runaway success in Italy and Goblin—in one form or another—would provide the sonic scares for Argento for films such as 1982's *Tenebrae*, 1984's *Creepers/Phenomena* (starring Jennifer Connelly), 1989's *La chiesa* or *The Church* (sharing credits with Keith Emerson[2] as the Goblins), 1985's *Demons* (Claudio Simonetti is credited solely), and again in 2000 for *Non ho sonno*, briefly reuniting a deeply splintered band.

With one lineup or another, Goblin would cut a studio album (*Roller*) in 1976 and score films for other directors (i.e., Ernest Pintoff's *St. Helens* starring Art Carney in a command performance as stubborn

Chapter Selections

1. Program Start / Main Titles
2. Servant Of Satan
3. Holy Slaughter
4. The Church
5. Legion
6. The Parchment
7. "The Devil is everywhere"
8. Little Liar
9. Apparitions
10. Hell Unleashed
11. Possession
12. Noise At The Window
13. Demon Lust
14. Reflection Of Evil
15. Confession
16. Dark Rites
17. Fountain Of Terror
18. Bloody Bride
19. Deadly Secret
20. Subway Splatter
21. Young And Beautiful
22. Lotte's Memories
23. Bride Of The Devil
24. Guided Tour
25. End Credits

Goblin and Italian horror film soundtracks are practically synonymous. Here, for *The Church*, the progressive rock band shares credit with ELP's Keith Emerson.

Washington State resident Harry Truman; the European release of Richard Franklin's 1978 thriller, *Patrick*, released in the midst of a 1970s telekinetic killer craze [including 1976's *Carrie* and 1975's *Psychic Killer* starring Paul Burke and *Creature from the Black Lagoon*'s Julie Adams], the U.S./Australia version of which featured music by Queen's Brian May; the European version of George Romero's *Martin*, a.k.a. 1976's *Wampyr*, putting forth a plot involving a confused boy convinced he's a vampire; and Enzo G. Castellari's 1977 crime drama, *La via della droga*, which expanded on the band's familiar electronic rock by including elements of jazz-rock, world, and funk).

The music for the aforementioned *Profondo rosso* is among Goblin's very best, and most effective, scores. Indeed. Goblin had placed themselves well within the horror-film soundtrack tradition while also influencing its direction. For one thing, it's difficult not to make a connection between the icy opening riffs of this score and Mike Oldfield's "Tubular Bells" used in *The Exorcist* from late 1973, and even the heart-racing theme in 5/4, composed by John Carpenter, pulsing through the young filmmaker's genre-redefining classic *Halloween* (1978).

Dario Argento's *Suspiria* features some of Goblin's best work.

Electronics and good ole Mediterranean flavored prog rock offered prospective filmmakers and, specifically, horror filmmakers, a rich color palette of sonic textures, supporting, but never overtaking, the visually disturbing images beamed onto the silver screen. Often the band's work of the mid- and late 1970s reveals a strong Yes and Genesis influence, not to mention contemporary classical: ingredients that had also shaped the sound of the band's direct precursor, Cherry Five (which once counted drummer Carlo Bordini, of *Opera Prima* fame, among its members).

Goblin's classic writing team consisted of keyboardist and multi-instrumentalist Claudio Simonetti, percussionist/pianist Agostino Marangolo, bassist and acoustic guitarist Fabio Pignatelli, and guitarist/bassist/mandolin player Massimo Morante. This hellfire squadron produced a diversity of sounds and moods for movies, beginning with *Profondo rosso*, music for which was initially done by jazzer Giorgio Gaslini. When he dropped out due to disagreements with Argento, the filmmaker showed enough confidence in Goblin to greenlight their involvement with the production.

Perhaps the group's two greatest single works were for George Romero's *Dawn of the Dead* (*Zombi* outside the U.S.), the sequel to 1968's *Night of the Living Dead* (the Everest of brain-munching zombie flicks), and, no surprise, Argento's beautiful and eerie *Suspiria*. The latter film's almost Disney-esque cinematic scope marries perfectly with Goblin's occasionally creepy, layered, symphonic approach, making for a rare instance of synchronicity, and a masterpiece of sound and vision.

As of this writing, Claudio Simonetti's Goblin was on tour in North America, performing the soundtrack to *Dawn of the Dead* at various venues screening the classic film.

The Exorcist (1973)

Despite the raw cold, lines circled around the block in Manhattan movie theaters when the film opened around Christmastime 1973. Mike Oldfield's "Tubular Bells," already a hit on the college circuit (and the album from which the single was derived, released through Richard Branson's infant Virgin Records label, climbed to number one in the British charts in July 1973), was forever and indelibly linked to the film. (A single of the main theme from "Tubular Bells" performed by the Mystic Sounds, b/w "Iraq," an excerpt from the soundtrack, was released in Japan via Warner Bros.)

Stretching the studio to its very limits, "Tubular Bells" was composed and recorded thanks to hundreds of tracks and a ton of patience. "I had a track sheet, which was a roll of paper that we would scroll out on the floor, and was divided into blocks of a minute or something like that, in colored crayons to mark which track musical bits were on," says Simon Heyworth, one of the engineers for "Tubular Bells."

Italian Cult Bands

Inside the Making of Two Classic Records

S o much attention has been bestowed upon Italian progressive rock bands such as Premiata Forneria Marconi, Banco del Mutuo Soccorso, Le Orme, and Procession—and for good reasons. Generally speaking, the abovementioned bands helped to forge what we today consider *Progressivo Italiano*, a romantic musical style of prog rock that's held an unusual allure for Western listeners since the 1970s.

Yet, as historically significant as these artists were, the scene was heavily populated by a slew of, dare we say, equally talented bands flying just below the radar, having released only one or two records before dissolving.

Bands such as Osage Tribe, Capsicum Red, Della Festa Mobile, Città Frontale, Flea, Corte Dei Miracoli, the jazz-rock outfit Rocky's Filj had criminally short shelf lives despite the skilled songwriters and musicians within their ranks.

Few Italian prog records have been as mysterious and held in as high esteem as 1973's *Zarathustra* (which, for decades, remained Museo Rosenbach's only studio album) and *Opera Prima*, the lone LP recorded by the organ-and-drums duo Paolo Rustichelli and Carlo Bordini.

Rustichelli, son of the famous Italian soundtrack composer Carlo, has worn many musical hats throughout his career, having worked in the smooth jazz, notably with Miles Davis and Santana, 1970s prog rock, and film score fields. Q&As with Museo Rosenbach co-founder/bassist Alberto Moreno and Paolo Rustichelli follow.

Note: Although Museo Rosenbach's Moreno is fluent in English, he was most comfortable responding to my inquiries in Italian. The author has translated his words and checked these translations with the artist for clarity and accuracy.

Alberto Moreno (Museo Rosenbach) Q&A

WR: Please describe how, where and when Museo Rosenbach was formed?
Alberto Moreno: Museo Rosenbach was formed in Bordighera [northern Italy], a seaside town in the Liguria region, a few kilometers from the French Côte d'Azur, in December 1971. The group evolved from a cover band called Quinta

grog
records

LATO 1
SRML 2004
(GRL 04)

CORTE DEI MIRACOLI

1. ···E VERRA L'UOMO(7:00)
2. VERSO IL SOLE(6:34) 3. UNA STORIA FIA FIABESCA(6:52)
(F.Scogna-M.Scogna-A.Feltri)

Registrazione Effettuata Su
16 Piste Presso Lo Studio G Di Genova. Tutti
I Brani Sono Pubblicati Dalle Edizioni Musicali Eletta.
Prodotto da Mauro Scogna Su Etichetta Grog
record Della Off.SIDE Di Genova.
℗ 1976
Licensed and Distributed by Si-Wan Records Ltd. from King Records Ltd. Japan. Made in Korea.
All trademarks and logos are protected.

Corte Dei Miracoli (loosely translated as "the court of miracles") was issued in 1976 via the short-lived Grog label founded by New Trolls' Vittorio de Scalzi. The "court of miracles"—the ghettos of seventeenth- and eighteenth-century Paris, France—served as inspiration for Victor Hugo's novel *Les Misérables.*

Strada, featuring drummer Giancarlo Golzi, guitarist and soloist Pierluigi "Pit" Corradi, guitarist and lead vocalist Walter Franco, and myself on bass. [*Note: "Pit" is an abbreviation of Pierluigi.*] Essentially, we were a cover band, playing Led Zeppelin, Grand Funk Railroad, Jimi Hendrix, and Cream tunes. When Walter Franco left the group for military service, we searched for a new singer. While in the military Corradi was transferred to Genoa ... where he met Stefano "Wolf" Galifi, an R&B singer, who was performing James Brown, Chicago, and Joe Cocker songs. At the same time, in San Remo, drummer Ciro Perrino, bassist and vocalist Luciano Cavanna, Hammond organist Floriano Roggero, guitarist Enzo Merogno, and the flutist and saxophonist Leonardo Lagorio left their band, Il Sistema. Moreno, Golzi, and Corradi asked Merogno and Lagorio to join Quinta Strada and changed instruments, because "Pit" decided to play the Hammond—the very Hammond that Il Sistema's Roggero was selling. When the two factions of Il Sistema and Quinta Strada united, it was clear that we were in need of a lead singer. Corradi, in November 1971, reached out to Galifi in Bordighera for an audition. "Wolf" sang some songs in his repertoire, but, frankly, there was some doubt if the bluesy qualities of his voice would mesh well with the compositions that I was writing at the time. It was agreed that the musical and commercial viability of this union was uncertain, because the new songs we were performing were very classical in nature, in the vein of the Nice. However, and it may seem surprising to you, "Wolf" became part of the new group, which, at the end of 1971, had six members: Wolf, myself on bass, drummer Golzi, Hammond organ player Corradi, guitarist Merogno, and Lagorio on flute, sax, and piano.

WR: I know you were not in the band . . . But how important was Il Sistema to the Italian progressive rock scene?
Moreno: Il Sistema was an interesting symphonic rock group that certainly would have gone a long way in the music business, had they stayed together. One of their strengths was bass player/singer Cavanna, a great composer and live performer. The band was already doing Mussorgsky's "A Night on Bald Mountain," a version of Bernstein and Sondheim's "America" à la the Nice, and was also working on original compositions. They'd appeared at the Loano Rock Festival and got the attention of record label executives. But after performing a few shows and after trying to take their music to a national level, the group disbanded. When Merogno and Lagorio joined Quinta Strada they brought with them the musical material they were working on. Most importantly, with the permission of the authors, of course, I used the suitable parts of this material for a suite I was writing, called "Zarathustra." So, really, Il Sistema and Quinta Strada gave birth to Museo Rosenbach.

WR: Why the band name, Museo Rosenbach?
Moreno: Our new band was preparing material for a full-length record, but by early 1972 we were still without a band name. It was some sort of trend back then to link band names to buildings—banks [Banco del Mutuo Soccorso], bakeries [Premiata Forneria Marconi], theater houses. So, we followed suit with a museum. The name Museo Rosenbach was chosen purely at random. I was actually in a library one night, reading a biography of Ottomar Ernst Rosenbach, a German publisher. I liked the fact that the surname, Rosenbach, meant "River of Roses" in Italian. I suggested the name, "Inaugurazione del Museo Rosenbach," but it was too long, and it was almost immediately shortened to Museo Rosenbach.

WR: How did you come to be signed to your original record label, Ricordi?
Moreno: During the winter and spring of 1972 Museo Rosenbach tried out new compositions. "Dell'eterno ritorno" was the first one we tried, but with lyrics very different from what was recorded in 1973 for the *Zarathustra* album. The second song, "Dopo," we performed in concert, but it did not find its way onto *Zarathustra*. These two versions appear on a CD [*Live '72*], a bootleg released in 1992 by Mellow Records [MMP 102]. The third piece was "Della

natura" that evolved from a riff I wrote for saxophonist Lagorio. You can hear this version on the CD *Live '72*, released by Mellow Records. Our band, then a six-member group, performed concerts in 1972 composed largely of cover material. We certainly weren't doing anything "progressive." Some of the songs we were playing included "It's a Man's Man's World" by James Brown and our own interpretation of Donovan's "Season of the Witch." During the summer of 1972 we wrote the suite "Zarathustra," which included some material we had inherited from Il Sistema. By September Lagorio left the group—for professional reasons—and that forced us to change several of our arrangements. It was then that we decided to purchase a Mellotron M400, which featured three prerecorded sounds: flute, cello, and strings. Museo Rosenbach completed the "Zarathustra" suite in November 1972, and recorded a demo of what we were working on, except for "Dopo." We sent the tape to the prestigious Casa Ricordi, because they had released two albums we greatly admired: Banco's *BMS* and *Darwin!* We sent them the tape and within a week they had gotten back to us with a response. So, in early January 1973, we reconvened to perform some material for the record company. These versions can be found on the CD *Rare and Unreleased*, issued through

The "controversial" cover of Museo Rosenbach's *Zarathustra*. "In Nietzsche's book *Also Sprach Zarathustra*, Zarathustra was the prophet of the 'Superman,'" says Alberto Moreno. "Unfortunately, Nietzsche's concept of the Superman was simplified and distorted by anti-Semitic Nazi propaganda. Nietzsche proposed an evolution of man in a philosophical, *not* biological, sense. I wanted to present this much-misunderstood point of view on *Zarathustra*."

Mellow Records [MMP 103]. The material convinced the heads of the label to sign us to a three-record deal, the first of which needed to be ready by April 1973 in order for us to make an appearance at Il Festival di Musica d'Avanguardia e di Nuove Tendenze in Naples, which was running from June 7 to June 10. We went into the recording studio in early February [1973], and the recording lasted fifteen days; mixing was done in five.

WR: You wrote a twenty-one-minute or so title composition for *Zarathustra*. What is the title song about and how does it relate to Nietschze's *Also Sprach Zarathustra*? Had you just finished reading Nietzsche's *Also Sprach Zarathustra/ Thus Spoke Zarathustra*?

Moreno: In those years I studied philosophy at the State University of Milan, so I have an in-depth knowledge of Nietzsche's works, having read all his books. When we recorded the LP we immediately thought we could have a concept album, similar to Banco's *Darwin!* We used the character of Zarathustra—Nietzsche's fictionalized version of the historical figure—because the language of the book, *Also Sprach Zarathustra*, is rich in evocative images. The structure of *Also Sprach Zarathustra* is based on "speeches" given by Zarathustra. We decided to build a suite that recounted Zarathustra's descent from the mountain after a period of meditation and his encounters with certain characters, who represent different schools of thought that the prophet criticizes. The composition of the music, however, occurred in fragments, in the sense that I was composing melodic themes for the piano that were then applied to each instrument or voice of the band. We demoed the piece in a variety of ways, experimenting with various adaptations that featured one choral development in which each element would play a precise part, as happens in classical music. The band members were attempting to play interlocking instrumental parts to build up the composition and recall the sound of an orchestral symphony. The use of Mellotron helped in this regard. Of course, we were a rock band, so the challenge was to balance the dynamism of classical music with the bite, the harshness and volume of rock.

WR: The opening bars of the title composition remind me (a little) of Strauss' *Also Sprach Zarathustra*. Were you influenced at all by Strauss when writing the music?

Moreno: Before we took the stage for our concerts in 1972, we used the prelude of *Also Sprach Zarathustra* as a brief introduction. I was impressed by Stanley Kubrick's 1968 film, *2001: A Space Odyssey*, and the director's use of classical music, including *Also Sprach Zarathustra*. I'm also fond of Kubrick's 1971 film, *A Clockwork Orange*, which employed Elgar's Pomp and Circumstance #1. We actually closed our concerts with a portion of that composition. When we were considering the intro to the *Zarathustra* suite we intended to create a powerful section that would paint an image of a curtain rising, revealing a powerful, evocative opening scene. The text was written during the recording process for the album by myself and Mauro La Luce, who had worked with the band Delirium. On the whole, though, the general thrust of the lyrics remained intact.

WR: There was a bit of controversy in connection with the album cover.
Moreno: For the album cover art we initially prepared a collage of images representing Zarathustra's face. Elements of this collage were fragments of Greek temples, Roman walls, etc. The result was a face formed by archaeological ruins. When we were presented this art by the record label we said the concept was good, but the images needed to be a bit stronger, more powerful. Graphic artist Wanda Spinello modified the image using the elements you now see on the cover. Frankly, we were all so engrossed in making the recording to raise too many objections. We were also young and inexperienced. The label did embark on an extensive marketing campaign around the album cover that appeared, at least initially, to be rolling out very smoothly. Controversy did occur regarding the cover, however.

The use of black color and a bust of Mussolini on the cover created a fine political mess for us. In those years the political climate in Italy was very unforgiving and we were immediately accused of being fascists. The disc was then "banned" from the radio and the promotional campaign suffered a lot. Then, when we played "Zarathustra" during our concerts we felt a degree of hostility directed toward us. When you're onstage you can't offer too many explanations about your music or your cover artwork, so we remained, for a long time, a band labeled fascist, especially in Italy.

WR: What can you tell me about each movement of the title song, "Zarathustra"?
Moreno: The suite is composed of a series of dialogues Zarathustra has with some characters, symbols of humanity. In the intro Zarathustra appears and we follow his descent from a mountain cave, his home for a decade. "L'Ultimo Uomo" is sung by Walter Franco, the lead singer of Quinta Strada. We used a distant echo on the vocals to conjure the image of Zarathustra's words echoing through the valley; the echo also represents the distance Zarathustra must travel in order to show humanity the light. "L'Ultimo Uomo," a representation of humanity's contentment and lack of creative evolution, says to Zarathustra that his journey will be useless because the world will not abandon its traditional beliefs on life, good and evil, and the afterlife. The prophet responds that the essence of existence lies in living it intensely with joy; it also lies in the concept of "eternal recurrence" of events in a person's life repeating over and over and that person embracing life, with all its pains and joys.

The dialogue is created by the contrast of two musical elements. Wolf's solemn voice expresses the prophet's sincerity, passion, and deep conviction. There's a short intermezzo, that's slightly muted, played on piano and Mellotron; a Moog takes the lead for the second dialogue during "Il Re Di Ieri," interpreted on synthesizer by Giancarlo Golzi, who is featured on vocals in "Il Re Di Ieri." Here,

Raccomandata Ricevuta Ritorno (or RRR) released only one record in the 1970s, the concept album *Per . . . un mondo di cristallo* (For a Crystal World), based on "a poor astronaut, who returns to Earth only to see that it's been destroyed," says RRR vocalist Luciano Regoli. "His thoughts about the destiny of humankind provide the narrative thread for the album's song cycle. Each track takes into consideration the various causes for this apocalyptic situation and the events that led to the destruction of the planet."

too, was the need to create a multifaceted voice. The king of "Il Re Di Ieri" thinks he rules by divine right and calls on Zarathustra to stop preaching, telling him that what he's looking for is represented by his [the king's] authority. The vocals are gentle and fragile, because the king is a man who has not evolved; he's stuck on his ancient and anachronistic beliefs. Zarathustra strenuously objects to the king's belief system as well as his rabbis' dogma, and explains that the true god is the man who is honest to his nature and without need of an afterlife or a heaven. Nietzsche believed that concepts based on the otherworldly notions were holding man back. This episode develops Nietzsche's theme of the death of the traditional God. Here Wolf's voice recalls Peter Hammill of Van der Graaf Generator and the music itself is at its most aggressive. The emotional tension rises, but is immediately diffused by a section that recalls the work of composer Giovanni "Nino" Rota, a film scorer I particularly love.

The third and last dialogue occurs between Zarathustra and the clergy. In "Al di là del bene e del male," the chorus reminds the prophet that moral law has been written in stone and has survived for centuries. To give an idea of the mass of the priests who denounce Zarathustra, nearly everyone in the band sang during this part for the studio version of the song. Zarathustra responds by criticizing the hypocrisies of religious men who preach on piousness and purity but behave badly. Once again, we return to Nietzsche's theme—proposing that humanity surpass the time-honored moral laws of civilized society. The music in this section grows in strength; it becomes more robust, more rock-like, approaching, I think, something similar to the music on Jethro Tull's *Thick as a Brick.* Guitars and keyboards mix and alternate. This sonic battle lies at the crux of the conceptual thrust of the entire album.

In "Superuomo" Zarathustra experiences a moment of weakness and begins to doubt himself and his mission. He becomes sick that nihilism—nihilism from his point of view—is destroying humanity. Here the music is as open and as empty as the soul of the prophet. That is until Zarathustra's strength of will prevails and the prophet is renewed, refreshed. In "Il Tempio delle Clessidre," Zarathustra enters the temple to better understand the passing of time. He is at peace with the knowledge that if he were to return, after his death, as the same person and feel the same joys and sadness he would gladly do it again for all eternity. Musically, the band incorporates some of the musical ideas that were kicked around by Il Sistema prior to the formation of Museo Rosenbach. An instrumental crescendo builds, interweaving guitars and keyboards conjuring the image of a labyrinth-like maze that knows no time—no future, no past. Only "the present" exists. Throughout, there are musical references to King Crimson's *Lizard,* in particular the little march, the *marcetta,* that launches the finale of the suite. At this point the music returns to the theme of "L'Ultimo Uomo" and the atmosphere is decidedly epic, featuring a symphonic crescendo. The three songs [on the second side of the original LP] that follow do not relate to the Zarathustra dialogs, but are presented as discourses on specific topics. In this way, the "concept" is carried through via an in-depth analysis of some of the thoughts inherent to Nietzsche's Zarathustra. "Degli Uomini" was composed a few days before the recording of the album. I had prepared what became the final part in which Wolf sings accompanied only by guitar and swaths of Mellotron samples. The lack of percussion expresses the empty feeling of the lyrics. In fact it's a discourse on the human race, which is unable to curb its instinct for war. It is this same theme that is developed for Museo Rosenbach's 2013 studio record, *Barbarica.*

The initial riff was a collaboration on the part of the entire band, built on the basis of some of the ideas given by guitarist Enzo Merogno, while the rondo centerpiece was proposed by Pit Corradi, and arranged in the manner of librettist John Gay's/arranger Johann Christoph Pepusch's *The Beggar's Opera.*

WR: What happened to the band immediately after the release of *Zarathustra?*
Moreno: The record label heavily promoted the album and we were booked on the main Italian music-festival circuit at that time. In addition, the album

garnered numerous reviews, which highlighted the complexity and novelty of the work. The band, however, was not fully satisfied with the recording. When the record was banned from radio broadcast there was a lot of nervousness about our future.

The material on the record officially debuted in Naples, at Il Festival d'Avanguardia e Nuove Tendenze. The concert was disrupted by a political protest, which had no connection at all to the band, but made it difficult for us to properly perform. We had already played "Dell'eterno ritorno," "Della natura," and parts of "Zarathustra." The public, disturbed by the presence of the police, showed no great enthusiasm for what we were doing onstage. The festival failed to do what we thought it would for our careers at that time. We returned from Naples very discouraged. There was a proposed summer tour of Italy, but we were totally exhausted and deflated. Plus, some of the creative choices we made in the following months were cause for serious band discussions—and creative differences. The record label continued to propose gigs for us to play, but in the summer of 1973 we only performed together five or six times. In September we had a band meeting in which we decided to take a break until the end of the year. The label reminded us that our contract dictated that we still owed two more records. All was in vain. Our break lasted until 1995!

WR: Why did the band dissolve?

Moreno: By the autumn of 1973 each one of us was busy with our lives outside of Museo. Galifi was working at a hospital in Genoa; Corradi, Merogno, and I had to finish university. Corradi eventually moved to Genoa and I to Milan. Golzi was due to leave for military service. Finally, the heads of the label accepted that Museo Rosenbach was dissolved and no longer supported us.

WR: Why did you want to re-form Museo Rosenbach in the late 1990s?

Moreno: In 1987 I proposed to Golzi and Galifi that we write and record a studio album of original material. Merogno and Corradi were very involved in their professional careers and were not interested. Galifi was particularly excited, because he managed a pub and was in a band playing blues covers. Golzi, however, instead of accepting the invite to record with us again, he joined the pop group Matia Bazar. After finding a singer, Andrea Biancheri, we started playing some new pieces along with covers in small clubs. In 1996 we added a keyboardist, Marioluca Bariona, and by December of 1998 we began to record *Exit*, which was released in the year 2000 on the Nuova Carisch label. The label signed us, yes, but there was no real budget for promotion, and the record company didn't press very many actual records. Not to mention the fact that Museo Rosenbach fans were not very enthusiastic about *Exit*.

WR: Have you seen interest in *Zarathustra* grow over the last few decades?

Moreno: From the time we broke up in 1973 until the early 1980s, around 1981, I had heard very little about *Zarathustra*. I didn't have any regrets about the whole experience, but I knew the record—and that entire time period—were part of the past. I began working as a teacher of philosophy [in Liceo Linguistico] and listened to a lot of reggae music. In 1981, a Japanese label reissued *Zarathustra* [Seven Seas, K22P-280], and from that moment on, interest in the band and the record has grown.

WR: Stefano Galifi is currently in a band whose name was inspired by one of the pieces in the "Zarathustra" suite. What are your impressions of Il Tempio delle Clessidre and its keyboardist Elisa Montaldo?

Moreno: When Galifi, with Il Tempio delle Clessidre, performed "Zarathustra" live onstage, Golzi, Marco Balbo, and I were working on *Barbarica*. We had a lot of material, but the structure of the music was not very defined. Il Tempio delle Clessidre's version of "Zarathustra" impressed us and we had discussed, among ourselves, how they had solved the issue of performing certain parts of the record live onstage. One evening, during the rehearsals for *Barbarica*, with Andy Senis on bass, Sandro Libra and Marco Balbo on guitars, Giancarlo on drums, myself on Mellotron, and Fabio Meggetto on Moog synthesizer, as a joke, we jammed to "Al di là del bene e del male." Everyone, more or less, knew the parts of the song. Andy even handled Wolf's vocal part. I think after we finished playing the song, right then and there, we looked at each other, and without saying a word, we knew, prior to recording *Barbarica*, we had to resurrect "Zarathustra." I called Wolf the day after our rehearsal, asking him if he would sing with us. He was very enthusiastic about it. Marco Balbo, however, preferred to write new material and wanted to avoid any sort of musical revival, and he decided to leave to pursue other creative paths. We tried another guitarist, Max Borelli, who came onboard in June 2012. Wolf left Il Tempio delle Clessidre and Museo Rosenbach was officially re-formed. In October of 2012 we recorded a new version of "Zarathustra," live in the studio.

Paolo Rustichelli Q&A

WR: What was it like growing up with a film composer and what was your first introduction to music?

Paolo Rustichelli: I started listening to classical music and used my grandfather's gramophone. I was listening to Toscanini [conducting] the big orchestra . . . I was impressed by the music of Beethoven. I was also hearing my father [Carlo] composing; he was always working and was a . . . prolific composer. At the time, Cinecittà was powerful—equal with Hollywood. I didn't know jazz at the time. I started playing piano, getting lessons, and my father bought me a little organ, a Vox Farfisa, when I was about ten years old. I also played bass about the time the Beatles were hitting. At the same time I had a little band and we were playing outside on the street. We had a house with a big balcony and we made a kind of exhibition, playing repertoire of the Rolling Stones and the Beatles. At the time I was singing and playing a Hofner bass, which was exactly the same bass Paul McCartney used. I spent twenty years in L.A. but I came back to Rome and I forgot everything, now being in Rome. [*Note: At the time of this interview, Rustichelli had been living in Rome from more than six years. "Though I'm preparing soon to go back in the U.S.," Rustichelli says.*]

My father was using a Hammond, Novachord, but also, for special movies, like science fiction movies, something like the theremin, called ondes Martenot, or "musical saw," as well as the Thomas Organ, which was part of Fono Roma studios instruments arsenal where he recorded a lot of his scores. In addition, my father was really proud to have used in the sci-fi movie *La morte viene dallo spazio* [*The Day the Sky Exploded*], one electric blender (smoothie blender). So I got involved with the C-3 and asked my father to buy it. He needed it for work, anyway, so I started playing the organ, which began with me listening to Keith Emerson and Jon Lord. Well, I had heard Emerson before he was with ELP, of course, so this style was part of my playing, but the organ was already part of my world. I also saw the Doors when I was in L.A. They were in the charts at that time with "Light My Fire" and I saw them at the Roxy. I was young. I'm not good with dates, but I was thirteen or fourteen years old, and, as far as I remember, Ray Manzarek was playing a Continental, which I had played, too.

But then I shifted from the bass and embraced the Hammond organ, and we made a band. Several years we tried to make it . . . We prepared the repertoire that became the *Opera Prima*. We were auditioned by some producers and . . . at the time RCA was the main label here in Italy. To make it short, I wanted to go ahead with label backing, with the drummer, Carlo Bordini. At that point the sound was completely different because the guitar and bass were out and I was the singer. So we decided to do it in a duo format.

As the band Cammello Buck, we rehearsed for two to three years before being contacted by RCA to sign with them. But Cammello Buck split, mainly for continuous frictions, heated discussions, creative differences, etc., with producers Lilli Greco and Paolo Dossena, who were assigned to us by the main bosses at RCA. This continuous state of stress and animosity among us and them came to an end with the split of the band. Guitarist Pino Belardinelli and bassist Mauro Morlacchi didn't want to sign the deal with RCA, and vice versa. The final album—*Opera Prima*—was not reflective of the arrangements made with the band. It took a lot of work with many, many recording sessions and overdubs.

WR: How easy was it to translate the band's music to a two-piece?
Rustichelli: At the time I was more into experimenting. The president of RCA asked me to sing like Joe Cocker style.

WR: Almost a strained vocal approach . . .
Rustichelli: I can sing this way or [sings high pitched], so my voice was flexible. You must understand that, again, at that time I was really young and

"During the making of *Opera Prima*, RCA played a strong role directing the words of the songs, through their lyricist Paolo Dossena and
producer Lilli Greco," says Paolo Rustichelli. "However, the basic
ideas were mine, and the whole album was dedicated to the 'universal
life power.'"

RCA dictated mostly the way to go in production. Producers Lilli Greco and
Paolo Dossena ... wanted me to sing with a raspy tone. In particular, having
a really flexible voice-tone range, I deliberately exaggerated my raspy vocal
performances in order to "discourage" Greco and Dossena to use my voice that
way. Instead they were delighted and enthusiastic with those takes, and then
that voice remained. I tried then to buy the master tapes from RCA in order to
remix and sing the songs again but I was unable. If I had known they were going
to take the raspy voice I would have done something different, better.

WR: Were you compared to your father initially?
Rustichelli: You have to compromise yourself a little and, especially with the
shadow of my father, and I'm being frank by saying that people had asked me,
several times, to compose something in the way of my father. I say, "Yes, if a
scene requires a Rustichelli style." In the end it became a very obnoxious thing
to be asked this, and I wondered if I had made a mistake in going into scores
and being Carlo Rustichelli II. Maybe.

WR: How did you come to the attention of Miles Davis?

Rustichelli: I was lucky that he listened to the demo I made so he started this new project that changed my life in the direction of smooth jazz. I went to the U.S., and recorded with Santana [the song "Get On"] . . .

WR: What can you tell me about recording with Miles Davis?

Rustichelli: "Get On," as you know, is part of the album *Mystic Man*. It's a song dedicated to Santana, with a typical cha-cha rhythm. Miles is also playing the Harmon trumpet. It was, unfortunately, a really fast session with Miles because he was busy and his health was bad. Carlos plays beautifully . . . and he always wanted to play with Davis. We recorded in L.A. and in San Francisco at Record Plant Studio in Sausalito.

WR: How was the *Opera Prima* record tracked?

Rustichelli: We tried to do it like it was a live concert. I played the C-3 and the bass with the Moog or with the ARP 2006, a monophonic synth. I also had a Mellotron. Most of the time we tried to emulate a live concert. When it was impossible we did some overdubs. Later, when I had my studio in my house with MIDI without the sequencer, I had to do all overdubs. That was much more difficult. Everything was synced with SMPTE . . . Today, with sequencers, you can play everything from one keyboard. I also use plug-ins now, so I can use a C-3 plug that recreates the Hammond sound. Plus, my old C-3 disappeared in the U.S. I was really mad at the time.

WR: How did it disappear?

Rustichelli: I gave it to Keith Emerson when he composed the soundtrack for *Inferno*, the Dario Argento movie. They needed a C-3 organ, Hammond.

WR: Are you saying Keith didn't give it back?

Rustichelli: No! He gave it back to me, but then years later I went to the U.S. I thought it was safe, gave it to some people to take good care of, but it was stolen. They said it was broken, but I believe it was stolen.

WR: Getting back to *Opera Prima*: Is the album a concept record?

Rustichelli: The album has several songs that were written over a few years, so it was not a concept album. In fact, after this album, I had an idea of doing a progressive, classical rock album, taking some famous classical pieces and interpreting them. But then, the president of RCA didn't like it. During the making of *Opera Prima*, RCA played a strong role directing the words of the songs, through their lyricist Paolo Dossena and producer Lilli Greco. RCA decided to have an Italian version of the songs and the whole album had an Italian title. However, the basic ideas were mine and the whole album was ideally dedicated to the "universal life power." The song "Natività" was the opening song of the album, which implies a birth, a new human life. "Dolce sorella" is the name of life, which is like a sweet sister, who lives with us until the end of our human experience. "E svegliarsi in un giorno" is the day after you're born, your adolescence, good years, like a day full of light.

"E svegliarsi in un giorno" was composed by me to be part of the repertoire of Cammello Buck. Originally, the text was in English. A version of the song, not played by the band though, but by me and other people of the film score orchestra, was used in the movie *Don Camillo e i giovani d'oggi*. The movie version of the song, in the original English version, called "To Wake Up in the Morning," was recorded at Fono Roma studios, because the movie scored by my father was recorded there.

WR: Why didn't RCA's president like the idea of taking classical pieces and interpreting them in a rock style?

Rustichelli: He wanted to add words to make it more commercial. For example, I did the Vivaldi piece, *Spring*, and was asked to add words. I said, "To put vocals on this music would make it grotesque." Then he said, "We don't do anything, then." So, I broke the deal with RCA. People said I was crazy to do that. The label was great, but it was not for me. At this point I shifted to soundtrack work.

I would like to clarify, also, that RCA imposed the notion that the songs on *Opera Prima*, those with words, needed to be in Italian language. Then the lyricists working with RCA translated more or less the original English version of the songs that I composed and wrote the words.

WR: Why did you write the song "Cammellandia," which I believe translates to "In the Land of the Camel"?

Rustichelli: The song was long—nine minutes—and the idea was to make a video with an animated camel walking across the desert. Actually, it would have been dancing. I had a vision of a camel dancing and clicking its hoofs, following the rhythm of the music. It never happened, though.

WR: Regarding imagery, the cover photograph is iconic.

Rustichelli: The cover was chosen by the president of RCA, as a kind of romantic picture. Now it makes me smile, but at the time me and Carlo were pissed about it.

WR: I've heard about things such as Hobbit Camps. What can you tell me about the connection between J. R. R. Tolkien, prog rock, and the political climate in Italy in the 1970s?

Rustichelli: It's "disturbing" for me remembering past fights, putting music second, in the name of this fucking useless politics. Also, it pisses me off, thinking of what we, the Italian progressive bands, could have done had we been adequately supported by the Italian media. In Italy, it was a fact that in some minds prog rock was considered belonging to fascism. This is pretty much the same problem Tolkien encountered with critics around Europe and this is why his masterpiece was considered a "bible of fascists." As I said about synths, you need to understand, that a lot of things drastically changed around that time: synths are now a common thing and political ideology has become somewhat obsolete. But at the time the situation was completely upside down. The era from 1960–1970 was full of ideological and political tensions. The flower-power hippie movement was the U.S.'s answer to Vietnam. In Europe, the tensions were mainly among communists and fascists. If you were not communist you were considered most likely a fascist.

Crafty Hands

Happy the Man

S tanley Whitaker, son of a U.S. Army colonel, and future Happy the Man vocalist and guitarist, spent two years in Spain with this family before moving to Germany where he lived out his high school years of the late 1960s and early 1970s.

Whitaker's experience in Germany afforded him the opportunity to witness, firsthand, the spread of progressive rock from his catbird seat in central Europe. "I saw a number of bands on their first European tours when I lived over there," Whitaker says. "I saw Yes in Frankfurt at the Zoom Club, ELP, Gentle Giant. . . ."

When Whitaker and his family returned to the States in 1972, the young guitarist attended Madison College, now James Madison University, hearing the echoes of prog rock in his ears.

"I was living in Germany when I applied for school, and signed up as a guitar major," says Whitaker. "Well, after being accepted they told me that they didn't offer a guitar major. They told me I had to change instruments. I went to violin, although I never played it before. They did alert me to the fact that they had a jazz program and that I should get into that."

As it so happens, an up-and-coming musician and future Happy the Man keyboardist/horn player, Frank Wyatt (born Frank Crawford),[1] was the tenor sax player for the program's jazz band. Wyatt was a self-taught keyboardist, and an unorthodox piano player at that, who composed music with nearly indecipherable jazz-like chord structures. "I met him and we clicked," says Whitaker. "We became roommates."

Indiana Connection

Meanwhile, in the Midwest two musicians were fixing to enter the professional music world when fate stepped in. "Rick [Kennell] and I grew up together, and played in Fort Wayne, Indiana, with Cliff [Fortney, vocalist/flute player]," says Mike Beck, drummer/percussionist. "I joined a band called Monolith and about that time Rick went to the service [in Germany] and that broke up our partnership. That's when he met Stanley."

Kennell, still in the military, informed Beck and Fortney of Whitaker. (Kennell joined the band upon returning from military service.) "Next thing

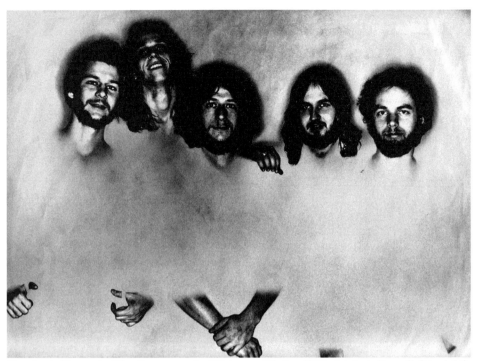

The classic Happy the Man lineup, on the LP sleeve of their self-titled debut album (left to right): Mike Beck, Stanley Whitaker, Frank Wyatt, Rick Kennell, and Kit Watkins.

we knew we were living out in Harrisonburg, Virginia," says Beck. "At that point Stanley and Frank were in a dorm and we camped with them and started rehearsing."

While they hadn't really found a suitable keyboardist (David Bach, a member of Shady Grove, Whitaker's German-based band, was the keyboardist for a brief time), a local Harrisonburg whiz by the name of Christopher "Kit" Watkins had come to the attention of the fledgling band. "His technique was fantastic," says Wyatt. "Both of his parents are classical piano teachers. All his life he was raised with playing classical piano. Then on the Moog he was like Jan Hammer and Rick Wakeman and Keith Emerson."

In the years before the band was signed with Arista, HTM experienced some personnel turnover, usually involving lead singers. Fortney was one of the band's original vocalists. (Some of the band's early material with Fortney, such as "Don't Look to the Running Sun" and "Passion's Passing," can be found on *Beginnings*, released via Cuneiform Records in 1990.)

Dan Owen, a singer whose name is spoken of in hushed tones in progressive rock circles, and who'd go on to record with Fort Wayne, Indiana–based progressive rock band Ethos, became HTM's vocalist for a brief period. "Dan was in Atlantis, our high school band," says Wil Sharpe, former guitarist with Ethos and head of Sharpe Entertainment. "A killer singer, and he also played bass. Just an angelic voice."

"I grew up with Dan," says Beck. "Magnificent singer and a magnificent songwriter to begin with, and a great person. A reclusive person, stays to himself; a perfectionist."

Happy the Man's fusion of orchestral and European musical traditions, sly wit, a sense of the ridiculous, and upbeat jazz (perhaps featured most prominently in guitarist Stanley Whitaker's searing solos and Wyatt's melodic sax work) was gaining popularity in the northern Virginia/D.C. area live circuit. The band's fluid, technical chops and command of odd times and polyphony floored some who saw them.

The band was constantly pushing itself to new creative heights. One of HTM's more serious creations, "Death's Crown," developed into a multimedia extravaganza. Written in 1974, "Death's Crown" was envisioned as an entire theatrical production, complete with lighting and dancers, which was originally staged in Harrisonburg, Virginia.

"'Death's Crown' was about a forty-five-minute production," remembers Wyatt, "and we had dancers, a central character, and media projection. It was really about one of the cards found in the tarot, the Hanged Man. The story went that a guy gets killed and the plot follows his trip into the afterlife. As he's leaving his body, flashing before his eyes are certain isolated events of his life."

"The theater in Harrisonburg was set out in the woods," adds Beck. "We had friends of ours, modern dancers, and we rented out a theater for several shows. We had this big bulk of music that . . . we crafted into a live performance. Some tunes were broken up that way. 'Open Book' [from 1978's *Crafty Hands*] was part of the larger piece. . . ."

Although the work didn't get much further than the local production, at least at that time, it provided a great resource for the band: HTM siphoned off sections of the masterwork for their live performances. The music for the show had never been released in its entirety until 1999, when Cuneiform Records issued the CD, *Death's Crown*, which contains a thirty-eight-minute version from a band rehearsal.

Today, Wyatt admits that he had other plans for the work. "After Happy the Man split up I was hoping to get some financial backers to put on the production [in New York]," says Wyatt. "Eddie Kenestrick, a New York theater director, who was working at Madison College when we were there, was trying to give us stage direction and help us with our stage presence. He had moved back to New York and . . . we were going to produce this production, an Off-Off-Broadway production. Then the backers pulled their money out, because they had some commodities option come up. I got a job in . . . the cabinet-making business and I became a carpenter and general contractor."

Goodbye to Dan

Despite writing the lyrics to HTM's most brazen composition, Owen decided to call it quits. "We played out a few times with him," says Beck. "I can't answer why Dan left. It just didn't work. It was a chemistry thing, and we were so tight at that point, but something just didn't lock in."

"When we went to New York to record some songs for RCA, pre-Capitol, Dan Owen couldn't deal with the pressures of New York City, being a small-town Indiana boy," adds Sharpe. "He ended up quitting the band [Ethos] at the time, which hurt because he was the voice."

It wouldn't be the last time the HTM gang would circle in Owen's orbit. "Kennell has been courting Dan to get his original tunes to get them out," says Beck. "But Dan does his thing at home and is happy doing that. After Happy the Man broke up, Rick, Dan, and myself formed a band in New York. We had had a house rented and we were working on his tunes. We were going to get a deal, but that didn't work out. That was the last time I worked with Dan on a serious note."

Instrumental Fundamental

The band bounced around the D.C. area in towns such as Reston, Arlington, and Harrisonburg, living, working, and playing out—as a largely instrumental band. Difficult as it is to believe today, HTM was breaking through to an audience, even in the era of soft rock, disco, and the emergence of New Wave or punk. Before long HTM was represented by the venue Cellar Door, which had developed into a management company.

Adding to the band's live appeal, percussionist Beck brought a certain acrobatic flair to HTM's performances and quickly became the focal point of the show. Beck's setup was impressive—it was really two kits in one: a rock kit and behind it another station for his percussion equipment and odd bits of gear. "Everybody called it the Cage," says Beck, who says he was influenced by King Crimson's Jamie Muir and Bobby Colomby from Blood, Sweat & Tears. "It might have been twelve feet wide by twenty-five feet long. The front room, and I called it a room, because I would walk to get to the timpani and chimes, the orchestral stuff. I ended up wearing dancing tights because I was active. I was doing this almost theatrical performance kind of thing. . . . I saw myself as a percussionist in an orchestra."

With enthusiasm building for the band's show—and sensing HTM's confidence—Cellar Door sent the band on auditions for labels such as Passport and Arista. "Cellar Door Management got us the showcase at the Ritz in Manhattan," says Wyatt. "It was a showcase for Clive Davis."

Arista liked what it saw but didn't commit right away. And just as Happy the Man was waiting for the company to produce "papers," and officially seal the deal, some very interesting developments were occurring. Former Genesis

vocalist Peter Gabriel was considering HTM as his backing
band. It's believed Gabriel was
aware of the band because members of Genesis' tour crew were
longtime friends of Kennell and
Beck, and periodically, the HTM
guys would slip cassette tapes to
them in the hopes that, maybe,
Genesis would listen to them.[2]
Apparently, Gabriel did.

"I remember Peter coming
over to Reston, Virginia, where
we were living, and rehearsing
'Slowburn' and 'Here Comes the
Flood,' which wound up on his
first solo album," says Beck.

"I think there were two or
three bands in England and two
or three here in the States Peter
was checking out," says Whitaker.
"We had heard all these other
horror stories in which he would
spend ten or fifteen minutes,
get flustered at a rehearsal, and
leave. Anyway, it was the day after
my birthday, June 28, 1976, and

Stanley Whitaker, August 2013, in Bluemont Vineyard,
Bluemont, Virginia.   *Photo courtesy of Peter Princiotto*

I was 22 years old. We got to rehearse with him for seven and a half hours.
He wanted us exclusively, but we were ready to be signed to Arista. [Peter's
management would call] and I'd say the same thing every time: 'Happy the
Man has been together five or six years now, we have a record deal on the table.
It's not signed, but we are real close to signing our own thing. If we get your
project, we'll give you top priority and we will put Happy the Man on the back
burner. . . .' Ultimately he may have aided in Arista offering us our record deal
a little quicker. They were well aware that Peter was courting us. Peter made it
real clear that he wanted me, and Kit, mostly. He liked the other guys, but felt
he could get other people to fill those holes. I felt that was a no-no. Speaking
for Kit, I knew he wouldn't do that, either.

"Three years later," Whitaker continues, "he offered me a shot to play with
him, again, around 1980. At that point I was trying to get the band Vision up
and running. Vision was with Rick [Kennell] and a remarkable singer, Rocky
Ruckman, who I had found in Cumberland, Maryland. He had a voice to end all
rock voices. I had that already in motion when Peter's management called and

said, 'Peter would like you to send a tape over and be a part of this record. . . .' If I have any minor regrets it would be that third record."

"We worked so hard to get signed on our own accord," says Beck. "Tough choice. I would have loved to play with Peter. We had a great time rehearsing with him. We got signed to Arista and that was that."

Debut

Ken Scott, who was known for his work with acts such as the Beatles and Mahavishnu Orchestra, was the band's first-choice producer. The band remembers the sessions with Scott at A&M Studios in Hollywood as being educational but challenging—the experienced producer demanded near perfection from HTM.

"We didn't do a whole lot live in the studio," says Whitaker. "We might play a song live, but he would only take the drums and bass for the most part. [Scott] wanted every single note of guitar double tracked. So every single note of guitar on that first record is double tracked and all the solos, every guitar solo on that first record, he had me double track, as well. On 'Knee Bitten Nymphs in Limbo,' he had me learn the whole solo an octave lower and play it at half speed. I did that and he did his little tape magic and brought it up to full speed."

"We'd record a song and [Scott] would say, 'Can you play it from the second verse out?'" says Rick Kennell. "So we would play it from the second verse out. Then [Scott] would say, 'Can you play it from the bridge out?' And we would do that. Then he'd say, 'Can you play just that last section?' We'd do that and then go into the mixing room, and he'd say, 'Go play pinball. Get lost.' Then he would put it together and when he was done we'd listen to a perfect take of us playing the song. Really, the only song on the first album that we made it all the way through, with no edits is, believe it or not, 'Befrost' ['Upon the Rainbow']. 'Befrost' was one take, start to finish."

HTM's self-titled 1977 debut was an amalgam of tricky bits, difficult-to-play sections, and production wizardry, boasting such tracks as the Whitaker-penned, cartoon-inspired "Stumpy Meets the Firecracker in Stencil Forest," "Mr. Mirror's Reflection on Dreams," "Knee Bitten Nymphs in Limbo," and Frank Wyatt's "New York Dream's Suite."

"'Stumpy . . .' is a cartoon that I had in my head when I wrote that song," says Whitaker. "I never drew it out, but I have envisioned what he'd look like. The top of his head would be like the old Acme missiles in the *Road Runner* cartoons. The bottom part of him looks like a little stumpy mushroom with little legs and little arms.

"I've never been asked about 'Knee Bitten . . . ,' but that was a wacky title that was inspired by my time in high school in Germany," Whitaker continues. "It was just something silly that fifteen- and sixteen-year-olds were doing. We had, probably, partaken of certain substances and we discovered that biting a person's knee would create a very sensual, sensitive experience. I don't know about the ' . . . Limbo' part. It may have been something that the music evoked."

Wyatt's "On Time as a Helix of Precious Laughs" was developed from a sci-fi concept with which the songwriter had been working. "I was thinking about the concept of time," says Wyatt. "Sometimes you're working and time is dragging by. And then at other times, if you are sitting around with people and telling stories and laughing, time is no longer a part of the equation. That's why I figured that time is a helix of those precious laughs: those milestones are what help you escape the concept of time, by not being aware of it."

The closing song, "New York Dream's Suite," is among Wyatt's best and most evocative work, and was originally augmented with lyrics and vocals by Dan Owen.

"I was from a really small town, Galax, Virginia," says Wyatt, "and there's nothing but some furniture factories there. The first time I had been to New York was because Frank Levi, the roadie for Rick Wakeman with Yes, who I was talking with once, said, 'Yeah, come up to New York, mate, and hang out with us.' I was a kid from Virginia, a town for five thousand people, and seeing New York was just incredible. I was digging it. He was taking me around to all the premier places—Max's Kansas City, Village Vanguard. We had a blast.

"After this experience, I returned to New York, and I stayed with some friends in Staten Island," continues Wyatt. "I would get up early every morning and take the ferry. I'd be wandering around the city. Then I'd go back [to Staten Island] and sit down at the piano and ['New York Dream's Suite'] is what came out. That was my impressions of being in Manhattan, being on my own, just wandering around, and sticking my nose in places, exploring."

"I was really sad that we had to rework that one without vocals, because I really liked that one a lot," says Kennell. "We had Dan playing bass on that as well. Two bassists."

Despite some deeply personal—and otherworldly—playing, the record did not make much of a splash on the charts. The issue with Happy the Man was never their playing: it was finding the right venues and booking the right kinds of concerts in order to properly target an audience receptive to their style of art-rock.

"Cellar Door was okay at the time, but they didn't know what to do with a progressive rock act," says Whitaker, "or they would have brought us to Europe. We were getting stuck on the strangest shows . . . We did the arena in Commack, Long Island, opening for Hot Tuna. I remember we walked out and got pelted with beer bottles. You know, 'Hot fucking Tuna. Hot fucking Tuna . . .' There were a couple of shows that the manager of Hot Tuna said, 'Why don't you guys stay back and you'll still get paid.'"

The conspiracy theorist in the writer wonders if there wasn't more happening behind the scenes. Hot Tuna weren't nearly as technically adept as Happy the Man were. Over the years you hear stories about headliners sabotaging up-and-coming acts. I could find no evidence of this vis-à-vis Hot Tuna, but incidents such as these do seem suspicious.

Ryche Chlanda, also of an American progressive rock band, New Jersey's Fireballet (originally called the Fire Ball Kids), had similar experiences in the 1970s, and remembers opening for the likes of Black Sabbath and Alice Cooper.

"If you're a progressive band that has quiet passages with a guy playing xylophone, you don't want to support Black Sabbath," says Chlanda. "People will throw things at you. We were opening for Alice Cooper in upstate New York, playing an English-style rock. I remember the incident clearly. There was this beautiful girl. Second row, actually. She stood up, and I thought, 'This is nice. We have a fan here.' Then she whipped a Twinkie at me. A Twinkie was the worst thing in the world to get hit with. You can shake off a bottle. If you get hit with a Twinkie and hits your guitar neck, it turns into glue. You're done. I definitely think she knew what she was doing. I think we left the stage after that and gave it up."

Was this mischievousness or cruelty? Most likely, it was down to the fact that not everyone in the American recording industry had a great read on how to handle progressive rock acts. Beyond this, the road was tough for underground American progressive rock bands for other reasons. Although all the technical angles were covered, Kennell says that the emotional toll of playing the band's music was a hefty price to pay night after night.

"Part of the problem I had when we played this music live was that there's so much emotion that it became draining to play the songs," says Kennell. "Not physically draining, but emotionally draining. Sometimes I would go offstage and just collapse. I couldn't do anything for fifteen minutes except veg out. A good example would be the song 'Ibby It Is' [from 1978's *Crafty Hands*]. It goes through every emotional possibility from delicate and intricate sections to the balls-to-the-wall ending.

"If you were ever going to play one tune that's representative of the band, I think 'Ibby' would probably be one of my first choices," Kennell continues. "Frank Wyatt's girlfriend at the time, who unfortunately passed away a few years after the band broke up, during childbirth, I think, was an artist and art student and was working with Frank on an animated project. There were storyboards, even. I don't remember if I ever saw the final cartoon, but I know it was very ambitious. We had a road-crew guy named Izzy [thanked in the original LP's liner notes], and he was a cartoon character in himself, and Frank always says that Izzy was the inspiration, but he wanted to change the name to 'Ibby.'"

"'Ibby' was one of the most difficult things I wrote on piano for myself," says Wyatt. "It's about a cartoon character that wants to be a real boy. I had visions of this vaporous cartoon character, made up of rainbow-color mist. Then when approaching the possibility of actually becoming a real person, he discovered what it was like to be human and the less he wanted to do it.

"I remember I was playing piano," Wyatt continues, "and Kit was in the kitchen cooking breakfast and we were talking, 'What are we going to call this song?' We had this big roadie, whose name was Izzy. I didn't want to name this character after a real person. I said, 'How about Ibby?' And Kit said, 'Yeah. Ibby it is!'"

Despite the whimsical nature of the music, tensions were growing behind the scenes. For one thing, some members wanted the music to move in a slightly different direction. Beck, the band's percussionist/drummer par excellence, was the first to leave, under circumstances that are still not fully understood. The catchall "creative differences," ironically, probably best sums up the feeling in the band at the time. Beck was gone, and with him went an enormous part of the band's stage show.

"I had known Mike since I was twelve years old," Kennell says. "The live show *was* Mike. He was the star. He stole the show. But he got it in his head that this was the case and that got to some of the guys in the band. You know, 'We'll show you.' Of course it wasn't the same without him."

Beck's replacement, Ron Riddle, was a hard-hitting rock drummer with serious chops; the perfect person to succeed Beck as the drummer for the band. "We had played the Cellar Door in D.C., and I was out in the streets one day and Ron was tacking up some fliers for some clinics he was doing," says Beck. "We became friends and he used to come to the shows."

Prior to joining Happy the Man, Riddle was in a New England band called Waves with future Cars keyboardist Greg Hawkes. "Waves was an experimental jazz-rock fusion band with Greg on saxophone, flute, and clarinet," says Riddle. "Greg and I met at Berklee College. Waves really turned into the Cars. We hooked up with Ric Ocasek and Ben Orr and we started working on their material and the band was called Richard and the Rabbits at that point."

Riddle moved to the D.C. area after Waves fell apart and was teaching drum lessons. One night at the Cellar Door, watching Happy the Man, has stuck with Riddle. "Mike hit one of his wind chimes and a small piece of metal was sent flying off the stage and landed out into the audience, right at my feet," says Riddle. "I always thought it was a sign."

With Riddle onboard, the band rekindled their working relationship with Ken Scott at Chateau Recorders in North Hollywood for their second album, 1978's *Crafty Hands*, a more aggressive outing whose fire is not weakened by the band's increasing proficiency. "We had a lot more confidence for the second record," says Whitaker. "I also put my foot down about how I wanted to achieve my guitar tone and doing all of these overdubs."

Riddle brought in the song "Service with a Smile," cowritten by the drummer and Hawkes. "They liked the tune," says Riddle. "It's actually in 11/8. It's a very fun time signature to play in."

As much as Riddle was contributing to the band, he was beginning to feel a tad bit self-conscious. "Ken was not happy that I was playing drums," says Riddle. "He thoroughly expected to see Mike Beck there. And wasn't really in the loop. I think that threw him."

KIT & COCO
IN TIME

After HTM, Kit Watkins and Coco Roussel formed the keyboard and drum duo Kit & Coco. For 1985's *In Time*, recorded at Watkins' home studio, Kit "programmed drum patterns on a drum machine with some specific sounds," says Roussel, who used a host of percussion instruments for the recordings, including 13″ and 14″ circular saw blades in lieu of gongs.

"At the time, we didn't realize, but no matter how much we rehearsed it, Ron left a certain amount of room for spontaneity," says Kennell. "This is the concept of, 'Let Ron play it three or four times and one of the takes will be brilliant, and you use that one, and then we all mold ourselves to that.' He was a click track freak."

There's a famous story involving HTM and Scott and certain in-studio activities that won't serve anyone to repeat here. For one thing, the circumstances of which have been highly misunderstood, the author believes, and cast in dark light. In any case, Riddle picked up on this dark vibe.

"I was just remembering that that was the time of the Hillside Strangler," says Riddle, who has scored music for TV, including programs such as *Most Evil*. "I had this feeling at the time that we were exploring things musically, which was magical and mystical, but there was this other feeling, this dark energy, that was around at that time, as well. It was very intense."

Riddle's gut reaction proved prophetic. As was the case with their debut, *Crafty Hands* was not a major seller and HTM found themselves in a precarious position. "When we were working on *Crafty Hands* we found out that we had been dropped," says Whitaker. "It was like, 'Are you kidding me?' We had found out that Arista was not going to pick up our option."[3]

Riddle, who did not express any interest in touring, exited the band after the recording sessions. In fact, he wouldn't play live with the band until the year 2000, at the NEARfest prog-rock festival, for a HTM reunion.

Without a skinsbeater, HTM acted on the advice of bassist Michael Manring and keyboardist Gregg Karukas, friend of the band, who knew the French drummer Coco Roussel (Richard Heldon, Clearlight Symphony). Roussel jammed with the guys on the new material from *Crafty Hands* as well as that of the debut, and got the gig.

"Mike Beck was a percussionist and Ron Riddle was more of a rock drummer," says Coco Roussel. "My style of playing fits right in between. . . . There were some concerns at the beginning with replacing Mike. But I think these concerns were mainly from others in the band."

"My whole swan song with Happy the Man is that every record had a different drummer, and it has been hard for me, you know, as the bass player to adjust," says Kennell. "I had to get used to a different drummer with every recording it seemed like."

After working on music that would later emerge on their *3rd: Better Late . . .* record, from 1983, the band was clinging to some hope that they could still find a major label deal. None materialized. Around this time keyboardist Watkins accepted an offer to play with Camel, after Pete Bardens had vacated the keyboardist spot in that British prog-rock band, and entered into a situation similar to Happy the Man (i.e., dual keyboarders). Watkins did some recording with Roussel, including 1981's *Labyrinth* and 1985's *In Time*, but from the early 1980s or so on, Watkins had left the world of progressive rock.

"I think Kit grew weary of the rock world," says Mike Beck. "After he went with Camel and after having experienced some life-changing personal events, he withdrew from it permanently. Plus, Kit could do so much on his own. He was like Ron Riddle. He was happy doing that. He didn't need the embellishment at that point."

Without much support from either a label or management, without a star keyboardist, and with the sea change in the music industry that was already underway when the band was signed to Arista, Happy the Man didn't have a hope in hell. They split in 1979.

Happy Men, Again

Happy the Man may have been gone but they weren't forgotten. In subsequent years, the Cuneiform record label issued a few HTM records, including performances recorded in 1978 titled simply *Live*, *Beginnings*, *Death's Crown*, and reissued the band's posthumous third studio record, composed of demos, *3rd: Better Late . . .* , which includes bonus material.

The Muse Awakens, a studio record of new music, appeared in 2004 on Inside Out Music, featuring Wyatt, Whitaker, Kennell, and new members keyboardist David Rosenthal and drummer Joe Bergamini. (Riddle was asked first but scheduling and traveling distance from Ithaca to rehearsals in Baltimore made it near impossible to carry on as a unit.) Two years later Whitaker and Wyatt recorded their *Pedal Giant Animals* disc, which veers, on occasion, toward the mystical and esoteric, and organized a new prog band, Oblivion Sun, whose self-titled debut was released in 2007 and was followed by *The High Places* in 2012, featuring a title track that links conceptually with early work done by Oblivion Sun and HTM.

In both cases, Whitaker's and Wyatt's songwriting shine (as do Whitaker's vocals, especially on *Pedal Giant Animals*, which, incredibly, contains material rejected by the re-formed HTM band). In addition, Wyatt grabs the spotlight, for a change, coming out from Watkins' shadow as a keyboardist.

The D.C. Area Scene

In the mid-1970s, an eclectic progressive rock and avant-garde rock scene was gathering steam in the D.C. area, thanks to bands such as the Muffins, Happy the Man and However, who were playing music that was reminiscent of Gentle Giant, the Canterbury Scene bands, Zappa, and Henry Cow.[4]

The Muffins' were unusual, even for some of the more unusual D.C. bands. Their "live in the studio" approach undoubtedly impacted their overall creative direction in the 1970s and early 1980s.

Produced by Henry Cow's Fred Frith, the Muffins' hyper-frenetic *<185>* is seen as the band's high-water mark of their early years. Released just before the band split up in the early 1980s, the record contained moments of intense musicality and experimentation, such as "Zoom Resume" and "Under Dali's Wing," the latter featuring backward/reverse drum sounds. (Members of the Muffins played on Frith's 1980 solo record, *Gravity*.)

Soon after the release of *<185>* the Muffins disbanded. (They would return, however, in the 1990s after a long absence, exploding with material for their 1998 album, *Double Negative*. From an outside perspective, it seems the Muffins had their shit down, navigating an incredible diversity of compositions and doing it with a newfound energy. By 2012, the Muffins had released *Mother Tongue*.)

Another band, However, owes something to the likes of Frank Zappa and Weather Report (even the Windham Hill band from Chicago, Shadowfax). We shouldn't lose sight of the fact that Zappa himself was born in Baltimore, Maryland, in 1940, less than forty miles from D.C., and while he became an international figure while living on the West Coast, many of his lyrics, it would seem, were informed by his life in the Mid-Atlantic—everything from gas masks to the impact of the military industrial complex on our everyday lives.

"Progressive rock was strong here, in the D.C. area and the Northeast in general, for a number of reasons," says Peter Princiotto, bass player and songwriter for However. "We had some record stores here that carried imports. We had a station by the call letters WGTB, out of Georgetown University, that played a lot of progressive rock. . . ."

"There was also a confluence of musicians who ended up here, and it was a kind of incestuous community in which Happy the Man were here and the Muffins were here—we all sort of knew each other," says However guitarist Bill Kotapish.

However had its roots in the band Black Orchid, which featured Princiotto, the Muffins' Tom Scott, and drummer Tom Grignon. Eventually Peter met Kotapish, and saxophonist Ken Hitchcock, and went on to form Ancient Moon Orchestra, which covered music by ELP, King Crimson, Return to Forever, Mahavishnu Orchestra, Bill Evans, Charlie Parker, and Miles Davis, and also performed original material.

"There was a fair sprinkling of straight-ahead jazz [in our music], and we were able to get into some of these jazz clubs in Washington," Kotapish says. "We were way younger than any of the patrons. In fact, we wouldn't have been allowed in the clubs because we were so young."

The tight-knit D.C.-area progressive music scene of the 1970s produced some real musical gems, including However.

A few years later, future However vocalist/multi-instrumentalist Bobby Read and Princiotto were attending school at the New England Conservatory when Kotapish moved up to Boston in late 1976, and had mentioned the name However to the artist Mark Stuart Holmes. Holmes, who'd later create the cover artwork for the band's two early studio records, had heard about the band's debate regarding their name. Although some in the band were not convinced, at first, by the name However, Holmes later sent a postcard to the guys, addressed to However, which convinced them that this "evocative" name was the right choice.

Band members seemed to drift in and out in the late 1970s and early 1980s. The lineup that performed at venues with the most regularity was Princiotto, his brother, drummer Joe Princiotto, Kotapish, Bobby Read, and Don Berkemeyer (vocalizations and wind instruments). There weren't many options regarding venues in those days, so However created their own scene. For their first show, they rented McLean Community Center in McLean, Virginia. "We got permission to play there, promoted it ourselves, invited . . . family and friends, and whoever else we could drag there, and put on a show," says Kotapish.

After several shows, the band focused on studio work, recording their first album, 1981's *Sudden Dusk*, featuring all of the above-mentioned musicians (augmented by others), chock-full of spritely yet dense, challenging compositions, such as "Beese" with animal sound-effects clips from the National Wildlife Federation audio library, the quirky/herky-jerky "In the Aisles" built on dissonant chord shapes and decorated with a fuzzed-out bass solo, the subtly swung collaborative effort "It's Good Fun," and "Louise Sitting in a Chair."

The title track, which refers to the effects of a midday eclipse, is largely an improvised piece that was edited in the studio. It's unclear if the piece was inspired by chance methods, such as Oblique Strategies, which Brian Eno was making famous.

"The piece, 'Sudden Dusk,'" says Princiotto, "the first half was an improv, and then Bobby [engineer, saxophonist] edited it down to create a piece out of a longer improv [we had] on tape. He picked his favorite sections and literally cobbled it together. He did that all himself. . . . The second half was different. Bill came up with a guitar idea, these swelling chords, on the spot, I think. . . . Then Bobby put a bed of saxophones over that."

Although the original band was not together very long, However created a strange but endearing blend of musical styles that sounds fresher today than ever thanks to recent reissues (via the North American East Recordings label). However would record other material, but their first record, *Sudden Dusk*, stands as a rare gem of the late progressive era.

Blinded by the Lite?

A Look Inside Prog's Number-One Song

Long before Yes' surprising and triumphant comeback with "Owner of a Lonely Heart," and predating the meteoric rise of Pink Floyd's "Another Brick in the Wall—Part II" to the top of the charts in 1980, Manfred Mann's Earth Band reigned supreme as the only major progressive, or prog-pop, band to hit pay dirt with a number-one song in the U.S.[1]

There had been number-one albums on both sides of the Atlantic, written, recorded, and produced by progressive rock bands throughout the 1970s, from Yes and ELP to Jethro Tull, but "Blinded by the Light," a song written by Bruce Springsteen, rode on or near to the top of the charts, in both America and the U.K.

Released in the heady days of August '76, the heavily edited single for "Blinded . . . ," b/w "Starbird No. 2," saturated the airwaves as it roared to number one on the *Billboard* Top 100 chart in February 1977. (It went top six in the U.K. in August 1976).

"Blinded by the Light" wasn't, of course, Mann's first taste of chart success. It wasn't even the Earth Band's for that matter. Mann's version of "Do Wah Diddy Diddy," first recorded by the Exciters as "Do-Wah-Diddy" in 1963, was a number one hit in both the U.S. and Britain in 1964; "Pretty Flamingo," which featured future Cream bassist/vocalist Jack Bruce on four-string, Mann's "Mighty Quinn," a cover of the Dylan tune "Quinn the Eskimo (Mighty Quinn)," were also U.K. number-one hits.

By the end of the 1970s, Mann had interpreted the work of a wide range of artists, from John Prine and Gary "Dreamweaver" Wright (the Cream-meets-Crimson "Give Me the Good Earth" from 1974's *The Good Earth*), Lane Tietgen, and Sue Vickers (former wife of Mann band's Mike Vickers), to poet Christopher Logue, Harriet Schock, Billy Falcon(e), Dr. John, and Mike Rudd of Harvest label signees Australian blues rock/progressive rock band Spectrum (later of Ariel).

But, perhaps more than any other artist up until the mid-1970s, Mann had earned a well-deserved reputation for reworking Dylan, a tendency Mann nurtured as far back as 1965's antiwar warhorse "With God on Our Side" (a song heavily informed by Dominic Behan's "The Patriot Game," based on traditional Irish music).

However, with the arrival on the scene of Bruce Springsteen, considered by some of the rock intelligentsia at the time to be Dylan reconfigured for the gritty 1970s, Mann widened his scope to include some new blood. Prior to *The Roaring Silence*, the Earth Band cut a version of the Boss' "Spirit in the Night" for their 1975 *Nightingales & Bombers* album. The song reappeared on a rerelease of *The Roaring Silence* in both the LP and cassette formats (respective catalog numbers BSK 3055 and MS 3055, which featured a blue-tinted cover, distinct from the flesh-colored artwork previously used for the Warner Bros./Bronze release; the original 1976 U.K. LP format release [ILPS 9357] and the U.S. LP [BS 2965] did not include "Spirit in the Night").

Double Vision

The South African keyboardist seemed duplicitous, a musician nurturing double (competing?) artistic visions, feeding a fascination with the Top 40 as well as the baroque (and jazz). Mann's jazzy slant can be heard on records stretching back to 1968's *Mighty Garvey!* and 1967's ill-received *Soul of Mann*, which contained instrumental tracks from Mann's time with the His Master's Voice (HMV) label. Mann and his frequent collaborator drummer Mike Hugg (born Michael Hug) had shown their love for jazz earlier in the 1960s, stretching back as early as the Mann-Hugg Blues Brothers (formed in the early 1960s).

It wasn't until Manfred Mann Chapter Three, a direct precursor of the Earth Band, however, that the keyboardist seemed to be following a full-on jazz and jazz-rock path. Manfred Mann Chapter Three (previously known as Emanon), co-led by Hugg, not only dabbled in jazz but mixed in funk with their rock—a far cry from the pop ditties that the world had come to know and love from Mann.

Some will no doubt take issue with this, but tracks on the band's self-titled 1969 debut (on Polydor), such as Mann's "Konekuf" and Hugg's "Devil Woman," "Where Am I Going" and "Time" were laying the very foundation of jazz-influenced prog rock. (Interestingly, Phil Collins once auditioned for Chapter Three. Didn't get the gig, but wound up playing in a little band called Genesis.)

"After all the hits, it was like [Mann] was saying, 'Okay, fuck it. I'm going to do what I want to do,'" muses well-known Chicago jazz drummer Paul Wertico, who bought the first Chapter Three record when it was first released. "His old drummer, Mike Hugg, is playing piano and singing, as well, and there's this amazing horn section with Harold Beckett on trumpet. The [first] Chapter Three record is unbelievable. I think it's one of the lost masterpieces of that time period."

"Our drummer from my old band, Procession, Craig Collinge, joined Chapter Three," says Earth Band guitarist/vocalist Mick Rogers. "Manfred nicked him, which we didn't approve of at the time. [laughs] The other thing that happened is, there's a song called 'One Way Glass' that Manfred recorded with Chapter Three and then we did with the Earth Band [which was cowritten by Chilli Willi drummer Pete Thomas, later of Elvis Costello, which appears on the Earth Band's 1972 album, *Glorified Magnified*]. Prodigy took the horn parts and put that on their album." [*Note: Kanye West also sampled a Manfred Mann's Earth Band's song, "You Are—I Am," from the Earth Band's* Angel Station, *for his "So Appalled."*]

"It was funny because [Procession] started off as a backing band for ... Norman Rowe," Rogers continues. "That's how I got out to Australia. It was called Normie Rowe and the Playboys. Norman is a big pop star in Australia, like a David Cassidy and, in fact, looks a little bit like David Cassidy. I joined that band in England and then went to Canada, in Montreal, about 1967, for the World's Fair. Then went to Australia to do a tour. What had happened is Normie had gotten called up to Vietnam, the Army, and out of the Playboys was changed a couple of personnel and we called it Procession. It was myself and Trevor Griffin, the keyboard player, who loved jazz, Brian Peacock, the bass player, who wrote for the band, as well as myself and Trevor. The drummer liked the Archie Shepp Band and really avant-garde jazz, and if you put all those influences together you have Procession."

Procession, Mick Rogers' Australia-based, pre–Earth Band group, evolved from Normie Rowe and the Playboys.

After a second Chapter Three record failed to chart, and a third was recorded and never saw the light of day, Manfred needed some stability. For a time, he was operating under the banner of Manfred Mann (a holdover from the old pop days of the 1960s) before making a conscious attempt to distance himself from his earlier work by changing the group moniker to Manfred Mann's Earth Band in 1971. (The eventual Earth Band had actually operated as Manfred Mann for a brief period. It's urban legend that artist and former Mann band member Klaus Voormann may have inspired the Earth Band moniker.)

The Earth Band wasn't "out there" musically, but far enough where pop music seemed like a foreign concept. The tension among the ranks seemed to create a hybrid progressive pop rock that included bits of jazz, classical, and blues. Of course, cynics might say that while part of the band wished it could play music in the vein of Mahavishnu Orchestra, or even Frank Zappa, Manfred was "blinded by the lite," in search of hit records hoping to move beyond jazz-rock or prog-rock musical territory. It was a source of frustration for some in the band and even led to one seismic personnel shift in the mid-1970s.

"We kept trying to pull Manfred in that direction," says Rogers.

Primer Prog

Perhaps to get a better understanding of the events that led up to the Earth Band's commercial success, we should backtrack a few albums. Albums such as *Messin'* and *The Good Earth* are colored by varying degrees of complexity, studio effects, and even prophetic lyrics and themes, such as the near-ten-minute environmentally aware "Messin'" (a holdover from the Chapter Three days), a psychedelic reworking of Chain's criminally underappreciated "Black and Blue," a number-one Australian hit, and "Buddha," a kind of Yes-meets-Black-Sabbath amalgam, propelled by a spiraling opening guitar riff anticipating Boston's "More Than a Feeling."

What Mann and the Earth Band did so effectively is erupt with classical-music-informed jazz-rock and synth-based prog-rock passages, which are seemingly launched from out of the blue. 1972's *Glorified Magnified*, which boasts Mann's "Meat," so to speak (also appears with the title "Can't Eat Meat," as the B side of the U.K. Vertigo single, 6059 083, containing A side, "Joybringer," a rock adaptation of "Jupiter, the Bringer of Jollity" from Holst's *The Planets* suite) is a jazz-rock number with spaced-out synth effects.

Meanwhile, the Chris Slade–penned bluesy number, "Look Around," makes overtures to something more complicated. The band never quite get there, however, but this could be an example of what Yes/King Crimson/Genesis/etc. drummer Bill Bruford termed "lurking" when describing how Crimson appeared poised to do something, but "[w]hether something actually happened or not seemed immaterial . . ." wrote Bruford in his 1988 book, *When in Doubt, Roll!*

Solar Fire

That damnable prog kept rear-
ing its head. When it came time
to organize the next album and
write new material, the Earth
Band would venture further out
into the musical cosmos than
they had ever before. Rogers says
that the group were influenced
by Pink Floyd at the time, and
the Earth Band's planetary concept has roots in the music of
Procession.

With the release of 1973's
Solar Fire, the Earth Band had
joined the ranks of the heavier
progressive bands of the day.
"People, in those days, were
doing albums that had a theme
about them," Rogers says.
"With Procession I used to do
the theme from 'Joybringer'—
'Jupiter,' from *The Planets* suite by
Holst, and that was a drug song
when we did it: [sings] 'Make
your stash, be careful when you
do it . . .' Then I . . . brought it to
the Earth Band. We were looking
for a single and Manfred liked
the melody, as did the rest of the
guys, and we said, 'Let's try this.'
Because it was Holst and *The
Planets* suite, we thought, 'Why
don't we stick with that planetary
theme. . . .' Bear in mind that we
were the Earth Band, right? It all
sort of tied in."

The newfangled prog-pop
outfit the Earth Band were
beginning to break ground in
the U.K. in 1973 with the Top 10
single "Joybringer." (The song

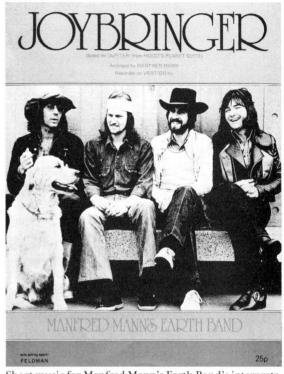

Sheet music for Manfred Mann's Earth Band's interpretation of "Jupiter, the Bringer of Jollity," from Holst's *The
Planets* suite.

"Joybringer": Classical rock at its finest.

was included on the band's 1973 concept album, *Solar Fire*, but only in certain regions.)

The Earth Band kept building its repertoire, creating more musically muscular tracks for each successive record. For instance, material on 1974's *The Good Earth*, such as "Earth Hymn" and "Earth Hymn Part 2," both cowritten by Chris Slade and Mann; "Sky High," which virtually foreshadows *The Roaring Silence*'s "Waiter, There's a Yawn in My Ear"; and the Christopher Logue poem set to music, "Be Not Too Hard," which Donovan had previously covered, had edge but never lost their pop appeal.

"'Sky High' was going to be a B side," says Rogers. "I can't remember . . . who had the melody first, myself or Manfred. But he and I would sit around a piano and I would have an acoustic guitar or something. A lot of that material happened like that. It was just sitting there and playing."

The Good Earth is perhaps most famous for the badge stamped across its front—a message congratulating the consumer for buying the record. The story goes, if you bought the album you were, in fact, purchasing a little square piece of land in Wales. According to Rogers, this was not a PR stunt.

"It's all preserves in that area," says Rogers. "There's a big TV show, *Countryfile*, and we were featured during the whole program about this, actually. Apparently *Countryfile* is one of Prince Charles' favorite shows. Whether he saw the show we were featured in, I don't know. I'll send a copy to Buckingham Palace to see what reaction I get. . . ."

After records such as *Messin'*, *The Good Earth*, and *Solar Fire*, which skillfully combined elements of pop, fusion, and prog, Manfred began to get antsy for another breakthrough cover song. He attempted to introduce "Blinded by the Light," but it was largely rejected by the trio of drummer Chris Slade, guitarist Rogers, and bassist Colin Pattenden.

Whatever power struggle existed within the band wouldn't exist for long. Reading the writing on the wall, Rogers and Mann had a sit-down to discuss the future direction of the band. "I had an offer to [play with] Zappa and got to know him fairly well and played with him," says Rogers.[2] "I became too much for the band and, I think, I had to go. It was like I was being destructive in as much that I wanted to play other things, you know? It was probably a midlife muso crisis. I worked through that. Earlier in my career I had lived in Australia and I went back through there, hooked up with some friends of mine, who are fusion players. We used to do some crazy stuff, like Ornette Coleman stuff. One moment we would be playing Ornette Coleman and the next I would be doing something from the 1950s. I'd be doing a couple of Elvis things. Even with the Earth Band, now, I do 'Shake, Rattle and Roll' on my own. I went to Los Angeles for a while, too, and got the muso stuff out of my system and rejoined the Earth Band in 1986 and I've been there since."

New Band

Exit Rogers, enter New Zealand singer and guitarist Chris Thompson and lead guitarist Scotsman Dave Flett, both of whom cover for the position left vacant in the wake of Rogers' major withdrawal from the band. (Rogers does appear on *The Roaring Silence*, but as a backing vocalist.)

Flett remembers his early days in the Earth Band: "It got to the point where Chris Slade, Colin Pattenden, and Mick Rogers, they loved the jazz-rock, the progressive type, everything had to be in 5/4 or some strange time signature," says Flett. "Manfred said that for a year before Mick left, he had tried to present 'Blinded by the Light.' Manfred told me that every song he came up with the band said, 'Nah, nah.' I mean Mick Rogers and Chris Slade were real Frank Zappa fanatics. That was valid, but there was already a Frank Zappa. When Chris came in with this great voice and I was more like a Clapton melodic type player, the whole balance changed."

Weeks after the new recruits joined, the Earth Band were on tour of the States. "*Nightingales & Bombers* was released, and when Chris [Thompson] and I joined we'd done an American tour without recording," says Flett. "I remember, on tour, we did a few tracks from the *Nightingales & Bombers* album, including 'Spirit in the Night.' We also did [Dylan's] 'Father of Day, Father of Night,' and a couple of the newer ones, what would wind up on *The Roaring Silence*, to see how they went down."

Recorded at Mann's Workhouse studio in Old Kent Road in London, *The Roaring Silence* runs the gamut from disco to a strange hybrid of classical music, techno rock, fusion, and soul.

The first song on the record is the disorienting, synth-heavy "Blinded by the Light," boasting a stream-of-consciousness narrative inculcated with events from Springsteen's early life as an up-and-coming musician performing in seedy nightclubs in New Jersey. We're introduced to a whole freaking crew of music business and Jersey-Shore phonies, cronies, shysters, and oversexed creepizoids. This sleazy adult-oriented imagery, which sometimes appears in the form of double entendre, seems tailor-made for Mann's musically lush, psychedelic-progressive pop audio visions.

The symbolic, streetwise lyrics, which have been continually misinterpreted and/or misheard, contribute to the disorienting, carnival-like atmosphere the song evokes. (More about this gloriously unfortunate circumstance in a moment.)

Not since "Louie Louie" had there been so much confusion about what a vocalist is actually singing in a pop/rock song. The line "Revved up like a deuce, another runner in the night" has been hopelessly mangled by fans and critics alike. The lyrics have nothing at all to do with playing cards or a certain feminine hygiene product. Springsteen's version, of course, reads, "Cut loose like a deuce," which obscures the meaning of the line a bit, but the automobile

The re-released "blue" version of *The Roaring Silence* included two songs written by Springsteen.

imagery seems pretty unmistakable, whichever version we're considering.

The song also dimly recalls the hazy surrealism of the Beatles' halcyon daze a decade earlier, typified by "Lucy in the Sky with Diamonds" and "A Day in the Life" from *Sgt. Pepper's*. These songs take listeners safely on a form of psychic "tripping."

Breathy, synth-effected voices shine like shafts of lights. Flett's note-dribbling, swirling MXR phaser-inflected guitar work (and the hissing white noise that seems to shadow it) melts into Mann's intelligent use of synth—making it one of the most iconic guitar solos and instrumental breaks of the 1970s rock era. Chris Slade's sixteenth-note hi-hat beats propel the music.

"We had come back from America and we bought some equipment there," says Flett. "One was a MXR Phase 90, an orange box that was a phaser. If you listen to the 'Blinded by the Light' solo, all of a sudden I [click] this phaser and I was just trying it out, thinking I was going to do the solo, again. I did it just to see what the effect was like and it cut the volume. I went, 'Ah, shit.' I played other solos after that one, but Manfred said, 'Nah, let's stick with the original take.' I said, 'You can't do that. The volume drops because of the phaser. . . .' He said, 'Yeah, Dave, but it sounds like a real guitar player.' That phaser on 'Blinded by the Light' is almost a complete accident. I have a feeling that solo was done live, because I never really liked it. I can remember being terrified. I was thinking, 'When the band plays [this solo] back in the control room they'll hear every mistake.'"

Flett was using his famous, and then-newly-acquired Gibson "flying V" reissue model for the song. Pattenden, who went shopping with Flett in New York, had fashioned the vibrato tremolo unit on the guitar for Flett and swapped out the pickups for humbuckers. (For the band's next album, *Watch*, Flett had borrowed John McLaughlin's double neck and also his acoustic for tracks such as "California" and "Chicago Institute.")

"The strange thing was, even though it was my first time in the recording studio, sometimes Manfred would go home at the end of the day and he would tell me: 'You played the solo for two and a half minutes and we only need a minute and a half. You edit it,'" says Flett. "I would stay with the engineer and we'd cut this solo and Manfred would come in the next day, hear it, and go, 'Yeah, that sounds fine. Next!' That was a joke about my solos, Manfred would say, 'That's the trouble, Dave. You want the notes to be perfect, but you are much better when you play off the top of your head.' He said, 'Once you start thinking about it, you lose it.' Manfred had been at it longer than I had been. Before I joined the band I was driving a laundry truck!"

The electronic whirring madness of Mann's keys captures the sounds of a whirling-out-of-control merry-go-round and the wheezing broken calliope referenced in the song. (Interestingly Wikipedia refers to Mann's Moog riffs on the ten-and-a-half-minute tune "July Morning" from Uriah Heep's 1971 album, *Look at Yourself*, as being of the "calliope" variety. Ken Hensley's notes to the original LP, written July 1971, seem to suggest that Mann appeared on more than one song on the album.) In addition, Chris Hamlet Thompson's voice, which teeters between gruff and smooth the entire song, an effect not weakened by the fact that drummer Slade provides backing vocals, crops up in interesting spaces in the stereo image, helping to give the song dimension or "depth."

The Earth Band revisited "Blinded by the Light" several times, trying out different options for the chorus and even chopping up the song. "I turned to Manfred and said, 'I'm not complaining, but why is it taking so long to do this track?'" says Flett. "Manfred said, 'On the day that we release this album, if you think about your average kid, who maybe has a paper route and maybe can afford to buy an album a week, or an album every two weeks, the day we release our album, Genesis, Paul McCartney, Santana, and Eric Clapton could release their albums. The kid has enough money to buy one album.' He was right."

The album or "long" version of "Blinded by the Light" contains bits from the nineteenth-century waltz "Chopsticks"—a dissonant tune geared toward beginner piano players that celebrates or, perhaps more precisely, "enforces Western diatonic tonality," writes Scott Burnham, a professor of music at Princeton University. (Yes, "Chopsticks" was actually *composed* by someone—sixteen-year-old British girl Euphemia Allen.) In more ways than one, the song seems quite a peculiar tune to have reached the top slot on the Hot Singles chart: it captures the spirit of psychedelia while almost standing outside it.

Despite his mentor status, Mann made great use of the songwriting talents within the band's ranks. Pattenden and Slade had already proven themselves in the past, and they were called on, again, for *The Roaring Silence* as was Chris Thompson. Songs such as "The Road to Babylon," "This Side of Paradise," and even the classically informed tunes such as "Questions" and the funky fusion track "Starbird No. 2" were cowritten by Mann and Earth Band members. "Starbird No. 2" features choir-like counterpoint vocals and a melody ripped from Igor Stravinsky's *The Firebird* ballet.

The biggie, the breakthrough: "Blinded by the Light."

The Earth Band covers the Incredible String Band's Mike Heron's "Singing the Dolphin Through" featuring Colosseum's Barbara Thompson on sax, and performs a five-and-a-half-minute jazz-rock workout, "Waiter, There's a Yawn in My Ear,"[3] (partially taken from another Chapter Three holdover, "Fish"). It's the jazz-rock instrumental that may have inspired Shirtsleeve Studio, or vice versa, to create the iconic cover for *The Roaring Silence*, which is reminiscent of Hipgnosis' giant ear motif for Pink Floyd's *Meddle*.

"The record company, they came up with all these album covers," says Flett. "They said, 'Can you call it *Roaring Silence*?' One illustration had someone reading in the library and, in the back, a bookshelf falls down and, like dominoes, the next shelf falls and so on."

If cynics believed that prog had lost its way in the mid-1970s, then "Blinded by the Light," while being a massive hit for the Earth Band, manages to embody the grandeur and silliness, the headlong dive into keyboard technology, the "everything and nothing," that mainstream progressive rock seemed to have been at the time.

By early spring '77, "Blinded by the Light" and *The Roaring Silence* both had achieved gold status. Prog, it seemed, had finally gone pop, and what better ambassador to the mainstream world than the king of the (doo wah) ditty himself, Manfred Mann?

Mann's chart success would continue, at least in the U.K., with the number-six song, written by John Simon, "Davy's on the Road Again" from *Watch*, an album title inspired by a trip through Sweden. "I can tell you that we were walking through an airport in Sweden, I think, and we were seeing all these local artists' paintings on the wall," says Flett. "In one of them there was this guy running along an airplane runway with his arms outstretched. I said to Manfred, 'Look at that one.' He said, 'What caption would you give?' 'Watch. Look what I can do . . . Watch this!'"

Flett remembers the collaborative efforts being very fruitful throughout his time with the Earth Band, especially regarding the creative process for the band's next album, *Watch*. "Chris Slade had written 'Drowning on Dry Land,' and Manfred gave him a help on that. Being a drummer he wasn't instrumentalist, and six weeks before we could hand in the album, we didn't have a solo or middle piece for 'Drowning on Dry Land.' I had been messing around with something I'd come to call 'Fish Soup,' which was in the same key as 'Dry Land,' and we had been playing it. The good news was Chris' song was finished. The bad news was that Chris didn't write the whole song himself. [The song is credited to Slade, Mann, and Flett.] Chris, at that time, was into martial arts and eating brown rice and practicing tai chi. We nicknamed him 'The Guru.' He didn't drink or eat meat—he was a vegetarian. So, I decided to call it 'Fish Soup.' No big, deep meanings there."

Bassist Pattenden had exited prior to the recording of *Watch* and Thompson said farewell to the Earth Band in 1979 to form his own band, Night (only to return in the 1980s, just in time to work with future Yes man Trevor Rabin, witness the brief but memorable stint of guitarist/lead singer Steve Waller, and a mini–Earth Band resurgence courtesy of the group's cover version of Ian Thomas' "Runner," a Top 30 hit in the U.S. in 1984).

"I believe the reason Manfred has endured is because he is open to changing," says Flett, whose 2014 solo recording, *Flying Blind*, features Mann—the first time they had worked together in decades. "He's not frightened to step outside the box and try something new."

Prog Gets Punk'd

What Caused the Decline of the Genre?

D id punk rock kill prog? That's a complex question that requires more than a simple "Yes" or "No" answer. It's difficult to consider the rise of a populist movement like punk, that supposedly put power back in the hands of the disenfranchised "little guy," without discussing the dismal state of Britain's 1970s economy.

Sluggish economic growth and rising OPEC oil prices (which actually halted production of vinyl records in 1973) left Britain vulnerable to strikes by coal workers. Despite amassing 18 million tons of coal, the U.K. was in a precarious situation when the miners did indeed strike in 1972, and again in 1974, resulting in the commercial use of electricity being limited to three days per week (i.e., the Three-Day Work Order).

Public offices were required to cut their energy consumption by 10 percent so that the country as a whole could survive the winter. School children were sent home; law enforcement officers were urged to walk and not drive to, or during, work; office buildings were required to keep their temperatures below sixty-three degrees Fahrenheit; the BBC and ITV abided by a nightly curfew; and, like an image from Genesis' song "Me and Sarah Jane," the street lights were dimmed by 50 percent to conserve energy.

Perhaps the political and financial standoff was ideologically driven: Prime Minister Edward Heath, largely due to his stance on inflation and wage increases (Phase III), did not budge, and leaders of the National Union of Mineworkers flatly rejected the National Coal Board's offer of a 17-percent pay hike. (Things got heated in the run-up to the coal miners' strike: Heath had briefly considered halting unemployment benefits for the miners' families, if they decided to stop work, and one miner went on record as having admitted that what the union was proposing was "blackmail.")

Many adults who stood in solidarity with the miners left their lights on in protest, and smart-aleck youths went around the house turning on appliances or lightbulbs to poke their finger in the eye of "the man."

Writers for television programs did not hide their support for the miners, either, and artist Jamie Reid, who'd later design controversial album and single covers for the Sex Pistols, created retail-store posters that advised shoppers to buy now, before the collapse of "monopoly capitalism."

Historian Dominic Sandbrook, in his book *State of Emergency: The Way We Were: Britain 1970–1974*, theorizes that some of the effects of the oil crisis, the three-day work week, rise in unemployment, and power shortages have been overstated or misremembered by the populace at large. This has some validity, as Sandbrook convincingly makes the case for the fact that some people may have been recalling their hardships of 1970 or 1972, not 1974. In addition, the winter of '74 wasn't nearly as harsh as expected. Yet, the psychological damage was done, and other historical events, such as deadly IRA bombings, loomed like a dark cloud over Britain's political and domestic concerns throughout the 1970s.

Revolution

The table was set for revolution by U.K.'s disaffected and disenfranchised youth, convinced that the West's socioeconomic and political systems were rigged against them.

"The thing about punk in the U.K. is that it was very much in tune with the sociological conditions at the time—high unemployment, a real sense of no future," says former punk producer Mick Glossop, who worked with the late '70s Brit bands the Ruts and the Skids, the latter having featured a young Stuart Adamson, pre–Big Country fame. "The feeling was that there was no point in going to university to have a career because there weren't many jobs. That nihilistic attitude was very much a part of the new, younger generation zeitgeist."

"What women started saying, from the Slits, X-Ray Spex, Honey Bane, this amazing expression came out of punk, something the likes of which had never been heard before about a kind of existential discontent, but also very specific about sexism and women's roles," says Gretchen Phillips, an Austin, Texas–based musician involved in the Stateside punk scene in the early 1980s.

Brits Siouxsie & the Banshees and the Members struck at the heart of the middle class, railing against the soulless lives and materialism of suburbanites (a demographic from which prog rock drew its greatest supporters). John Lydon (a.k.a. Johnny Rotten), in his autobiography, *Rotten: No Irish, No Blacks, No Dogs*, lamented the fact that prog rock was "devoid of any reality. How on earth were we supposed to relate to that music when we lived in council flats?"

"The music that had gone on before [punk] for ten or fifteen years was more like one big happy family; it stressed inclusiveness," says ambient/electronica maven Toby Marks (mastermind of Banco de Gaia), who grew up on prog rock and included covers of King Crimson, Hawkwind, and Pink Floyd songs on Banco's 2009 double record, *Memories Dreams Reflections*. "With punk, it was very much about 'us and them.' It was confrontational."

"Out back of the design studio in Soho was a little rehearsal studio and we used to hear loads of bands rehearse, Bad Finger and all that," relates Richard Evans, in-house layout artist for design firm Hipgnosis, a name synonymous with progressive rock and Pink Floyd. "Po [Aubrey Powell, cofounder of Hipgnosis]

A late '80s Sex Pistols cassette of *The Mini Album* unabashedly boasts the politically incorrect image of Hitler's face as artwork.

was doing a photo shoot with Olivia Newton-John, before she moved out to the States. She was this young singer trying to make it in this country. We did an album cover for her, which was very un-Hipgnosis. It was a portrait, done in the studio, and it was summer. We had the windows wide open and we hear this awful noise coming out the back windows. It sounded like people clearing their throats. We stopped the shoot. We looked out the window and it was Johnny Rotten and Sid Vicious leaning out their window across the yard spitting into the yard. Po said, 'I'm trying to do a photo shoot here, would you mind not doing that,' and Johnny Rotten said, 'Sorry, mate. We're just practicing for our act. Now fuck off.' That was when we knew the game was up, you know?"

Sign(ing) of the Times . . .

Growing weary and wary of long compositions written by progressive rockers, labels looked to convert the dissatisfaction of Britain's youth culture into big cash. The industry's push for the Next Big Thing helped to change tastes, listening habits, and even friendships.

Future Pendragon frontman Nick Barrett remembers the punk trend sweeping through his school. "The strange thing was, some of these kids just completely dumped their Yes record collections," Barrett said in a 2008 interview. "I can think of one friend who just completely turned his back on it. I said, 'How could music that was so influential in your life suddenly stop being such?' I think he was kind of kidding himself, because he was looking for more of a social standing by making a statement."

Lee Abrams witnessed the kind of pressure placed on artists to mute their arty tendencies and streamline their approach in order to reflect the changing times. "[Yes] were getting a lot of pressure from the record company and the industry," says Abrams. "You know, 'The kids are dancing now. You have to make three-minute records that they can dance to.' I told them, 'No. Don't do that. That's not what you're all about.' Gentle Giant, they knew I was working with Yes and they were about to be dropped. I was introduced to Derek Shulman and I traveled over to England to meet the rest of the guys. The band eventually recorded *Civilian*, which was not really in the Gentle Giant style. They were just trying to see what would work. It was a mixed reaction. It was an interesting experience, but it was a little too late for them."

An individual needed very little money to be in a punk band. Keeping up with the latest keyboard technology was not a job description—musical training unnecessary. "Punk allowed, because it was affordable, for you to begin playing immediately," says Gretchen Phillips. "You didn't have a drum kit that had a million toms. You didn't have a Moog. You had your guitar and maybe a shitty amp."

ROI was the name of the game. According to an article published by *Circus* magazine in July 1976, the Ramones cut their self-titled full-length debut for around $6,400, having completed the fourteen-track album in less than a week, something the writer viewed as a gutsy move for a young band. Of course, in the mid-1970s, $6,400 went a lot further than it does in the twenty-first century. Nevertheless, the astronomical production costs—a whopping $600,000—was seen as "downright obscene."

With these sums of money being spent on recording rock acts, Sire Records, in a similar manner, was matching revenues to expenses, realizing that doing business with punks was a no-brainer. Sire cofounder Seymour Stein, sometimes credited with actually coining the phrase "punk rock," branched out as well, signing punk, NYC punk, and art-pop punk types such as the Ramones, the Voidoids, Johnny Blitz, the Dead Boys, Richard Hell, and Talking Heads. (Ironically, just a few short years earlier, Sire achieved its first real hit with Focus' "Hocus Pocus." Sire, it should be pointed out, continued to carry Renaissance on its artist roster.)

Chrysalis, which had been cofounded by Jethro Tull manager Terry Ellis, signed bands such as Cleveland's Pere Ubu and New York's Blondie and turned the latter, CBGB regulars, into stars who'd mix New Wave, disco, hard rock, and pop into a commercial success.

One of the more ironic about-faces in modern recording-business history was Virgin Records' rejection of the more experimental bands the label had signed just a few short years earlier, such as Hatfield and the North and Henry Cow.

After being dropped by EMI and A&M (rumor had it at the request of Rick Wakeman and others on the label's artist roster), the Sex Pistols signed with Virgin, a record company with little experience promoting punk bands and one that had supported experimental rock music in the early and mid-1970s.

"I know Virgin had signed a bunch of punk bands—the Pistols and a lot of other younger bands like the Ruts and the Skids," says Glossop. "The label used to try to convince the bands to record at Virgin studios to cut down on costs."

"[Virgin] was built on the success as a mail order distributor—unique and far-sighted at the time," explains Fred Frith, guitarist/composer for the avant/prog rock bands Art Bears and Henry Cow. "I think there was a lot of idealism [at the label], the kind where they were saying, 'Well, if only we had the same resources as these boring major labels, we could actually make this music that we like more popular.' Richard [Branson, founder] supported that one hundred percent. If Michael Oldfield hadn't hit it shockingly big with *Tubular Bells*, which came out of the blue, I doubt if the label would have survived beyond a couple of years, anyway. But it kept the label afloat long enough for them to grasp the hard reality that their early signings, like us [Henry Cow], were never going to be mainstream in a million years. At that point the label, rather than continuing to try to bring the mainstream to Virgin, lurched over to the mainstream themselves. In the end there was a bottom line, and Richard did need to see profitability, being a businessman."[1]

Across the pond nascent prog bands were feeling the noose tighten, as well, not only from the encroachment of punk and disco, but also from so-called "arena" rock bands, such as Journey, Foreigner, and Boston, who, ironically, had taken theatrical and musical cues from prog.

"I can't speak for Boston or Journey, but I can tell you that Foreigner songs were geared toward radio and the idea was to have hit records," says Ian McDonald, former member of both King Crimson and Foreigner. "Foreigner had different priorities and objectives from King Crimson. I certainly am not knocking it. I feel very privileged to have played arenas. We were one of the biggest acts in the country at one time. But it was a different kettle of fish."

One New York progressive rock band, Cathedral, spurred on by the likes of Yes, Genesis, and Gentle Giant, applied European classical music forms to the rock idiom regardless of the trends. "We were based on the Southern Gold Coast of southern New York, on Long Island in Suffolk County," said Tom Doncourt, keyboardist and stage builder for Cathedral during the mid-1970s. "I think growing up around mansions, even though we didn't actually grow up *in those mansions*, gave us a clue into European opulence and the romantic English countryside. Peter Gabriel had the ruins and remnants of Roman occupation and we had Heckscher State Park."

Both Doncourt and Fred Callan were members of the Long Island band Odyssey, but had seen Cathedral become much more financially successful, having grown a rabid following even among complacent Long Island crowds, who'd just as soon pay bottom dollar to see some bar-circuit cover band. Cathedral scheduled a fateful meeting with Atlantic Records in New York to discuss a possible record deal.

"Atlantic said, 'You guys are powerful, but we can't sell twenty-minute songs,'" Cathedral bandleader/bassist Callan told me in 2008. "We were just not on the same page. Atlantic told us, 'You have to package it, keep your music to three minutes.' I knew what they wanted, but we were what we were, and not everyone [in the band] wanted to go in that direction. This was really the demise of Cathedral."

For this and other reasons no deal was struck. (One story related to me by a band member blamed not only external factors, but also the band's presentation to the label and the culture at Atlantic at the time.)

Although Cathedral continued to perform live, without major label support, it was as though the life had been sucked out of the band. (It would take a 1990s reissue of Cathedral's 1978 Delta Records label release, *Stained Glass Stories*, by Syn-Phonic, and a new attitude toward prog, to convince the band to re-form, which they did in 2003. Four years later Cathedral cut *The Bridge*, their first studio album in nearly thirty years.)

Label owners, who failed to see a viable future in songs many of these artists were crafting at the time, ironically, locked American prog bands out of the American Dream. In some ways, the spirit and inventiveness of prog rock had come from the up-and-comers, the underground talents, who were pushing their art—and the genre—into different areas. Given the climate of the recording business in the mid- and late

Known for its complex, counterpoint-heavy progressive rock . . .

. . . Gentle Giant responded to the changes in popular music by streamlining their approach, beginning with the album *The Missing Piece*.

1970s, many bands who were either established or attempting to get off the ground fell by the wayside.

Scorched Earth Tactics

The first rule of take-no-prisoners political campaigning is to demonize your opponent to maximize your own value as the "new" guy on the block. If you alienate your opponent and make him/her/them illegitimate or unacceptable, the voting public will undoubtedly recognize the ultimate potential you represent. The course of action taken by punk bands—or the moneymen bankrolling them—was tantamount to a "scorched earth" policy: set aflame nearly anything that came before in order to level the playing field.

"I was in a band called 64 Spoons," adds Jakko Jakszyk (King Crimson). "I remember we did a gig at the University College of London, and the support band were one of these newfangled punk groups that had come up from Brighton. We were onstage, sound check, and I'm mucking about with the amp and tweaking it a bit, when suddenly I became aware of someone standing too damn close. I turned around and saw this spiky-hair vision, less than a foot away from my face, chewing gum. He did this thing where he was talking to his mate without taking his eyes off of me, you know? He said, 'Kevin, get this bloke. He can play the guitar really well. What a wanker.' Suddenly everything I had ever believed in was the most meaningless currency in the world overnight."

Paul Fishman, the mastermind behind Absolute Elsewhere and its controversial instrumental electronica/prog record *In Search of Ancient Gods*, featuring drummer Bill Bruford, saw the writing on the wall, as well. "After *In Search of Ancient Gods* the band name was shortened to Absolute and I recorded another album for Warner Bros. called *Playground*," says Fishman. "It was with a different drummer, Andrew McCulloch, who, like Bill, was a drummer in King Crimson. It also featured the guitarist Phil [Saatchi] and bassist Jon [Astrop]. It was different from the first record but also more complex, the music was much more intricate than Absolute Elsewhere. Needless to say it was shelved. It never came out. There was a stage where it was a problem, because if you showed up at a record company and they thought you could play it was not desirable."

"It did change quickly," says Mark Hitt of Rat Race Choir, a New York–based cover band. "The only way I can describe us maintaining credibility with our fans was being true to our form. But, I have to say, that every once in a while we pulled 'My Sharona' out of the hat. We felt we had to."

The Great Divide?

Myth-making is the lifeblood of any good entertainment endeavor, and the thought of projecting an image of the sloppy, don't-give-a-shit rocker held its allure.

Although it's true that many musicians working in the punk era were not virtuosos on their instruments, others seemed to belie this fact. Drummer Marc Bell (a.k.a. Marky Ramone), for instance, had recorded several records prior to joining the Ramones and possessed a wicked right-foot kick drum technique, which he tweaked during various performances of his late 1960s proto-metal band Dust. Glen Matlock, the original bassist for the Sex Pistols and a one-time art school attendee, reportedly understood the value of melody and composition, helping to bring structure to the Pistols' songs. (He was, of course, famously sent packing from the band before they hit it big.) Even the official Sex Pistols Web site (www.sexpistolsofficial.com) reports that Sid Vicious became a bit more serious about learning the bass and "practiced like crazy." As the story goes, "other circumstances soon began to get in the way of any budding ability . . ."

"Much of that punk and New Wave music is, with the benefit of hindsight, highly crafted, well-executed and surprisingly musical," says keyboardist Nick Magnus (Steve Hackett, Autumn). "I'm sure they'd have been mortified at the time to discover they were actually doing it very well."

At the same time, artists such as David Bowie, Robert Fripp (who lived in Hell's Kitchen and played with Blondie), Ultravox, and Visage (both progenitors of the New Romantic movement) made overtures to New Wave art-rock and even so-called punk trailblazers the Damned, who many credit with having released the first "punk" single in the U.K., in the fall of 1976, called "New Rose" (via Stiff Records), were being labeled toward Goth. (The band was also influenced by Krautrock and their ill-fated foray into psychedelia, 1977's *Music for Pleasure*, was produced by Nick Mason.) Additionally, to a degree, Brian Eno (who'd released a "no wave" music compilation, *No New York*, in 1978, and would go on to produce Talking Heads) blurred

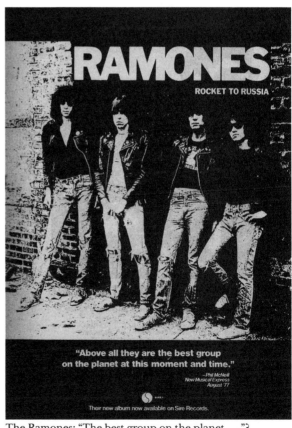

The Ramones: "The best group on the planet . . ."?

"Hippies just sit around and smoke dope. If I see someone like that in an audience, I'll jump out and kick him. You got to be alive, man."
— Stiv Bators

In 1978, rock 'n' roll is alive and kicking hard, in the capable hands and hearts of Stiv Bators, Jimmy Zero, Cheetah Chrome, Jeff Magnum and Johnny Blitz.

THE DEAD BOYS
In *Young Loud and Snotty*
Produced by Genya Ravan for Sire Records
marketed by Warner Bros. Records, Inc.

Punk gained your attention by any means necessary. An ad for the Dead Boys.

the lines between punk, electronica, and art-rock.

In America, Television and Sonic Youth straddled genres, as well, as bands working outside cultural epicenters of New York and Los Angeles caused major regional buzzes. Along with 15-60-75, Mirrors, Tin Huey, Frank Zappa favorite Devo, and Human Switchboard, Cleveland's Pere Ubu helped to put Ohio underground music on the map. Ubu, which evolved from the legendary Rocket from the Tombs (formed by David Thomas and regional icon Peter Laughner), combined garage-band riff rock, noise, Dada-esque humor, and studio experimentation for records such as "30 Seconds Over Tokyo" (a single released on the band's own label), *The Modern Dance*, *Dub Housing*, *The Art of Walking*, and *Song of the Bailing Man* in the late 1970s and early 1980s.

"The Cleveland scene . . . was based on the hothouse environment of the competing record shops," Ubu frontman Thomas once told the author. "All the major figures of the day worked in record stores. The competition between record stores to stock everything and to be versed in everything was intense. . . . It was about taking it all in and being the best band in the world; doing what no one else was doing."

"I've always loved [prog rock]," says the Tangent's Andy Tillison. "As much as I enjoyed punk, punk was always presented as the great choice. You know, 'You don't have to like that stuff anymore. Here's punk.' I kind of looked at the world and said, 'Is there anything wrong with liking both?' It seemed that there was. I'm probably one of the few people who saw Yes and the Sex Pistols in the same week.

"I wrote a letter in 1977 to the *NME*, actually," Tillison continues. "It was amazing. They had been harping on for weeks the fact that punk rock was for the kid on the street and prog rock wasn't for the kid on the street. I wrote them a letter, a kid who is on the street, and I told them that I saw Yes 'this week' and saw the Sex Pistols also in the same week. The only thing was that there were about three thousand more kids on the street for the Yes concert. They didn't publish the letter."

Perhaps the most famous crossover example was John Lydon's ironic admission, in an article titled "A Punk and His Music: An Evening with John Rotten," from *Sounds*, July 23, 1977, that he was a fan of Van der Graaf Generator's Peter Hammill. Admittedly, Hammill generated a pre-punk-like psychotic energy, but Lydon befuddled critics by immunizing this underground prog-rock icon him from his venom.

Lydon wasn't alone. In 2007, years after the fact, Pistols guitarist Steve Jones admitted his dirty little secret to *Rolling Stone* magazine: he loved Queen, Journey, and Boston, even at the height of the Pistols' success.[2] At the time, of course, none of the Pistols could bring themselves to say such a thing.

Punk was not invincible or immune to PDAs (public displays of appraisals). As prog had done before it, punk soon attracted its naysayers and detractors. Reportedly, Pistols concerts were canceled and contracts ripped up, allegedly due to nasty personal behavior.

"The Sex Pistols risked a lot, physically," says David First, whose Philadelphia-based band, the Notekillers, released one 45 single, on Ed Bahlman's indie label 99 Records, which influenced Sonic Youth and held the fascination of pioneering No Wave guitarist Glenn Branca. "You can say all you want to say about Malcolm McLaren, but he wasn't beaten up and stabbed on the street."

Street Cred

Punk certainly had cultural relevance, but, it can be reasoned, the music fit snugly inside an existing record-industry template. If punk was closer, musically, to rock and roll and its roots, then promoting it meant reverting back to classic business tactics: exploitation and lowest common denominator.

Because prog artists hardly, if ever, made claims to being social revolutionaries, there was no inherent contradiction in their making great art and also pursuing their own financial interests. In other words, concepts such as selling records and creating art-rock weren't mutually exclusive, whereas punk represented, dare we say, anticapitalism and antimaterialism, ultimately boxing them into a corner.

Some writers, even back in the day, were able to peel back the curtain and correctly identify the inherent or *seemingly* inherent contradiction and hypocrisy of punk bands wanting to identify with their disaffected audience, yet, willingly signing on the dotted lines as directed.

In the October 1977 issue of *Trouser Press* Ira Robbins reasoned that the British punk bands became "too successful to continue to claim the political integrity of being just like their audience—kids on the dole with no future."

Although the article was written by an obvious punk fan who points to the fact that mainstream culture co-opted the movement, Robbins doesn't shy away from calling out punks, who won't admit what they were after in the first place: hitting the Big Time. "[F]ew bands have made serious attempts to stem the tide [of fame and fortune]," Robbins wrote.

One could argue that the progressives held their ground, artistically, for a longer period of time than the punks did. The progressive era was populated with fewer recording artists willing to make concessions regarding their music. In retrospect, and quite ironically, it was prog, not punk, that turned the industry on its ear.

As it turns out, sometimes radicals don't have as much of an impact on a lifestyle or political system as they—or anyone else—might think. Sure, they can fuck things up for a little while, but to effect long-lasting change and artistic influence requires more skill than simply mindless bomb-throwing—no matter how impassioned or unpredictable. It's the old debate about working inside or outside the system. Which option achieves the greatest results?

Progressive rockers were ordinary people playing extraordinary music— music that transcended boundaries and time. Because of this, for the historic period prior to the rise of punk, the music made by the progressives, some of them, at least, could not neatly fit into a mold designed for mass-produced widgets. Instead, for a time, the industry bent to the prog rockers' wills and deferred to their artistic sensibilities. An often-baffled rock music business, still fairly young in the early and mid-1970s, was forced to follow the leader—*not the other way around.* In some respects, prog helped to create a new type of framework, supported by AOR and FM radio, that put old-school marketing men back on their heels. In the 1970s, it seemed to work.

"You couldn't tell a Robert Fripp or a Jon Anderson to limit the song to two minutes and thirty seconds," one-time Atlantic Records radio promotional man Phillip Rauls confessed in an interview I conducted. "They would tell you to stick it up the wazoo. When they wrote a song and recorded it, they didn't want their artistic work tampered with. It was a musical score. It took a gazillion debates . . . to try to get the musicians to buy into the concept of the two-and-a-half-minute single."

"A hit could crucify you," Keith Emerson told me. "We'd want to stay away from that."

"I can tell you that these progressive-rock artists, for the most part, didn't care about commerciality," says Mark Hitt. "They had a statement to make and they made it."

"There's a zeitgeist about why [prog rock] started and about why it finished," adds Andy Tillison. "If we're going to get into why it finished, first, I think it dealt with this global reining in of product. Essentially, what we had in the world of artistry, and I'm not just talking music, we have a situation that was very close to what I would call creative anarchy. In the world of music, the musicians . . . were making the decisions about what kind of music they were going to make. *Topographic Oceans* is a good example. Record companies couldn't control Yes; they couldn't control Emerson, Lake & Palmer. They couldn't get a five-minute pop single and a slot on *Top of the Pops*. What they wanted was control of the rock market."[3]

Did punk kill prog? No doubt that the vast majority of prog artists felt the sting, if not directly, then indirectly, and the genre as a whole was forced underground by the early 1980s. (Prog would see a kind of resurgence in the 1980s with British neo-prog bands such as Marillion, Twelfth Night, IQ, and Pendragon, among others. This is to say nothing of the ongoing orchestral, avant-prog, and Rock in Opposition scenes populated by the likes of Univers Zero and others.)

Whatever role punk played in bringing down some of the major progressive rock bands, they had accomplices in a hostile press searching high and low for Robin Hood–like false messiahs, and a leviathan, known as the record industry, hoping to gobble up easy money.

Perhaps the most damaging part of the punk legacy relates to something far more insidious. Certain well-positioned individuals willing to capitalize on the ever-shrinking attention span of youth—a marketing strategy, which continues to prey upon our art-as-disposable-commodity, digitized society—may have, in retrospect, ignited the bomb that exploded inside popular culture in the mid- and late 1970s and has done irreparable damage. The progressives were, and still are, by the very music they make and had made, diametrically opposed to such strategies.

It took commitment to listen to the progressives and, by the same token, it took a commitment to excellence to make the music. The true rebels were, and are, the acts that challenged the listener and represented a more substantive form of popular music—a concept that stood in opposition to what the record business symbolizes and had represented, perhaps, from its earliest days.

Heavy Horsesh#$!

Examining Prog's Criminal Record and Critiquing Critical Reaction

From the moment John Peel declared ELP's performance at the Isle of Wight festival in 1970 a "waste of electricity and talent," progressive rock has been fighting an uphill battle against outspoken critics in the media, who staunchly opposed the marriage of classical and rock since the early stirrings of prog's embryonic stage.

In the 1970s there were few options to neutralize negative press, other than granting an interview to the very same publications denouncing prog artists in the first place. Outlets such as the Internet were still decades away; full-page advertising was never as effective (or budget-friendly) as press-generated publicity; and TV appearances were a luxury. Worse still was the thought of being ignored—a situation that could potentially do more damage than any nasty write-up could.

Conversely, punks did no wrong. To hear music scribes of the time tell it, Patti Smith should attempt walking on water, the Ramones were the "best group on the planet," and Sex Pistols' frontman John Lydon's contorted bodily movements and maniacal facial expressions were a mixture of Jagger-esque cocksure strutting and "Dionysian irrationality."

In many cases, critics not only attacked progressive music, but the listeners who valued it. For instance, the Moody Blues, in a *New York Times* article titled "Mushy Blues" from October 29, 1973, were indicted as "paragons of turgid transcendentalism," pandering to "phony high culture." To paraphrase this review: ignorant suburban audiences consumed vapid, overblown commercialized crap while sitting motionless in stifling arena atmospheres, thinking what they were inhaling was actually art.

With this kind of coverage it's a wonder prog found its footing at all. "It all struck me as being amusing," Jakko Jakszyk (King Crimson) told the author once. "As the music got more and more simple, the verbosity of the journalists writing about it got more and more fuckin' florid and preposterous. All the things that they were accusing the bands of the prog era of being, they became the literal equivalent of. They [were writing] about a couple of geezers from Dartford playing a D-minor [chord] through a fuzz box—and not very well. But they viewed it as being imbued with this kind of portentous sense of angst."

Not all bands were mistreated. They were shown some level of respect, even if it was fleeting. *Rolling Stone* published a positive feature on ELP in April 1974, and again, in July 1977, presenting a slightly more sobering look at the bombastic trio filtered through the extravagance of their *Works* tour. (However, Lester Bangs, writing for *Rolling Stone*, blasted the band's live performance during their 1974 *Brain Salad Surgery* tour.) Opinion leader the *New York Times* reviewed ELP's late 1971 live record, *Pictures at an Exhibition*, praising the trio for channeling an "original mode of expression," only to largely change their tune about the band later in the decade.

Yes and Rick Wakeman fared moderately well, receiving some good press in particular from *Rolling Stone*. However, Wakeman and the band did have their well-placed champion or champions at the magazine. Cameron Crowe, for instance, future Hollywood screenwriter and film director, seemed to generate most of *Rolling Stone*'s positive in-depth features on Yes and Wakeman.

It perhaps goes without saying that bad reviews accumulated as the 1970s wore on. In the wake of punk and disco, critics smelled blood in the water. "The British press definitely wanted the death of prog, I think, because they were uncomfortable with dealing with musicians who were more intelligent than they were," former IQ member Martin Orford once told me.

Prog took its lumps well into the 1980s, as well. Supergroup Asia and neo-prog hitmakers Marillion absorbed their share of public trashing. And who could forget *Musician* magazine's infamous one-word review of the 1986 GTR album ("SHT")—a sentiment echoed by *The Rolling Stone Encyclopedia of Rock?*

The intent of this section is not to target specific publications or writers; on the contrary. Scribes had every right to print their opinions and speak their minds. Having said this, there was plenty of material from which to choose, so much so that the author could not print all of the negative reactions he encountered. In some cases rebuttal "arguments" are presented for effect and to offer a more balanced view.

King Crimson: *Lizard* (1970)—*Evening Standard* (December 12, 1970)

Although the band did win praises from some in the British music press for this record, the sentiment toward the band's third studio offering was far from unanimous. The *London Evening Standard* ripped into the band, saying the LP was abysmal, the perfect gift for " . . . the person you like least of all, but are forced, for one reason or another, to buy them [*sic*] a present."

ELP: Fillmore East show, 1971—*New York Times* (May 2, 1971)

Color the *Times* unimpressed. Ringing in the band's New York debut with a Bronx cheer, the paper dismissed ELP's performance as little more than a Nice sequel. Emerson is taken to task for playing "too many notes with too little idea of what to do with them . . ."

ELP: *Pictures at an Exhibition* (1971)—*Circus* (April 1972)

Slamming the fusion of classical music and rock as being "genuinely awful" and "pretentious," the reviewer's ultimate judgment about the record was a fait accompli. The review goes on to insult the awareness and intelligence of the audience, saying ELP borrows the best portions of Mussorgsky's work and bends them "to suit their own needs." No big deal, it turns out, because, says the reviewer, their audiences wouldn't know the difference, anyway. . . .

ELP: *Trilogy* (1972)—*Newsday* (August 4, 1972)

Again, ELP—and their fans—are targeted. "Anyone who buys a record that divides a composition called 'The Endless Enigma' into part one and two deserves it."

Jethro Tull: *A Passion Play* (1973)—*Melody Maker* (July 21, 1973)

Most fans know the story of Tull's reputed technical difficulties at Château d'Hérouville, a studio outside Paris in which Anderson and the boys were recording their follow-up to *Thick as a Brick* in August 1972.

Anderson was supposedly so disgusted with audio quality of the technical standards of Château d'Hérouville that he dubbed the studio "Chateau d'Isaster." (Ironic, since Elton John had just titled his 1972 studio release *Honky Château*, in honor of the place.) Were the tapes so atrocious that Anderson decided to abandon the work that was already completed there and head for home? It's been reported that, aside from the supposed technical glitches, the band was feeling a bit of homesickness.

"I don't think anyone enjoyed being at that studio," says recording engineer Robin Black. "The vibe just wasn't good for the band. I think some of the playing was excellent and would love to get my hands on those tapes again."

Years later, as legend grew around these recordings, Anderson changed his mind about the entire debacle, if it could rightly be called such, and released the tracks from that time, titling them "The Chateau d'Isaster Tapes," which appear on the 1993 compilation *Nightcap*.

"I think Ian listened to the tapes sometime later and realized that they were far better than he thought," says Black.

But back in 1972, those tracks were scrapped and Tull went full-steam ahead with another dense, and far more cryptic, concept record, *A Passion Play*. The album was packaged as a mock theater program, similar in its elaborate presentation to its predecessor, *Thick as a Brick*. In this program, the fellas assumed fictional identities. Interestingly enough Anderson was "Elvoe" (picking up on his old nickname from his Blackpool days).

What irked some observers was not the cover design but the music and Tull's overall artistic approach. The nearly indecipherable story line of a soul's

The content of Jethro Tull's "The Chateau d'Isaster Tapes" appeared on the 1993 compilation *Nightcap*.

journey in the afterlife (and the choices it faces), along with the absurd, Monty Python–inspired vignette, "The Story of the Hare Who Lost His Spectacles," left most critics cold and stunned, but not at a loss for words.

Arguably, the article featured in this entry was the mother of prog-rock (possibly even rock) criticism. In a *Melody Maker* review titled "Tull: Enough Is Enough," the band is skewered for being good technicians but little more. This well-known, scathing indictment, penned by veteran music journalist Chris Welch, had long-range ramifications. It was reported in the press at the time that Tull was ready to give up touring due to negative reviews. (Tull manager Terry Ellis even issued a statement saying, "The abuse heaped upon the show by the critics has been bitterly disappointing to the group . . .") However, as it turns out, all of this was public theater: frontman Ian Anderson later admitted that the band's perceived anger was a misguided ploy for press coverage.

Unfortunately for Tull, the attacks were real. Welch said he was so shaken by the quality (or lack thereof) of the music appearing on *A Passion Play* that he would seriously consider never listening to another rock album by a British band, ever. "If this is where ten years of 'progression' have taken us, then it's time to go backwards," wrote Welch.

Yes: *Tales from Topographic Oceans* concert at New York's Nassau Coliseum, February 1974—*Newsday* (February 15, 1974)

After attending this Yes show, respected rock critic Robert Christgau, in a review titled "No, No, No, No, No, No," called Yes "deceptively fatuous," emotionally bankrupt, and a mediocre example of classical rock. As was common practice for many prog or classical rock bands of the day, Yes decided to play their new album in its entirety: four pieces clocking in at ninety minutes. True, this tested even the most ardent of fans' patience, but in this review the music was flatly denounced. Bored to tears, the reviewer wondered if the audience members, particularly those attempting to listen intently, were not simply displaying a form of "phony gentility."

The piece then introduces a classical music writer on the *Newsday* staff to drive home the point that Yes *only projects* an image of musical sophistication. The expert dismissed the presence of tempo changes in Yes' music, saying that the band performs only in "uncomplicated" odd time signatures, such as 12/8, 6/8, and 3/4, all but putting the band down as mangy hybrids.

Some might take issue with the expert's definition of "uncomplicated" and, in any case, Yes often and seamlessly shifted through trickier time signatures such as 7, 9, and 10, as well. (No mention of this, though.) There were more sophisticated bands than Yes in the prog world, but as Kevin Costner said (when portraying New Orleans D.A. Jim Garrison in Oliver Stone's 1990 movie *JFK*): "That's like me saying Touchdown [the dog], here, is not very intelligent, because I beat him three games out of five the last time we played chess. . . ."

Strawbs: *Hero and Heroine* (1974)—*Rolling Stone* (April 25, 1974)

Dave Cousins, fearless leader of Strawbs, once told the author that due to critical reaction to records, such as 1974's *Hero and Heroine* and 1975's *Ghosts*, the decision was made to change the group's signature sound. In other words, when Cousins got wind of some of the reviews, such as this one dubbing Strawbs' music "melotraumatic," the band shunned the Mellotron. (Brilliant keyboardist John Hawken also left the band not long after.) *Hero and Heroine*, which reached the top 100 on *Billboard*'s Top 200 Albums chart, was labeled "unbalanced and irresolute." Although the review did point out some of the record's assets, the verdict read mixed affair.

Jethro Tull: *Minstrel in the Gallery* (1975)—*Rolling Stone* (November 6, 1975)

The premier music mag found the only soulful (and unintentionally ironic) aspect of this Tull record was the ending interlude of the fifteen-minute track, "Baker Street Muse." The song concludes with audio of Ian Anderson attempting to exit the studio, but failing miserably and shouting, "I can't get out!" Said *Rolling Stone*, "That's roughly the same feeling that this listener got about midway through" the first side of the record.

As biting as this criticism was, it paled by comparison to what the magazine printed less than a year earlier about Tull's 1974 effort, *War Child*. One hint: "Tull rhymes with dull." (The nickname Jethro Dull was perhaps popularized by *New York Times* writer Loraine Alterman in her somewhat playful August 19, 1973, critique of *A Passion Play*.)

Larry Fast: *Synergy: Electronic Realizations for Rock Orchestra* (1975)—*Creem* (October 1975)

An odd one to be sure: a positive review of an art-rock/electronic record that takes a swipe at prog's Caped Crusader. "Everything that [Rick] Wakeman wants to be, but hasn't got enough sensitivity or class" to accomplish.

Creem wasn't alone in using this tactic. Fixated on artists they despised, critics reached across genre lines to gut the latest trending prog rocker. One feature in New York's *Newsday* (November 26, 1972), extolling the virtues of Johnny Nash's 1972 number-one "comeback" hit, "I Can See Clearly Now," subtly, but mysteriously, victimizes ELP.

King Crimson: *USA* (1975)—*Rolling Stone* (July 31, 1975)

Perhaps Crimson's definitive live statement, recorded in Asbury Park, at the Fun Palace, on June 29, 1974, and Providence, Rhode Island, June 30, 1974 ("21st Century Schizoid Man"). Arguably the edgy, noisy qualities of "Lament" and the majestic sustain of Fripp's guitar ("Exiles") quite possibly help these live versions transcend or, at least, rival their original LP counterparts. *Rolling Stone*, however, did not hear it this way, and pointed out that Wetton's vocal performance "pales next to Greg Lake's originals" on "Schizoid Man." *USA* is generally seen as Crimson's last band record of the 1970s (although a double LP compilation called *A Young Person's Guide to King Crimson* later emerged). According to *Rolling Stone*, Crimson left not with a bang but a whimper.

Mike Oldfield: "Tubular Bells" (1973)—*New York Times* (February 21, 1975)

Oldfield's signature and breakthrough composition is "decidedly inferior" to the music of meditative avant-garde composers, such as Stockhausen, Ligeti, and minimalist Terry Riley, this critic theorizes.

Admittedly, the repetitive and cyclical aspects of Riley's "A Rainbow in Curved Air," even Steve Reich's "Piano Phase" from 1967, seem to be forerunners to "Tubular Bells." But, "Tubular Bells" and Oldfield's shrill electric guitar tones and vibrato are miles from the so-called New Age genre that critics often link to Oldfield's music.

Rick Wakeman: *Criminal Record* (1978)—*Creem* (March 1978)

This brutal, relentless review advocates for Wakeman's "noggin" to be "bashed with a hockey stick until it's a gorgeous pool of pulpy gelatin." This perceived outrage stems from, the author believes, the fact that Rick—and his A&M labelmates—were responsible for the Sex Pistols getting the boot by the record company. (The author could not verify.) The article took Wakeman to task for unleashing on the public a totally lame and anachronistic artistic vehicle—the concept album. (In this case, all the songs were said to be linked

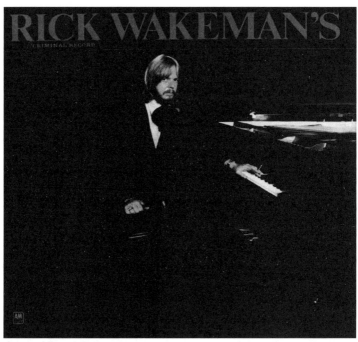

Criminal Record: In some music critic circles, Rick Wakeman was persona non grata in the late 1970s.

thematically via the dastardly deeds of history's greatest villains.) Although Wakeman himself has said that *Criminal Record* didn't live up to expectations, the review dabbles in mighty strong words and violent, disturbing imagery. Criminal record, indeed!

Jethro Tull: *Heavy Horses* (1978)—*Creem* (July 1978)

Heavy Horses, the linchpin of Tull's so-called folk trilogy, is the victim of a fierce critical lashing. Branding Tull frontman Ian Anderson as a "stupid clod fink [with] the flute," the reviewer's critique drives a spur into the collective side of the band, a band that is, evidently, totally incapable of "[crashing] an auto [even] if it sped into Dead Man's Curve." Bizarrely, it's reported in the very same issue of *Creem* that, despite their supposed retiring image (and, presumably, retiring music), Ian and the boys were kicked off an airplane for "hassling" a stewardess. The reviewer, apparently, wasn't buying any of the reports of Tull's red-blooded and boorish male behavior, and one succinct phrase sums up the writer's feelings on this matter: "Heavy Horse-shit."

ELP: *Love Beach* (1978)—*Creem* (March 1979)

Although the review never directly addresses the music appearing on ELP's final studio album of the 1970s, it does refer to the "three idiot grinning figures" on the cover (that's E, L and P to you). Admittedly, *Love Beach* may not be the best example of a prog-rock crossover album, and certainly by far one of the worst cover concepts in rock history. Part straight-ahead rock songs, part tone poem, *Love Beach* is a snapshot of a band unsure of itself and in transition. But, in retrospect, the record does have some merit (the Peter Sinfield lyrics, alone, in the twenty-minute "Memoirs of an Officer and a Gentleman," must evoke some response), and readers could have benefited from the perspective of an objective (hell, even a slightly interested) critical voice.

Presumably operating under a pseudonym, the writer paints a not-altogether-unfunny fictional (autobiographical?) portrait of a teen who hides his growing drug habit, penchant for petty theft, and rebellious love of punk rock from his music-critic father. It seems Dear Ol' Dad receives records, such as *Love Beach*, in the post, yet, little "Tommy," unfazed by this exclusive access to new music, wouldn't waste his time using such items as "butt wad."

Genesis: *And Then There Were Three* (1978)—*Crawdaddy!* (July 1978)

This review tears apart Rutherford's guitar playing as being "clumsy," his bass pedal work as "overkill," and Banks' compositions as rife with "dog-eared romantic clichés." (In the critic's mind, synths exist only to liven up "relatively weak melodies.") In addition, Collins' vocal performances are "insipid," his drumming uninspired. Given his work outside Genesis (namely Brand X), the reviewer muses, Collins must be creatively exhausted and incapable of making any coherent rhythmic statement on this record.

These bold statements prompted one Missouri-based *Crawdaddy!* reader to pen a letter to the editor, scolding the journalist for his lack of objectivity as someone who obviously "hates Genesis." As the appearance of this letter seems to indicate, most of the naysayers, who thought the trio were finished, underestimated not only fans' passion for their favorite band, but also Genesis' ability to write hits.

Genesis: *And Then There Were Three* (1978)—*Creem* (July 1978)

Both the *Crawdaddy!* rant and the *Creem* review pick up on Genesis' shift into pop music territory. Here, Genesis is far too sanitized—and lucky—to do anything risky or outrageous. When referring to Phil Collins' vocals in "Deep in the Motherload," the reviewer writes: "[Collins] can deliver the words 'mother's milk' in a way that makes you think he's singing about iced snot." Whatever that means, it sounds unappealing. . . .

U.K.: Concert at New York's Palladium, 1979—*New York Times* (March 26, 1979)

In a post-punk music world, no prog-rock band was safe from critical ridicule, not even a so-called supergroup. In the opening grafs of this article, the *Times* writer refutes the claim that U.K., then reduced to a trio (John Wetton, Eddie Jobson, and drummer Terry Bozzio) is prog rock's "great white hope." Progressive rock, of the kind that's been perpetrated by the likes of Yes and

Slammed in 1979, U.K. returned in 2012 to wide acclaim. *Night After Night*, the title of a 1979 U.K. live album, was adopted for the band's comeback tour.

ELP, is an exhausted idiom that "persists only to be bastardized by American groups like Kansas."

When the writer actually gets around to describing aspects of the show, we learn that Jobson performed "pseudo-classical flourishes . . . ," Wetton's bass tone "lumbered like Godzilla" while his vocals were "excruciatingly strained and off pitch." Lest rhythmatist Bozzio thought he would come away unscathed, U.K. is called out on its use (misuse?) of odd times as a failed attempt at creating rhythmic complexity within the structure of their songs. Indirectly, the review pronounces prog all but dead and U.K.'s music "pretty vacant," a sly reference to the Sex Pistols' tune of the same title.

Not everyone agreed at the time, of course. When bassist/vocalist for the Texas-based progressive metal band King's X dUg Pinnick saw the British supergroup in Chicago in 1978, he was stunned by the band's control and technique. "They came onstage and were devastating," says Pinnick. "They played and left. 'Take that, muthafuckas.' I feel like that was what they were saying to us. 'Try to follow that,' you know?"

Chris Poland, former guitar player for Megadeth and prog-metal act Damn the Machine, said U.K. was on a whole other musical level. "I mean, Wetton's voice, and the fact that he could play those bass parts in 7 or 9 and sing on top of it?" Poland told the author in 2010. "I almost quit playing when I heard [the debut]. A bass-player friend of mine, Doug Burlison, who was in a band called Felony, played me the first U.K. record. He looked at me and said, 'You know we're never going to be this good, right?' I think I listened to that record two years straight."

Kansas and Molly Hatchet: Boston Garden concert, November 1980—*Boston Globe* (November 11, 1980)

Said this reviewer, Kansas, an American "aberration," is "unwittingly parodying what progressive rock used to mean." Layers of synth tones and numerous time-signature changes were "predictable," and the band's "silly" musical pretentions inevitably collapsed into a "swirl of cosmic jive." Lead vocalist Steve Walsh and violinist Robbie Steinhardt are about as sincere as "Wink Martindale," the sort of rock-star caricatures Todd Rundgren "pokes fun at."

Yes, an Implosion?

The Behind-the-Scenes Drama of a Rock Powerhouse

S tories extolling the virtues of prog rock's death have been greatly exaggerated. Whether they were desperately trying to respond to the punk movement by purposely streamlining their approach or simply churning out more commercial music—or both—many of the major prog bands were failing to take on new fans—and failing to produce their best work.

The time frame that birthed ELP's compromised and schizophrenic *Love Beach*, Gentle Giant's *Civilian*, Yes' *Tormato*—the late '70s through early '80s—finds our heroes incorporating various musical elements, tinkering with their musical style—and not always for the better.

ELP had just finished *Love Beach*, and were in the midst of organizing a farewell tour, but couldn't find enough common ground to agree on anything. As a result, Emerson pursued movie soundtracks, Lake embarked on a solo career, and Palmer, prior to forming Asia, established the band PM, which cut the 1980 studio album *1:PM*, a Berlin Bowie-meets-the-Cars prog-funk effort aimed at the skinny tie crowd.

It was a strange time, indeed. Jethro Tull was nearly set to enter its electronic phase, largely diluting their more acoustic (and folk) tendencies, and Genesis, reduced to a trio, crossed into mainstream consciousness with its first Top 10 British single ("Follow You Follow Me"). Even some progressive acts occupying the genre's musical outskirts gravitated (albeit slightly) toward the commercial center. It wasn't long before Rock in Opposition band Stormy Six released the New Wave-ish *Al Volo*, and even the grand masters of Zeuhl, Magma, led by Christian Vander, unleashed *Attahk*—what might be their most accessible work.

Because of Yes' high profile, the band was perhaps more sensitive to both outer and inner stressors and shifts in the marketplace. Undeniably the music industry attitude toward this new style of music impacted Yes, but hairline fractures were visible during the band's *Tormato* phase and exacerbated by the attention given to punk.

"Yes were all over the place," says Lee Abrams, known as the father of the AOR radio format, who helped guide Yes in the late 1970s as the cofounder of the music industry consulting firm Burkhart/Abrams. "They weren't thinking cohesively. It was this confluence of negative energy coming together for one album. I know a lot of the guys didn't like Jon's direction, particularly 'Arriving U.F.O.' and, in particular, 'Circus of Heaven.' If it was *Fragile* they all would be thinking about every bar they recorded."[1]

Some of what made Yes classic does slip into the final cuts for *Tormato*, however. In the hypnotic instrumental break of "Future Times/Rejoice," perhaps the record's most dramatic song, drummer Alan White shuffles along in odd time signatures, accenting pivotal beats that propel the track. Others such as "Circus of Heaven," inspired by a Ray Bradbury short story and featuring Anderson's son (Damian), Chris Squire's pleasant "Onward," Yes' answer to punk, "Release, Release" and "Arriving UFO," which seems to vibrate in sympathy with Klaatu's "Calling Occupants of Interplanetary Craft," seem to divide fan opinion.

Except for the very early days, Yes had existed largely as five individuals sharing a common interest. While the band members were not always on the same page, Yes always found common ground to produce superior material. But, as the 1970s wore on, the personal and musical differences were becoming increasingly difficult to reconcile. Although *Tormato* reached the top 10 on *Billboard*'s Top 200 Albums chart, and Yes embarked on a tour to support it, these factors only delayed the inevitable.

After touring Europe in 1978, Yes ventured out for a three-month stint in North America for their in-the-round stage production. Prior to this tour, the band members were once again circling in their own orbits: Wakeman and Howe were stoking the flames of their solo careers, Anderson hooked up with Vangelis (for the recording of *Short Stories*), and at his home studio Squire was busy compiling taped performances for a live record, what would become 1980's *Yesshows*.

The simple and mystical title *Tor* was transformed, via a chucked tomato, into *Tormato*.

Perhaps because the bandmembers were scattered throughout Western Europe, it was decided that Yes would descend on a centralized location, Paris, for the recording of their next album, the follow-up to *Tormato*. From the beginning it seemed that factions within the band were pulling Yes in different directions.

"Yes was highly recommended by their manager [Brian Lane] to bring in Roy Thomas Baker, who funnily enough produced their 2014 studio album, *Heaven & Earth*," says Abrams. "He had been working with Queen and Foreigner and the thinking was that it might help get Yes a hit record."

That was the thinking, yes, but putting it into practice was another matter altogether. "Baker and the band started recording in Paris and the whole thing completely imploded," says Abrams. "I went to a couple of those sessions. They weren't talking to one another. Musically, Chris thought Jon was writing wimpy songs and Jon thought Chris was just an . . . Well, anyway. Rick probably was a little bit on Jon's side and Steve and Alan may have been in the middle. It was very strained relationships. It was almost *Spinal Tap*-y.

"I was living at Chris Squire's house for six months, because we were recording a band on MCA called Critical Mass, which was Green Day about ten years before it happened," Abrams continues. "I saw the whole thing first-hand and it was ugly. It was sad. It was this great band and they were at each others' throats. The Roy Thomas Baker experiment was a complete disaster, but it was happening at a point when the band was falling apart internally, anyway."

After Anderson took some time off in Barbados, the members (all, less Wakeman) attempted to reunite in the U.K. in 1980 at Redan Recorders. Far from helping the band achieve a consensus, the break aggravated an already strained situation: festering personal differences, career frustrations, tour exhaustion, creative depletion, and possible internal financial concerns all seemed to overwhelm the band. Not surprisingly, Anderson was gone (either asked to leave or exited of his own accord) and Rick seemed to float in and out until (the story goes) manager Brian Lane placed the call issuing his dismissal.

With Anderson and Wakeman out of the picture, Yes needed to act, and act quickly, in order to fill the void. Squire recruited the electronic pop duo the Buggles (i.e., keyboardist Geoff Downes and future producer extraordinaire Trevor Horn, both Yes fans)—a studio band that had stunned the pop world with its 1979 number-one U.K. (and Top 40 U.S.) hit "Video Killed the Radio Star."

As it so happens, the Buggles were also managed by Lane and working on their next album in the same studio in which Yes were rehearsing. Horn had played Squire a song he'd written, called "Fly from Here" (a.k.a. "We Can Fly from Here"), and thought he could sneak it onto the next Yes album. The minute Squire heard the track he was hooked.[2]

Squire invited Horn and Downes to rehearsal. Thinking Anderson and Wakeman would show up any day, the Buggles guys believed they were simply running through the song's arrangement with the band, when, eventually,

Squire asked them to join the band permanently. It was reasoned that Horn had proven that he could project a high-pitched, nasal vocal quality that recalled Anderson's famous singing voice, and Downes, who had studied at Leeds College of Music, could nicely fill Wakeman's shoes via his command of chords and keyboard textures.

What followed was a protracted, nine-month recording process for Yes' *Drama* that produced such tracks as the monolithic "Into the Lens" (earmarked for the second Buggles disc), "Machine Messiah," "Tempus Fugit," and "Does It Really Happen?"

"Trevor said to me the other day that 'Tempus Fugit' was remarkable," Steve Howe told the author in 2005. "You know what is remarkable about it is that we hadn't even met Trevor and Geoff when we had recorded that. They overdubbed on top of it. That's how Trevor remembers it. We could look back now and see that it was the heaviest album that Yes had done. It was like it was in your face. It was attitudinal. And that was good."

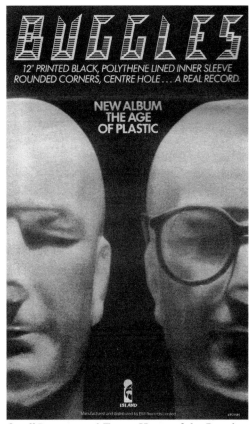

Geoff Downes and Trevor Horn, of the Buggles, helped to reenergize Yes in the early 1980s.

Although the songs were not without their appeal, and some of the record retains the classic Yes sound, there were lingering doubts as to the credibility and durability of the music. Recording engineer (and Yes fan) Gary Langan, who worked on *Drama*, remembered the sessions with a mixture of frustration and disbelief.

Langan recalled the making of the album for the author: "They were clutching at straws trying to keep the whole thing together," said Langan in 2008. "It was tragic for me. It was a lot of hard work. I always thought they were trying to make something out of what they didn't really have. Fish [Squire], Alan [White], and Steve [Howe] were desperate to hang on to the fact that Yes had to carry on. They had to do another mega American tour and there had to be another Yes album, you know?

"There were times on *Drama* when the rows were just enormous," Langan continued, "and there would be caustic notes left from one member to

glass hammer : chronometree

The musical paths of Yes and Georgia-based progressive rock band Glass Hammer intertwined in the late twentieth century and throughout the twenty-first. GH's 2000 studio album, *Chronometree*, uses Yes' *Close to the Edge* to playfully probe the concept of alien contact; Jon Anderson appears on GH's 2007 studio release, *Culture of Ascent*; and Yes' nineteenth studio album, *Heaven & Earth*, produced by Roy Thomas Baker, features GH vocalist Jon Davison.

another: 'I think this should be . . .' Or, 'How dare you . . .' It was just . . . like a bunch of kids. We ended up [recording the album] in shifts, me and Julian Mendelsohn . . . I'd come in and do three or four nights of the night shift. That meant working with Fish and doing bass overdubs and vocal parts and things like that. Julian would have been working with Steve Howe during the day. I used to come into the studio in the evening and think, 'Oh, God, what has been going on?' Unless you were there you wouldn't believe half the shit that was going on. I always used to think it was aptly named: Yes, it was a complete *drama*."

Although *Drama* went to the top of the charts in the U.K. and would be supported by a largely successful world tour, including sold-out shows at Madison Square Garden in New York, Horn always felt uncomfortable performing songs originally written and sung by Anderson—just one of the many signs that Yes' days were numbered.

Liner notes to the Yes boxed set *The Word Is Live*, written by *Yes Magazine* editors Doug and Glenn Gottlieb, posits: "Surely if they withstood the onslaught of punk and disco, Yes would have easily held its own against the likes of New Wave and the infant stirrings of hip-hop."

It was not to be, however. The band officially broke up in 1981, the members scattering to the four corners, as they say. Howe would soon form Asia with John Wetton, Carl Palmer, late of ELP, and his bandmate, Downes. Horn would become one of the most sought-after producers in England, and Squire and White hadn't given up hope of fronting a stadium-rock band.

Keyboardist Dave Lawson (session man, Greenslade), through personal contacts, met with Squire and the rest, as they sometimes say, is (almost) history. "After hearing me play on a Synclavier [sampler synth] in the studio, [Squire] asked me to come out and meet Alan White," Lawson told the author. "I've got some recorded tracks of us playing, still. After I did a film called *Death Wish II* with Jimmy Page, I mentioned playing with Chris and Alan to Jimmy and Jimmy knew of Chris. In fact, Jimmy put some guitar tracks on the recordings we did. I've never heard the guitar version, but it appeared as though we were becoming a band [called XYZ]." [*Note: Rumor had it that Robert Plant, who was only marginally involved in the project, was going to be the group's lead singer.*]

Lawson described the tracks as "aggressive" but retaining some of Yes' complex qualities—what was essentially a marriage of blues-based hard rock and Euro folk influences from the Zeppelin side and classical music and jazz, largely from the Yes camp. The song "Mind Drive," which appears on *Keys to Ascension 2*, was based on a demo recorded by XYZ.

In an era of supergroups, XYZ would have stood apart, perhaps even more than Page's star-studded, mid-'80s post-Zeppelin project the Firm. "Unfortunately, the band never happened because of political reasons, and that was the end of that," Lawson said. "But a while later, when Yes started to put the band together again, it was assumed that I would join. Alan White even said, 'I'm begging you . . .' when I said I couldn't do it, because I was so busy with sessions." [*Note: When Zeppelin reunited in 2007 for a performance at the O2 Arena with Bonham's son, drummer Jason, Rick Wakeman, Keith Emerson, Chris Squire, and drummer Simon Kirke of Bad Company were scheduled to be the opening act. Due to a Jimmy Page injury, the concert date was moved and Wakeman had to drop out due to scheduling. However, Yes' Alan White was recruited and joined the opening band.*]

Although the supergroup never materialized, Squire and White released a single around Christmastime, 1981, called "Run with the Fox," with lyrics supplied by Pete Sinfield. It became a holiday hit.

Within a few short years, Yes would reunite, with Horn at the console and young South African composer/singer/guitarist Trevor Rabin (Manfred Mann's Earth Band, Rabbit) taking the command role as lead songwriter, completely redefining what it meant to be Yes, and reshaping it through the marvels of studio experimentation and production savvy for a new decade. A U.S. number-one hit, "Owner of a Lonely Heart," would emerge in 1984, resurrecting Yes' career.

Wise After the Event

An Anthony Phillips Q&A

Even those who were closest to him largely misunderstood his early departure from one of the most influential progressive rock bands ever assembled. A combination of stage fright and health concerns forced original Genesis guitarist Anthony Phillips out of the spotlight, off to the sidelines, and into the studio, where he's largely worked, tirelessly, for over four decades.

Because Phillips' exit from Genesis was so abrupt, and so early in the band's career, we tend to forget the contributions the versatile guitarist made to Genesis and its recordings, such as 1970's classic *Trespass*. Through their combination of six- and twelve-string acoustic guitar melodies and overdubs, Phillips and guitarist Mike Rutherford were responsible for creating the very foundations of the eerie, dreamlike qualities in Genesis' music so revered by fans.

Indeed. Through his songwriting craft Phillips (born 1951) played no small role in steering Genesis toward a more cerebral, pastoral, and idiosyncratic progressive rock path, while helping the band shed its Bee Gees–like vocal style, largely thrust upon it by *From Genesis to Revelation* producer Jonathan King, a graduate of the prestigious public school Charterhouse, where he had discovered and later christened Genesis.

Although his unexpected evacuation from Genesis nearly permanently damaged his relationship with his friend Mike Rutherford, Phillips continued to exchange ideas and record tracks with his former bandmate for what would eventually become his first solo record, 1977's *The Geese & the Ghost*, which features Phil Collins, who'd joined Genesis after Phillips had waved good-bye to touring life.

Since the release of *The Geese & the Ghost*, Phillips has been prolific and active—some might even say hyperactive—as a "homespun" recording artist, releasing dozens of studio albums and compilations of archived material.

Below is a Q&A with Phillips, who discusses his time with Genesis, *The Geese & the Ghost*, some unlikely sources of inspiration, and how—and why—he felt simpatico with Nick Drake.

WR: Some of the material on *The Geese & the Ghost* dates to the early Genesis days.

Anthony Phillips: Quite a lot of material on *The Geese & the Ghost* dated back to Genesis. The instrumental "The Geese & the Ghost" itself had a lot of bits that came from 1969, which we then added extra sections to later. I wrote some of the "Henry: Portraits from Tudor Times" bits just after I left Genesis in 1970: "God If I Saw Her Now," "Which Way the Wind Blows," and a song we later included [on the CD reissue], which wasn't on the original, called "Master of Time," from 1970. "Collections" was from '69 as well. All the basic material was from 1969, 1970—the stuff that Mike [Rutherford, Genesis guitarist] and I hadn't managed to get through the group.

WR: What was it about the material that wasn't coming together for Genesis?
Phillips: I should explain that "Henry . . . ," almost all of it, was after Genesis. "Collections" was for [the band], but didn't fit in. I think some of the only bits were "The Geese & the Ghost" instrumental and we had lots of material in that style. In Genesis we had a piece called "The Movement," parts of which were used for "Stagnation" [from 1970's *Trespass*]. We did have quite a lot of stuff that there wasn't room for. In fact, Mike and I, before going on the road in '69, mucked around with demos for what later became the basis for "The Musical Box." I don't think it was ever played to anybody [in the band]. These were areas that we thought maybe too personal, or whatever, for the band. *Our* areas. During the time on the road, Mike and I stopped playing together outside the group. Something went out of it, really. We didn't listen to or play any of that material from September 1969 through to when I left. So, when I left, he must have come across this bit and thought, "Hang on. Maybe the revamped group could do something what that." He did—and very well, indeed.

WR: So, you helped to write that material, in essence.
Phillips: It is not a major issue. I wouldn't worry about it too much. I've let it go. I was only involved in the initial bits, a couple of initial bits. I should say there was another track called "Harlequin" [from 1971's *Nursery Cryme*] where something of mine was used. I think being a placid guy and the fact that they were battling it out on the road, doing all the hard work, I felt rather guilty—and I was making money from *Trespass*. I just never felt like rocking the boat. There was a mutual respect for each other and none of us would slag each other off or take each other to court or something.

WR: Could you have written material for the band without touring with them, like Brian Wilson did with the Beach Boys?
Phillips: I'll tell you what: Genesis was a sect, or religious sect. You were either in it or out of it. You couldn't be half in it, and I think that my departure was not very well understood by the others. I won't say it was bad blood, but the relationship wasn't brilliant afterwards.

WR: It took years to release *The Geese & the Ghost*. What can you tell us about how the album was recorded?

Phillips: The recording process and its subsequent release spanned three calendar years. It kicked off in autumn 1974 and didn't come out until early 1977. The first bit of recording was done at my parents' place, a studio at my parents' place. Mike Rutherford and I got hold of two four-track Teacs, which were using quarter-inch tape in those days, and we had DBX noise reduction units, and we recorded a lot of the basic guitar parts on that. I knew Mike was going to go off on tour, the *Lamb* tour. In fact, we only started it because Steve [Hackett] had managed to cut his hand on a wineglass and gave us a couple of weeks' grace. Otherwise we wouldn't have been able to start it at all. Then, Mike went off on tour and I didn't have many tracks

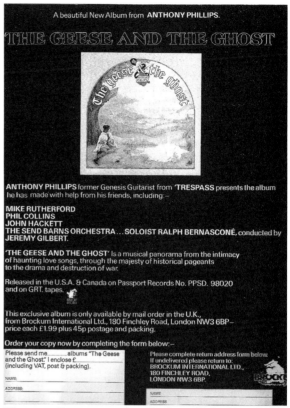

The recording process for *The Geese & the Ghost* (1977) spanned nearly three years. Ad from Genesis' 1977 world tour program.

to play with, as you can imagine with two, four-track Teacs. I did a few test parts on top [of what was already recorded]. Then, during the next phase of recording, we had two options: try to get a hold of an eight- or even sixteen-track recorder, or have a go elsewhere. It turned out we went elsewhere.

WR: I once spoke with recording engineer Simon Heyworth, who worked with Gong and Mike Oldfield. He said he had helped with the recording of *The Geese & the Ghost* and that you were working on a barge.

Phillips: It was a barge owned by Tom Newman, who engineered *Tubular Bells*. Richard Branson [founder, Virgin Records] had premises near. All of the Virgin [label] people used to drink in the local pub around there. Simon was the number two [engineer] on *Tubular Bells*, so that was the connection. That was the autumn '74 for the basic recordings, at which point Mike was away for six or seven months. We went fully on in the early summer of 1975 on this barge. But things kept breaking down all the time. Thank God it was a nice summer; we spent most of the time sunbathing. We actually [completed the record] at night. Well, I say night, but it was four or five o'clock in the late afternoon, early evening, most of the time. Being England, you get loads of sunshine at that time of day, still. Well, that is if the sun's ever out! It was really those two phases.

Everything was then transferred to a sixteen-track Studer, as I recall. Because it was an ambitious project—the instrumentals, in particular, required lots of tracks—we had to do some pretty dicey things. At that point Mike had to get ready for the next Genesis phase. Peter had left and Phil was becoming the singer. Mixing it, precomputer days, was an absolute nightmare.

WR: What makes you say that?
Phillips: Well, as an instrumental is flying through we'd have our positions ready [on the mixing desk] to suddenly switch where the bass drum becomes an oboe or something. Now, you can computerize it all. Mixing it was like flying on the seat of your pants. The interesting thing about those days was that, apart from the Mellotron, you had to create all the sounds yourself. Nowadays a lot of us rely on samples.

WR: Please talk about sonic experimentation as relates to *The Geese & the Ghost*.
Phillips: I remember trying silly little things like, there's one part of "Henry: Portraits from Tudor Times" in which we had fuzz electric guitar playing with a cor anglais. I mean, that's unusual, but that had to be thought out and planned and that wasn't a sample.

WR: Much of *The Geese & the Ghost* was inspired by events in English history, such the Tudor Dynasty. What was the fascination with the past?
Phillips: I think that was a pivotal point in history. So many [TV] programs and documentaries have been done about the Tudors since the release of the record that it's almost too much now. But it was a seismic time for England: moving away from the Catholic Church, and Henry VIII was nothing if not a dramatic character, so I found the people and characters were just so larger than life, really. There was great romance, intrigue, drama, blood-thirst . . .

WR: The story about your exit from Genesis has always been entangled with this idea of stage fright.
Phillips: It was my fault. I didn't really explain what was going on, partly because I was too disturbed by what had actually gone on, if you want me to be quite honest with you. I was very young, as well. . . . We didn't wash our dirty linen in public. There was none of that. But I think there was a slight bitter taste left in everyone's mouth. We didn't avoid each other. I used to go and watch their gigs. Maybe to them it's a bit like I had deserted. It wasn't that. I was told by medical people to leave. There was certainly no question of that. If you look

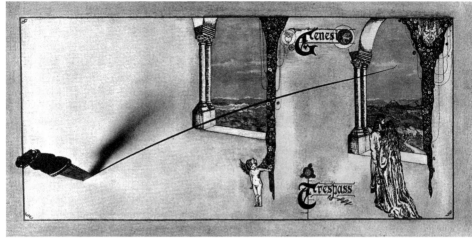

The full cover for *Trespass*, Anthony Phillips' final studio album with Genesis.

later on, Peter Gabriel left and didn't write for them; Steve Hackett left and didn't write for them. There has never been a precedent.

There were a few songs that started out on the road that died a death, as well. That was slightly sad. There were a few nice acoustic ones, bridge tracks, if you like, from *From Genesis to Revelation* and *Trespass*, but the kinds of gigs we were doing weren't conducive to those types of songs, because we were playing either noisy technical colleges where people wanted to dance, so you had to flatten them with a bit of volume, or nightclubs where people really weren't interested in that sort of acoustic guitar stuff at all. We played once at Brighton Dome and that was the sort of rare place where you could do that kind of thing. Something like "Let Us Now Make Love," which was one of our sweet tracks, but did not wind up on a studio album [*Trespass*], wasn't . . . It was kind of sad, because those songs didn't last that period. Someone like Nick Drake, who we'd come across at gigs, because he was managed by one of the agents, was subjected to playing completely the wrong venues. Poor old chap. Similar to us, I guess, in a way. Nick used to play with us at a lot of these tech gigs, and this guy was very shy and he was hunched over the guitar and had a husky voice. Nobody would listen, because it was not what they wanted. But when he found out that I was the premier writer of [bold "Let Us Now Make Love"], he actually came up to me and said, "Dangerous." I'll never forget that.

WR: A cult has built up around Nick Drake . . .

Phillips: I know. When people find out that we knew him or had gigged with him, they assume we went out to dinner after the show. It wasn't like that. We didn't have a lot of money. After the gig we would jump into the van and go home, because we had to unload the gear at the other end. There were no roadies doing it for us. I mean, we had a couple of mates working as roadies with us, but we were in it together. It was all hands to the tiller.

WR: Were you shocked by his death? [*Note: Drake's death is still shrouded in mystery. Some believe he'd committed suicide. Others theorize he died of an accidental overdose.*]
Phillips: It's not the act itself. It was what he must have been feeling leading up to it—neglected and nobody interested in him. Then you think about now how people see him now, it's bloody ironic. It's cruel. I mean, without getting maudlin about this, there were times, and I wouldn't say I have been close to that, but there have been times in which reaction to my own records has put me . . . in a pretty dark place, to be honest. I . . . always felt a strong affinity with Nick. Honestly, with *The Geese & the Ghost* I'd given up on it. It was not an easy time, because Genesis re-formed, had a huge success with *A Trick of the Tail* [a U.K. top 3 album], and went storming off into the sunset. *The Geese & the Ghost* with Mike Rutherford and Phil Collins sat on the shelf. Looking back on it, talking about Nick Drake, I'm not sure how I kept it together, really. I just threw myself into as much of the music as I could, and I was teaching quite a lot, too. I've been lucky, having fingers in other pies, and having a very active, vibrant, and remunerative life in TV music.

WR: Can you describe the critical reaction to your records in a bit more detail?
Phillips: I came back with *The Geese & the Ghost* around the time of punk; not good timing. In the States it wasn't the same sort of thing. Over here [in the U.K.] it was merciless. 1977 was a rotten time. I was away to the States around then [touring], and I had gotten some very mixed reviews. I remember being given a press sheet and one review read, " . . . a mellow rock classic," another wrote, " . . . music to wash dishes to." You hear stories of football players, who are told never to read the press. Believe you me you always remember the bad ones.

WR: The artwork for your album contributes greatly to how the entire package is perceived. This is especially true of *The Geese & the Ghost*. It seems you have a symbiotic relationship with illustrator Peter Cross.
Phillips: The artwork for that one was very different from most albums. *The Geese & the Ghost* was done, and that meant that Peter was given the finished article. Often someone would be asked to do a cover on the basis of the title alone, and maybe a few demos, but [the musician and illustrator] would have to work in tandem in this sort of guessing game. He created artwork completely from his own auspices from those tracks. He took all the elements, predominately using the pastoral, Tudor England aspect of it.

WR: This has been talked about, but why the title?
Phillips: I wish I could tell you it was something imaginative. It wasn't. There were two sounds on the record: one was very thin, wraith-like, ghostly, and we used to call that "ghostly." Then there was another sound, this repeat echo and panning sound that goes across the stereo speakers that we called "geese." The record was actually going to be called *Lostwithiel*, which is a wonderful sounding place in Cornwall, which . . . is not as lovely a place as it sounds. [laughs]

Anyway, no disrespect to the inhabitants of Lostwithiel, but *The Geese & the Ghost* is a slightly better title.

WR: You had hinted at this already: *The Geese & the Ghost* was released at the height of the punk movement in the U.K. How did this impact you personally and your music?

Phillips: Like all things in life the record industry was ruled by extremes; it was one thing or the other, which was ludicrous, really. You had this nonsense that the Virgin staff were arriving one day with skinhead haircuts, because they . . . were frightened of the young turks. I had nothing against punk, and if I were ten years younger I'm sure I probably would have been doing it myself [playing punk rock], but the idea that everyone had to do short-form pop songs with lots of balls, as they kept saying, was a complete joke. In fact, *Sides* [solo album, 1979] was a pisstake. *Sides* was going to be called *Balls*. You know the cover of *Sides* was a football table [table soccer]? [Peter Cross] had to change it, because it was called *Balls*. I was so fed up with people saying things about me like, " . . . oh, yeah, but he doesn't have enough balls . . ." It was such bollocks, pardon the pun. In fact, the track "Um & Aargh," a lot of people didn't realize is me really having a go at the A&R people at record companies. They were notorious for not knowing what the hell they were on about, half of them. I remember one quote from a guy about an album: "It's too good to go out." That's why the lyrics of "Um & Aargh" are lines like, "'It's too good for the people,' he said." [laughs] It was me having a go . . . just as the Genesis song "The Knife" [*Trespass*] was an anti-revolutionary song. It was a pisstake, really. A spoof. But people took it up as revolutionary.

WR: Most of the members of Genesis were, at one point, from the public school Charterhouse.

Phillips: Yes. We were quite traditional boys. Don't get me wrong: we weren't right-wing Tories sitting around saying to each other, "We don't like these revolutionary chappies . . ." It wasn't like that at all. It was Peter's lyrics, and I helped him with the second verse, I think. It wasn't pro-revolution. It was having a little gentle dig at the naïveté of it.

WR: Getting back to punk, it did seem as though the recording industry was looking for the Next Big Thing, something out of step with the rock of the day . . .

Phillips: I will say that some of the progressive music had gotten quite esoteric. Maybe there were some younger people who needed something more urgent and direct. I think it was the fact that yesterday's heroes were turned on and knifed in the back, in this sort of palace revolution that shocked people. That did them a terrible dishonor. I can't blame the people in the record industry for looking for a new Beatles, and I can't blame them for wanting to embrace a younger market, but the two should have been able to coexist. Funnily enough, at the age of twenty-six I found myself being called an old fart, which was rather extraordinary.

WR: Was *Wise After the Event*, from 1978, recorded in response to the changing times?

Phillips: When I did *Wise After the Event*, I wasn't being ordered to do short pop songs, and have hits. It was more of, "Write an album of songs and perhaps try to have a hit." We got a deal from Arista, but by the time it came around to *Sides* it was very much a question of, "You gotta have hit records. . . ." Disco was in by then, as well. I always felt I should have been carrying on developing *The Geese & the Ghost*–type stuff. I think one of the sad things for me is the time had passed for that kind of music. What would have been great would have been to take *The Geese & the Ghost* and move further into that terrain. By the time it was released, there was this demand for simple pop songs, again, and to get away from overblown classical, pomp rock. Although it had its aficionados, *Wise After the Event* wasn't the right direction to go in, enjoyable though it was, working with Rupert Hine, John Perry, Michael Giles.

WR: How quickly did they work?

Phillips: They were super quick. It was difficult to get Mike to do the show-y stuff. I like Mike's wild, wild strange fills from "The Court of the Crimson King." Loved it, but Mike was quite reticent. He wasn't a showman. He was a less-is-more man. He would hang back. You'd have to really force Mike to let go. He's sort of, you know, a correct Englishman.

WR: What inspired the title *Wise After the Event?*

Phillips: I'm trying to remember. Let me backtrack. One of the [song] titles came about because I met a girl in Cleveland [during the promo tour for *The Geese & the Ghost* following its March 1977 release], who explained to me what "moonshooting" meant. That's why I chose the title for that song. Most of the titles were not inspired by any real events. "Regrets," that was about a failed relationship. But "Wise After the Event"? Not sure really. It was slightly psychedelic, I suppose, the lyrics were. A line like "Four monks . . . in a maelstrom . . ." was quite bizarre. I wasn't taking any drugs, either.

"Now What (Are They Doing to My Little Friends?)" was written as an anti-hunting song, because I had seen a hunt in Devon, which was disgusting, and there was a story in the papers about these guys killing almost the last of these endangered species called the spectacled bear. So, that was the inspiration. In fact, that line about "bespectacled and brown" may sound ludicrous, but it's not. There's a species of bear, called the spectacled bear, so called because it had rings around his eyes. From South America, I believe. That took two days to mix that track, because we really worked on that song and stripped it down, so each section had its own arrangement. There wasn't too much going on and then it builds to this climax. If I'm proud of anything on that record, it's that track.

WR: I have to backtrack: "Moonshooter"?
Phillips: It means to bare your bum.

WR: Like, mooning someone.
Phillips: I had never heard the phrase. It's an American term, maybe?

WR: Well, maybe it was popularized here . . .
Phillips: She was talking about moonshooting and I asked her what it was. She was quite wild. I had been to the States a couple of times . . . and I had just had such a wonderful time meeting all of these wonderful people all over the country. It was fantastic.

WR: "Pulling Faces": What inspired that?
Phillips: That is pretty surreal. That was mainly space. There was a whole lot of astronomical stuff in there. We had a wonderful old character, Patrick Moore, who used to do a program called *Sky at Night*, which we used to watch as much to see Moore's wild eyebrows and hear his strange speech. He was a real classic English eccentric who died recently, sadly. Astronomy was the one form of science that I really loved.

WR: You came up with *Private Parts & Pieces* series to release your older material. Why?
Phillips: Around the time when everything was headed into the more commercial world, I pleaded to see if it was possible to do more homespun music, simple acoustic guitar music. [Passport] agreed to give away *Private Parts & Pieces*, and at that stage it was a limited edition. The first thousand people who bought *Sides*, I think it was the first thousand, got that record for free. [*Note: Phillips' own website,* www.anthonyphillips.co.uk, *reports that it was the first five thousand copies.*] Then it got released separately in the States [June 1979]. Then, it became a kind of series. I thought that the cover by [illustrator] Peter Cross was an absolute masterpiece.

There were quite a few pieces from the early 1970s that I hadn't been able to find a home for. I mean, the piano piece "Autumnal" [*Private Parts & Pieces*, 1978, 1979] and the acoustic guitar piece "Field of Eternity" [*Private Parts & Pieces*] were two of Mike Rutherford's favorite pieces of mine in 1972 when we were starting to fraternize again, before we thought about *The Geese & the Ghost*. When the record deal dried up, the *Private Parts & Pieces* series was the only practical thing. It's all about simple home albums using limited resources and costing limited amounts of money. That was really the pattern for the 1980s and when I came over to the States in the 1980s, I found out that what I was doing was being called "New Age." I had been doing it for ten years at that point. On the basis of that I was able to do the *Slow Dance* album [1990]. . . . I hadn't done a full-scaled album like that one in years.

WR: Your album *Twelve* from 1985 is interesting. Why do a concept record based on the months of the year?

Phillips: That came from Peter Cross. When I first saw Peter's work, he had a book based on the twelve months of the year with a sort of story line with these animals: trumpets being the goodies, grumpets the baddies. There were these wonderful animals, at times at peace, at times at war, very funny, but it was a mixture of incredibly beautiful pastoral landscapes and very strange guns and machinery. That's what I saw and what inspired me, so that's what led me to ask Peter, initially, to do *The Geese & the Ghost*. But I'd also wanted to do a record of music that was inspired by his book project. As it happens, his book came out in a slightly different way from the version I had seen, and years later I was stuck for an idea for a twelve-string acoustic album. A twelve-string album seemed the most practical thing to do at that junction given the nature of the resources available. So, although I was initially inspired by Peter's work, I never managed to fully tie it together with his story line, which is a shame.

WR: What would you say was one of the most challenging songs for you to record or write?

Phillips: Gosh. All of it is difficult. Recording is never easy. You get to record and as soon as the red light is on you start freezing. I'm slightly joking, of course. But, I remember the guitar part on "Nightmare," from *Sides*, was difficult. There have been a couple of acoustic albums that I've had to give up on a couple of tracks, because they've beaten me. I couldn't nail them. While working on material for *Field Day* [2005] there were two classical guitar pieces that were too difficult for me, so I had to let them go. It's one thing to strum an idea rough, but it's another to have it perfect, smooth, all the tones right. Sometimes the gap between the initial bit of writing and the finished performance is very different.

WR: So these songs never surfaced?

Phillips: Absolutely not. I can't remember them.

WR: Let's go back to Genesis. What can you tell me about the recording of *Trespass* and John Anthony's production style?

Phillips: Well, we had been playing these songs for nine months, and it was difficult to get any particular inspiration. We were a well-drilled unit by that stage. We could play these songs backwards, although I'm not saying we were bored. The most memorable thing about the recording sessions for me was recording the twelve-string, because I had this particular way of recording twelve-string. I had my own signature twelve-string sound. We featured twelve-string guitar as a sort of harmony, slightly classical instrument. I remember I had gotten my sound and Robin [Cable], the engineer, said, "That doesn't sound like a twelve-string." I said, "It does." He moved the mike and then I kind of moved it back again. The way I set up was part of the group sound. That was a bit tricky. Aside from that it went fine. We weren't great at backing harmonies, but we just about supported Peter. John Anthony was a nice guy, but we were not allowed to drop in. Mike had an idea for "Stagnation," a classic guitar pattern that came in about the seven-minute mark, and he had to sit there for seven minutes waiting for the moment when he could play. By the time he had gotten there he could hardly play. I don't know why John Anthony had a thing about not being able to drop in. It was pretty strange. We had recorded *From Genesis to Revelation* [1969] in such an amateur way, and here we were at Trident Studios pretending to be Big Boys. [John Anthony] very much helped us with that. We played the songs so much on stage that he helped us to reinvent some of them.

WR: When you say reinvent . . .
Phillips: It was more of, "We can try this effect on this track . . ." We had been signed by Charisma, and we didn't really want to start ripping apart songs that [the label] knew.

WR: The early Genesis had written a song called "The Mystery of the Flannan Isle Lighthouse." Do you remember why?
Phillips: Wasn't it about the lighthouse where people disappeared?

WR: Yes.
Phillips: That idea came from Peter [Gabriel] and Tony [Banks]. We were looking for interesting lyrical ideas. [Producer] Jonathan King whipped us into shape and made us try to do more pop songs. But we started experimenting with longer tracks. We were doing four- or five-minute things, taking bizarre subjects, a million miles away from boy-girl relationship subject matters. Look at "A Day in the Life." Hardly a pop song. Look at "The Fountain of Salmacis," later. There is a direct link to some of those songs. They are a bit clumsy and they are a bit boyish. But in terms of looking at mystery and length of development there is a link there. If you cut up the Jonathan King period of singles, it's almost a seamless procession, if you like, from piano-vocal stuff to fully arranged material with mystery and development.

Shock to the System

Henry Cow and Rock in Opposition

A lthough the original Rock in Opposition (RIO) coalition lasted for only two years, the impact of its influence remains incalculable.

Henry Cow are one of the pillars of what's been labeled the avant-prog movement, a style encompassing a wide range of artists, from the Muffins to Guapo, Hamster Theatre, Alamaailman Vasarat, Art Zoyd, Univers Zero, Sleepytime Gorilla Museum, Doctor Nerve, and Miriodor, among others, who keep the spirit of the original RIO bands flying.

Reinforcing the belief that avant-rock pioneered in the 1970s continues to be relevant in the twenty-first century, an RIO festival, established in 2007, is held annually in France, and promotes music ranging from rock, free jazz, and noise to chamber and contemporary classical.[1]

To better understand RIO we should take a brief look at Henry Cow and its music.

Formed in 1968 at Cambridge University by guitarist Fred Frith and saxophonist/keyboardist/guitarist Tim Hodgkinson, Henry Cow were turning the underground on its ear and running in the same circles as Pink Floyd (even opening for them).

"Henry Cow formed because Tim and I liked each other after we met and played together, and being in a band seemed like a good idea," guitar Fred Frith says flatly. "I'd already been in bands since I was fourteen, and I was missing it. So we got together and jammed with other folks that we met.

"We were constantly listening to everything that was going on at a time when there was an unprecedented availability of all kinds of music, live and on record," Frith continues. "In 1968, the year we started, I discovered Indian music, Balinese music, Beefheart, Zappa, John Cage, Berio, Stockhausen, and went to hear John Lee Hooker at a bar in Hull in Yorkshire. You could do that then. At some point we started to get better at what we were doing, and then we had a name, and we started to take ourselves more seriously.[2] Then suddenly we weren't students anymore, and so it took on a different character, the birth of thinking more professionally, I suppose, in our cack-handed way."

After some personnel changes, seeing the likes of bassist Andrew Powell and drummer Dave Atwood move through the band's ranks, Henry Cow became a more solidified group. The new, more stable lineup, which included Frith, drummer Chris Cutler, John Greaves on bass, wind instrument player Geoff Leigh, and Hodgkinson (with the addition of Lindsay Cooper, bassoonist/ flautist/oboist) was to be the core of the band for the next few years.

Henry Cow appeared to be ahead of its time; some of Cow's early performances were multimedia crossover events, which gained notoriety via word of mouth, bringing them to the attention of the fledgling label Virgin Records.

"There was a buzz around us in London in 1972," says Frith. "We'd been on John Peel for the second or third time and it had gone down well. Respected people like Robert Wyatt were singing our praises and suddenly it looked like we were on the verge of something. That's what record companies are always looking for. We were actually negotiating with another label, but we'd come to the conclusion that they were primarily interested in us as a tax write-off. I did like Branson . . . Plus, the way he successfully stood up to the BBC over their archaic refusal to allow Robert Wyatt to appear on *Top of the Pops* in a wheelchair, for fear of 'upsetting' viewers, earned my undying respect."[3]

For some observers, Henry Cow's mixture of rock, free music, jazz, and contemporary music was unlike anything on the British scene at the time. Ray Smith, an artist who would design the famous paint-line "sock" for the cover of the band's debut album, made appearances at these performances, prior to the band even being signed, to "add a dimension to the whole experience" taking place at events dubbed Cabaret Voltaire and the Explorers Club.

"One of my favorite pieces opened an evening with Henry Cow and Gong at the New London Theatre," says Smith. "I began by walking to the center of the stage at the beginning of the evening dressed in a dark suit. I had some gaudy pink material attached to one of my arms. The material was dropped to reveal a glove puppet, which mimed enthusiastically 'You are my heart's delight' and I then walked quietly off the stage. Another evening at the Rainbow Theatre, where I had put on a white shirt and a dark suit, I set up an ironing board stage left and spent the whole evening on the stage quietly ironing."

Smith, at the Hammersmith Palais, also "read out short passages of discontinuous text between each piece of music," he says. "It was interesting how one passage could so transform another. I later proposed a series of visual activities which included working with text, film, and performance. The activities did not specifically 'choreograph' the music."

"I saw them live and they played one song for an hour and a bit," says King Crimson guitarist/vocalist Jakko Jakszyk. "It was all of their numbers segued in between all of these bits of free improvisation. As an impressionable teenager, I got a perverse enjoyment for that. At the time I loved the alienating aspect of the free improvisation. I could sense people in the audience saying, 'This is bollocks. I don't like it'—the way it would meander into this complicated music and it was played beautifully."

The writing, at times, was extraordinary. Songs on the band's debut, 1973's *Leg End* (a.k.a. *LegEnd*, a.k.a. *Legend*) such as "Nirvana for Mice," the "Teenbeat" suite, the political "Nine Funerals of the Citizen King" (foretelling the

Henry Cow Concerts: Robert Wyatt (Soft Machine, Matching Mole) makes an appearance.

band's foray into the world of RIO), and "The Tenth Chaffinch" were nearly indefinable, fusing what seemed free improvisation with structured composition.

"The Tenth Chaffinch" is particularly bonkers, sounding like a conversation between a Ligeti chorus section on LSD and drunk Buddhist monks. "We're just improvising," drummer Chris Cutler says.

"I heard 'Nirvana for Mice' a million times, and I thought I knew it," says Jakszyk. "But then I took it apart on paper and, I mean, there's a whole section in the middle where it goes into 21/8 and stays there. They keep messing around with the bottom measure. They keep flipping from 5/8 and 5/4. But, it doesn't sound like the other kind of fusion stuff that was starting to happen where people were wearing that kind of cleverness on their sleeve. This music sounded terribly organic. And when you stripped it back that was when you'd realize how complicated it was."

Henry Cow's next record, *Unrest*, opened up more production possibilities for the band, as they were, more or less, left to their own devices in the studio, so to speak. Aside from the engineers, one of them being Mike Oldfield, Henry Cow took the reins for the recording and produced *Unrest* themselves. As with *Legend*, most of the first side of *Unrest* was done with limited overdubs, "live" in the studio. The second side was assembled via studio experimentation (i.e., sixteen-track loops involving the band holding pencils in different locations of the studio and playing back mixes at half-speed by accident for parts of "Deluge"; it wouldn't be until Frith and Cutler formed Art Bears that they worked with clicks and overdubs). These bold steps would hint at the sense of freedom and musical independence the collective unit and the individual members would demonstrate in the near future.

"At that point we were being pretty experimental," says Frith. "We didn't know where it would lead, and a 'producer' might well have been too anxious about the result. Who knows? I've been a producer on numerous occasions, and worked with producers too. I'm open to anything. But back then it felt right just the way it was. To be honest I think most producers would have thought we were nuts, and that's probably why it remains our most successful record, in my opinion."

In one example of the way their left-of-center minds were operating, Frith used the Fibonacci series to compose a piece called "Ruins," an ironic title for such a mathematically neat and metrical piece.

"'Ruins' has . . . various phrases that are palindromes with specific numerical values, and other mathematical elements that I no longer remember, to be honest," says Frith. "It was composed on paper, and I don't have the score anymore. The instrumentation in the middle is dictated by what instruments we could play. I wanted it to be somewhat classical-sounding. So violin, bassoon, and xylophone were as close as I was likely to get. The fact that the violin was so badly played [by Frith] is a matter of some sadness to me, and it would be interesting to have another shot at it with Carla Kihlstedt [Sleepytime Gorilla Museum] playing, but I doubt if I'll ever have the energy or motivation to go that far. But I do like the fact that very different compositional and improvisational approaches are contained within the same piece."

Why did Frith use the Fibonacci series to begin with?

"Why not?" replies Frith. "It's a supremely elegant and simple ratio that's found throughout nature, expressed in myriad forms. It can be a kind of tool, if you like. I had just read a biography of Bartók, which spoke at length about how he used it to structure his compositions. As has often happened with me, I thought, 'Okay, let's try that.' I was as much inspired by the fact that Bartók kept pinecones on his desk as anything else. My interest in the series was to see whether it might lead me to some new creative areas, and it did, which is kind of the beginning and the end of that particular story, though I've continued to use it off and on ever since. . . . Over the years I've used it to determine harmonic ratios, structural ratios, rhythmic ratios. I started looking at it for exactly the same reason that I used chance methods to compose 'Nirvana for Mice' after reading John Cage—curiosity."

The details of the comings and goings of the band circa 1974 through 1976 might be best handled at some other later point, in another capacity. However, briefly, the band played and recorded with Robert Wyatt (the double live album *Henry Cow Concerts* recorded in England, Italy, Netherlands, and Norway), toured extensively, and merged with the experimental band Slapp Happy, also on Virgin, fronted by singer Dagmar Krause, an association that produced two records, *Desperate Straights* (1974) and *In Praise of Learning* from 1975.

Henry Cow began to incorporate written words into their music and made overt gestures toward a more left-leaning political agenda, a situation that was fueled, at least in part, by their affiliation with l'Orchestra, an Italian musical cooperative begun by the band Stormy Six, formed in 1966 as a folk act, and later of the RIO coalition.

"There were two main reasons for bringing about l'Orchestra," says Franco Fabbri, native Brazilian guitarist/vocalist of Italy's Stormy Six. "The first was that the Italian music industry was lagging behind compared to other countries; and, on the other hand, political parties were exploiting musicians emerging in the movement, and the only independent labels and organizations were closely related to folk revival and topical songs."

This may, or may not, have helped to plant a seed in the mind of drummer Chris Cutler's mind regarding the establishment of the RIO movement, which sought to sidestep the industry altogether and benefit members of its coalition through mutual support.

Unrest

Times were changing, and Virgin was developing rapidly in due course. No longer the great supporter of experimental music they once were, the quick fix seemed to be the order of the day. This meant Henry Cow was an afterthought.

Cutler maintains the band was largely ignored by Virgin after the first year or year and a half, and that Cow didn't so much as walk out on a contract with the company as slink away from it. "[Virgin] became more of an impediment than an aid," Cutler says, "and we just took back control of our own affairs without further reference to Virgin. Subsequently, neither of us mentioned the rest of the contracted recordings, since they obviously weren't going to happen. By the time we had reason to annul the contract, we'd had nothing to do with the label for a couple of years."

"The really strong motivating force behind our moves towards self-sufficiency and independence were not so much the label as all the structures they tried to create around it," says Frith. "Touring in a bus with Captain Beefheart and his . . . managers of the time, realizing that the real power of a label wasn't in A&R, but in the people, who were actually selling the product into the stores—and they hated us from the beginning—seeing how the industry worked from close quarters, how getting a review was a function of paying for advertising rather than any genuine interest, talking to journalists who simply didn't have a fucking clue what we were talking about—it was a very good education. And it didn't so much shatter our idealism as much as strengthen our resolve to stay out of the whole mess."

By this point Henry Cow had gotten a reputation for espousing certain noncommercial attitudes. Some might even call them socialist or communist principles. However, what Henry Cow was objecting to was, perhaps, not so much the money that they *could make* as signed artists, but the dilution of intellectual property by commercialism.

Although we cannot ignore the inherent contradiction of a band actually signing with a commercial entity and then marketing commercial records—and then denouncing the structure that supports such products—the point is, Henry Cow would not compromise their sound.

Was Virgin's move to the center a travesty or a liberating experience for Cow? "Oh, I think we felt completely liberated, especially as it became clear where Virgin was headed," says Frith. "In a way it's ironic, since Virgin, more than anything else, was what put us on the map;

An ad for Richard Branson's Virgin label, which was once a bastion of experimental music and progressive rock.

they cheerfully supported us, spent money promoting us, put us in their wonderful studio for weeks at a time, and gave us time to figure out who we were musically and where we were going. The fact that this turned out to be way to the left of them shouldn't blind one to the fact that they were instrumental in our early success, a fact that is sometimes forgotten."

So there may not have been a single incident in which Cutler and crew decided to establish the so-called RIO coalition, but rather a series of events—a perfect storm—linked with what the band experienced with its flirtation with the corporate music industry.

"The impetus was not so much an incident as an accumulation," confirms Frith. "As an independent British band we became all too aware of how much easier it was to tour in other countries than it was for bands from those countries to tour in the U.K. This appeared to us largely a result of what we identified as a form of cultural imperialism based on the fact that at the time the U.S.-U.K. entertainment industry axis was dominant everywhere. It seemed odd to us that

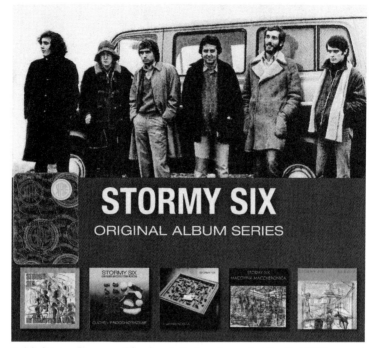

Italy's Stormy Six, one of five bands that performed at the first RIO concert
in London in 1978, composed both serious avant-garde music and a parody
of such, as evidenced by a song such as "Enzo," from 1980's *Macchina
Maccheronica*. Pictured: Warner Music Italy's 2012 *Original Album Series*, a
five-CD set.

groups felt compelled to sing in English, not their native language, in order to
be successful."

On the road Cow had met groups that had impressed them, and believed
them to be kindred spirits. "It seemed natural to pool our resources," says Frith.

The very existence of Rock in Opposition was an indictment of the economics of the record business. RIO wasn't without its conventions to socioeconomic
norms, as it was as much a way to survive the music business as a method by
which a select group of artists could build a competing and perhaps ultimately
more compelling *economic system* to maintain a level of exposure (i.e., regular
gigs).

But what exactly was RIO?

"Rock in Opposition was a wholly practical project," Cutler maintains. "It
was born to organize events, arrange LP distribution and theoretical discussion,
and to support independent production and innovation in what we thought of
as rock music. . . . [T]he economic power of a few American and British record
companies had ensured that only British and American bands and styles got
any exposure—and that only their version of rock was thought of as authentic."

The first Rock in Opposition (RIO) concert saw Henry Cow (England), Univers Zero (Belgium), Etron Fou Leloublan (France), Samla Mammas Manna (Sweden), and Stormy Six (Italy) perform on March 12, 1978, at the New London Theatre in London. A second concert was held in Milan in the spring of 1979, followed by two more concerts in Sweden and Belgium, but not before the "members" attempted to draw up a constitution to better define membership qualifications and guidelines.

It was decided that not everyone could join RIO—they had to meet certain requirements. For one, prospective bands must exhibit a level of "musical excellence"; actively help other bands in the RIO circle get and maintain gigs and record (i.e., a "social commitment to rock"); and work "actively outside the music business."

"The criteria were essential, I think," says Cutler. "Rock in Opposition wasn't an anything-goes club; it was severely rigorous. A free-for-all would have made a different point, a purely political point, but [RIO] was also making an aesthetic point: the five bands were chosen precisely for who they were and what they did. That's why, when we had our first meeting, and the issue of expansion was raised, the question of criteria was important—and difficult."

"There were, as far as I remember, just two criteria," adds Fabbri. "One was independence from commercial record companies, and lyrics, if any, needed to be sung in one's own language. We also agreed on a common commitment to aesthetic quality, in all aspects: lyrics, composition, recording, performance, but no stylistic requirements were ever considered."

The requirements for Italy's l'Orchestra were similar. "Well, yes and no," says Fabbri. "The requirement of independence was very strict, and we also required musicians to be closely related to the antifascist political and cultural movement. We also expected groups to sing in their own language, although most groups were Italian. But l'Orchestra also had non-Italian members, like Henry Cow, Etron Fou, Sogenanntes linksradikales Blasorchester, and was open to amateur groups. Although we tried to help these groups improve their musical quality."

After a meeting in Switzerland, a symbolic neutral ground if there ever was one, three more bands were added to the RIO roster, including Art Bears, a band that Henry Cow appeared to be transitioning into (featuring Cutler and Frith and Dagmar Krause), Art Zoyd from France, and Aqsak Maboul (Belgium).

From an outsider perspective it seemed as if RIO was a viable vehicle, but in just under two years there were already signs that the foundation was crumbling. As it happens, this closed society couldn't really agree on much. Despite their best efforts and surface similarities, deeper differences were becoming more and more apparent.

By 1980, the lifeblood of RIO had been drained out of the "organization," and the coalition dried up. "There was never a falling out, just a falling away as that moment passed," says Cutler. "Subsequently the term has been appropriated by others to mean all sorts of things, things we would never have been involved with."

"Maybe, also, Rock in Opposition was affected by changes in groups who had a prominent role in the organization of events, tours," says Fabbri. "Henry Cow was transforming into Art Bears, Chris [Cutler] had founded ReRecords [Recommended Records], which absorbed most of his energies. . . ."

"We all at least got to play in each others' countries," says Frith. "This was by far the most important aspect of Rock in Opposition at the time—the pragmatic one. And if you scratch the surface you find quite different ideologies and points of view across the [RIO] groups, who often had little in common, after all. I feel that [RIO] has taken on a philosophical-political significance in retrospect that it maybe didn't quite manage at the time."

18

Jack the Ripper and Other Musical Villains

Univers Zero's Daniel Denis

Belgium's Univers Zero (UZ) is the most enduring of all the multinational groups that established the original Rock in Opposition coalition in the late 1970s.

Daniel Denis, the band's leader, chief songwriter, and drummer, has been a mainstay and key figure on the avant-rock scene for nearly forty years. Denis has played with the likes of Magma; Present (with former UZ guitarist Roger Trigaux); UZ, which he formed in 1974 (and was named for Belgian author Jacques Sternberg's 1970 sci-fi novel of the same title), and its forerunners, Arkham and Necronomicon; as well as the French avant-rockers Art Zoyd, led by violinist/viola player/keyboardist Gérard Hourbette, a member of the original 1970s RIO movement.

Although UZ split in the second half of the 1980s, Denis remained active through performances with Art Zoyd and releasing his own solo albums (*Sirius and the Ghosts*, *Les Eaux Troubles*) before coming back full blast with a reconfigured UZ in the 1990s. As of this writing UZ had been a going concern for over fifteen years and just released a new studio album, 2014's *Phosphorescent Dreams* via Japanese label Label Arcangelo/Disk Union.

With his approval, I translated Denis' responses from French to English. Our exchange is below.

WR: I'm going to go out on a limb and say that you see images/visions in your mind when composing. What visions did you see when writing a piece such as "Triomphe des Mouches" [*Ceux du dehors*], "Emmanations" [from 1988's *Uzed*], "Dense" [*Ceux du dehors*], "Xenantaya" [*The Hard Quest*], etc.?
Daniel Denis: In general, images don't come to my mind before I, or we, begin the composition of a song. The inspiration and the construction evolve progressively over the course of a song being completed. I'm particularly attentive to rhythmic patterns, the harmonies and, above all, the development of a

composition's structure and the consistent themes that should run through a particular piece of music. The initial image that a piece of music evokes does little more than act as a guide. As we create the piece it sort of stimulates the imagination, creating visual images that we had not foreseen. Also, titles of songs are not necessarily indicative or representative of the pieces that emerge. "La Faulx" [from 1979's *Heresie*], "La corne du bois des pendus" [from 1981's *Ceux du dehors*] and various other pieces of this type may have emerged from a specific theme at the outset. The darker, mysterious side of songs is quite evident in retrospect, but I can tell you that I was not necessarily in a dark or depressing state of mind when I wrote these songs. And I'm not depressed in my daily life. Actually, it's quite the contrary. Ironically, I want the music to be very positive, uplifting and alive, in its own way, even if aspects of the music don't always necessarily reflect this idea.

WR: You've said that you don't necessarily consider your compositional style to be "dark." However, some listeners and observers have suggested that 1981's *Ceux du dehors* was less dark than Univers Zero's previous releases. *Bonjour chez vous*, for instance, seems pretty scary, and some of Andy Kirk's writing sounds like it was written by the Orcs of Middle-earth. The band, in the past, had even joked that one of its musical influences were serial killers, like Jack the Ripper. Did you make a conscious decision to "lighten" the music?

Denis: If the music of Univers Zero expresses moods, whether they are disturbing or mysterious, then that's what gives these pieces their personality, their identity. There's no desire to constantly compose music in the same musical

Univers Zero, 1977, once counted serial killers among their "influences." Bandleader/ drummer Daniel Denis is second from the right.   *Courtesy of Cuneiform Records*

vein. A piece such as "Toujours plus à l'est" [from 1983's *Crawling Wind*] and "Dense" [1981's *Ceux du dehors*], like a lot of UZ's music, was inspired by some traditional dances, giving it a sometimes cheerful feel. It's mainly the multitude of emotional shades within a song that give it its value. I have always been opposed to the idea that Univers Zero's music was depressing, off-putting, and obscure.

WR: You also said that some members pushed the "dark" angle a bit more than perhaps they should have (if the band wanted to reach mainstream audiences). Bassist Guy Segers even appears, for dramatic effect, in a wheelchair in PR shots. What could bandmembers have done to tone down the "darkness"?
Denis: We wanted to express our opposition to show business in the easiest way possible, and presenting ourselves as being dark and mysterious was one way of doing so. We also wanted to have a way of making sure our music was differentiated from commercial music that was being made at the time. There was, obviously, a lot of humor in what we did, even if most people didn't really get the joke.

WR: You said once that you don't read or write musical or drum notation. How did you, then, communicate musical ideas for a monster piece, such as "La Faulx"?
Denis: My compositions, dating back to the early days of Univers Zero, took a while to successfully develop to my liking. What's more, I did not have the latest, most up-to-date recording technology when composing the music. I had to make do with cassette players, which required an unusual level of patience. We spent a lot of time on small sequences that I'd transform from their original state and develop as part of a larger piece of music. I should also make clear that each member of the band arranged his own particular part of these compositions. The opening section of "La Faulx" is the result of combining a series of improvised ideas that arose during our live performances. As I became more and more familiar with writing on the keyboard, I could improve and tweak certain musical ideas, which had inspired me at the moment. Because the sounds of current software instruments are close to the real analog instruments, I already have an idea of what the song will sound like. When I deem a song finished, Kurt Budé [saxophonist/wind instrument player] will take each of the various parts of the song, write them out, and make them understandable for each musician. I always liked the idea of working as a "traditional" music composer, and for this reason I never studied musical theory.

WR: You once said that your writing has been influenced by the occult. What did you mean by that? You'd mentioned that you based some of the vocalizations on *Heresie* on the Enochian language, or something like it, I suppose, à la Magma.

Denis: There's no attempt on my part to integrate aspects of the occult into the music of UZ. This was done more for effect than anything else. It's true that I'm interested, although not very deeply, in the alchemy of the Middle Ages, because people had a roundabout, but I believe genuine, spiritual way of understanding the world around them. I fear that spirit has completely disappeared. I had been, at a certain time, very attracted to fantastic literature, like the writing of H. P. Lovecraft, and this is reflected in the music I compose, but is only one of a multitude of influences I've had in various periods of my career. I will say that I am interested in the work of C. G. Jung, who seemed to have put his finger on some of life's biggest mysteries.

WR: Of course, there are certain musical currents that ebb and flow in your music. Even variations of musical concepts are present. But I would love to hear from your point of view about the musical and rhythmic structures that went into composing a song, such as the twenty-five-minute track "La Faulx," from *Heresie*?

Denis: It's difficult to dissect music I write, because so much of it involves improvisation, and I do not adhere to established rules of composition. Because the music is so angular, and the fact that I'm self-taught, I can understand why someone would perceive UZ's music as appearing to reflect some form of subversion on my part. But the pieces I write don't reflect a nonconformist attitude. There's no secret to it. I listen very much to contemporary music, also, and my ears are adapted to this music. A lot of different music inspires me— Charles Ives, Krzysztof Penderecki, Edgard Varèse—as well as Béla Bartók, Igor Stravinsky, Claude Debussy, Miles Davis, Hendrix, Beefheart, and on and on.

WR: How did you come to be signed to Cuneiform Records in the 1980s?

Denis: Wayside Music/Cuneiform distributed our records at the time, which were out on Recommended Records/Atem and Madrigal. Once we dealt with them, little by little our work appeared on the Cuneiform label. I think I remember that *Heatwave* [1986] was one of their first productions. [*Note: It was within the first ten records released on Cuneiform.*] We were probably a little impressed that this is an American label, which was not only familiar with our material, but that also wanted to support us. Still, after signing with them, I found that we were caught in a kind of trap.

WR: Why do you say this?

Denis: I think that Cuneiform is always content to remain in the service of their customers without really trying to open up new markets or trying to push music on their label for wider publicity beyond the faithful fans.

WR: Why did you record UZ's latest release, *Phosphorescent Dreams*, for a Japanese label?

Denis: Well, this is a whole other experience. We'll have to wait and see the results.

WR: Chris Cutler once told me that at the first meeting of the RIO coalition, criteria for inclusion into "the club" were discussed. Chris pointed out that a band such as Stormy Six had little to do with (he actually said) Univers Zero. If bands were so vastly different, musically speaking, how did everyone arrive at criteria for inclusion?
Denis: Some groups were more politicized than others. This was not the case with UZ.

WR: Despite the fact that there's an annual RIO festival, the originators of the RIO "sound" had long ago dissolved the fellowship. Chris told me that there was not so much a falling out but a falling away of the original RIO coalition. Is this the way you remember it, too? If so, why did the bands fall away from one another?
Denis: The Rock in Opposition Festival offers a concert programming full of groups who are making music outside the usual parameters of popular music. Rock in Opposition, at the time to which you were referring, was more an approach that these bands shared regarding how we would organize ourselves. Of course, how we organized ourselves was based upon each of the bands having the same concerns and problems in relation to the recording industry and live concert business, in general.

WR: How did you help each other?
Denis: By inviting foreign groups to our respective countries to play. It was an interesting movement, but it was also a different time. It can't be repeated and the RIO festival that you see today has nothing to do with what we were doing in the 1970s.

WR: You were briefly in Magma, as a second drummer, playing with Christian Vander. How did you coordinate performances?
Denis: I was in Magma for a short time, shorter than a month. Our group Arkham had opened for Magma in Belgium in 1971 and later Christian Vander had invited us—[keyboardist] Jean-Luc Manderlier and myself—to join Magma in March 1972. Jean-Luc was there more than a year. Personally, I was very young and probably not quite ready to appreciate the experience to the fullest.

WR: By the time you were recording records such as *Uzed* and *Heatwave*, I sensed a confidence in your compositional abilities. The music seems to have more definition; the players seem more sure of themselves.
Denis: Certainly. Each musician who has participated in the group has collaborated on some level for the greater good of the band. They've helped to evolve the group in their own way through their energy and involvement. Nothing is

more annoying for a music group than to fall into a routine, or to always work from the same guidelines. You're just spinning your wheels in that case.

WR: In the early days UZ's material was written by, essentially, two composers. By the 1980s . . . *Uzed* was written totally by you . . . and the majority of the material appearing on later albums, *The Hard Quest* and *Rhythmix*, was written by you. Would I be correct in assuming that you want to "spice" up the band's sound by having more band members contribute material?

Denis: It really depended on which period we're discussing. During the period of *Uzed*, for instance, I was the only person to compose music. However, I remain convinced that several composers in any given group affords the band a richer sound and richer compositions. However, the musician must be aware that the composition he's writing must fit within the framework, even if that framework is a very wide one, of the style of music the group creates. This is the case now with Kurt, who offers a musical vision different from mine. This is very good, in my opinion.

WR: I think you've said something along the lines that playing with Art Zoyd helped your compositional chops. But how do you think the French band benefits/benefited from your presence?

Denis: Art Zoyd had asked me to be part of the group after the departure of cellist and saxophonist André Mergenthaler [in 1985]. I played percussion at the concerts for Roland Petit's ballet *Marriage of Heaven and Hell*, in 1985, for multiple productions at the Champs-Élysées in Paris and L'Opéra de Marseille in Bordeaux and Grand Théâtre de Bordeaux. After a few concerts without the ballets I parted ways with the group to concentrate on UZ again. I did think it was interesting to participate in a group that was already up and running. In fact, I welcomed it. I created all the drum parts, but with Art Zoyd, the music was all composed, the structure was built, 100 percent. It was a very nice experience, and I especially enjoyed working with the concept of composing music for existing silent films [i.e., *Nosferatu, Faust, Häxan*] in the 1990s and 2000s. With Art Zoyd I also discovered an attraction for [sound] samplers that I have applied to Univers Zero since I left Art Zoyd.

19

The Defector's Dream Team

Steve Hackett—His Exit from Genesis and His Musical Triumphs

I n the nearly forty years since he left Genesis, guitarist Steve Hackett appears more prolific than ever, issuing an unprecedented amount of original material and globe-trotting with musicians who have a considerable history with the guitarist.

Hackett has never stopped challenging himself as an artist, and his output is arguably the most diverse of any of the Genesis band members' individual recorded material. "Steve has had his own band with a fixed personnel for some years now, with Gary O'Toole on drums, and works very closely with [keyboardist] Roger King," says Steve's brother, John Hackett, flutist. "He has good people he's comfortable with. If you look at the number of records he's produced and the quality of what he's produced over the years, it's just astonishing. And he's still going."

Undoubtedly. But the flurry of recent activity generated from the Hackett camp turns our mind back to another time in Hackett's career. For a decade, starting in the late 1970s, Hackett's solo records were fairly successful affairs: *Please Don't Touch*, *Spectral Mornings*, *Defector* (a Top 10 album in the U.K.), *Cured*, *Highly Strung*, *Bay of Kings*, *Till We Have Faces* all entered the British charts at various positions along the scale of the Top 100. Hackett returned to the charts in the twenty-first century with releases such as *Beyond the Shrouded Horizon* (number 133 on the British album charts) and *Genesis Revisited* (number 24 in the U.K.).

But it was Steve's albums of the late 1970s and early 1980s that, arguably, had laid the foundation for his longevity in the business, both as a bandleader and solo artist. In particular the two albums, 1979's *Spectral Mornings*, which contains Hackett's signature tune, and 1980's *Defector*, mark the first time the guitarist commanded a genuine recording and touring band outside of Genesis, which he left in 1977 during the mixing of the seminal live recording *Seconds Out*. (In Hackett's own words, he was "forced into giving them ultimatums": either a percentage of his material is used within the band context or he's out. We all know how this fairy tale ends.)

Of course, prior to these albums Hackett had released both *Voyage of the Acolyte* and *Please Don't Touch*, the former while still a member of Genesis, but it was *Spectral Mornings* and *Defector* that represent Hackett's first real solo efforts apart from involvement by ex-Genesis members and a parade of guest artists. Dare we say that these records contain some of Hackett's greatest work, which has helped to keep him afloat as an artist to this day. If this is the case, he surely didn't do it alone.

The lineup of drummer John Shearer, bassist Dik Cadbury, vocalist Pete Hicks, keyboardist Nick Magnus, and Steve's brother, John Hackett, on flute and Moog Taurus bass pedals, was a versatile crew that could play nearly anything that was set in front of them. "I think having a band was a great plus," says Hackett. "It made a tremendous difference. For a start, we were touring. Whatever I was recording and whatever I was writing there was always a view toward, 'Let's try to do it live.' I think it produced some of my best stuff."

One could argue that Hackett, fresh from Genesis, *needed* to collaborate, to bring in guests, such as Phil Collins, Mike Rutherford, Richie Havens, Kansas' Steve Walsh and Phil Ehart, etc., to help achieve liftoff. Heck, even Steve's brother, John Hackett, provided a helping hand thanks to his Tandberg reel-to-reel tape recorder capturing certain bits and pieces and musical ideas—from guitar riffs to multitracked flute—that found their way onto *Voyage of the Acolyte*, a themed album centered on the tarot deck. But by 1978 and 1979, this collaborative approach of presenting numerous variations on a studio band blew up. Hackett was convinced that he wanted a band, again, but needed to ensure that there would be some principal changes in how this band would operate.

"Committees can come up with very good things," Hackett says, "but at times you can have the best of it and worst of it. The worst of it means what you have are people operating to the lowest common denominator, coming up with things that least offend and you get alliances building up in bands, of course, where some people will always vote with their crony."

"Steve's band wasn't a democracy, quite understandably, because Steve had been in that situation," says John Hackett. "Why should he want to go back to that? He was a strongly creative person and had a vision of what he wanted to do, so he put the band together. Quite rightly he was clearly the main man and leader. Obviously at times we would give creative input, as we should, but it was clearly his band."

Virtually one by one, the band members were pulled from various points in England. John, of course, had been playing with his brother since they were in their teens, and even appeared on *The Road*, a concept album recorded by Quiet World in 1970, one of Steve's first bands. John was even present for Steve's audition for Genesis.

"Peter Gabriel and Tony Banks came to our flat and we sat in our bedroom, and I was privileged to be in on the audition, if you call it an audition," says John. "It seemed a very relaxed affair. Steve had a twelve-string and that impressed them. I remember he was playing some interesting chords. Peter

Gabriel played flute and so I guess there was an instant connection with twelve-string guitar and flute and the general attitude towards not always doing the obvious chords. It was after the audition and they were playing a gig at the Lyceum, and they had Mick Barnard on the guitar, then. It was great. There was no question that Steve join them should they offer him the chance."

Scottish drummer John Shearer, son of a football player, moved down to England when he was a teen and began gigging professionally almost immediately with a band called Hampton Court, based in Daventry, Northamptonshire. Eventually Shearer, who counts Buddy Rich and Carl Palmer among his early drumming heroes, hooked up with the band Moon, which signed to CBS Records in 1976. (Simon Frodsham, a former press agent at CBS Records, says that Moon was a "seven-piece with a strong rhythm section, punchy horns, and probably one of the world's great undiscovered singers in Noel McCalla. During that time I got to know John [Shearer] quite well. He was a terrific player, brought up in showbands. He had learned how to capture an audience, which added an extra dimension to his ability.")

With or without Shearer's drumming ability Moon didn't last long beyond the release of their second album, and Shearer was looking for a new career direction. "I called Genesis' manager, Tony Smith, and said, 'If Phil Collins ever drops dead or leaves, I'm the guy!'" Shearer says. "[Smith] said, 'I have to take your name. This is far out.' Apparently he passed my number on to Steve. . . ."

Shearer remembers the strange set of circumstances that led to his joining Steve's band. "Simon [Frodsham] used to wind me up, tease me, and phone me up every now and again, in a disguised voice," says Shearer. "He would phone me up and say, 'Hi, is this John Shearer?' I'd go, 'Yeah?' 'This is the

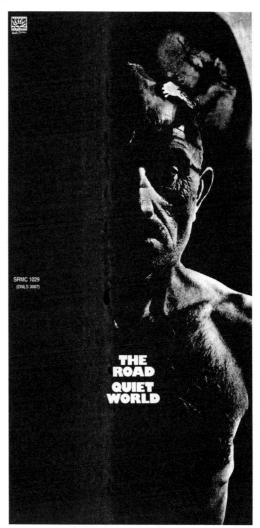

Steve Hackett played electric and acoustic guitar and harmonica on Quiet World's *The Road*, a concept album (as far as the author can surmise) that details a spiritually transformative process. Steve's brother, John Hackett, also appears.

English Tax Authority . . . and we haven't gotten your taxes . . .' And, of course, I'd fall for this every bloody time. One day I am practicing, and I get this call and the person on the other end of the line says, 'Hi, can I speak to John.' I said, 'Speaking.' 'Hi, my name is Steve Hackett.' I said, 'Simon, f— off,' and I slammed the phone down. I got back to practicing and the phone rang, again. 'Yeah?' 'Sorry, my name is Steve Hackett . . .' I said, 'Simon, I haven't got time for this. Now go away.' I can't believe he called back a third time. He said, 'Look, I really need you to understand that my name is Steve Hackett and I am a guitarist.' I said, 'Simon?' He said, 'No.' I said, 'Steve?' He said, 'Yes.' I said, 'Shit. Really? You don't have to tell me who you are, Steve, I'm practicing to you right now. I'm practicing to "Afterglow,"' . . . which was one of my favorite tracks that Steve ever did."

The guitarist apparently didn't mind the exchange because he sent a truck to pick up Shearer and his expansive twenty-four-piece stainless-steel-shelled kit for an audition, just drums and guitar. "When I was in a studio and rehearsing with someone, I just concentrate on playing the music and forget who they are and where they're from," says Shearer. "Sometimes I forget how big this guy is in terms of guitar fame. I played and said, 'Follow this . . .' and went into some odd time thing. Steve just looked at me and went up and down the fretboard, 'No problem.' I went, '7/4,' and he played again. I was really, I suppose, trying to lose him, and he said, 'You got the gig. Anybody who tries to lose me has got to be worth employing.'"

Bassist Dik Cadbury, formerly of Decameron, a folk-rock outfit with progressive rock leanings, is a classically trained vocalist who would arranged vocal harmonies on Steve's solo records of that time. "Steve's producer, John Acock, was a friend of mine," says Cadbury. "He had told me that Steve was putting a new lineup together, that he'd recommended me for the bass job and to expect a call. I got the call, went for an audition, and Steve and I started with a sort of blues jam. Then Steve asked if there was anything I wanted to play, and I asked him to show me the riff in 'A Tower Struck Down.' Five minutes later we were playing that, and Steve told me that the session player took about an hour to learn it. That's when I got the offer. Maybe it was also my mention of the vocal work I'd done with Decameron that helped?"

Nick Magnus, a vital component of Hackett's recording and touring team, had come onboard almost by accident. "I was in my band, Autumn, which was an unknown prog outfit in 1978, struggling against the backlash of punk," says Magnus. "We decided it was time to disband, so I advertised in *Melody Maker*, well known at the time for its 'Musicians Wanted' classified ads. They published the ad with the wrong phone number, so I got them to reprint it in a subsequent issue—with the correct number. It was that reprinted ad that Steve saw and responded to. If *Melody Maker* had got it right the first time, he would never have seen it."

Finally, vocalist Pete Hicks was invited onboard and the band, one of considerable talent, skill, and depth, a kind of Dream Team, was assembled. The band barely had time to catch its breath: rehearsals were up next and a tour, Hackett's first as a solo artist, was waiting for them.

"I left Sheffield University in 1978 and went straight into rehearsing with Steve and the band and we went off on the road," says John Hackett. "Oslo, Norway, was the first gig, on October 4, 1978. I'd only just left college that summer and we had just rehearsed with the guys, and off we went on tour. For me it was my first tour. I had only done university stuff, orchestral stuff, mostly playing flute and chamber music, and some folk, but nothing of this level in front of that number of people. It was big news, too: Steve had just left Genesis."

Despite this being the height of the punk and New Wave movement in the U.K., Hackett's band was somewhat insulated from the fray; they were finding an audience, scoring gigs, and continuing to record, in large part due to Hackett's rock pedigree and the smoking players in the musical unit. "We partied like hell all the time," Hackett admits. "It was an interesting time with a very dedicated audience. I was nervous about heading out on my own after Genesis had been such a success. After the first gig, it went down so well, I felt that, that was going to be the future."

After glimpsing the future, the band decamped in Hilversum at Phonogram Studios to record what would become 1979's *Spectral Mornings*, produced by John Acock, who'd worked on Steve's previous two albums.

Some members of the Dream Team remember the experience vividly.

"It must have been a horrendously expensive album to make," says John Hackett, "because we were going abroad and staying in a hotel and guys sitting around while tracks were being laid down. It was a multitracked album, so it was done in bits. The snow there was thick on the ground. There was a lot of sitting around and there was a drinks cabin, as I remember, we got through quite a lot of Scotch whiskey over that period."

"It was a beautiful setting, with a large frozen lake by the side of the studio," says Magnus. "The ice was thick enough for people to drive cars on it, doing spins and hand-brake turns for the entertainment of onlookers. Otherwise, there was little else to distract us from the task at hand—total immersion. We tended to work at night and sleep during the day. The studio complex was very cozy, and became like our home."

"The band were a bit straight and I would go out with the roadies, because I was a bit of a party man," says Shearer. "We probably used to go to Amsterdam after recording. You know what I mean? As a young man that was quite an eye opening for me."

"The studio in Wisseloord, Hilversum, was amazing," adds Cadbury. "Brand new, vast, and hi-tech, with innovations from Philips and all the gear we could possibly need. I believe we had every single noise gate and compressor in our studio for John Shearer's massive drum kit. The sessions got later and later until it was suggested that this was counterproductive and wearing us out, and that perhaps setting a cutoff time might be a good idea, so we could come back fresh. I think it was Charlie Watts who summed up his time with the Stones as

'Five years of making music and twenty-five years of hanging around,' which is probably a fairly accurate summary of the recording process."

Immersion can do wonders for a musician's focus. Hackett had already experienced this a few years earlier with Genesis' *Wind & Wuthering*, also recorded in Holland, under similar isolated circumstances. It's no surprise, then, to find that, similarly, *Spectral Mornings* appears thematic, perhaps not with recursive musical ideas (like *W&W*) but lyrical ones. References to war abound, from a skirmish in the First World War, to a downed airman to "Lili Marlene," a song popularized during World War II.

Is *Spectral Mornings* a thematic work?

"I was trying to write something cohesive that would run through a number of the songs," says Hackett. "I didn't start off with the idea of doing a concept album, but in a sense the album is a concept album, in that the one constant is death. Well, death and survival. That's something that made me write [the title] piece. I thought of the title of "Spectral . . . ," of something otherworldly and ghostlike, and I was thinking of the release of the spirit after death, an after-death flight of the spirit. I was thinking of this great release and something that was hugely optimistic. I felt that perhaps spirit was with me when I was doing it."

The album imagery captures these two moods almost perfectly. The cover painting, by Steve's ex-wife, Kim Poor, presents Steve's ghostly, almost ghoulish visage through the ether; flip the record over and there's a photograph of Steve, in the flesh, at the microphone—a portrait of the survivor. These are, essentially, virtual mirror images—the earthly self and the spiritual self, occupying both sides of the LP jacket. Kim could have easily been working from the same, if not a similar, photo from the one shown on the back cover.

"Clocks—The Angel of Mons" is a great example of a song making all stops along this conceptual train. Mons, Belgium, was the site of the first British battle in the First World War in 1914. (A clock rests on the bell tower of the City Hall building there.) The British, despite being heavily outnumbered and forced to retreat, suffered fewer casualties than the advancing German army absorbed, prompting some to call the military action a minor miracle. Legend has it that the specters of longbow men who fought the Battle of Agincourt in 1415, a crucial skirmish won by King Henry over the French in the Hundred Years' War, nearly five hundred years earlier, assisted the British, helping to save the lives of untold valiant soldiers.

Arthur Machen in *The Angels of Mons: The Bowmen and Other Legends of the War*, which first appeared in the *Evening News*, September 29, 1914, linked this legendary war story to the image of St. George, England's patron fighting saint. Hackett's research in the library of the Spiritualist Association of Great Britain helped to inspire some of the songs on the record, including "Tigermoth," which tracks the consciousness of a downed airman, and "Clocks . . ."

"The idea of angels fighting on our side intrigued me," says Hackett. "It's basically mythological, but I felt that it really fit in with the spirit of the album, with the idea of ghostly occurrences. At the time I was a member of the Spiritualist Association of Great Britain—the SAGB, Number 33 Belgrave Square, in London. The building was given to the association by Sir Arthur Conan Doyle and this was something he owned, and it's a huge townhouse which exists alongside various embassies. I used their library for research and I was reading Lord Hugh Dowding's memoirs. Dowding was the commander-in-chief of the Battle of Britain and claimed, because he was an ardent spiritualist, that although he was not a medium himself, he'd had encounters with various mediums in which the spirits of discarnate airmen, who had been killed very suddenly in air battles, would talk to him through various mediums. Many of these spirits were in a confused state, it seems, and were only too happy to be talking to Dowding, who would talk to his insignia and say, 'You know who I am, and you have to face up to the fact that you are no longer living. . . .' If you take it all literally or metaphorically, whether you take the cynical view, which is to say that this was war propaganda, nonetheless, it's very interesting. I did quite a lot of research with mediums and sat in a circle at one point and I found there was something to it. It was not your normal kind of boy-meets-girl album style. In a way it was perhaps more personal and it was an area that not many people were touching at that time."

In the studio Hackett was as experimental and cutting-edge as ever. His use of guitar technology stretches back to *The Lamb Lies Down on Broadway* (with the EMS Synthi Hi Fli to produce kazoo sounds on "Cuckoo Cocoon," a device that was also used by David Gilmour). Hackett also sprinkled guitar synth over tracks appearing on *Please Don't Touch*, making his guitar sound like a harmonium.

"The Synthi Hi Fli did afford a wider range of sounds than what a regular guitar could do," says Hackett. "It enabled me to play forwards, turn the sound backwards, for instance. It also had some interesting vibrato functions and I haven't really found too many things that do that. That was a very interesting device. I could play bass on it at the same time. I could do these enormous chords and have a sound that was very nearly like Syndrums by employing a kind of rasgueado right-hand technique. It allowed me to sound like a keyboard player, plus a drummer, and you could do it all in one go. I used to start out the show with that. Halfway through what used to be Side Two, on 'Tigermoth,' you have that sound on its own and it sounds like a number of things playing at once. That was the Roland GR-500. There are a few weird and wonderful sounds where you can't tell what the sound source is. I used to spend a lot of my early life impersonating keyboard. I believe it is the instrumental section that opens the tune."

"The GR-500 guitar synth," says Magnus, "provided textures that the keyboards couldn't do. I didn't have any polysynths then, so as such it was an innovative and unique sound. By the time we did *Defector*, I had a Prophet 5, and we discovered that the guitar synth, Prophet, and Mellotron blended well to create luscious orchestral effects, best demonstrated on the second half of 'Hammer in the Sand.' We rather enjoyed blurring the distinction between guitar and keyboard, so that it was not always obvious who was playing what.

The *Till We Have Faces* album [1984] saw Steve using a different guitar synth, the GR-300, to produce trumpet-like tones, which had an unusual liquid quality due to Steve's playing style and the singular technique the GR-300 demanded to get anything from it!"

"Dave Simmons, who invented the Simmons drums, he brought some down for me and for John Bonham, who was next door," says Shearer. "John Bonham said, 'Fuck off. I'm not using electronic drums.' I loved the sound. Around that time they got out, because Donna Summer was using them on her tracks. I think I used it only on one track, which produced descending notes and that was the only track ["Every Day"]. We thought it sounded a bit disco so we stopped using them, really."

After recording wrapped, Hackett and his team went back on the road, touring Europe throughout the spring, summer, and fall of 1979. "I very much enjoyed the role in Steve's band, and also played second guitar," says John Hackett. "The arpeggio parts Steve had recorded in 'Spectral Mornings' for the album, I would be playing live. These second guitar parts are sometimes quite tricky, actually. It was great because it varied the role, switching from flute to guitar and bass pedals."

"Half the album, if not more, was doable live and struck a chord with audiences," Hackett says. "'Every Day' became a favorite live number and we did 'The Red Flower of Tachai Blooms Everywhere,' and that became a live number, strangely enough. "'Clocks . . .' as well. It works like the Genesis tune 'The Knife.' Not subtle, but it possesses an all-out nature. John was always completely exhausted after ['Clocks . . .']. He . . . used to put everything into it. He would literally fall over, in pain, every time he did it. A great personality live. Audiences loved him."

"'Clocks . . .' was a feature for the bass pedals, as well, that I used to play raised up on a stand," John Hackett says. "Genesis had used bass pedals and Steve was keen on the sound. I used to really enjoy playing the bass pedals because it was a bit of a Jekyll and Hyde thing, because the flute is generally seen as a gentle instrument. But the bass pedals, my goodness: they pack a punch."

Defector

Hackett's next studio record, 1980's *Defector*, was recorded at Wessex Sound Studios, at 106 Highbury New Park, London—the very same recording space that King Crimson burned their influential debut over a decade earlier. *Defector* was a bit more of a rushed affair relative to *Spectral Mornings*.

"Wessex Studios, by contrast to Hilversum, was in London," says Magnus, "so the mere fact of going home at the end of each day made the experience not quite as totally immersive as Phonogram. The studio was pleasant enough, not as geared up to 'client luxury' as Phonogram, but they did have a gorgeous Bösendorfer in the main studio, which I tinkered on whenever I had a free moment, and is the one I used on 'Hammer in the Sand.'"

"I seem to remember doing lots of shows and writing on the run," says Hackett, "and walking into the rehearsal room one day and saying grandly, 'We are not going to leave here today until we've written three new tunes. I'm happy to do it with anybody, but we're really up against it time-wise and we have to come up with something.' Although at the end of the day we didn't leave with three tunes, by the end of the following day or by lunchtime the following day, three new tunes had been written. 'The Steppes' was written, 'Sentimental Institution,' and 'Hercules Unchained,' which was a spoof punk song, which became a B side on a single, the flipside of 'The Show.' I often wanted to have a day, one day in the life, where you write a whole album in a day and make it cohesive by the time you have recorded the whole thing."

The record hangs together nicely, despite the hurried nature of the recording process. The songs seem poised and even carry a kind of self-referential quality (i.e., the main melody of "The Steppes" recalled on acoustic guitar for "Two Vamps as Guests"). It's a technique that's reminiscent of the variation on and recapitulation of melodies whirling around Genesis' *Wind & Wuthering*, released three years earlier.

"It's something that we did quite naturally in Genesis," says Hackett. "I seem to remember doing this around the time of *A Trick of the Tail*, as well, where we had an acoustic version of a tune and then it came back as an electric version. You have a recapitulation of the riff from 'Squonk' that returns with the Mellotron choir at the end of 'Los Endos.' That's an idea that's common to classical music as well as that era of rock."

"I felt there was something symbolic in the use of the word and name [*Defector*]," says Hackett.

As with *Spectral Mornings*, album and song titles seemed to hint at overriding themes present in the work. Historically, there were a number of defectors from Russia and Eastern Europe to the "West" around the time of the *Defector* record (circa 1978–1980), including author Viktor Suvorov, who defected to the U.K.

"I think during the writing of *Defector* I was spending quite a lot of time in New York City," says Hackett. "It was a case of political turmoil. It was a tricky time for the world, never mind America and Iran. As I say, looking back on that I was struck with the idea of leaving Genesis and feeling like a traitor to the cause. The defector idea came to mind at that point. I felt there was something symbolic in the use of the word and name. I was trying to research what that meant and was thinking of certain people. I was influenced by a Bernardo Bertolucci film called *The Conformist*. I remember seeing films of [Rudolf] Nureyev when he first defected. There was also a movie, with Montgomery Clift, called *The Defector*. I was influenced by all of those ideas. If *Spectral Mornings* had to do with a potential afterlife then *Defector* was firmly rooted in an earthly setting. In a way they are two halves of the same coin: same band, same era, and perhaps two years between them."

Defector was Hackett's highest-charting album, breaking the Top 10 in the U.K. He'd done it: great success outside and independent of Genesis. Yet, despite this high note, Hackett, ironically, was bleeding money. Something had to give, change. Due to budgetary reasons Hackett dispensed with his Dream Team and went on to record 1981's highly programmed *Cured*.

"I believe it was over a coffee—or maybe a pint—that Steve and Bill Bruford were bemoaning the cost of running a permanent band and the decision was made to disband Steve's 'Dream Team,'" says Cadbury. "Nick was into technology and programming on a big way and it seemed logical that Steve should retain his services and exploit his genius at drum programming to deliver the next album."

"When I first joined Steve in 1978 it felt as if we had a degree of 'immunity' from the anti-prog movement," says Magnus. "We could still sell out large venues, and album sales were strong, although that immunity began to falter after *Defector*, and had patently failed by around 1984."

Hackett was on the road in the fall of 1981, but with some key personnel changes. Cadbury was gone (in favor of Chas Cronk) and Shearer exited, replaced by future Marillion drummer Ian Mosley. Shearer went on to play with Iron Butterfly and, later, to open the world-famous, now-defunct drum shops in the U.S. and U.K., John Shearer's Talking Drums. Magnus and John Hackett remained, providing a form of continuity in Steve's touring and recording. In a few short years Steve himself would become acclimated, albeit briefly, to a new situation: as one of two mega-guitarists in the supergroup GTR, with Yes' Steve Howe.

"I'm still very fond of *Spectral Mornings*," says Hackett, "and I think of that as one of my favorite albums. It's a solo record. But, you know, calling something a solo record isn't quite right. Obviously the influences of people I was working with were hugely impactful."

Key Tracks

A quick glance at some pivotal tracks appearing on *Spectral Mornings* and *Defector.*

"Clocks—The Angel of Mons" (*Spectral Mornings*, 1979)

"I love African music and Zulu drummers and I had this idea," says John Shearer. "I thought, 'How could I be a tribe of drummers on my own?' Because I had studied independence, I'm fortunate that all my limbs can move independently of each other. That is what 'Clocks . . .' was initially. I was practicing and Steve walked in, if I am not mistaken, and said, 'What's that?' I said, 'Just an idea.' He said, 'We gotta use that, John. We gotta use that.' A lot of people came to the gigs to see if I could perform 'Clocks . . . ,' because people thought I had overdubbed drum parts. I didn't."

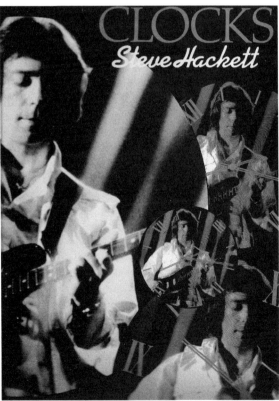

Nick Magnus plays the spooky, horror-show Mellotron notes; John Hackett punches Moog Taurus pedals to achieve those deep ominous tones. Completely locked in with Shearer, Steve mutes the strings by placing his left hand on the fretboard and, with his right hand, performs two surgical strikes on the strings resting over the bottom or body of the guitar to produce subtle, but well-timed, sonic "bumps." The synchronized intermingling of the woodblocks, crotal bell, and Hackett's "tick-tock" guitar bumps underscore the theme of the song. Later in the track, Shearer conducts a chorus of drums, evoking a traditionally African "call and response" rhythmic conversation.

"I had toured with the top Dutch session drummer Louis Debij when Fungus toured with

Clocks: A three-track 12″ disc featuring the title track, "Tigermoth," and an acoustic set, including Hackett live staples "Blood on the Rooftops" and "Horizons."

Decameron in 1975," says Cadbury, "and I bumped into him the morning after we'd recorded the drum solo on 'Clocks . . .' He came into the studio to listen and asked John how many overdubs it had taken. John said, 'None,' and Louis replied, 'What are you—fucking octopus?'"

"The Ballad of the Decomposing Man" (featuring "The Office Party") (*Spectral Mornings*)

Steve's West Indian accent is spot-on. That is to say he assumes the role of a suicidal, graveyard-shift factory worker dreaming of a Caribbean holiday and speaking in a faux West Indian accent. Kitschy delivery, to say the least. In essence, Hackett assumes the role of a character assuming a role.

"I remember wondering if we'd get away with Pete Hicks quoting that line from *Grease*, 'You're the one that I want . . .'" says Magnus. "No one was sued in the ensuing thirty-five years, so I guess we did. . . ."

"Aah—'The Office Party,'" says Cadbury. "I was on Taurus bass pedals for that one and I couldn't get it. My father's retirement trip took him and my mother to the Caribbean and they came back with an album entitled *Carnival in Trinidad*. I loved the bass lines on that and tried to capture that vibe. I abandoned the attempt on day one, but came back after thinking it out and nailed it the following day."

"Spectral Mornings" (*Spectral Mornings*)

Hackett had intended "Spectral Mornings" to be a vocal piece, but when he played the song for singer Pete Hicks and the other members of his band, they encouraged him to keep it as an instrumental.

"Spectral Mornings" is the standout song on the record and Hackett's signature song, communicating a similar sense of spiritual freedom as Peter Gabriel's "Solsbury Hill" from 1977. Both were recorded in the wake of their stint with Genesis and both songs are declarations of independence, charged with an electrifying sense of the new day's possibilities.

Shearer says that "Spectral Mornings" came about when Steve told him, "'I want to imagine curtains opening in the morning on a snowy day.' At that time we were rehearsing and recording in Holland, in deep snow, and I think we were in a hotel in the middle of a bloody lake. I used a bell tree for atmospheric percussion, signaling the curtains opening. You would probably only know this if you knew the thought behind the track."

"The Steppes" (*Defector*)

"I remember we put drums in a church [adjacent, St. Augustine's Highbury], and recorded them," says Shearer. "The song was like a Zeppelin track,

'Kashmir.' I believe I can remember Steve saying, 'I want to imagine a camel train going across the desert.'"

"Slogans" (Defector)

"There are about seven different time signatures in the same sequence," says Shearer, "and in those days I would have been coming from a technical side first. I was adamant about playing this song and never going away from a paradiddle. . . . I think I went into the studio to show Jonathan [Mover] of GTR what I did on one of the tracks."

"I'd just acquired a Roland VP-330 Vocoder," says Magnus, "and we were intrigued to see what we could get it to do. That guitar-tapping section where the Minimoog doubles Steve in harmony was also a blighter to learn. Basically we rehearsed the structure sufficiently to get the drums down, then built the track up from there."

Any Colour You Like

A lthough not as musically adventurous as *Aqualung*, *Thick as a Brick*, and *A Passion Play*, the material written and recorded during Jethro Tull's late 1970s period helped to solidify the band's staunchly loyal fanbase. Releases such as *Songs from the Wood*, *Heavy Horses*, *Bursting Out*, and *Stormwatch*—viewed a single body of work—represent an organic evolution of a style, which mixed folk, hard rock, classical, and blues.

Bassist Tony Williams, who toured with Tull through North America in 1978, having replaced an ill John Glascock just prior to the latter's death, remembers having to come up to speed on very difficult material. Certainly Williams had his work cut out for him. Glascock's legend has grown in the last few decades, and he remains one of the genre's best bassists.

"That was bloody hard work," says Williams. "Some of those songs were very difficult to play. A lot of the bass root notes are not what a rock bass player would go for. They're more what you'd hear in an orchestral piece, what the bassoons might be playing or a double bass."

Glascock was a member of the prog-y Flamenco-rock band Carmen, formed in 1970, who opened for Tull during dates on the band's *War Child* tour. David Bowie was a huge fan of Carmen and there was talk that someday soon, Carmen would appear on the same bill as the Thin White Duke. Due to timing, Carmen, instead, accepted the support role on Jethro Tull's 1975 North American tour. Impressed with what he saw, Anderson extended an invite to Glascock to join Tull, which he did in November 1975.

Glascock and the beautiful Angela Allen, his girlfriend and Carmen founder David Allen's sister, would appear on Tull's 1976 concept album, *Too Old to Rock 'n' Roll: Too Young to Die!* (Angela was a backing vocalist on "Crazed Institution" and "Big Dipper," helping to advance the album's story line involving Ray Lomas, an aging rocker who's alienated from the pop culture trends of the day. Lomas, a friend of David Palmer, kindly lent his name to the project. Lomas' lifestyle, or life story, was intended to be the basis of a theatrical production, but this project was later abandoned.)

Glascock was a more versatile player than his flamboyant predecessor, Jeffrey Hammond-Hammond, and his confidence helped to solidify what some consider Tull's strongest lineup: Anderson, Martin Barre, Barriemore Barlow, John Evan, and second keyboardist David (now Dee) Palmer. On tracks such as "Pied Piper" and "Taxi Grab" Glascock locks into Barlow's beat patterns and even weaves around string parts in "Quizz Kid" with an economy of notes.

Barlow's playing, as well, was stellar during this time period. "Barrie used to rehearse, I know for a fact, with those old-fashioned drum machines that you used to sit atop a Hammond organ and press a button and you'd get a quick step, waltz, fox-trot, and then some corny rock and roll," says Williams, Barlow's mate in a band called Requiem prior to his work with Tull. "Barrie would sit with one of those plugged into a tape machine. He would press a button and play a waltz for five bars. Then he'd hit fox-trot and then go into rock and roll. He'd learn it all. It was weird."

The lineup was stellar, no one denies, but after Glascock's death there was a major band split. Many theorists have speculated as to why, citing personal problems as being the culprit, but most have concluded that Ian was interested in

This 1976 four-track EP, celebrating England's pre-Christian pagan past, kicked off Tull's so-called folk phase.

indulging his fascination with electronic music. (Others, off the record, have said that Ian was affected by the change in music in the late 1970s and early 1980s and wanted to be, if not ahead of the curve, then riding the wave. Tull, more than anything else, was a business. And for a business to be effective, one needn't appear to be complacent.)

"When you're chasing other people's [musical] territory it's an unruly state," keyboardist/arranger Dee Palmer told me in 2009.[1] "I couldn't see why Ian wanted to throw away something we had forged for ten or so years."

John Glascock was a member of Carmen and the Gods prior to joining Tull.

"When John Evan left Tull [circa 1980], they were thinking about recruiting Kerry Minnear, keyboardist of Gentle Giant," says producer Mark Mancina, who's worked with Yes and ELP. "I would have loved one album with Kerry playing keyboards and Ian at the helm. I mean, Kerry's percussive approach with Jethro Tull? Come on. [Guitarist] Martin Barre told me about Kerry, back in the mid-1990s. I had just gotten out of the hospital with appendicitis and I was at his house. He was showing me all the guitars he used for every one of the Tull records. He saved each guitar in a case." [*Note: I checked with the Minnear camp to determine if there was any validity to this story. When I made contact with Lesley Minnear, Kerry's wife, she informed me that Kerry had not been asked to join Tull at the time of the band's big split. As far as the author can surmise, this story has been circulating since, at least, 1990, when Minnear had first heard of it.*]

Tull albums such as *A* (originally meant to be an Ian Anderson solo record), *Broadsword and the Beast*, Anderson's unfairly undervalued 1983 solo album *Walk Into Light* (i.e., a techno-rock song, such as "Fly by Night," fades out as Anderson performs something akin to Konnakol vocal rhythmic patterns, lending the song, and portions of the record, an '80s Peter Gabriel vibe), *Under Wraps*, and *Crest of a Knave*, which won a controversial Grammy for Best

Hard Rock/Metal Performance in 1989, all contained a move toward electronic music and either prepped Tull, or kept them competitive, for the new techno decade.[2]

Enter Eddie Jobson, formerly of Roxy Music, Zappa, and U.K., who joins Tull on the heels of U.K.'s split, and his keyboard work is prominently displayed on the *A* album. "The biggest influence on that album [*A*] is Eddie Jobson," Martin Barre told the author in 2003. "He was very powerful with his ideas and very upfront. A lot of that album is [Eddie]."

Jobson toured with Tull, a tour that's immortalized by David Mallet's concert film *Slipstream*, shot in downtown L.A. with upwards of nine cameras. Interestingly, Jobson replaced Darryl Way in Curved Air, and he was charged with having to learn Way's original violin parts in "Heavy Horses" for Tull's 1980 stage show.

Barre went as far as to say that some fans were resentful of Jobson for being another star at the front of the stage. Some speculate that perhaps members of Tull agreed. Whatever the real story, it's been long believed that Jobson put himself at a distance from the band, and never claimed to be a full-fledged member.

"When [the military] put special forces—groups of soldiers—together, troops of four, those four are screened to make sure they are complementary in every way," Palmer told the author in 2009. "When you start a string quartet, they will spend months and months playing together. . . . Up until Eddie [Jobson] appeared, we used to know what we were."

After this Tull experience, Jobson joined Yes, briefly—he was scheduled to perform on the *90125* tour (when Tony Kaye exited, briefly) and can even be seen in the background of Yes' video for "Owner of a Lonely Heart" (he's visible on a couple of occasions, although barely so, behind Alan White's kit and Jon Anderson).

With his Zinc band Jobson continued in this *A*-like techno-rock musical direction with 1983's *The Green Album*, featuring Gary Green of Gentle Giant and guitarist Michael Cuneo. *The Green Album* came out, but [Eddie] didn't tour to support it," says the drummer Michael Cartellone, who got to know Jobson well in the mid-1980s. "In mid-1984, not being sure what he was doing, or if he was going to continue the Zinc project, I just took the initiative to send him a resume and video. At the time, I was still living in my hometown, Cleveland, Ohio, and playing in bar bands. Eddie liked what he saw and we began corresponding, during which time he was doing advertising and soundtrack work. He told me he would revisit Zinc and, at that time, he would audition me."

As it happens Jobson wasn't quite ready to resurrect Zinc, but had called Cartellone back in 1985. "The audition finally happened in Connecticut," says Cartellone, "where Eddie was living at the time. There was a good chemistry and we really clicked, and even though he wasn't ready to resume Zinc, he told me I would be involved, when he did. So, a few months later, I moved to New York City, and before long we were doing demos, the songs intended for the second Zinc album, *The Pink Album*."

In the ensuing years, *The Pink Album* has taken on a life of its own. Some have said, and understandably so, that the record, or even pieces of it, didn't even exist. That it was a myth generated to create an aura around Jobson; something that was only talked about, and a record that never got beyond the planning stages.

"Each of Eddie's records was intended to have a different color," says Cartellone. [*Note:* The Green Album *was issued via EMI/ Capitol Japan on green vinyl.*] "Unfortunately, *The Pink Album* never materialized."

The intended *Pink* band was going to be Jobson, Cartellone, and Rat Race Choir guitarist Mark Hitt. "Actually, Eddie, Michael, and I did a fair amount of arrangement rehearsals for that project," says Hitt, "but I personally never laid any tracks."

But, says the drummer, demos do exist. "They ended up being a full album's worth of material," he says. "I continued to work with Eddie well into my time with Damn Yankees. If memory serves, the last demo Eddie and I recorded was in 1991."

A snippet of a song Cartellone recorded with Jobson can be heard on the drummer's site (www.michaelcartellone.com) and on a YouTube video of Cartellone's paintings called "The Four Davids." The YouTube video employs a fade-in and fade-out of the song "Transporter," from Eddie's/Zinc's *The Green Album*, which book-ends the hard-edged "unreleased" music. (When pressed for possible or working song titles of this or any music, as well as access to tracks, Cartellone declined to offer an invitation to help make some of this material public.)

"I have it all," Cartellone says. "Maybe I'll play you something from it someday."

Encouraged by people around him, Jobson pressed on, and in 1985 he released the highly improvised, instrumental electronic studio album *Theme of Secrets*—a Synclavier synthesizer special—through the Private Music label, produced and co-engineered by Tangerine Dream's Peter Baumann.

"I had a few themes written before [I went into the studio]," Jobson said. "I spent two or three weeks programming [the bouncing ball sounds] and some of the sliding sounds ... But it was just put together in the studio, building up parts."

Although *Theme of Secrets* was not a commercial breakthrough, it seemed to capture the imagination of some in the commercial music business, helping to further facilitate Jobson's crossover into TV scoring. "After a short period of time I was given this Volkswagen commercial [to score to] by this U.K. [band] fan," Jobson said. "The next thing I knew, he awarded me this huge national Amtrak campaign."

21

My Own Time

Highlights of John Wetton's Journeyman Career

P rior to his career as a solo artist and frontman of Asia, bassist/vocalist John Wetton was the quintessential British progressive rock journeyman.

Born in Derby, and raised in Bournemouth, Wetton was smitten by the beautiful melody and round-robin vocal technique employed by Brian Wilson for the Beach Boys' song "God Only Knows," a U.K. Top 2 single (Top 40 in the U.S.).

Guided by the strong presence of church music in his life, Wetton went on to forge a pop, or prog-pop, songwriting style that conveys a cathartic sense of spiritual awakening. Wetton's extensive experience and musical background, having recorded and/or toured with King Crimson, U.K., Renaissance, Roxy Music, Family, and Uriah Heep, has helped him to remain competitive, something that was more than just a little useful when he was jumping from gig to gig in the second half of the 1970s.

"What gives John an edge over his contemporaries is that he started off as a kind of gun-for-hire bass player, and not for a band," says It Bites guitarist John Mitchell, who has been playing with Wetton since the year 2000. "He didn't grow up in the Yes camp, finding success, more or less, within a few years. John was a session musician and has a different perspective on the whole thing."

Indeed. Martin Orford, a former member of the prog band IQ, was a member of Wetton's touring band and remembers some of the sketchier days of Wetton's solo career, around the turn of the century.

"We went to some very strange places," says Orford. "We did some very weird gigs in all manner of places all over the world. We went to both extremes of rock and roll. I remember we once played a huge festival in the Hague in the Netherlands. There was something like 250,000 people there. But a couple of weeks later John had tried to ask the promoter to get us some warm-up shows for an American tour [which started] in San Diego. They booked us in this really small bar where we played to fifteen people. We couldn't get anyone off the pool table all evening. At the end of the night this guy came up to John [Wetton] and said, 'You're not bad.' Since we were playing Asia material he said, 'You know, you do sound a bit like that guy from Asia.' John just looked at the guy and said, 'I *am* that bloody guy from Asia.'"

Like any great pugilist Wetton can't be counted out, even when it appears he may be on the ropes. Somehow, from somewhere, he finds the resources to overcome adversity and in so doing manages to deliver honest messages of love and loss, and, most importantly, hope.

Here's some often overlooked (non-Crimson and non-U.K.) projects Wetton has contributed to, both as the solo artist and as a group member/sideman.

Edwards Hand: *Stranded* (1970)

This recording for Edwards Hand (Roger Hand, Rod Edwards) has been referred to as Wetton's first professional recording date as a session musician. And what an auspicious beginning.

Produced by George Martin, *Stranded* (with cover artwork by Klaus Voormann, the artist who designed the cover of the Beatles' *Revolver*) was

Wetton appeared on a number of records throughout the 1970s, including (clockwise from top left) Edwards Hand's *Stranded*, Jack-Knife's *I Wish You Would*, Uriah Heep's *High and Mighty*, and Roxy Music's *Viva! Roxy Music*.

recorded at the newly minted Morgan Studios, the site of numerous classic progressive rock titles, from *Tales from Topographic Oceans* to Pink Floyd's *Meddle*, and mixed at Martin's unfinished Air Studios.

"We were working musicians and had built up relationships with other really talented musicians of like mind," says vocalist/keyboardist Rod Edwards. Edwards Hand was converting from a psychedelic folk duo to something resembling folk-influenced progressive rock, a transition facilitated by the capable "side" musicians featured on the record. "It's sometimes helpful to escape the confines of one's own talents and tap into those of some fellow travellers, from both the world of fellow groups and bands, like [guitarist] James Litherland and [bassist] John Wetton, and . . . [drummer] Clem Cattini," says vocalist/acoustic guitarist Roger Hand.

Stranded is surely the first concept album Wetton had ever helped to record. The album examines U.S. society, particularly its negative or regressive side, which was symbolically summed up by Voormann's original LP cover artwork (for the U.K. version) of a potbellied, gun-toting lawman most likely patrolling a certain civil rights–challenged region of the country. The image was clearly inspired by the song "Sheriff Myras Lincoln," which drops the "N" word—for effect and social commentary.

The album is book-ended by two suites: "Suite U.S." and the masterwork "Death of a Man," the latter being a great example of Wetton's sure-handed bass playing, which would help catapult him to rock royalty in the coming years.

"The U.S. was both a dream: the place to be—California sun, New York life, the birthplace of twentieth-century popular music—and a nightmare: Vietnam, imperialism, segregation, inequality," says vocalist/guitarist Roger Hand. "The juxtaposition of the romantic dream and the nightmare, as seen by young outsiders, was a point of interest then and remains so today."

Mogul Thrash: *Mogul Thrash* (1971)

Taking its name from Spike Mulligan's show *Mogul Thrasher*, this funky, soul-drenched early progressive metal band, originally called James Litherland's Brotherhood, featured guitarist Litherland, demon organ player and producer (Oblivion Express') Brian Auger, horn player Malcolm Duncan (Average White Band), guitarist/horn player Michael Rosen (AWB), drummer Billy Harris, saxophone player and horn arranger Roger Ball (also later of AWB), and, of course, hotshot bassist/vocalist Wetton.

"Those guys were really talented," Auger told the author in 2008. "Their album was actually a number-one play on Radio Luxembourg for a month. They had John Wetton on bass, great bass player, a couple of saxophone players who turned up in the Average White Band . . ."

The album, engineered by Eddie Offord in Advision Studios in West London, occupied a strange sector of the British musical landscape— somewhere halfway between Cream and Sly and the Family Stone. Wetton's unmistakable voice appears on "St. Peter" (a track with piano contribution from Auger), a song Wetton cowrote with Alan Gorrie, later of Average White Band.

The band showed a lot of promise, but, said Auger, "they kind of lost their minds at one point. The Scottish part of the band, from Dundee, which was the saxophone players, unknown to me, went behind my back, and they were successful in taking [drummer] Robbie McIntosh . . . from my band. Very nice. We were helping another band called Forever More, which had Alan Gorrie and Onnie Mair [a.k.a. McIntyre, later of AWB]. They succeeded in pulling both of those bands to pieces and also messing up a deal that we were able to complete with CBS for my band and theirs. I lost my deal with CBS because of that, too."

It appears that Mogul Thrash was doomed from the start. But none of this reflected poorly upon Wetton. "He was a very cool bass player, man," Auger said. "I think . . . he had a great bass tone. He seemed to know exactly what he was doing. He was a great support in the rhythm section . . . I just thought he handled himself very well and he seemed to be a good guy. He was kind of an exceptional player."

Family: *Fearless* (1971)

Family continued to invent their own musical vocabulary, even as they tempered much of their progressive sensibilities with their left-of-center interpretations of acoustic folk, electric R&B, and soulful vocal entertainment.

Recordings such as 1969's *Family Entertainment*, 1970's *A Song for Me*, 1971's *Fearless* and the partially live *Anyway*, and 1972's *Bandstand* feature an intriguing and aggressive mixture of R&B- and blues-based rock with traditional Western and exotic Eastern musical modalities. Some of the sonic textures the band achieves are downright grating and animalistic, especially on *A Song for Me*, which echo the adventurous sounds established on *Music in a Doll's House*.

Prior to Wetton's joining, there were a few pivotal personnel changes within the Family ranks, and the band had very little success breaking America. (The story goes that Roger Chapman swung his microphone and hit Fillmore honcho Bill Graham; and Family was booed while performing at the Fillmore. "We died at death [in the U.S.]," Chapman says. "Ric Grech [bass/violin/cello/vocals] says he was leaving to join Eric [Clapton] and Ginger [Baker] and Steve [Winwood] in Blind Faith. Really good news for a debut American tour. I'm afraid to say it was curtains. . . . They slaughtered us in the States.")

Before beginning work on their third album, *A Song for Me*, Family was introduced to Eric Burdon and the New Animals guitarist John Weider, by Peter Grant, Led Zeppelin's manager. "Peter was also our co-manager," says Chapman. "I assume he had some dealings with Eric or something. John joined us and rehearsed in the Bowery and did the remainder of the tour [in the U.S.], and came back to the U.K. John moved his gear back to the U.K. and we started *A Song for Me*. Halfway through that we started to have problems with Jimmy [King, saxophone/vocals], he was sick and not very well . . . And we couldn't all function in the same room together. Jim left and we asked [Deep Feeling's] 'Poli' [John Palmer, vibes/piano/flute] to join. We did that for the next couple of albums, and changed again, after *Anyway*, and John Wetton joined us."

Although some credit Palmer as the reason the band was reenergized, Wetton may have been just as stabilizing a force, at least on the surface. The bassist's vocals and use of double-neck guitar/bass added a certain amount of musical firepower to rehabilitate the band's energy and rejigger their style. (Guitarist and songwriter John "Charlie" Whitney also used a double neck on stage. Talk about firepower.) The result, *Fearless*, is one of the band's strongest efforts, alongside *A Song for Me*, showcasing the band's penchant for a wide range of songs, from jazz-rock to blues rock.

The experience seemed to impact Wetton musically. The line from the Asia song "Only Time Will Tell"—"The brightest ring around the moon will darken when I die"—is a variation on lyrics sung by Wetton featured in "Spanish Tide," written by Roger Chapman and Poli Palmer. How much input Wetton had on the song (or whether the singer/bassist simply liked the wording) is unclear.

Roxy Music: *Viva!* (1976)

Because both Wetton and Bryan Ferry of Roxy Music were managed by E.G., a casual meeting at a pub was set up between Wetton and the art-glam rocker. Inevitably, the question arose: Would Wetton join Roxy until the band could find a permanent bassist? Wetton was still in King Crimson at the time and had planned on touring *Red* with the band in the fall. But when Crimson collapsed the tour never materialized, and Wetton's bread and butter was gone. It also meant that Wetton was free to pursue other avenues, and dove right into working regularly with the likes of Uriah Heep, Phil Manzanera, and, of course, Roxy.

Wetton fit so well within Roxy's ranks that the other members thought he had joined full time. The truth was Wetton never made his intentions fully known and felt stifled in the band, having virtually no creative input. He never appeared on a Roxy studio album, for example. Wetton told the band, in no uncertain terms, that he hadn't joined, and their thinking otherwise was a big misunderstanding. For John, Roxy was a career move in the strictest sense: it was a paying gig. (He also appeared on Ferry's 1974 solo outing, *Another Time, Another Place* and 1976's *These Foolish Things*.)

Nonetheless, his time with Roxy, essentially in a support role to singer Bryan Ferry, was an eye opener; a reminder of what he had hoped to achieve, if the industry would ever afford him the opportunity to become a frontman.

Viva! presents Roxy at its most vibrant, and at times raucous and ridiculous. Hearing Bryan Ferry drone on, in a faux-Transylvanian accent, about a vinyl blow-up sex doll ("In Every Dream Home a Heartache"), straddles a line between outrageously kitschy and downright menacing.

Although Wetton does not appear on every track—it was recorded in spurts from 1973 through 1975, at Glasgow's Apollo theater, London's Empire Pool at

Wembley, and Newcastle City Hall (site of ELP's *Pictures at an Exhibition*)—sharing the stage with violinist/keyboardist Eddie Jobson, who joined Roxy when Brian Eno jettisoned for a solo career, eventually led to the formation of U.K., less than two years after the release of *Viva!*

Arguably it was his experience on tour with Roxy and the band's focus on the visual presentation of a live show (the complete opposite of Crimson) that may have helped Wetton navigate an ever-increasingly commercial (and hostile) music industry. After all, in the 1980s, which weren't too far off, image was everything.

"It was quite educational," Wetton said.

Uriah Heep: *High and Mighty* (1976)

What a run-up to this release. Wetton, who replaced bassist Gary Thain in 1975, was electrocuted while performing onstage with the Heep at the St. Paul Civic Center in Minnesota in 1976. (Singer David Byron escorted Wetton offstage.) After catching his breath, Wetton braved the stage again, and, again, within minutes, collapsed and was sent to the hospital. Ironically, Thain, who had bouts with heroin (and who had died in 1976), was also electrocuted while on stage with the Heep during a concert in Dallas in 1974. (Adding more injury to insult, Mick Box had fractured his wrist in three places during this time, and he, too, sought emergency medical attention.)

As he had done with Family, Wetton helped to breathe new life into the band he'd just joined (possibly similar, in ways, to Thain's and Kerslake's presence reenergizing the band for 1972's *Demons and Wizards*). The fantasy-laced hard rock of 1972's *The Magician's Birthday* and the orchestral stylings of *Salisbury* (1971) were things of the past, but 1975's *Return to Fantasy* and 1976's *High and Mighty*—both featuring Wetton—despite containing material that was largely penned by keyboardist/guitarist Ken Hensley, could quite possibly be Heep's most accessible yet varied albums, closely recalling the diversity of 1973's sometimes overlooked *Sweet Freedom*.

Much like Deep Purple of the same time period, Heep straddled the line between hard rock and prog. These divisions virtually disappeared when Hensley employed Moog synth and lead singer Dave Byron commanded the musical foreground with his vocal prowess.

The band's moniker, lifted from the hypocritical con artist of the same name appearing in the Charles Dickens novel *David Copperfield*, spoke of a need to connect with the past (and things traditionally English), a trademark of most mainstream British progressive rock bands of the 1970s. In addition, Heep's overtures toward serious works shared a kinship with their progressive rock contemporaries. For instance, *The Magician's Birthday*, intended to be a full-blown concept album, was inspired by a fictional story written by Hensley, which told of a wizard who invites his supernatural rivals to his birthday party to demonstrate a battery of magical spells cultivated over five hundred years. (Remnants of that initial concept can be detected on the official release, especially the ten-plus-minute title song, but the thematic approach was ultimately abandoned.)

Perhaps most importantly, Roger Dean's artwork, which graced the covers of some of Heep's most beloved early efforts, signaled the band's aspirations toward Wagnerian multimedia artistic expression. (Dean called his work for *Demons and Wizards* "an allegory of cosmic eroticism," which anticipates the iconic gatefold waterfall image printed in Yes' *Close to the Edge*—a nature scene inspired by Dean's trips to Scotland and Venezuela. The vibrant cover of *The Magician's Birthday* was pieced together from three separate images, one of which was revealed in the inner gatefold of the original LP and later the CD booklet for 812 298-2.)

So, it was a slightly different Uriah Heep into which Wetton

Crimson's mid-'70s break up led Wetton to join the hard rock/quasi-prog band Uriah Heep. Pictured: an ad for Heep's *Return to Fantasy* tour.

was recruited. One would hardly recognize the band hearing tracks on *High and Mighty*, such as the Afrocentric rhythmic patterns in "Can't Stop Singing," the spacey, almost Floyd-ish "Weep in Silence" (cowritten by Wetton), the vaudeville-esque "Woman of the World" (Wetton's bubble-icious bass line is more reminiscent of Jaco Pastorius than Thain), and the riff-based "One Way or Another," featuring Wetton, who shares lead vocals with Hensley (in the absence of a very ill Byron).

Just as Heep was arriving at exotic musical ports of call, Wetton was in need of a different headspace—a reaction to what had happened within Crimson and its sad demise. But a confluence of dark circumstances, including the record's lack of commercial appeal and internal discontinuity, was tearing the band apart. Byron's spiraling alcohol addiction and rock-star attitude did little to ease tensions, and the band was eventually forced to relieve the singer of his duties in July 1976. Reports blamed dissension among the ranks for the split, brought on by Wetton's appearance, but Byron's volatility and the band's unwillingness to proceed any further with the troubled singer can't be overstated. Putting a lie to some of the contemporary accounts, and in what may be interpreted as a show of solidarity, Wetton followed the booted Byron out the door.

Despite the traumatic events leading up to and surrounding the record and the aftermath of its release, much of *High and Mighty* holds up after nearly four decades. This is true, no doubt, due to Wetton's hand in arranging these tunes (with Hensley) and the musical collaboration he forged with the keyboardist/ multi-instrumentalist.

Years later, Hensley and Wetton teamed up for one night in London, in December 2001, an event that was documented by the 2003 CD and DVD releases titled *One Way or Another* (focusing on Wetton's set featuring Hensley) and *More Than Conquerors* (i.e., Hensley's showcase highlighted by Wetton's appearance).

Jack-Knife: *I Wish You Would* (1979)

Richard Palmer-James, a native of Bournemouth, was the former lyricist for King Crimson in the Wetton-Bruford (and Cross) era of the band, and the two teamed up once again for this release—a mix of original compositions by Palmer-James and Wetton and revamped blues warhorses by Willie Dixon, John Lee Curtis Williamson (a.k.a. Sonny Boy Williamson I), Alec "Rice" Miller (Sonny Boy Williamson II), Billy Boy Arnold, and John Lee Hooker, which venture into New Wave.

Palmer-James and Wetton had known each other for years from outfits such as the Corvettes and the Palmer-James Group, before their collaborative efforts made an impact on the Crimson catalog.

I Wish You Would, recorded in Munich over a ten-day span in February 1978, was a Bournemouth Special, containing material that the project's musicians once played in local clubs in the late 1960s, and featured keyboardist John Hutcheson, formerly of Tetrad, a late 1960s band of which Wetton was a member; and drummer Curt Cress, once of Orange Peel and later of Triumvirat. (Peter Bischof of Orange Peel lends vocals, Michael Lohmann is on sax, and Christian Schultz tickles keys on the Minimoog for the sessions.)

Once again, Wetton's bass performances surprise, first for their fluidity, and secondly by their funkiness and aggressiveness. His figures, especially on the title track and Palmer-James' "Mustang Momma," mesh well with Cress' assorted percussion and deep pocket—the spicy ingredients of a killer, albeit short-lived, rhythm section.

Released via PolyGram/EG.

Atoll: *Rock Puzzle* (1979)

After U.K.'s dissolution, Wetton had flirted with joining the French jazz-rock/prog-rock group Atoll, which was transitioning from a Mahavishnu

Orchestra–like fusionoid outfit, as witnessed by 1975's *L'Araignée-Mal*, to a funky, hard-driving, rock-oriented act exhibiting flourishes of musical virtuosity.

Initially, Atoll had wanted Wetton to produce their next studio album following *Rock Puzzle*, but things developed rapidly when the former King Crimson bassist/vocalist expressed genuine interest in becoming a member of the band.

Demos were recorded in early 1981 in Paris' Polydor Studios. Three tracks emerged but were not released until the CD era. Included on the reissued version of *Rock Puzzle* are "Here Comes the Feeling," "No Reply," and "Eye to Eye," which feature Wetton on bass and vocals. If the titles of some of the aforementioned songs seem familiar there's good reason: "Here Comes the Feeling" and "Eye to Eye" were forerunners to songs that would appear on Asia's 1982 debut and its 1983 follow-up, *Alpha*. (The music for "No Reply" and "Eye to Eye" is credited to keyboardist Michel Taillet and drummer Alain Gozzo, and lyrics to Wetton; Wetton wrote "Here Comes the Feeling.")

The French band's plans of having the former King Crimson bassist/vocalist join quickly faded when negotiations among management representatives stalled, a circumstance that may have inadvertently led to Atoll's breakup in 1981. However, the brief summit produced tracks that, for years, represented something akin to a Holy Grail for Wetton fans.

Asia: Now (1990)

After Wetton and Downes made an initial, unsuccessful attempt to regroup Asia in the late 1980s, Wetton and Palmer reunited as Asia for live performances in Germany in 1989. A show in Nottingham, England, at Central Studios in June 1990 with San Francisco–based guitarist Pat Thrall, was recorded and released as a promo disc titled *Now*. Wetton's voice was as powerful as ever, and the band was tight on such favorites as "Voice of America," "Wildest Dreams," "Open Your Eyes," "The Heat Goes On," and "Only Time Will Tell." (*Now* would eventually be reissued in 1997 with different packaging as an official release on the Blueprint label.)

The response to the shows was so overwhelming Wetton was convinced (as was Downes, Palmer, and the band's then-label Geffen Records) of the commercial possibilities of a reunited Asia. To capitalize on this Asian Renaissance of sorts, in August 1990, Geffen released *Then & Now*—a best-of collection of classic songs plus new studio material, featuring the surprise hit "Days Like These," an anthemic song ruminating on the cycle of self-empowerment, which reached *Billboard*'s Hot 100 singles chart.

Further testing the waters, Wetton, Downes, Palmer, and guitarist Pat Thrall recorded Asia's very first official live album in November 1990 in front of twenty thousand fans at Moscow's Olimpijski Stadion. The performances, recorded over two nights, were filmed and later released on both video and CD as *Live in Moscow 09-XI-90*. Asia even shot a music video just outside the Kremlin for "Prayin' 4 A Miracle," cowritten by husband and wife songwriting team Sue Shifrin-Cassidy and former teen heartthrob David Cassidy of the Partridge Family fame. Both songs appear on *Now* and *Then & Now*, and bear the hallmarks of Wetton's unwavering optimism in the face of desperation and despair—a template for the singer/bassist's solo career throughout the 1990s and 2000s.

Ironically, this briefly rejuvenated Asia lacked the fortitude—and one key original member (Howe)—to continue. Wetton himself, in an interview the author conducted a few years later, had pronounced the band deceased: "Asia? . . . Asia is a dead duck," Wetton said flatly. "It's just the way I feel about it."

The original members of Asia would, of course, reunite in 2006 and as of this writing Wetton, Palmer, and Downes continue to tour as a unit with guitarist Sam Coulson, 27, who appears on the band's 2014 studio album, *Gravitas*. Aside from cuts heard on *Live in the 'Hood* recorded in 2000 (released in 2007) by the band Qango (an alliance between Palmer and Wetton arising from the ashes of a failed Asia reunion), *Now* and *Live in Russia* might represent the best of Asia's live material.

John Wetton: *Battle Lines* (1994)

Originally titled *Voice Mail* (and prior to that, *Raised in Captivity*—a title Wetton fans will recognize as the name of John's 2012 solo album), *Battle Lines*, recorded in two locations from April to July 1993, is the quintessential Wetton solo album.

"*Battle Lines* was four years in the making," Wetton told me not long after the record was released.

For all intents and purposes, Wetton was finished with Asia (at least that's the way it appeared at the time) and spent nearly two years in California working on *Battle Lines* (a.k.a. *Voice Mail* in the Pacific Rim). Wetton had written forty-six songs, he told me, and whittled those pieces down to ten.

Battle Lines, which was produced by Ron Nevison, mixed by Chris Lord-Alge, and earmarked by Virgin Records America for release, features Robert Fripp, drummer Simon Phillips, Michael Cartellone (Eddie Jobson, Damn Yankees), and veteran session guitarist and Toto founder Steve Lukather.

"One of the people I wanted to get on that album there was Robert Fripp," Wetton said. "He's someone I've known for the better part of thirty-five years. I desperately wanted to get some connection between me and my past."

The impressive crew Wetton assembled was rounded out by keyboardist/programmer Bob Marlette (Alice Cooper, Saliva, Marilyn Manson, Tony Iommi, Black Stone Cherry) and arranger Paul Buckmaster (Elton John, Shawn Phillips).

Songs such as "Right Where I Want to Be" (nobody does sincere positivity the way Wetton does), "Crime of Passion" (cowritten with John Young, later of Qango), and "Hold Me Now," a tune Wetton wrote about the icy relations he had with his mother, are all vintage Wetton. Wetton's signature passionate

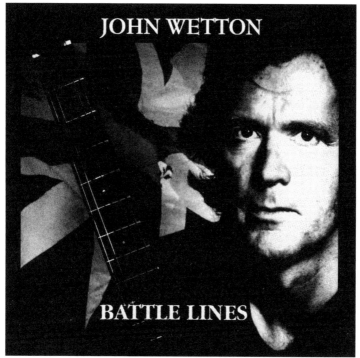

Battle Lines: The quintessential Wetton solo album?

and pained vocal delivery affords the lyrical content of the track considerable dimension, depth, and meaning.

Aside from Simon Phillips' pistons-poppin', tour-de-force double-kick-drum extravaganza on "Jane," Cartellone's drumming throughout the album grounded these tracks without stepping all over the song or Wetton's vocals. Cartellone, who had just finished recording a Damn Yankees record with Nevison in the same studio, was focused and efficient.

"I learned during Damn Yankees how important it was to stay out of the way of the vocals," Cartellone says. "I entered the recording process at the last moment. Basically, they would give me a demo of two songs the night before, I'd go home and listen to them . . . come in the next day . . . we would run through them once or twice . . . and cut it live as a four-piece band: drums, bass, guitar, keys, with John playing bass. We did this four or five days in a row and the rhythm tracks were finished. I feel that's why they have so much spark to them."

But after finishing the record, Wetton was shocked to discover that EMI had bought Virgin Records and that his services were no longer required. "The fact is that Virgin Records America signed me to do a record for them—and I did that," Wetton told the author. "Whatever it was. I was then told I was not needed anymore on Virgin Records America. So, I was pleased to get my record back for nothing. That was very nice of them for shit all. It was a crucifying blow. If you can imagine how I felt, having spent two years in California making this record for Virgin and then to be told it wasn't required. I felt pretty crushed. I felt absolutely sliced. I had then . . . the grisly task of getting different deals in different territories."

In the meantime there was some good news: produced by Bob Carruthers and directed by Graham Holloway, the 1994 period film *Chasing the Deer* featured two versions of the song "Battle Lines." With the credits rolling on the film, Wetton appears on camera, "singing" and playing bass as the electrified version of the song "Battle Lines" spins. (An acoustic version of "Battle Lines" is featured on the movie soundtrack.)

Wetton would, of course, secure deals for the global distribution of *Battle Lines*, and hit the road to promote the record. "In the words of the song, 'I picked myself up, dusted myself off . . . ' and I went out on the fucking road and did gigs," Wetton said. "It was great. I found that people were smiling at me."

In retrospect Virgin may have done Wetton a huge favor. The near disastrous situation motivated, perhaps forced, Wetton to hit the road, devise a stage show (boasting both an acoustic and electric set), and cut another album, *Chasing the Dragon*, recorded live in Japan, released in 1994 via the now-defunct Mesa label.

Although *Chasing the Dragon* was similar to Asia's *Live in Moscow*, a few years earlier, Wetton's career seemed to be experiencing a new beginning. Indeed. Arguably, *Battle Lines* was the cornerstone upon which Wetton has since built his career. Well, we should say his latest new career as it exists in its current incarnation.

Welcome to Heaven (2000)

The cover shows a heat imprint of, presumably, Wetton's hand; a more personal touch could not have been chosen for an album that seems to breathe and quake with a kind of intense intimacy. Despite the turmoil encircling Wetton's life at the time, namely his alcoholism, this is one of the journeyman's strongest solo efforts, nearly rivaling *Battle Lines*.

Former Crimson cohorts Ian McDonald and Robert Fripp appear, as do collaborative songwriters that include Ringo Starr, guitarist/producer Jim Peterik (the Ides of March, Survivor), Steve Hackett (on harmonica), and David Cassidy and his wife Sue Shifrin. One of the record's strongest songs, "Silently," is graced by the vocals of Beate, Wetton's then-partner with whom he had a child, Dylan. Beate can be heard sweetly singing the title phrase during the song's chorus. The tune, a plea by Wetton to his partner to return with him to a time before the couple began bickering, is chillingly prophetic. A few years later Wetton and Beate would part company.

Welcome to Heaven, titled *Sinister* outside Japan (the Japanese version contains two bonus tracks, including a makeover of "Space and Time," from *Battle Lines/Voice Mail*), contains three songs, cowritten by Canadian songwriter Jim Vallance (Bryan Adams, Aerosmith)—"Heart of Darkness," "Say It Ain't So," and "Where

Do We Go from Here?" These songs were taken from demos, what Vallance dubbed "quick and nasty" recordings, that he and Wetton had cut at Vallance's Vancouver-based Cabana Studios in 1991 and 1992. They were later used by Wetton for this 2000 release.

"The demo recordings and the tracks you hear on *Sinister* are 95 percent identical," says Vallance. "John on keyboards and bass, me on guitar and drums. John Mitchell added some guitar parts when John got back to England, but other than that, there was no change to the music. In fact, I assumed we were working on demos, audio templates, nothing more. I thought John would go into a proper studio with a producer and a top-notch band and cut 'master' recordings. I was very surprised when he decided to release the demos. They were never intended to be heard."

John's chronic battle with the bottle was flaring up around the time of *Welcome to Heaven.* How much of John's personal demons impact the recording/ writing process?

"I've worked with lots of people who had drug or alcohol issues," says Jim Vallance. "Sometimes it affected the writing sessions, sometimes not. In John's case, there was no evidence of alcohol abuse at all. Nothing. He was sober, focused, and one of the most pleasant people I've ever worked with. And that voice! It was a thrill to sit in the same room and hear the resonance when he sang."

Amorata, DVD (2003)

Arena and Wetton were playing on the same bill at Studio Krzemionki in Krakow, Poland, April 11, 2003. Guitarist John Mitchell (It Bites) was pulling double duty that night and sat in with Wetton's band for this recorded performance.

At the time Wetton was touring music from his *Rock of Faith* album, recorded in 2002 and coproduced by Clive Nolan (Arena) and Carl Brune (Theshold), with a stellar band, including keyboardist/flutist/backing vocalist Martin Orford (IQ, Jadis) and drummer Steve Christey (Jadis). (Wetton has said that there should be no confusion about the title of *Rock of Faith*: it's not meant to be taken as religious, but rather personal and spiritual. "Like taking words out of my diary," Wetton said. Wetton also covers "God Only Knows" for the Japanese version of the album.)

For the concert on this DVD, Wetton performed songs including his solo material ("Nothing's Going to Stand in Our Way," "Emma," "Battle Lines"), King Crimson gems ("Red," "Book of Saturday," "Starless," "Easy Money"), Asia tunes ("Sole Survivor," "The Heat of the Moment," "The Smile Has Left Your Eyes"), even U.K. classics ("In the Dead of Night," "Rendezvous 6:02").

Mitchell admits to not being completely familiar with the setlist prior to taking the gig. "I had Asia's first record, but I didn't know anything about U.K.," says Mitchell. "John basically said, 'It's all very well, and you can learn the Allan

Holdsworth solo note for note, but what would be the point in that? I know a lot of people like that solo, but I got you in the band because I like your playing. Do John Mitchell playing 'In the Dead of Night.' . . . It is not that I couldn't be bothered, it is because [John] encourages people to do their own thing."

Amorata was filmed in the time just before Wetton had sworn off alcohol altogether, remembers Mitchell. "John talks quite openly about it now," Mitchell says. "He has a tattoo on his arm of the day he gave up [drinking]. He's very committed. He's a lovely guy, anyway. My dad was a massive alcoholic, a two-bottles-of-Scotch-a-day kind of guy, and he died because of it, of a brain hemorrhage. I was twelve when he died and, the sad thing was, he had been going through a drying-out period. John has battled his demons and has been sober now [nearly ten years].

"At the end of the eighties, [Wetton] went through a period of sobriety that lasted five years and fell back off . . . I believe at this point he has had enough wake-up calls. John had . . . a triple heart bypass due to years of abuse. I don't imagine he will ever go back there."

Icon: *Icon* (2005)

The songwriting partnership of Wetton and Geoff Downes is renewed with this refreshing project. Although hyped as the return of the two creative giants of that supergroup, the 2002 release *Wetton-Downes* followed by Wetton's own *Rock of Faith*, which contained two Downes songs, actually got the ball rolling. Nontheless, this modern-day Downes/Wetton partnership was the trial run for the return of the supergroup Asia, which has become a global success.

Icon's debut was followed by the concept album called *Rubicon*, based loosely on the historical tale of Julius Caesar crossing the titular river, an act of defiance that eventually led to the establishment of the Roman Empire. In many ways, Icon was a point of no return for Downes and Wetton, and they have not looked back since. This came after decades of being apart. Wetton has gone on record as saying that if Asia had not re-formed Icon would be on the road as often as schedules allowed.

"One of the things of the twelve-step program is that you have to make amends with people you . . . have fallen out with in the past," Mitchell relates. "John has done dates with Eddie Jobson as U.K. It's about building bridges, and I think that's one of the reasons he wanted to do it. His career is going from strength to strength. John has managed to do what my dad never did, and I'm proud of the fact that he has managed to overcome it all."

Other Notables

Throughout his long career John Wetton has performed, written music, and recorded with a vast array of progressive-rock icons including Phil Collins (i.e., "Knights (Reprise)" on Peter Banks' solo record *Two Sides of Peter Banks*), former Genesis guitarist Steve Hackett (i.e., *Genesis Revisited, The Tokyo Tapes: Live in Japan, Genesis Revisited II*), and Family's Roger "Chappo" Chapman (i.e., 1974's *Streetwalkers* recorded by the blues-rock outfit Chapman-Whitney, which featured a revolving cast of impressive musicians from Britain's hard rock and art-rock scenes; in addition, the tune "Into the Bright," co-composed by Wetton, Bob Marlette, and Chapman, appears on Chappo's 1996 record, *Kiss My Soul*).

Here's a brief list of some additional key releases illustrating the depth and breadth of Wetton's work.

Peter Banks—*Two Sides of Peter Banks* (1972)

Phil Manzanera—*Diamond Head* (1975), *K-Scope* (1978)

Roger Chapman—*Mail Order Magic* (1980), *Hyenas Only Laugh for Fun* (1981)

Wishbone Ash—*Number the Brave* (1981)

Wetton/Manzanera—*Wetton/Manzanera* (1987)

Steve Hackett—*The Tokyo Tapes, Live in Japan* (video, 1999)

Wetton (solo)—*Akustika: Live in Amerika* (1996)

Wetton (solo)—*Raised in Captivity* (2012)

John Wetton + Richard Palmer-James—*Monkey Business* (rarities collection reissued in 2014 on a single CD with Jack-Knife, containing the King Crimson song "Doctor Diamond")

22

Asia "Minor"?

John Payne Discusses His (Largely Underappreciated) Years with the Prog-Pop Band Asia

T he founding members of Asia are nothing if not shrewd.
Despite their status in the progressive rock world, bassist/vocalist John Wetton, guitarist Steve Howe, drummer Carl Palmer, and keyboardist Geoff Downes rightly ignored audience expectation to reclaim a part of their musical legacy.

Realizing that the pomposity of '70s prog held little, if any, currency in the fast-paced, highly commercialized techno-savvy Reagan-Thatcher Era, each member seemed to be making an effort to streamline his approach, going out of his way to curtail musical excess that could be misconstrued as having anything to do with the so-called pretentiousness of prog rock.

The risk paid off. Having sold over four million copies of its 1982 self-titled debut in the U.S., alone, and watching its 1983 follow-up, *Alpha*, earn platinum status, Asia appeared to be on solid musical and business footing. Although hardcore progressive rock fans bemoaned the fact that Asia was veering away from more creatively challenging material, *Alpha*'s performance at the cash register, while not matching the breakout success of the debut record, was still very much the stuff of rock and roll dreams.

Despite outward signs of success, by the mid-1980s, Asia was mired in messy personal, contractual, creative, and professional entanglements, which threatened to render the band just another music-business stat.

After working on demos for songs that would appear on their then-upcoming album, *Astra*, Howe was asked to leave in September 1984, citing creative differences, and Krokus axe-cranker Swiss-Canadian Mandy Meyer was recruited for the recording of *Astra*.

Although *Astra* displayed glimmers of musical dynamics typical of Wetton's previous band U.K. (i.e., "After the War," "Too Late"), much of the material seemed even more formulaic than the unabashedly pop *Alpha*. Astra reached number sixty-seven on *Billboard*'s Top 200 Albums chart, but the band was on life support in the eyes of record company bigwigs, and dangerously pivoting toward irrelevancy in the fickle and highly competitive mid-1980s pop world.

Due to lack of interest and label support, the quartet refused to underwrite a tour to support *Astra*—a circumstance that did little to resuscitate the band's flatlining career. The fanfare that trumpeted in the release of their debut had faded in just over three years, and Asia slipped away quietly, presumably forever, in the months following *Astra*'s November 1985 release, some of the band members claiming they never wanted to speak with the others again.

Or so some thought.

After numerous tries to get the band up and running with various original members, Downes hadn't given up on Asia, despite all pop culture signs pointing to the fact that Asia was a relic of some bygone era, a guilty pleasure for prog fans.

With little holding them to the past, and no longer signed to a major label, Asia was resuscitated by Downes with the help of guitarist/vocalist/bassist/producer John Payne, ostensibly Wetton's replacement. Although Asia was no longer the commercial force it once was in the 1980s, the duo kept the Asia banner flying—in a big way. From the early 1990s through the early 2000s, fans were bombarded with a slew of Asia anthologies and live and "official bootleg" releases of varying sound quality, featuring past and then-present members of Asia, including double-disc sets *Anthologia: The 20th Anniversary/Geffen Years Collection (1982–1990)*, *Gold* (i.e., original remastered recordings of the classic Asia catalog), *Live in Buffalo* (an early Asia live recording from 1982), the single disc *The Very Best of Asia: Heat of the Moment (1982–1990)*, *Archiva* (a two-volume set containing then-unreleased material dating back to the early 1990s), *Live: Osaka, Japan 1992* (featuring Steve Howe), *Live in Köln—Germany*, and *Live at the Town & Country Club* (recorded during a Payne/Downes acoustic duo tour of America in the early 2000s). This is to say nothing of the John Payne–era Asia's studio efforts (*Aqua, Aria, Arena, Aura, Silent Nation*).

After a dozen or so years, the creative relationship between Downes and Payne had virtually disintegrated. Increasingly, Payne was shouldering more and more of the songwriting duties, a fact made apparent with the release of 2004's *Silent Nation*. The album's title, Payne once told the author, was partly inspired by the use of patriotic rhetoric to silence political opposition (and what Payne interpreted as a general indifference to speaking truth to power). Given the internal turmoil of the band, however, it could also reflect the extant communication breakdown between the band's two protagonists. "Geoff had lost a lot of interest in music full stop," says Payne. "It obviously was time for [Downes] to do something else, in my opinion."

Perhaps Downes agreed. Looming in background since the late 1990s were rumors of the possibility of the four original members of Asia reuniting. (In actuality, the band, less Howe, had planned to stage a comeback in 1999, but, depending on your news outlet of choice, either Payne nixed it over rights to the name or the day-to-day band operations may have proved stressful for certain members, and a 3/4-Asia reunion was DOA.)

Then, in 2006, the impossible occurred: Wetton, Howe, Downes, and Palmer toured together for the first time since 1983, making Asia a global success, once again, and further fracturing Payne's relationship with Downes. After a protracted legal bout over ownership of the band name, Payne was given clearance to tour as "Asia Featuring John Payne," and in 2012 the digital single "Seasons Will Change" appeared. (2014 brought the covers album *Recollections: A Tribute to British Prog*.) Although Payne told the author in 2009 that his version of Asia had signed a deal with Sony Japan and "we're currently recording a new [studio] album," as of this writing, the multimedia, theatrical classic rock production *Raiding the Rock Vault*, appearing nightly at Las Vegas Hotel & Casino, had taken up much of Payne's time.

Below is a portion of the conversation the author had with Payne involving the most pivotal points in Asia's history, the events leading up to the original-member reunion, and his sixteen (largely underappreciated) years of service to the cause.

WR: Take me through the story of how you worked out a deal with the four original members of Asia.

John Payne: First of all I had been with the band longer than anyone, other than Geoff. At the time I had joined, John Wetton said he didn't want anything more to do with Asia again. He would never get back working with Asia. Geoff told me at the time that he would never work with John Wetton again. . . . Steve had already sold his shares of the name—they bought him out in the early days. Carl had sold his rights to the name. John had blamed Steve for his departure in the early 1980s, so when he returned for the *Astra* record, it is my understanding that Steve had to go. Geoff had walked out during the recording of what was going to be our new record, then titled *Architect of Time*. He then decided to get back with the original members and tour. I was in the middle of working out a deal with the label Inside Out and they had offered us quite a large advance to record the album. We had signed a three-album deal. But since Geoff had left, I had to basically give them the money back. But since I own the company that ran the band, we were forced to go to litigation. Then for a period of maybe two years we were battling over the name, and eventually we settled. What we agreed upon was that they would call themselves the Original Members of Asia and myself, Asia Featuring John Payne. Although we did go through a painful process, sometimes in these situations this is the only way things can be decided. I made sure that part of the deal was that my name would only take up 25 percent of the band logo.

WR: What was your perception of the public reaction to Asia Featuring John Payne in the wake of the legal wrangling over the name?

Payne: When we first went out as Asia Featuring John Payne we did a show in Los Angeles and several thousands of fans turned up. We did a set that was one hour and three-quarters. We get a lot of young people coming to the show and even their dads, who were into the band. We do material from both eras of Asia—music from the first album and material that's right up to date.

A rendition of Asia Featuring John Payne's logo sent to the author in 2009.   *Courtesy of John Payne*

WR: How did you join Asia in the first place?
Payne: I met Geoff [Downes] when he was working with a friend of mine called Phil Spalding who was in a band called GTR, the supergroup with Steve Howe and Steve Hackett. Geoff had been working on a series of songs that GTR vocalist Max Bacon had sung. John Wetton had come in and sang some of songs. That's when I started working with Geoff. This project was something we were developing, which we were going to call Rain, which didn't work out, and after that I went to ELO Part II. That's when Geoff called me to ask if I would be interested in joining Asia. He said, "[The band] would just be you and I with various people playing on the tracks."

WR: How long did the entire process take, from the time you were working with Rain to joining the revitalized Asia?
Payne: It was only about six months after [Rain] that Geoff asked me to join [Asia].

WR: What can you tell me about your relationship with Geoff just prior to—and just after—the original Asia reunion?
Payne: I used to know Geoff very well. We had worked together for sixteen years; we often shared apartments and things like that. Since he left what, ostensibly, was the band, I have had no contact with him whatever. I've tried to, but it was just like he was there one minute and was gone the next.

WR: Did you receive any warning signs from Geoff that he intended to re-form the original Asia?
Payne: I think with *Silent Nation* [2004 studio album] Geoff had lost a lot of interest in music full stop. Pretty much all the songs that appear on *Silent Nation* I wrote. I tend to write a lot on acoustic guitar and I pretty much brought all

the songs to Geoff rather than us sitting down and collaborating from the very beginning. It definitely seemed difficult for him to collaborate at that stage, even though at that time we were sounding great and had just come off a tour with Dio.

WR: A signature element of the music of the original Asia was the layered vocal/ vocal cluster or church choir vocal effect. Your version of Asia perfectly captured this effect, particularly in a track like "Darkest Day" from 2004's *Silent Nation.*
Payne: Fair enough; an interesting point. I had a Catholic upbringing and it was only halfway through my childhood that masses went from Latin to English. There weren't English-language masses that you could attend. So, the Gregorian chant was something that subconsciously came to mind. The Latin term *caligo dies* translates to "darkest day." I think I must have recorded myself forty times. It sounded like a choir of monks, basically.

WR: You've actually worked with nearly all of the original members. What are your impressions of the guys?
Payne: I think that Carl is a straight guy. . . . He drinks cappuccino and he is constantly picking at you like a mother hen. [laughs] Steve . . . has the occasional glass of wine. John used to drink to absolute oblivion. But the party animal was always Geoff. Not all the guys have said nice things about each other. How they initially got to work together, I don't know. The first record was a good record. It was a really good record. Collectively it worked.

WR: A cynic would say that Asia was cooked up in a corporate boardroom.
Payne: A lot of this was [former Geffen label A&R man] John Kalodner's idea. Those four guys would never have bumped into each other in a bar and said to one another, "Let's start a band." In the 1980s, the industry had money to spend; it was the start of MTV, video marketing was a fact of life, payola was still alive and well and relevant to radio station airplay. Financially it was a very wise decision.

WR: Post-litigation it couldn't have been easy to perform, essentially, as "Asia" knowing that the four original members were out there, touring also under the Asia banner.
Payne: It's been a hard struggle. It was two years of not earning any money. It was horrible. Prior to the original-member reunion things were going really well. We had a South American tour booked . . . Despite the difficulties that went down with the two bands, I would still be very open to a dual tour with them. I doubt it would ever happen, though. The thing is it wasn't I who decided to split and walk out on the band.

WR: Forgive the comparison, but I see you as the Billy Sherwood of Asia.
Payne: Yeah. Interesting comparison. Billy and I have been through very similar things. Billy, who is a friend of mine, is extremely talented. There's material

on [some of the Yes] records where you think certain people are playing—and they aren't. It was Billy.

WR: Both of you helped to keep your respective bands alive . . .

Payne: Sixteen years is a long time with the band. [*Note:* Aqua, *Payne's first album with the band, appeared in 1992 and the original member Asia reunion occurred in 2006.*] For a lot of that material, essentially from the early 1990s through the mid-2000s, I didn't have collaborations with anyone else. I engineered, produced, and mixed most of the records as well as doing the lion's share of the writing. It really was down to me to keep it going. You can't stop anybody wanting to leave. I'm fine about that. But I would have just liked to have finished the project we were doing.

WR: 1992's *Aqua* was Asia's first studio release since the mid-1980s. Did it surprise you when it began to make some noise?

Payne: We had quite extensive airplay in Europe and America with a song called "Who Will Stop the Rain?" [CD EP, Great Pyramid Records 7 3333 36006-4]. I remember it went Top 3 in Japan. It sold 75,000 units in Germany in two weeks. Although *Then & Now* [a 1990 release featuring new studio material and greatest hits] had been released just prior to *Aqua, Aqua* was the first fresh studio release by Asia since the mid-1980s. Then, again . . . Geoff never actually played on the original songs appearing on *Then & Now* . . . Steve never played on it either; it was a bunch of session guys with John Wetton in America. The song "Prayin' 4 A Miracle" was cowritten with David Cassidy's wife [Sue Shifrin]. [*Note:* Aqua *featured a cast of players, including original members Carl Palmer and guitarist Steve Howe on a variety of stringed instruments, drummer Nigel Glockler (Saxon) and guitarist Al Pitrelli, of Alice Cooper and Megadeth fame. "As a session player the pressure was on me to deliver, but that's as far as it went," recalls Glockler. "I think the pressure was on Geoff and John Payne, as it was the first record of the revamped lineup and, I think, they wanted and needed to make a tremendous record."*]

WR: Why was the work of outside composers featured on *Aqua?*

Payne: One of the songs, "Love Under Fire," was written by Greg Lake [ELP] and Geoff, because at virtually the same time, if not three months before, Geoff was working on a project with Greg called Ride the Tiger, which never really properly came to fruition. That's where that song came from and that's pretty much where *Aqua* came from—songs that I had and songs Geoff had from working with other people, like British songwriter Johnny Warman and Greg Lake, mostly.

WR: Do you consider *Aria* a concept album?

Payne: It was very much four people—Al Pitrelli, Geoff Downes, Michael Sturgis, and myself—actually writing meaningful songs that had some form of thread connecting them. There were songs on *Aria* like "Summer," which, on the surface, seems like it's about a season of the year, but I actually wrote it about my father coming towards the end of his life. There was also quite a military thread going through the album with the appearance of "Military Man" and "Remembrance Day." Lyrics have always been very important to me. Three people could listen to a song like "Summer" and get three different meanings.

WR: How did the recording sessions for *Aria* proceed?
Payne: We wrote the songs over a month in rehearsals in a place called E-Zee Studios in London. Then we went to Parkgate Studios in the south of England in, funnily enough, Battle, where the Battle of Hastings was fought, 1066. [*Note: Additional recording was done at Maison Rouge, London.*] We didn't leave the building for three months. . . . I think I went into the town center three times in three months.

WR: *Aura* is sometimes seen as the John Payne–era Asia's pinnacle. Thoughts?
Payne: I had been listening to a lot of Steely Dan before writing songs for that record. We'd tried to make Asia a four-piece band again with *Aria*, but the lineup was not stable. It just didn't work. Geoff and I knew it was down to the two of us, again. So, we thought, "Let's put together a rock Steely Dan album where we would work with a number of different people in the studio." We got quite a large record advance and bought ourselves a big residential studio in South Wales [Loco]. I wanted one of the greatest drummers in the world to play on it—Vinnie Colaiuta. He played on it and so did [bassist] Tony Levin, [drummer] Simon Phillips, Elliott Randall [guitarist, Steely Dan], Pat Thrall [Asia], and Steve Howe. It's a record that goes through huge changes from pop-y rock AOR to something that's heavily progressive. For most of it we had an engineer/producer called Simon Hanhart. We butted heads slightly, because I wanted to sing the songs a bit harder and he simply didn't want me to. . . . There were a few compromises in the performances. . . . Maybe it was a little too polished, in retrospect. But it's still a record that I'm proud of.

ELP's *Black Moon* Rising

Romantic Warriors in Enemy Territory

I t's not as bad as you've heard. File it one notch above *Love Beach*, for sure. ELP's 1992 studio album, *Black Moon*, deserves some respect, if for nothing else but the fact that this was the product of a classic British progressive rock band staging a comeback—and making bold statements doing it—in the era of grunge.

In large part, ELP's comeback was tied to the fortunes of classic rock in the late 1980s and the establishment of Victory Records, an American subsidiary of JVC, which offered a (semi) safe harbor to ELP and Yes, a band Phil Carson, head of Victory, had signed three times over the course of his career. (Carson re-signed Yes after they were dropped by Atlantic U.S., against the wills of the American office, and the resulting album, 1971's *The Yes Album*, was a Top 10 hit in the U.K.)

Emerson and Palmer's collaboration in 3, with bassist/vocalist Robert Berry, had ended, and the drummer was in the studio, again, with Asia, recording *Aqua* with the new lineup spearheaded by Geoff Downes and John Payne.

It's been reported that ELP was brought together to record a soundtrack for Carson, but this never materialized. Some question whether this story had any validity at all. "It wasn't easy getting the band together for the recording," Carson confesses, "but I remember being in a hotel in London. At the moment we were meeting Desert Storm broke out. That was the moment we were trying to re-form ELP."

Emerson had the mind to work with producer Kevin Gilbert (Toy Matinee, Giraffe), but when this wasn't in the cards, Mark Mancina, a confirmed progressive rock geek and former member of the American prog band Handel, emerged to occupy the producer's chair. Mancina "lived" with the band, working alongside them, day in and day out, for months in England, to prepare them for the recording.

"We were together twelve hours a day," Mancina says. "This was a difficult time for them. Keith was turning fifty. They felt the world was waiting for an ELP record—and I knew differently. I thought, *The only way we are going to hook people is if [ELP] goes back to the band's roots and they play the real stuff.* I said, 'You guys can get on MTV and play as an acoustic three-piece. People might respond to that. But if you guys get up there with synthesizers, glossy over everything and overproduced tracks and drum machines, you guys will fade out.'"

The early 1990s were tricky times for most bands. The alternative/garage rock/grunge movement was a tsunami, swallowing everything in its wake, mirroring, in some ways, the shockwaves the industry absorbed at the advent of punk rock nearly fifteen years earlier. History does repeat itself. Most execs in the industry were looking for the next Nirvana. Any hint of prog rock and your band would be S.O.L., at least as far as winning a major-label contract.

In the pre-Internet, pre-democratization of recording technology age, prog-rock festivals were still a few years away, and most of the prog-rock labels either hadn't yet come to prominence or weren't yet established. A metal band with progressive rock roots and leanings called Damn the Machine, signed to A&M Records, featuring Chris Poland, formerly of Megadeth, was a typical example of a great band lost in the shuffle of corporate realignment and cluelessness.

"We had a dinner with [A&M] and they told us, 'This year we're going to focus on Damn the Machine,'" says Dave Clemmons, former vocalist and guitarist with DTM. "This was after our record had come out, so they were referring to our next studio album. Weeks later, something along those lines, they dropped us. They were getting conflicting reports on what was happening with the industry. One week we were in and, literally, the next we were out. You know, some assistant tells his boss, 'I was wrong: this shit is dying, and you better get out from under it quick.' The A&R guy got dumped at A&M, as well, at the same time, strangely enough."

"It was timing," confirms recording engineer Patrick MacDougall. "I think timing is everything in whatever market you're trying to invade. Music certainly has its ebbs and flows, and at that time things were going toward that Nirvana-esque sound. What I found interesting is that after that wave, who come out of that? Porcupine Tree and the Mars Volta and other progressive rock bands that had a different sound."

Executives had little patience for lack of performance or success, to say the least, which is something Mancina had witnessed first-hand. "I remember Phil grabbed me by the collar and held me up against the wall and said, 'You better fucking deliver a hit song.' This happened. I am not speaking metaphorically."

"From the point we started talking, to the day we opened the record label . . . the sea changed a lot," adds Carson. "We ended up in a situation that in 1990, the week we opened up the record label, the Seattle sound broke and it was the end of classic rock music for a certain period of time. In a way, my timing was not exactly stellar for the formation of that record label."

Pressure was mounting to make this record all it could be. No one wanted to make a mistake for fear of putting the wrong foot forward in such a risky musical environment. "Greg held off singing until the very end, and I felt he should have been singing the whole year to get his voice up to speed," says Mancina. "His voice had changed radically."

Phil Carson signed Yes and ELP to Victory Music at a time when British progressive rock bands from 1970s held very little currency. Pictured: the albums *Talk* by Yes and *Black Moon* by ELP.

It's been noted that Frank Sinatra's voice changed in the 1960s, having accumulated a kind of patina, a darkness, that enriched the words he was singing. Perhaps Lake's vocal quality was similar. "It worked on 'Farewell to Arms,'" says Mancina, "because he had a kind of Father Time gruffness that works for that track."

On the whole, *Black Moon* is a solid and very listenable affair. The record features tracks such as "Changing States" (originally titled "Another Frontier" in its demo stage, it was intended for Emerson's solo album, which was going to be produced by Gilbert),[1] "Close to Home" (based on another Emo demo, originally titled "Ballade"), and "Affairs of the Heart," a song Lake wrote in Venice and had been earmarked for Ride the Tiger, his collaborative project with Geoff Downes. (The song is credited to both Lake and Downes.)

Other key tracks included "Romeo and Juliet" (titled "Montagues and Capulets," again meant for Emerson's solo album), "A Blade of Grass" (which was the B side of the "Black Moon" single, and appeared on the Japanese version of the disc, and was later included as a bonus track on the 2008 Shout! Factory reissue of the album), "Farewell to Arms," and one of the record's brightest musical moments, "Burning Bridges."

"I had written the song 'Burning Bridges' for Trevor [Rabin]," says Mancina. "While I was working with Trevor on Yes' *Union*, ELP called and said they had heard 'Burning Bridges' and wanted to record it. I thought 'Burning Bridges' was the best thing they did [for that album]. It's funny: I saw Greg at a swap meet about five years after that, in Santa Monica, and we went back to his house and opened a bottle of wine and he said, 'You know something? You want to know the best song on that album?' I said, 'What is it?' And he played 'Burning Bridges' about five times in a row."

When we spoke with Mancina he confessed that, even to this day, he was not totally satisfied with the end result. "If you listen to the record there's a lot of Hammond and there's a lot of stuff I did that I pushed so hard to get them to do, that they didn't want to do. But I was hoping we'd go in a more *Unplugged* direction."

Although the record may be compromised, it was a far cry from the dross invading *Love Beach* or the studio effort following *Black Moon*: the tossed-together, bloodless pastiche (putting it kindly) *In the Hot Seat*, which Palmer has always called "dreadful." Arguably, had ELP the ability to record and release *Black Moon* in the late 1970s (in place of *Love Beach*), it's possible they would have held themselves together a bit longer—and they would have fared better in the punk shitstorm hitting around that time.

"We made the record and the unfortunate thing was, of course, that we went with the wrong single ['Black Moon']," says Carson. [*Note: "Affairs of the Heart," b/w "Better Days," was also released as a single.*] "We went with something that was typical for ELP, the way they were, as opposed to the way the business was changing. If we would've gone with 'Paper Blood' it would have been a better choice. When I re-formed Yes back in the days of Atlantic, we went with 'Owner of a Lonely Heart,' which was nothing like the band was in the past. It reestablished the band, and was a number-one record. That was quite an event for them. We could have had a similar thing with ELP."

"[Lake] said, '['Burning Bridges'] was the best thing we had done in twenty years,'" says Mancina. "Greg said, 'We didn't release it because you wrote it, and we didn't want to put out something we didn't write. We felt that wouldn't be good for us.'"

While the record would not prove to be an overwhelming commercial success, *Black Moon* stands as a milestone in the band's career: as they had done in the 1970s, there was no making any excuses or apologies for its musical excesses, no matter how untrendy or unhip.

ELP toured the globe beginning in 1992, and the following year the stellar 1993 boxed set, *The Return of the Manticore*, appeared. *In the Hot Seat*, produced by Keith Olsen, followed.

Carson was counting on a hit, somewhere along the line, whether it was *Black Moon*, Yes' *Talk* or, even, *In the Hot Seat*, but nothing could save the record company from going under. "I did what I was supposed to do, which was to sign two of the biggest progressive-rock bands ever—ELP and Yes [who would record *Talk* for Victory in 1994]," says Carson. "By the time the records were ready, less people cared. That was unfortunate. The reality was that ELP had no thought of re-forming, but I had a relationship with all three of them, and was able to get them all in one room and make it work."

Carson's support of the band, however stressed and strained, helped ELP maintain a presence through the final years of the 1990s. "I saw [Carson] years later, at the Grammys," Mancina says, "after I had won, and he said to me, 'I owe you an apology.' I said you don't owe me one. 'I was a kid. I was young and I was trying to get a hit out of [ELP].' I took that band, man, and they never would have gotten a record out like that. It took a lot of work to get that record out. If you listen to their subsequent albums after that, I don't think anything comes close to it."

24

Änglagård

Riding the Third Wave

While Pennsylvania-based prog band Echolyn were breaking down barriers and making strides in the commercial recording world, Swedish band Änglagård, one of the leading lights of prog's so-called Third Wave, became the 1990s poster children for grassroots progressive rock, signaling that they're more interested in substance than style.

Their performances at historically significant festivals, such as ProgFest in 1993 and 1994, occurred at a pivotal moment when an underground musical movement was just starting to catch fire. The band's evolution and rising fortunes, it seemed, mirrored the genre's predicted ascendance to mass appeal and eventual acceptance by a mainstream audience.

One could argue that two decades on, prog rock is still battling for credibility in the mainstream psyche and Änglagård's best years are likely still ahead of them. While these circumstances may explain the cult-like following the band enjoys in the States and in corners of Europe and Japan, Änglagård nonetheless remains a bit of a mystery to this day.

One can't rightly call the band visible on the circuit, as they've remained dormant for long stretches of time, not touring extensively in any shape or form. In fact, 2014 marks the first time the band performs in the U.K.

Their music has appeared on various CD and/or video compilations, but the band hasn't been particularly prolific, issuing only five major releases since forming in 1991: 1992's *Hybris*, 1994's *Epilog*, *Buried Alive* (documenting the band's performance at ProgFest '94), and their most recent studio creation, 2012's *Viljans Öga*, a collection of busy and hypnotic tunes possessing, in its quieter and more minimalistic moments, an undercurrent of dark, knotty beauty that's a hybrid of acoustic chamber rock, electrified prog, and mid-twentieth-century classical. (May 2014 also saw the release of another live album—a double-disc extravaganza, *Prog på svenksa—Live in Japan*.)

What, then, makes this largely instrumental band so popular among progheads? Perhaps it all boils down to one unassailable point: Änglagård is notorious for their internal conflicts (i.e., their notable and numerous breakups, personnel changes, and legendary, if slightly perverse, by-committee writing and recording methods) and have willingly and admittedly created a contentious environment that feeds creativity as much as it threatens to snuff out the band's very existence.

Things may be changing, however. Given its history, it's almost inconceivable, but the band appears more active—and stable—than ever. (As of this writing Änglagård are guitarist/vocalist Tord Lindman, bassist Johan Brand, wind instrument/Mellotron player Anna Holmgren, drummer/percussionist Erik Hammarström, and keyboardist Linus Kåse.)

Scheduled to tour far from their home base throughout 2014, and stressing the need to release music with more regularity, Änglagård seems to have squared itself with its past. For how long this situation will last is anyone's guess, but when Johan Brand spoke with me he was cautiously optimistic about Änglagård, its creative process, and future prospects.

WR: What's currently happening with the band?

Johan Brand: The band has never been more alive than it is today. 2012 came the new studio album, *Viljans Öga*, and Tord Lindman came back to the band. New members pulled double duty: Linus Kåse performed on keyboard and soprano sax, and Erik Hammarström on drums and percussion. Änglagård did a lot of concerts in 2013, which resulted in a double live album from Japan, *Prog på svenska*, set to be released in May 2014. Änglagård is writing new material for an upcoming studio album and new concerts plans will be advertised continuously.

WR: So much has been made of the band's democratic method of recording and writing music. What were the early rehearsals like with the band?

Brand: Early rehearsal sessions were based very much on long jam sessions. Everyone in the band, besides Mattias [Olsson, former drummer], wrote music for the debut album, *Hybris*. It usually started with someone coming in with some themes, ideas. We played through the themes, saved the parts we liked, added other band members' interesting themes, and the puzzle was completed.... Änglagård has always written material in this way, and we still do, because everyone wants to contribute. We have no main composer. I'm convinced that this painful and time-consuming process helps to create our unique sound.

WR: I've seen some of the behind-the-scenes videos for the recording sessions of the band's last studio album, *Viljans Öga*. It seems every time a decision is made by two or three people in the band, a third person objects to it. How does anything get done in the Änglagård world?

Brand: Many strong wills, many conflicts, many tears . . . but in the end we make pretty interesting music, we think. Democracy has always been a key word in the band, and, yes, it takes a long time to produce a new Änglagård album. But we think it's good that the material grows slowly. The major challenge has been to keep the band together until we're ready with a new album. Today, with the new lineup [including Hammarström and Kåse], we don't suffer from that problem. We have a completely different harmony these days.

WR: Since 2012, has anyone in the band emerged "the leader"?
Brand: Änglagård has never had a leader, and still doesn't. The band does not work under such conditions.

WR: My understanding is that you have had offers from major labels over the years, but turned them down. Why?
Brand: We simply want to have full control of what we do and release.

WR: I'm interested in some inside info about how you write and record. For instance, can you describe how a song such as "Kung Bore," from 1992's *Hybris*, was written?
Brand: Tord Lindman wrote large parts of "Kung Bore." The song is based around the lyrics and created slowly from there. As usual we put our musical personalities into it and in the end it became a long composition.

WR: How did you approach recording pieces such as "Sista Somrar" and "Höstsejd" from *Epilog*? Did you record them in three or four different sections and then edit them together?
Brand: The acoustic sections we recorded separately. The other tracks were recorded live in the studio.

WR: Both *Hybris* and *Epilog* contain concepts relating to nature. Is there any thematic connection linking some of the material I hear on *Epilog* and *Hybris*?
Brand: Nature has always been close to us, so it has a natural connection to Änglagård's music and album covers.

WR: Is there a connection between the anthropomorphic "face" on the cover of *Epilog* and the one I see on *Viljans Öga*?
Brand: The cover to *Epilog* was created by Swedish artist Rut Hillarp. Rut did not use computers—she used a double exposure technique and worked hard in the darkroom with different techniques. Sadly, Rut passed away many years ago and I wanted to pass on the feeling in her imagery when I created the cover art for *Viljans Öga*. The difference is that I have created all double exposures, or layers, in Adobe Photoshop.

WR: For a while your material wasn't available to the public. Are there rare or "vaulted" tracks that you'd like to release at some point in the future?
Brand: There was a period when the records were out of print, and during this period, no one was actively working with Änglagård. Everything was dormant. Now more productions are in the pipeline.

Änglagård, one of the leaders of prog's so-called third wave. Left to right: Erik Hammarström, Linus Kåse, Tord Lindman, Anna Holmgren, and Johan Brand (born Högberg).

Courtesy of Änglagård

WR: Guitarist Jonas Engdegård and former keyboardist Thomas Johnson were members of a band called Minstrel. What convinced you that they were the right musicians for the band you were then forming?

Brand: Me and Tord had a musical project that we called Metaforara. We had some demo material that we were playing for Thomas and Jonas first time we met them. I think we realized pretty quickly when we heard each others' material that it would be an interesting fusion to create music together.

WR: You've said that you are influenced by a fairly obscure New York progressive rock band from the 1970s called Cathedral. Since some people, even in the U.S., are not familiar with them, when did you first hear their independently released 1978 record, *Stained Glass Stories*?

Brand: It was through Greg Walker's record label Syn-phonic that we heard Cathedral the first time. Greg released *Stained Glass Stories* on CD in the early 1990s. We listened a lot to that album during those early years. I personally love that record for the dark, mysterious atmosphere they've managed to capture on tape.

WR: Can you explain the concept behind *Hybris*?

Brand: *Hybris* has no clear concept, but I think the foreword to *Hybris* says a lot about the musical climate at that time of the band. The music was built on a very human basis—through conflict—and the pot is cooked by six fanatic cooks, each one a victim of hybris . . .

WR: I believe at one time the band was writing a song based on *The Fellowship of the Ring* (from *The Lord of the Rings*). Whatever became of this and did you ever consider writing a concept album on *LOTR*?

Brand: Thomas wrote some music and text that was loosely based on *The Lord of the Rings* when we wrote material for *Hybris*. These music pieces were quickly chopped into small pieces and were converted into the first embryo of "Vandringar i vilsenhet." We've never had the idea of doing a concept album based on *The Lord of the Rings*.

WR: How important was Roger Skogh to the band's early career?

Brand: Roger Skogh was like a father to us all during the recording of *Hybris*. We got in touch with Roger by a funny coincidence. I was hunting for a genuine Mellotron and rang desperately every little studio in Sweden and asked if they had an old Mellotron that was forgotten in some corner. In the end, I called Roger Skogh at Studio Largen and he said he had recorded some strange Mellotron sounds on an album in his early days. We became friends immediately and not long after that conversation we were in Studio Largen and recorded the first demo tape, "I från klarhet till klarhet."

WR: Talk about ProgFest.

Brand: Greg Walker of Syn-phonic Records called us late one evening in 1993 and said he had heard Änglagård's debut album *Hybris*. The next sentence was, "I want you to come over to Los Angeles to take part in my festival," which was ProgFest 1993. That was a very successful journey for Änglagård. I would say we have partly Greg Walker to thank for Änglagård's success in the U.S.

25

District 97 Q&A

Gender Politics and Prog

P rog rock was kind of a boys' club, it's true," Annie Haslam of Renaissance once told the author. "I was one of the few female singers around in the genre. There were others, like Fairport Convention, who had female singers. But these bands were all very different from one another."

Haslam has a point. Few females were members of prog-rock bands in the 1970s, but, it seems, the ones who did break prog's glass ceiling were larger-than-life, difficult-to-ignore personalities.

A trailblazer such as Curved Air's Sonja Kristina (Sonja Kristina Linwood) seemed to go out of her way to attract attention, relishing her sex-symbol status, and accentuated her considerable physical beauty.

Kristina wasn't some demure female frontwoman singing peacefully acoustic ballads about green pastures, and she certainly didn't shy away from controversial, if not gender- and adult-oriented topics in her songs, whether it was drug addiction ("Melinda (More or Less)" from 1972's *Phantasmagoria*) or young lust ("Back Street Luv" from 1971's *Second Album*). Kristina even cowrote the rather lighthearted and risqué commentary on modern society, masturbation, and pornography, "Not Quite the Same" (*Phantasmagoria*).

However, never let it be said that Curved Air, formerly Sisyphus prior to 1970, wasn't serious about their music. As some have pointed out, Kristina won the gig not because of her sexy figure, but her strong sexy voice.

The band that would become Curved Air, most of it, anyway, met at London's Royal Academy of Music in the late 1960s. When drummer Florian Pilkington-Miksa, bassist Rob Martin, and guitarist keyboardist Francis Monkman were established, they invited violinist Darryl Way to join, who then recommended Nick Simon, piano player. Simon left (enter bassist Ian Eyre, who was later himself replaced by Mike Wedgewood), Kristina auditioned, and the band changed its name to Curved Air (a reference to Terry Riley's "A Rainbow in Curved Air," a minimalistic composition containing mutating synth and organ patterns building upon themselves).

Curved Air quickly became a major player in Britain's bourgeoning art-rock/progressive-rock field, having signed for a reported six-figure deal with Warner Brothers. Britain, and the world, would go on to know Curved Air's unique blend of classical harmonies and melodies, the heavy beat of rock, traces of

Sonja Kristina (far right), one of the female pioneers in the field of progressive rock, in a Curved Air band photo from a 1971 Fillmore East program.

Eastern European folk, and electronic music in such bombastic gems as "Piece of Mind," "Marie Antoinette," "Metamorphosis" from 1973's *Air Cut* (written by Eddie Jobson, who'd replaced Way), and Way's violin's showcase, the band's pièce de résistance—a slab avant hard rock/classical titled "Vivaldi." ("The only direct musical reference to Vivaldi is the opening double-stopped violin figure, which comes from Vivaldi's 'Winter,' the section that refers to teeth chattering in the cold," Way once told me. "The rest of the piece is entirely my creation in the style of Vivaldi.")

It was clear that this band was not mucking about. The gloves were off, the musical action and technical ability of the musicians were high, and the sounds were, oftentimes, fierce. Not the type of environment one would expect to find a former theater actress.

"At the time there weren't really other female voices within that genre," Kristina told the author in 2008. "In America there was the Jefferson Airplane, so you had Grace Slick. She preceded me by a few years. I was still at college and I was aware of Jefferson Airplane. There was Janis Joplin, but she was doing her own brand of blues. Tina Turner was doing what she was doing. I came from a certain background, too, so I went into the melting pot of Curved Air. I became a progressive rock singer. I think having been in the British production of *Hair* . . . was the sort of bridge between my folky singing and the kind of performance I did with Curved Air."

For Kristina, it may have been a seamless transition from female folkie to fronting a prog-rock band, but Sidonie Jordan, cofounder of Empire, featuring Peter Banks, remembers females didn't always have the easiest time being a part of the boys' club.

"Being a female on the road: you get the applause and you are on this high when you come offstage, but when you go back to the hotel room, it was dead silence," says Jordan. "You are on your own. The guys go out drinking and pulling girls. It's not a life for a female to be on the road with out-of-control guys. I left Hollywood in 1981 and never went back."

Even in the studio, Jordan felt, at times, a bit alienated. "I'd be in the back of the studio, in the dark, in the sound booth, my only link would be feedback in my headphones," Jordan says, "and they would turn it off. I'd see them all lit up in the studio . . . they would be laughing at me. . . . I was not sure what was going on but they were having a laugh at my expense. I used to call it studio abuse. It was the guys trying to be guys, a little bit of bullying, I suppose."

In another story Haslam related to the author, she unwittingly courted a private audience during a dress change for the *Scheherazade* tour. "The lighting people would sit in different areas of the trussing," Haslam said. "They would sit up there and watch me change. If I knew that then I would have freaked!"

Surely boyish shenanigans still continue in rock, but the appearance of women in the prog universe is no longer such an alien concept. Consider this list: Moorea Dickason (the Bay Area's MoeTar), violinist/vocalist Andrea Itzpapalotl (Los Angeles' Corima), Carla Kihlstedt (Sleepytime Gorilla Museum), Melody Ferris (Inner Ear Brigade), keyboardist Anis Oveisi (Iran's Mavara Band) Hayley Griffiths (Celtic/prog band Karnataka), Anne-Marie Helder (Panic Room, Mostly Autumn and formerly of Karnataka), keyboardist Elisa Montaldo (Italy's Il Tempio delle Clessidre), Judith Rijnveld (of the Dutch prog metal band Kingfisher Sky, which also features cellist Maaike Peterse), and Iona, which is fronted by singer/acoustic guitarist Joanne Hogg.

The following is a Q&A with a modern progressive rock/metal band, Chicago-based District 97, featuring Leslie Hunt, a one-time *American Idol* contestant (and a Top 10 female finalist). Hunt, founding member/drummer/ songwriter Jonathan Schang, and guitarist Jim Tashjian discuss District 97's recorded output, single parenthood, and the reaction from prog audiences to a strong female presence fronting a prog band.

WR: Recently District 97 went out with John Wetton. How did you get the gig with him?

Jonathan Schang: We seem to have differing recollections on how this came to be, John versus me, but I'll just tell you the way I remember it: when the first album was completed and came out I was doing a blitz on any prog-related site I could find with a message board. I went to John's site and his message board and posted something there. I didn't realize that John had quite a strong presence on the site. He checked it out and liked the video for "I Can't Take You with Me"

[2010's *Hybrid Child*] a lot. Then . . . out of the blue, as I recall it, I got an e-mail from him asking us to send him a T-shirt to wear for a publicity shot. I did that and we e-mailed back and forth on occasion and around that time I wrote the song "The Perfect Young Man," which had a female and a male perspective in it. Leslie had been singing both parts but when it came time to record it, Patrick [Mulcahy], our bassist, suggested I ask John to do it. I e-mailed him and to my surprise he agreed. We sent him off the song and he added his vocals and it was an organic process from there. When we went to Europe it made sense to reach out to him again to see if he wanted to do some stuff. He did and it went well. That went well and we decided to do a tour.

WR: How does he remember it?
Schang: Well, he remembers that at some point we asked to use a quote about the band on our website. I'm not sure of the chronology. But I do know that the T-shirt request is what kickstarted the relationship.

WR: Was it John's idea to have you as a backing band and perform the music of King Crimson on tour?
Schang: He came to Chicago to open the U.K. reunion tour and so he decided to schedule a show around that when he was in town. Naturally, we were thinking of doing "The Perfect Young Man" with him and we started to think about what else we could do. I suggested a few Crimson songs and we decide to do "Lament" and that was what set the precedent for doing that kind of thing. We were playing these songs faithfully and some of them he had never done live with a band.

WR: How established was the band before Leslie joined?
Schang: I've got a long history with Patrick and Rob since we grew up in the same town and went to the same schools [in Chicago's District 97]. We have been playing together in different configurations for a long time, and it has been a long time since we'd played anything in the rock vein together because we were all jazz students at the Chicago College of the Performing Arts. It came to a certain point where it would have been nice to start a rock-based project, since we hadn't done that since high school. We recruited a guitar player, Sam [Krahn], who also went to the school and we started, trying to emulate Planet X, that sort of progressive metal/jazz approach. But it was loose and casual. I think we only had three songs, maybe four, before we got Leslie onboard. We only played a few shows. I started to write music that had vocals, which was another thing I hadn't done in a long time and I felt that in my heart more than all this instrumental music and I knew that I couldn't sing this myself. I thought she would be the perfect fit.

WR: Sam left early on. Why?

Schang: The primary reason is that Sam was looking to pursue graduate studies in music composition outside of Chicago at the time.

WR: It's interesting that a contestant on *American Idol*, a pop singer contest, ended up in a modern progressive-rock band. How did this come about and were you a fan of this style of music?

Leslie Hunt: My dad listened to a lot of progressive rock and jazz, so I grew up with that. It's music that goes to an atypical place. Just before I had joined I'd experienced a loss in my life: my sister [Lauren] had just died and the outlet was perfect. It was a great vocal challenge and there were emotions I wanted to express. Plus, I knew all these guys from the Chicago College of Performing Arts, so . . . I had a jazz appreciation as well.

WR: What were you studying at the college?

Hunt: I was a composition major. I only went for a couple of years, and . . . I wasn't super close with the band at that time, but that's how I knew these guys.

WR: What feedback have you been getting as a female singer fronting a progressive-rock band?

Hunt: I think it's been positive. If people had negative things to say they've spared me of that, which is nice of them. In the beginning, people actually said that it was a smart or savvy business angle. It wasn't the idea to do anything deliberate, but [having a female singer] does gives us an edge.

Schang: I think it's fair to say that in the live show Leslie is the focal point. Whether it's a male or female, she holds an audience member's attention. I've heard a few people say they prefer a more demure singer in this genre . . . I don't know if they can get with the female empowerment thing that Leslie embodies.

WR: I'd like to go back for a minute. Leslie, you said your sister died?

Hunt: Yeah. She died and I basically joined the band a month later or so.

Schang: I should mention that I took this trip to Japan with Patrick and Rob, June 2008, and it was there that I was discussing with them the idea of Leslie singing with us. They were skeptical because they had envisioned that we would have a male singer, and we had talked about it and the plan was that we had a show August first and Leslie said she would sing with us. As soon as we got back I had found out that her sister had died and I thought, "This is not going to happen, not for a long time, maybe not ever." But I got in touch with her and I assumed she would not be up for this. I couldn't believe it when she said, "Let's do it. When are we going to rehearse?" It was probably a few weeks after Lauren died that Leslie did "Mindscan" [*Hybrid Child*] with us for the first time. I really admired her for that and was pretty inspired by her fortitude.

Hunt: This is music that my sister would have loved to have been a part of. She was into metal, big time. When she died I think it was almost like trying to pick up where she left off.

WR: "Mindscan" is about alien abductions, but recalls *The Lamb Lies Down on Broadway* because of the psychological component of the lyrics . . .
Schang: I think the biggest similarity with *The Lamb* is the section called "Examination" [Part V]. It has these weird and generally creepy atmospheres I think definitely borrows something from "The Waiting Room." I'd say that's the most overt connection.

WR: There also seems to be more soul in your music these days. Leslie, you had collaborated with Jonathan on the first record but there's more of your songwriting on the second, *Trouble with Machines*.
Hunt: Yeah, the second record was, overall, more collaborative. Jonathan wrote all the music on the first album and then I wrote some lyrics for one of the songs ["Termites"], but the second one had a song by our bassist Patrick, and Jim, the guitarist wrote a song, and I had written some things. I wrote the first song on the album in its entirety and then Jonathan did a different arrangement on it.

WR: What can you reveal about the new record? Any song titles?
Hunt: We had a bunch of song titles but not for the album, yet. We are putting it all together.
Schang: We've nearly finalized all the music we'll be recording, so the sessions should start this summer. I think an early 2015 release is likely. There's no title as of yet. But that's why we're getting together today, because I'm going to show Leslie a new song. She's going to write the lyrics for that song.

WR: Any more details you can provide?
Hunt: We've got one, Patrick wrote a song called "Learn from Danny" and he doesn't like to talk about what it's about. It's more or less about the Great Leap Forward, the genocide that happened in China. He's very literate, so he's inspired by real-life events and fictional stories. There's one called "Snow Country" written about this epic love triangle that happened in . . . a book he read.
Schang: There's one called "All's Well That Ends Well," and it's about moving on from something, leaving something in the past, a broad meditation on that kind of concept. And Jim wrote one, "On Paper." I think it is about the gun culture in America. The last we've been playing is called "Handlebars," which I wrote the music for and Leslie wrote the lyrics, and she can tell you about that.
Hunt: The lyrics were really inspired by being a mom, and being a single mom, at that, and the limitations that come with that, but also the strengths. I was using this handlebar metaphor, you know, about going so far and when to let go.

WR: When did you have your child?
Hunt: She turned four a couple of months ago.

WR: You might hate this question, but how do you balance the career with raising a child?

Hunt: Well, lately, my life has been cake. [laughs] She's been in school for seven and a half hours a day, Monday through Friday. It hasn't been as difficult as it could be, because I'm not doing the behind-the-scenes work for the band. That's really on Jonathan's shoulders. He's the manager, booking agent . . . I am at home and I can just be with my daughter. My solo career, on the other hand, I'm not putting any work into at all. That is, unfortunately, a casualty of war, but . . . [laughs]

WR: There are sacrifices, but District 97 appears to be taking off . . .

Hunt: It is. I feel like we've worked really hard and it's happening at a nice pace.

WR: Do you still see your child's father?

Hunt: I do. He moved into a place in August [2013] and he is able to take her for overnights. Before that he lived in a studio apartment down the street. So he was

Leslie Hunt (center), a former *American Idol* contestant, brings soul and sex appeal to District 97's twisted and metallic brand of American progressive rock.   *Courtesy of District 97*

coming over and seeing her on my turf. But now she has a little place at Daddy's house and she loves it over there. Lately he's been shouldering a lot more of responsibility with her, which is awesome. We're fine. . . . We are actually flying to Phoenix for Thanksgiving [2013], the three of us, to spend time with his brother and his brother's daughter, and Eliza's cousin, which will likely be her only cousin, given that I don't have any siblings now and his other brother probably won't have any more kids.

Schang: When Leslie first joined the band, her first show led to all of this. Tommy [Faulds] was on the bill that night and I went up to the backstage area and Tommy said, "I can't believe you got Leslie Hunt singing with you guys. . . ." Eliza was born about a year after that.

Hunt: I've been told that there's an element of soul in my voice. I do love soul music and I definitely have that in there.

Schang: Earlier Leslie was ascribing all the behind-the-scenes stuff to me, and I do the lion's share, but I do want to give a shout-out to our label, Laser's Edge. Ken Golden really is the guy and he's been really good about helping us in any and every way he is able to, like taking ads out in prog magazines and stuff.

WR: How did you come to the attention of Laser's Edge?
Schang: We played a show at Martyrs' in Chicago and someone, who I'm now good friends with, author Charles Snider, who wrote *The Strawberry Bricks Guide to Progressive Rock*, he lives nearby and came to a show. I was talking to him after the show and I asked him for suggestions about what labels might I approach. He suggested Laser's Edge, which I had come across in my research but didn't know much about. But on Charles' suggestions I dropped something in the mail to Ken.

WR: I wonder who is the bigger taskmaster: Simon Cowell or Jonathan?
Hunt: Well, I sang a couple of songs live [on *American Idol*] and Simon had very little to do with me. I only saw him when we were on air in front of 37 million viewers, or something. There was no behind-the-scenes with Simon Cowell whatsoever. I saw him as this scripted judge, who basically said what he was told to say.

WR: Did any of the judges mentor you?
Hunt: Paula Abdul and I sort of had a little exchange on occasion. She might pull me aside and tell me what she thought I should do, like dress younger. Before that I was projecting this red lipstick and black dress vibe. I did dress younger, actually. I saw her after I left the show and she was sweet to me after I got eliminated.

WR: Was performing on *AI* as stressful as it appears?
Hunt: It was the craziest thing I've ever done. The hours were insane. I lived in a hotel, about two and a half months. They needed you to be in the lobby at like seven in the morning and hop into these Ford vehicles, because the

show was sponsored by Ford, and you don't get back to your hotel until about eleven [p.m.]. Most of it was waiting in these tiny dressing rooms all day to do something that might take a half an hour. And that was every single day. It was being in close quartets with all of these people, everyone trying to outsing each other. The food was . . . Then you get these tiny snippets of time where you're working with vocal coaches and . . . you have to be camera-ready all the time.

WR: After that ordeal, District 97 might look fairly tame?
Hunt: I received [a crash course] in Being Professional 101. Anyone who was late was chastised. I guess I'm still late all the time, so maybe I didn't learn anything, but . . . the guys in District 97 are my best friends and I didn't really make any friends on that show. I was kind of a loner. Really, what that show did more than anything was convince me that this was, for sure, what I wanted to do with my life—being a singer in any respect. I've been a full-time professional singer ever since, with no other side jobs.

WR: Had you, Jonathan, seen Leslie on the show and thought about her singing with you one day?
Schang: Well, she was on the show in 2007. March 1, 2007, she was off the show and it was about sixteen or seventeen months later that she was in the band. District 97, at the time she was on the show, was still in its infancy, and I wasn't thinking about getting a singer at that point. Part of it was me thinking, well, *If I have the singer from* American Idol, *I will be really well known.* Everyone knows that the people watching *American Idol* love progressive rock. [laughs] It was part of my thought process and I very quickly found out it wasn't going to be a help at all. Well, that's not necessarily true. It did attract people to the band initially, but once we were signed and had an outlet for publicity then we were able to use the *American Idol* thing. It may be a wash. It might have turned off some people and didn't allow them to take us seriously. You know, "*American Idol*: this must be a joke."

WR: What inspired the lyrics for "Termites"?
Hunt: At that time I was a staunch vegan and was so up in arms about the meat industry and how we know full well the environmental and physiological ramifications of a lot of meat and a lot of dairy as far as creating it for consumption and digesting it. Regardless, we eat it anyway because it tastes so good. That was my big rant, trying to get people thinking. Shortly thereafter I started to eat meat and dairy, so . . . But I was basically vegan throughout my pregnancy. . . .

WR: What's the trouble with machines?
Jim Tashjian: The concept is about the way the world seemed to be crumbling at the time—the economy, the government—not that it has gotten any better since. *Trouble with Machines* was inspired by a *Twilight Zone* episode that Jonathan

and I were fond of. We used that title as a way to talk about the shit we were pissed off about.

WR: Which episode was it?
Tashjian: It was called "A Thing About Machines" [written by Rod Serling].
Schang: It's about a guy who hates machines and he's alone in the house and all the machines started revolting.

WR: Had you read a lot of sci-fi?
Tashjian: When I joined the band Jonathan had been into crazy sci-fi stuff. My mom made me watch *Twilight Zone* and I hated it because she forced me to watch it. Jonathan was raving about it and lent me the DVDs. I ended up watching the entire series. I had a newfound appreciation for the show and how brilliant it was. It was the scariest and most intelligent show on TV at that time.

WR: What can you tell me about what you have been doing for the new record?
Tashjian: I feel like we collaborate to a degree on everything, no matter who brings the song in. Everyone throws in his opinion or how to adapt the piece to the band. But in the early days it was all Jonathan's writing. I've brought in previously written songs that I thought could be played by the musicians and some writing specifically for the group. I think the new material will rock hard and everyone's personality will come out in each piece.
Schang: We're currently working on a rather lengthy piece Rob wrote that will likely end up on the album.

WR: Will you record in town?
Tashjian: Unless we get a crazy offer we will most definitely record in the city, maybe where we recorded the last two records [Vault Lab]. Maybe somewhere else.

It's Worth Repeating

Minimalism, Steve Reich, and Radiohead

Minimalist composer Steve Reich has influenced three generations of artists working in the pop, rock, prog, and electronic fields, from David Bowie and Brian Eno to the Orb, Oneida, Bjork, Aphex Twin, James Murphy, and the National.

Reich's loop-based composition "It's Gonna Rain" from 1965 was a profound influence on Eno, and it hardly needs to be repeated that tape loops were the basis of Eno's collaboration with King Crimson guitarist Robert Fripp for recordings such as 1973's *(No Pussyfooting)* and 1975's *Evening Star*.[1] A signal delay system using two analog reel-to-reel tape machines would later be dubbed Frippertronics.[2] The result of this looping technique is a matrix of layered sound, on top of which the performer can add new information—notes—in real time.

The use of repeated patterns and phasing undoubtedly influenced Fripp as well, when he resurrected King Crimson in the 1980s with bassist/Stick player Tony Levin, drummer Bill Bruford, and guitarist/vocalist Adrian Belew. Tracks such as "Discipline" and "Frame by Frame" boast interlocking and interwoven guitar lines and place the music in the neighborhood of minimalist New Wave/ethno/progressive rock.

Author Hugo Wilcken, in his book on David Bowie's 1977 album *Low*, notes that Bowie's "Weeping Wall" slightly recalls Reich's minimalistic work. Indeed. The wordless vocals, pulsating synth beats, and what sounds like layered vibraphones all heard in the track perhaps owe a debt, Wilcken says, to *Music for 18 Musicians*, which Bowie saw performed in Berlin in 1976, prior to recording *Low*.

Although the composer employs different processes for *Music for 18 Musicians*, aspects of the work resemble Reich's famous piece involving the technique of phasing, 1971's *Drumming*. The piece is built up from a single beat until, gradually, the beats of each measure are substituted for notes, and as the composition progresses, a discernable and complete rhythmic structure emerges. This "build-up" is a cornerstone technique of Reich's compositional style, as is the reverse: what Reich calls "reduction" (i.e., substituting rests for beats until a single beat remains at the conclusion of the piece). In essence, all participating performers play a certain pattern even as it "undergoes changes in

KID A
BOOK AND COMPACT DISC

COMPACT DISC BY RADIOHEAD
BOOK BY STANLEY AND TCHOCK

Minimalist composter Steve Reich based his *Radio Rewrite*, a piece in five movements, on Radiohead's "Everything in Its Right Place," from 2000's *Kid A*, and "Jigsaw Falling into Place," which appears on 2008's *In Rainbows*. Pictured: Capitol Records' 6″× 6″ book and CD package of *Kid A*.

phase position, pitch, and timbre," Reich said. "[B]ut all the performers play this pattern, or some part of it, throughout the entire piece."

A now-famous visit to Africa in the early 1970s gave Reich "confirmation" that the cyclical, interlocking patterns he was working with had historical precedence and global implications. "Going to Africa was a big pat on the back," Reich says. "Same thing when I played Balinese Gamelan music with Balinese teachers. These rhythmic interlocking patterns are very highly developed—and I can learn from them, and I did."

In 2012, Reich turned his gaze to modern rock band Radiohead and composed *Radio Rewrite*, a piece, in five movements, that was inspired by Radiohead's "Everything in Its Right Place" (from 2000's *Kid A*, a record frontman Thom Yorke said was inspired by a fear that rock music was becoming extinct) and "Jigsaw Falling into Place" (from *In Rainbows*, officially released in 2008). We spoke with Reich about this and other topics.

WR: You've answered the question as to why you chose "Everything in Its Right Place" and "Jigsaw Falling into Place" for interpretation. But why not tackle something a bit more amorphous on, say, *OK Computer*, for your *Radio Rewrite*?

Steve Reich: I didn't listen to everything that the band did and I just heard certain things and did not make a complete survey of their music. I was definitely going for music and not electronics. So, if it were electronics I would have given it a fast-forward and skipped over it. "Everything in Its Right Place" is popular, it's three chords, but they are very unusually voiced. They don't really cadence and so they just keep on going. If you invert their order, which is what I did, you come up with a very different situation. That was intriguingly simple. What they did originally was very elegant and very well done. The other piece, "Jigsaw Falling into Place," was a beautiful tune and I felt totally invigorated. I almost wanted to get up and dance. It's harmonically interesting: it moves down a half step to begin with, which was unusual. In "Everything in Its Right Place," the most prominent aspect of the music that I take—aspects that you might relate with Radiohead—you will probably recognize. [Sings] "Everything . . ." I've said this many times before, but the I–V–I is the basis of Western music. That's the end of a Beethoven symphony. I'm sure that Thom Yorke did it spontaneously, just sitting at the piano or guitar, or however he wrote it, and this thing came up. That's the way real music gets written. But reflecting on it, "Everything . . ." *is everything*. The way he throws it out is marvelous, the casualness of it is wonderful. So, you'll hear allusions to that in the piece. In "Jigsaw" it's more in the harmonies. . . . [Sings] "Until the drinks arrive . . . ," that comes in the later part of the piece. Most of the time what you're hearing is harmonies underpinning the material that bears no relationship to theirs. A lot of people have a harder time tracing that tune than they do the other.

WR: Radiohead is not an acoustic group by any stretch of the imagination. Thom Yorke experiments with digital audio and the band's music is still very much related to electronica. Interestingly, Yorke's admitted to being influenced by Can, specifically Holger Czukay, and their recording and tape experiments. Yorke called it "[f]our-track gone berserk." Ironically, earlier in your career you experimented with electronics and tape loops, but you went the acoustic route for this piece.
Reich: I understand that and I know that, but they are blessed with basic sound musicianship, which got them going when they were kids. The tunes I picked, that's front and center. Maybe that's why I picked those tunes.

WR: Some have bemoaned the fact that Radiohead has gone, in some cases, too far into the digital audio realm.
Reich: I sit in front of a computer every day because I use Sibelius software to write my music. I have a piano keyboard next to me and I go back and forth. I work out in the mornings but I get exercise while I'm working. I've seen videotapes of Thom Yorke sitting down at the piano playing "Everything in Its Right Place," just hunched over the piano, completely unconscious of what is going on around him and . . . it's real music played by a real musician, totally involved with what he's doing, playing simple, or not-so-simple, piano chords

and singing beautifully with them. He's entitled to do whatever he likes to do and more power to him.

WR: I know you had referenced French composer Olivier Messiaen when discussing Jonny Greenwood's performance of your *Electric Counterpoint* piece at a festival in Krakow, Poland, which was originally recorded by Pat Metheny in 1987. Did you ever discuss Messiaen with Greenwood?
Reich: No, we didn't much talk about Messiaen. I just got the impression that he was interested in that composer when I heard his music for *There Will Be Blood.* I also knew he was at Oxford and studied viola. I did discuss Krzysztof Penderecki when we were in Poland because Krzysztof Penderecki was there at the time and they were hanging out and it was unusual to see a rocker hanging out with Steve Reich and Krzysztof Penderecki. We are living in a time when things are changing. Jonny Greenwood is an outstanding example, but he's not the only one. Bryce Dessner of the National has his own very interesting compositions played at the Barbican Centre in London. Here's an example of a guy who's a rocker, went to the Yale School of Music, he can read anything you put in front of him and Mark Stewart, guitarist for Bang on a Can. Mark went to the Eastman School of Music as a cellist and played the guitar for fun. He came down to New York City and realized that if you can read music as a guitar player, you can make a living, and so he started doing that and got involved with Bang on a Can. Then Paul Simon heard about him and said, "I want you in my music group," so he became music director for Paul Simon.

WR: Is there anything "wrong" with, as a contemporary classical composer, being inspired by popular musicians?
Reich: We're living in a time when notated music and non-notated music are reunited. It took a couple hundred of years of great composers, from Guillaume Dufay up to Palestrina, to feel obliged to use folk songs as the basis for a mass. A mass in those days was like writing a symphony. The Haydn Symphony No. 104, his big masterpiece, [sings] is an Austrian drinking song. Beethoven, Sixth Symphony First Movement, [sings] folk song. Béla Bartók, his entire musical output, you can't separate Serbo-Croatian folk music, which he collected and notated, from his abstract music. It's just embedded in his music. He didn't always tell the truth about it, but it's proven theory that Stravinsky's early Russian ballets—*Petrushka, Firebird, The Rite of Spring*—filled with Russian folk songs, more a credit to the great man. Charles Ives, *Three Places in New England*—filled with hymn tunes that he played as a church organist. That was his gig. George Gershwin. Is he one of our great composers or songwriters? Well, he's both, thank you very much. The window is open between the concert hall and street. When I went to school in the 1950s and 1960s, Stockhausen, Webern, Boulez, Schoenberg, Cage had slammed that window closed and it was the job

Reich, master of cyclical rhythms, such as those heard in *Drumming* and *Electric Counterpoint*, was impressed with Jonny Greenwood's interpretation of *Counterpoint* and his compositions for the 2007 movie *There Will Be Blood*.

of my generation to simply open that window. We didn't create a revolution. We create a restoration of normalcy.

WR: Why did they do that?

Reich: When things get too complicated we call it mannerist. Schoenberg was a great composer, but what he was doing was the death of German romanticism. Webern, too. Stockhausen and Boulez—it's been a long protracted death and mannerist phase. It's done by masters who are great craftsmen and great composers and their music will live. But it will live in a dark corner. That's okay. Not everybody is Top 40, but it should be understood that way. I think for those people popular music was irrelevant. It was junk. I think Schoenberg resented Kurt Weill and any success he got. But I don't think it went deeper than that. *Pierrot Lunaire* sort of has cabaret overtones in his work. Schoenberg wanted to get rid of harmony, and does, in the twelve-tone system. He wanted to get rid of toe-tapping rhythms and melody in any normal sense of the word. I love Bach, Stravinsky, bebop, John Coltrane, and I couldn't go on writing twelve-tone music, which you had to as a student. I have no love of that. I can admire it, but I have no time to listen to it. Life is too short.

WR: It's almost as if the listening part of the process wasn't part of the equation.

Reich: There was quite a bit of that. As a music student I can tell you a lot of people came to classes with these black scores—covered in notes—and they couldn't even play them at the keyboard. I don't think they heard them in their head.

WR: What inspired *Electric Counterpoint*?
Reich: At that time a lot of classical guitar players were coming up to me and saying, "Why don't you write a piece. Your music would be perfect for guitar because we pluck [strings]. It has a real attack and it would fit into the kinds of things you do." I said, "But the idea of writing for classical guitar seemed kind of boring," because I believe that the guitar in our day is really the electric guitar. I was having a chat about these things with Robert Hurwitz when he was the president of ECM in New York. He said, "Why don't we have Pat Metheny play it." We were labelmates at the time. [Hurwitz] hung up the phone and five minutes later I'm talking with Pat Metheny. We got together and I said, "I know the tuning, but I don't know anything about the guitar." He looked at me and said, "Write single notes. Watch the chords." I said, "Aye, aye, sir." And I did that. With eleven guitars going you can get a lot of chords going, just by writing single notes. It was a simple chart that I knew he wouldn't have a problem with. For Jonny Greenwood, to go back to that point, he put his touch on it, which was wonderful. The piece is very frequently performed, I have to say, because there's a lot of guitarists around who can read and a lot of guitarists who have laptops. When Jonny Greenwood did it, and he made his own [accompanying tracks], I was very impressed. We met in Poland and we immediately hit it off. I liked him and what he was doing. It has been a very positive human experience and a very positive musical experience.

WR: When you listen to *Music for 18 Musicians*, it is reminiscent of 1980s King Crimson. Can you comment?
Reich: I know of [Fripp] and I know he's worked with a lot of people, but I never heard that material. I can't speak intelligently.

WR: Fripp worked with Eno and Bowie . . .
Reich: Fripp and Eno, I know. At first I thought it was some special food: "Fripp and Eno on Rye." [laughs] Then I realized it was two guys.

WR: It's very much like *Music for 18 Musicians* . . .
Reich: If you listen to Tangerine Dream you'll hear a lot of that, too.

WR: There was something in the air in the mid-1970s through the early 1980s. These progressive rock and art-rock guys were listening to you . . .
Reich: 1976 was when the piece was written and it was released in 1978. It was released on ECM. Back in 1978 ECM was distributed by Warner Bros.—and it got a lot of distribution. When I would go into the record stores—and in those days there were record stores—I would find that my music was in the

Reich's tape-based experiments and concepts of rhythmic cycling influenced Brian Eno and, by association, Robert Fripp.

classical bin, it was in the pop bin, it was in the electronica bin, it was progressive-rock bin and it was in the jazz bin. That's really when my music began to infiltrate. We're having this conversation, because of what I'm telling you. That was the birth of my music finding its proper place.

WR: It would be interesting if a band like Radiohead ever went back and tried to redo that music via your interpretation using electronics . . .
Reich: They can't do it. They couldn't play it. There is only one electric bass part that one could play and that's it. I don't think anyone in that band plays flute or clarinet. Well, Jonny Greenwood could play viola and his brother could play bass. But that's cool. The window is open. They can do what they do and maybe they can pick up something that I've done and incorporate it into something that they do. Hey, be my guest.

WR: Most of the players in Radiohead can't read music, although I know Jonny Greenwood can . . .
Reich: But, you know, Thom Yorke is a fantastic musician. When I was teaching *Drumming* to my own ensemble I did it by rote. I didn't do it by notation, because the parts were so easy. The important thing was to demonstrate the feel of the piece and experiment with phasing to see if they could play [and create this phasing effect]. A lot of the experience of me transmitting the piece to musicians, although it was written down, it was to do it by rote, to do it by playing.

That's how things happen in rock groups. The non-notated tradition is the first tradition. We've been on the face of the earth for many thousands of years and musical notation only starts about a thousand or twelve hundred years ago. It's a latecomer to the party, and it has virtues of being able to . . . create things that would be impossible to create without notation. But non-notation is still there. Oral tradition is still there and it always will be. We are now at a time, historically, for most composers and almost all rock musicians, DJs, they are aware of this. Everything is in the room and everybody is trying to be as friendly as they possibly can be. . . . It's a model of peaceful coexistence and collaboration that I wish that other parts of the world would take note of.

WR: Will you interpret more of Radiohead's music?
Reich: No, I tend to be a one-off guy. I do something and then I try to go on to something else. On the level of subject matter, or going back to a project, I'm writing a piece now using electric bass. *Radio Rewrite* will be recorded April 3 [2014] and probably released, I would say, in the fall [2014], for sure, along with Jonny Greenwood playing his version of *Electric Counterpoint* and a brand-new recording of *Piano Counterpoint*, by Vicky Chow, who is a pianist in Bang on a Can. Right now the recordings that are floating around of *Radio Rewrite* are all pretty B-flat, in the sense of mediocre or dull. But [New York–based ensemble] Alarm Will Sound has been playing it, and they have the chops together now. I think we'll have a really good recording. My joke is, "I never repeat myself." Please, quote me.

27

Collins' Cosmos

Who, or What, Is Dimensionaut?

S imon Collins, son of legendary Genesis drummer and vocalist Phil Collins, has made some surprising and welcome career moves over the last decade. Collins' latest band, Sound of Contact, threw caution to the wind and completed an out-and-out concept album in 2013, titled *Dimensionaut*, which presents a sci-fi journey as a metaphor for spiritual transcendence.

Keyboardist Dave Kerzner, who runs his own sound sampling software company called Sonic Reality, was one of the chief architects of the Sound of Contact band and of the record *Dimensionaut*. Kerzner first met Collins in New York City in 2007 at rehearsals for Genesis' then-upcoming reunion tour.

"I was invited by Geoff Callingham, Tony Banks' keyboard tech, and we were talking about the possibility of maybe upgrading the samples of Mellotrons," says Kerzner. "Simon and I hit it off and that was just as much fun as watching Genesis. From that point we decided to do a cover of 'Keep It Dark' [from 1981's *Abacab*]. We made it available as a free download and received something like forty thousand downloads."

With this success as encouragement, Kerzner and Collins discussed the possibility of further working as musical collaborators, which they did for Collins' 2008 solo album, *U-Catastrophe*. (The title is a play on the J. R. R. Tolkien–invented term "eucatastrophe," which is roughly defined as a positive turn of events that benefits a story's main character, similar to the "deus ex machina" dramatic device.)

After conquering several personal issues, Simon set out on a new path—one of both spiritual and musical renewal. A far cry from the pop and hard-rock music found on Collins' *All of Who You Are* (1999), *Time for Truth* (2005), and *U-Catastrophe*, the ambitious *Dimensionaut* had been envisioned by Collins and guitarist Kelly Nordstrom as a melding of personal statement and abstract sci-fi plot.

Collins admitted to me that he began reading Carl Sagan, Deepak Chopra, and Brian Greene to have a better understanding of both the cosmos and inner space. Collins, along with Nordstrom, explored the nexus of these two concepts through music, and researched cosmology, astrophysics, and astronomy, to construct the rough outline of the *Dimensionaut* story (i.e., one character's journey to enlightenment).

Face value: Much in the same way his dad bared his soul in the early 1980s, Simon Collins sings about personal issues on *U-Catastrophe* and *Dimensionaut*, including some he hasn't even discussed openly in public.

The leap from *U-Catastrophe* to *Dimensionaut* was an organic evolution, Collins said, requiring the drummer and lead vocalist to step outside himself. Spiritual cleansing was, apparently, a major creative inspiration for Collins, and one he felt very strongly should be expressed through a bold artistic statement. Although keyboardist/songwriter Kerzner said he and guitarist Matt Dorsey attempted to talk Collins out of doing a space rock opera for Sound of Contact's first band recording, "[Collins] was ready for it," says Kerzner.

Kerzner would, of course, come around to the idea and even offered pieces he had already been working on, such as "Beyond Illumination," "Realm of In-Organic Beings" (reminiscent of Pink Floyd's "Great Gig in the Sky"), "Only Breathing Out" (including "Peter Gabriel–like yodeling," says Kerzner), and "Not Coming Down," penned for a fallen hero, a friend.

"I wrote that song with my friend Gene Siegel," says Kerzner. "It was originally about Kevin Gilbert [Giraffe, Toy Matinee, Sheryl Crow] and I wrote that in 1997, shortly after he died. I played it for Simon and he said, 'We have to do this. We have to make this fit into the story,' so we tweaked it a little."

For his part, Collins had been composing songs in anticipation of such a release, having written "Pale Blue Dot," "I Am Dimensionaut," and penning poetry and song lyrics. (Whatever written material wasn't used for the record was printed in the booklet accompanying the CD.) Collins also had dreamed up titles as such as "Omega Point," a song for which he collaborated with Kerzner on the lyrics.

The record's centerpiece—the nineteen-plus-minute theater-of-the-mind opus, "Möbius Slip," pieced together from several shorter ideas—reminds us of the psychological journey at the heart of Genesis' *The Lamb Lies Down on Broadway*, written forty years earlier. The author was told that the fourth section of the piece, "All Worlds All Times," was actually done in one take.

"We just decided to connect them all," says Kerzner, "and we split off into groups, because we were under the gun to get things done. Simon and Kelly went to write the first part of the song. That title, 'Möbius Slip,' was Simon's. Then I wrote the part, 'All Worlds All Times' . . . and we glued our visions together."

A Möbius strip is roughly defined as a two-dimensional plane with one surface. The strip can also be described as a symbol for infinity, much like the DNA double helix. An iconic symbol, for sure, but what's its purpose in the story line?

"What the 'Möbius Slip' is, or is supposed to be, is open to anyone's interpretation," Kerzner cautions. "Looking at it from an objective point of view, the Möbius strip is almost like a character in this story. It represents something that's beyond our comprehension. At the pinnacle of the story, the character, Dimo or Dimensionaut, is trying to traverse this strip, which is infinity."

Offering a simplified description of the plot, Kerzner dubs the song "a kind of head trip. It's impossible for Dimensionaut to traverse the strip, so he slips off. Then he sees the light. It's something along those lines. We can have long philosophical, metaphysical conversations about the whole thing."

This idea of suffering to reach heaven is a basic tenet of some Eastern religions. When I spoke with Collins he referenced the spiritual path of Buddha and his ability to

Not surprisingly, Simon Collins grew up listening and practicing drums to Genesis' live double album *Seconds Out*.

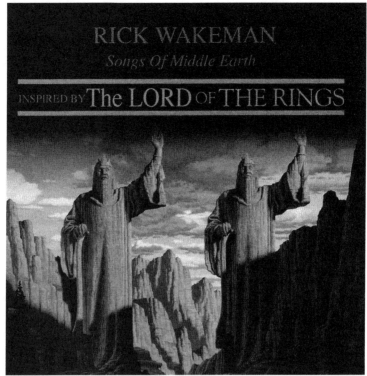

RICK WAKEMAN
Songs Of Middle Earth

INSPIRED BY The LORD OF THE RINGS

Prog rock artists other than Simon Collins have been inspired by Tolkien's writing, including Marillion (formerly Silmarillion), Rick Wakeman (whose *Songs of Middle Earth* is pictured here), Rush, Marco Lo Muscio, Spain's Galadriel, Barclay James Harvest ("Galadriel"), Bo Hansson, and even New Age composer/prog geek David Arkenstone, among many others.

free himself from a "prison planet" (a term used on the record, as well) by exploring altered dimensions of consciousness and astral traveling.

"If a songwriter tells you too much it can ruin it," Kerzner says. "If this were a movie, I would imagine seeing this kind of revelation on the screen of . . . the duality of our mortality and our connection to everything, and the character saying, 'I'm awake now.'"

The story could continue or, at least, the possibility is always open for this to occur with a little reworking and tweaking. "We actually recorded some songs that didn't make it on the record," says Kerzner, "because they didn't fit the concept—and they were good. They might see the light of day someday."

Carrying On

It's difficult to ignore the elephant in the room, so you may as well address it now: Collins' vocal inflections, on occasion, are a dead ringer for his dad's. There are moments in songs such as "Pale Blue Dot," "Only Breathing Out,"

"Closer to You," and "I Am (Dimensionaut)" that it very well could be Phil singing and we wouldn't know the difference. The apple doesn't fall far.

All of this is to say nothing of Simons' drumming abilities and *drum sound.* Simon had, for years, not only watched performances by his father and Chester Thompson, Genesis'/Phil Collins' touring drummer, but the younger Collins even played similar (and in some cases the same) equipment his father did, including open-bottomed concert toms, which helps to account, in part, for Collins' bombastic, booming sound. Of course, we should point out that Simon is a right-handed player, unlike his father.

Much like the progressive rock albums of old, the circumstances that shaped *Dimensionaut* can't be repeated. Indeed. Kerzner left Sound of Contact just prior to our talk, but says he's proud of his work with Simon and the project. Simon, who has been running his own label, Lightyears Music, since 2003, has a great creative team of people around him. And, like his dad, has the ability to seamlessly move with impunity between solo career and band projects.

"I could imagine making good albums together again," Kerzner says. "But I know Simon will carry on."

28

Scale the Summit

Sense the Adventure Metal—A Q&A with Chris Letchford

Formed in 2004 by guitarists Chris Letchford and Travis LeVrier, both former students at the Musicians Institute of Los Angeles, the Houston-based progressive metal band Scale the Summit (STS) has carved out a niche for itself, pushing their individual limits as musicians and traveling similar sonic terrain as Steve Vai, Dream Theater, TesseracT, Between the Buried and Me, the Dillinger Escape Plan, Meshuggah, and Cynic.

Although STS's approach might seem familiar, zeroing in on the exact term to describe the band's music proves elusive. Some have labeled it post-rock, prog-influenced instrumental rock, and progressive metal, but STS's own term, "adventure metal," seems to sum up the band's hybrid blend of instrumental polyrhythmic dual-guitar-based music perfectly.

Since unleashing their self-produced independent debut, *Monument*, in 2007, STS has continually honed its songwriting craft and technical prowess; they've toured the world, opened for Between the Buried and Me, appeared on Dream Theater's Progressive Nation tour in 2009, and released three full-length albums (2009's *Carving Desert Canyons*, 2011's *The Collective*, and 2013's *The Migration*, the quartet's first to reach *Billboard*'s Top 200 Albums chart and to feature six-string bassist Mark Michell, who replaced original member Jordan Eberhardt).

Having caught the attention of both the metal and progressive-rock worlds, STS has gained the reputation for its commitment to musicianship and keen understanding of theory. Here I talk with STS guitarist and songwriter Chris Letchford about the band's history, musical inspiration, and why STS will (likely) never audition another vocalist.

WR: Have you conceptualized songs, or riffs, that even you can't play?
Chris Letchford: Yes, but through the songwriting process. I'll write some parts throughout the album that I'm not able to play right then and there, but I eventually work up to it by the time we're set to record. Then they are really polished while on tour.

WR: What are some of the most challenging songs to perform onstage and why?
Letchford: I find that the songs with the most dynamic phrasing are the hardest. "Willow" [*The Migration*] is one of the toughest when it comes to dynamic phrasing live. There are parts throughout the entire song that I try to match exactly how I recorded them, but, of course, it turns out different each night. The other would be "The Traveler" [*The Migration*], just for the technicality. This song is pretty much straight sixteenth-note double picking with a lot of string skipping. "The Traveler" is also the most fun to play, as well, though it wouldn't seem like it would be to most since its so technical.

WR: What were the most difficult to get together in the studio?
Letchford: We always enter the studio with all the material written and pretty well rehearsed. There will be select sections that pop up here and there while recording that require more time and effort, but usually it's just some random part that you would never expect to be tough to record.

Scale the Summit's musical adventures seem to underscore a connection between odd tempos, the power of hypnosis, and Chaos Theory. "Riffs in 7/4 have always held such an awesome groove for me," says guitarist Chris Letchford. "I've been working on . . . a riff in 11/8, and I think it's one of the catchiest I've written, yet."

Courtesy of Prosthetic Records

WR: I sense an almost Bach-like mathematical basis for your music, especially on *The Collective* and the latest, *The Migration*. Did you compose music using mathematical sequences or formulas?

Letchford: I really just sat down and wrote, and what came out, came out. I appreciate the compliment, though; it means a lot. I have deleted so many sections, parts, and melodies over the years trying to become happy with a song, so it's nice to see others take notice of all the time and effort that goes into writing my music.

WR: You seem to reference geographic areas and even some imagined locales. What inspired "Black Hills," "Balkan," and "Secret Earth"?

Letchford: For "Black Hills" I wrote the music first and then titled the song. The middle section got me thinking of a very dry hillside, and what better than the "Black Hills"? The music for "Balkan" was written first, as well. The opening melody really made me think of vampires, and of course I would never name a song "Vampire" or "Vampires." That would be cheesy. After having done a little research I found a way to work in the theme [of vampires], but indirectly. The Balkan Peninsula, supposedly, is one of the first known places to make a record of vampires in that general geographic area. "Secret Earth" was the same thing: the song was written first. This one just felt "huge" to me. And there's nothing more epic than the word *Earth*, especially when paired with what I considered the mystery of the song.

WR: You titled your 2009 record *Carving Desert Canyons*. Why?

Letchford: We decided on this title purely around the idea that our songs were like water and images that pop up inside the listeners' heads, while listening to our music, were the canyons. It tied into our nature themes, but it was a way to help us also connect with our fans.

WR: How "live" are STS's records? Does the band record together and how many overdubs are typically done for a Scale the Summit record?

Letchford: Definitely not "live." We track all of our parts individually. I still write 24/7 when we're off the road, even if we aren't at the point where we have to be writing. I'm more into composing than jamming with band members. It gives me more time to edit and rework parts to have the compositions ready for the studio.

WR: I hear "The Great Plains" from *Carving Desert Canyons* as being highly representative of STS's music. Many of the band's signature elements are present, as is a great main melody. Can you explain how that song came together?

Letchford: We have always used the term "adventure metal" to describe our music, and this song was written to best present our "sound" to our audience. That song has really helped to pave the way for where we are today. I still enjoy performing it, even though we have played it live probably close to three hundred times already.

WR: Drummer Pat Skeffington hits all the many accents in your songs. Are there polyrhythmic figures in your music?

Letchford: There definitely are. Usually the polyrhythmic structure for certain parts, I think, fits perfectly again with the "adventure" theme, usually taking place between what the guitars are doing and the drums.

WR: Can you describe how you signed with Prosthetic Records in 2008?

Letchford: We met the Prosthetic crew back when one of our roommates, while at Musicians Institute, was also an intern [at the label]. We told him that we had an instrumental band, but never with the idea of being signed. We mentioned it in passing and, at the time, we wouldn't have fit on the label anyway. We also wanted to spend more time developing a solid foundation before we started shopping to labels. We self-released *Monument* [2007], our first full-length album around two years later, and did a lot of our groundwork for that album. Not only did we release and sell three thousand copies, but we also burned over three thousand CDs with half of the album on it to pass out as free demos. During this time I sent out over two hundred to radio and three hundred to reviewers, magazines, online blogs, etc., for reviews. Over fifty of the radio stations, mostly college and foreign, hit us back with stats that they actually played a few of our songs on the air. We then sent all of this information to Prosthetic, as well as a few other labels, which we did not hear back from. [Prosthetic] loved our music, vision, and, of course, the work ethic, which was the biggest seller for any label.

WR: I detect a distinctive cyclical, Gamelan/1980s-era King Crimson influence, especially in pieces, such as "Atlas Novus" [*The Migration*], "Bloom" [*Carving Desert Canyons*], and "Narrow Salient" [*The Migration*]. Writers often mention you in the same breath as Between the Buried and Me and Dream Theater. What are your influences?

Letchford: I grew up listening to Yes and Stevie Ray Vaughan. Yes' songwriting was what I appreciated the most. They had "prog" parts, and "prog" song lengths, but I just loved that the songs were still songs. I then found guys like Joe Satriani and John Petrucci [Dream Theater] and it was virtuoso playing from then on out. I wanted to get my chops up to hopefully one day become a guitarist people looked up to.

WR: You've said that the band does not want a vocalist, and never really did, despite auditioning singers at one point. Can you tell me when you were thinking about bringing in a vocalist and whether or not, from your vantage point right now, STS will continue as an instrumental unit?

Letchford: We had auditioned a few guys, but it wasn't going to be Scale the Summit anymore. This was back before we even had our first demo recorded. Travis [LeVrier, guitarist] was filling in for the band Into the Moat on a tour and, after the tour, told me he was planning on joining full time. I had no interest in looking for another guitar player, so I was just going to keep it a three-piece and find a singer. I thought, then, that there was too much going on with the music to have room for a singer. I had planned on reworking the current music to make room for vocals, which would have been cool, but my heart was in it for the instrumental music. After I finished tracking our demo with the song "Omni" and I sent it to Travis, he changed his mind and came back. He liked the solo in that song. We're now too deep into our sound to throw in a vocalist. I think it would be cool to do an album with a singer in the future as a side project, but it would be finding one that I really loved that I think would fit well with my style of writing. Who knows what the future holds?

Notes

Introduction: Signs of the Aprogalypse

1. "Geoff was a good friend, but also a very real human being who was good at relating to believers and nonbelievers alike," says Peter Gee, bassist of Pendragon. "Geoff inspired me to keep going in mainstream music and to write mainstream songs with spiritual meanings about God that would appeal to everyone, or at least get people to start thinking about their own beliefs. Geoff had a strong Christian faith, was a great musician and song-writer, a great vicar, husband, and father to his children."

2. In retrospect, we can uncover Christian-like themes on Spock's Beard's records such as *V* and the concept album *Snow*, but it would take the 2003's *Testimony*, Morse's first post-Beard solo release, for the songwriter to open up about his faith, and finally record material he had been writing since the *Snow* era.

   Centered on the fictional character John Sikeston—an albino teen with magical powers—the double album is, in many ways, the pinnacle of the Spock's Beard's creative output—a cross between *Jesus Christ Superstar*, *Powder*, *The Lamb Lies Down on Broadway*, and *The Dead Zone*. "The challenge of the *Snow* album was that my heart was changing, was in this process, and I was praying more and more and feeling the spirit of God more and more," Morse told the author in 2008. "I think Jesus said, 'Out of an abundance of the heart the mouth speaks.' What was going on in my heart was coming out of my mouth, so I was writing songs like 'Wind at My Back,' 'Love Beyond Words,' 'Open Wide the Floodgates.' The challenge was to take these ele-ments and make them a Spock's Beard album. That took a couple of years to write." (Note: Morse had written the Christian-themed pop song "God Won't Give Up" as the music for *Snow* was developing. It was later released in 2005 on Morse's album of the same name.)

3. Sam Taylor: "The band now claims that 'Pleiades' was the beginning of King's X. But they never played me that song when they showed eighty or so songs to me [when I first starting managing them]. For me, 'Wonder' and 'Power of Love' [from *Out of the Silent Planet*] was the beginning."

4. "We wanted a keyboardist, but when we couldn't find anybody we fell into the four piece by default," says Ray Bennett. "It was not something we wanted to do, but we started playing gigs as a four piece and got used to it. In fact, Patrick Moraz was one of the guys who wanted to join at that point before he joined Yes. When he said that, we realized, 'We don't want a

keyboard.' Prior to this, we found a guy who was rehearsing for the [debut] album and then dropped out at the last minute. He vanished on us. Then we had a recording scheduled and Pete said I'll ask Tony to come in and do it as a session. The only other guy who was kicking around at that time was Rick Wakeman, who was doing sessions. Jon Anderson actually said to me at the time, 'You should get Rick for Flash.' I said, 'That's a good idea.' A few weeks later we found out that he had gotten Rick for Yes."

5. The back of the original Sovereign/Capitol LP release lists the song as "The White House Vale." The LP label reads, "The White Horse Vale."

Chapter 1. Clockwork Soldiers: Are Proto-Prog Rockers Clouds the True Fathers of a Musical Movement?

1. Emerson's dazzling dagger displays weren't all pure showmanship. Emerson has said while with the Nice he wanted to "hold down two notes and sustain a fifth while [playing] another organ" in the band's cover version of "America," originally from *West Side Story*. Daggers, some say Nazi daggers, allegedly given to him by then-roadie Lemmy Kilmister (later of Motörhead), were the answer. One report from Japan said that the so-called Hendrix of the Hammond even slipped a samurai sword into the organ, much to the crowd's delight.

2. The band's official name, Nero & the Gladiators, led by keyboardist Mike O'Neill, actually covered the very same "In the Hall of the Mountain King," in 1961, years before the Lancasters.

Chapter 4. Mindcrimes and Misconceptions: Concept Albums (That Are and Aren't)

1. From 2010 to 2011 the author had been working on a separate project, a book focused on concept albums. Some of the research gathered for it came in handy for this chapter of *Prog Rock FAQ*. The interview with Gregg Geller was culled from that manuscript.

2. Stanley Unwin, the South African–born cunning linguist/comedian/writer, who created his own language of gibberish and mangled words, narrates the Happiness Stan suite on *Ogden . . .* , tying together all the songs appearing on the second side. This bizarre, Lewis Carroll–like verbal-ese, a vocabulary of gobbledygook (a word Unwin had, in fact, invented), and the hallucinogen-type trip it evokes, would later be echoed by progressive rock bands, including Jethro Tull for their homage to near-death experiences (1973's *A Passion Play*), Bruford (the *Alice in Wonderland*–inspired tune "Fainting in Coils"), and various rock artists for their reinterpretation of Prokofiev's *Peter and the Wolf*, narrated by Viv Stanshall (Bonzo Dog Doo-Dah Band).

3. Gabriel's proposed, large-scale, and now mythic conceptual album *Mozo* was shelved when it was apparent that there would be no financial backers

for such an endeavor in the late 1970s. As it turns out, Gabriel had been extracting pieces from the prospective work for years, slotting them into releases such as his first three solo albums, all titled *Peter Gabriel*.

4. If we believe the report, at the height of his success as a solo artist (in the mid-1980s), Gabriel owned an isolation tank, presumably to help unclutter his mind. Lilly referred to his LSD sessions as a kind of "pupation period," similar to the metamorphosis a caterpillar experiences prior to its transformation into a butterfly. Gabriel seems to refer to the entire *Lamb* trip in a similar fashion via the appearance of "Cuckoo Cocoon" and with the closing song, "it," which employs a "cocoon" image in the second stanza.

5. The penetrating, all-seeing Shiva eyes, fixed atop a towering white pyramid protruding from a tropical forest canopy, resemble those painted on a sacred Hindu temple in Kathmandu, Nepal. Dean, an army brat, spent his early life bouncing around the exotic environs of Cyprus, Greece, and Hong Kong, China, which were represented, in one way or another, in his album cover art for *Alpha*. Reportedly it was Howe who was quite taken with the pyramid eyes, a feature conceived by Dean's brother, set designer Martyn.

Chapter 6. The Gates of Delirium: Top 20 BIG Compositions

1. The line " . . . a million bright ambassadors of morning" has been repurposed by modern progressive rock band Pure Reason Revolution for its own twelve-minute epic, "The Bright Ambassadors of Morning."

2. Cardboard boxes were used on drummer Drumbo's cymbals, behaving something like a dampening mechanism, during the recording of Captain Beefheart's *Trout Mask Replica*, produced by Zappa. In addition, Zappa was turning his one-time recording space, Studio Z, into something of a film production house, and placed cardboard cutouts around the set.

3. Anderson has said that around the time of *Going for the One*, he read a book by Calvin Miller, *The Singer*, the first installment of a cosmic trilogy. In the novel the Christ-like figure uses a harp, a lyre, to spread the good word and play his "Star-Song," a phrase Anderson uses in the lyrics of "Awaken." In addition, the word *awoke* appears within the book's opening sentence.

4. Gomelsky seemed obsessed with the idea of establishing an alternative musical business structure as well as venues for the artists he represented. Gomeslky worked in France to do just such, and later, in 1978, established the Zu club in New York City where he promoted a twelve-hour Manifestival concert for avant-garde European bands.

5. Once and future Kansas members Phil Ehart and bassist Dave Hope were part of the Kansas I lineup and the band White Clover. Ehart, Hope, and Livgren would, of course, reunite for Kansas Mach III—the incarnation of the band that achieved stardom and included vocalist Steve Walsh and guitarist Rich Williams.

Chapter 9. The Cinema Show: Prog's Celluloid Heroes

1. Roger Dean's brother and sometimes collaborator, Martyn, designed what he termed a "Personal Pod," a controlled musical environment containing an upholstered interior as well as ten-inch speakers, that was glimpsed, albeit briefly, in Stanley Kubrick's film adaptation of Anthony Burgess' nightmarish sci-fi novella *A Clockwork Orange*.

2. ELP's Keith Emerson has composed music for films such as Dario Argento's *Inferno* and 1981's *Night Hawks*, starring Sylvester Stallone, Lindsay Wagner, Billy Dee Williams, and Rutger Hauer. The stenciled lettering featured on the cover of the *Night Hawks* movie soundtrack album revealed stills of scenes of the movie printed on the inner sleeve. Emerson sang on "I'm a Man" and used the Fairlight synth for "Tramway." Although soundtrack work hasn't been Emerson's greatest achievements, the 2006 CD *At the Movies* is a great three-disc collection containing nearly seventy tracks in total from *Night Hawks*, *Inferno*, the 1984 Italian fright flick *Murderock* by the controversial "Godfather of Gore" Lucio Fulci, 1983 Japanese animation film *Harmagedon*, *Best Revenge* (featuring late Boston vocalist Brad Delp), *Godzilla: Final Wars*, and *The Church*.

Chapter 11. Crafty Hands: Happy the Man

1. "Wyatt was my stepdad's name," says Wyatt. "I don't think he ever officially adopted me, so my real name is Crawford. Frank Crawford III. I changed it, though, when I was living in Reston, Virginia, when we were doing the Arista contract, because I wanted my legal name on the record deal. I changed my name legally to Frank Wyatt. I didn't know it wasn't my real name until I was twelve years old. They didn't give me that bit of information."

2. Although, contrary to common thought, Happy the Man *didn't* take its band moniker from a Genesis single of the same title (i.e., "Seven Stones" b/w "Happy the Man"), there are plenty of links connecting HTM, Genesis, Virginia, and Fort Wayne, Indiana. For one thing, Dan Owen became a tech for Genesis after playing in HTM and Fort Wayne's Ethos. Owen also appears on 1979's *Sides* by Anthony Phillips. In addition, Cliff Fortney, an original HTM vocalist, was rumored to have been considered for the position left vacant in Genesis after Gabriel left the band. Dale Newman, also of Fort Wayne, was Mike Rutherford's guitar tech at one time (he'd tune guitars, even twelve-strings, by ear), and Mike Ponczek, also of Ethos, worked monitors for Genesis. Craig Schertz, also of Fort Wayne, was the sound-mixing engineer for Ethos and Genesis. (In case you're wondering, the phrase "happy the man" is a Biblical reference.)

3. At least one of the band members disputes this and says the band was dropped less than a year after the record was released.
4. The Canterbury Scene generated music as diverse as psychedelic pop and British jazz-rock fusion. Bands purported to be a part of the Canterbury Scene range from Soft Machine and Gong to Hatfield and the North, Caravan, Egg, Robert Wyatt, and sometimes Henry Cow, Camel, and even Bruford. Wilde Flowers, which was formed in 1964 and featured such notable characters as Kevin Ayers, Richard Sinclair, Hugh Hopper, and Wyatt, gave birth to two influential Canterbury Scene bands: Soft Machine and Caravan.

Chapter 12. Blinded by the Lite? A Look Inside Prog's Number-One Song

1. "Another Brick in the Wall—Part II" reached the top slot in February 1980. (The song became a number-one song in the U.K. in December '79.)
2. Perhaps it's no surprise that Zappa had been interested in having Rogers perform with him. Both the Earth Band and Frank (and the Mothers of Invention) admired some of the same composers, such as Igor Stravinsky and Gustav Holst. The Mothers' song "Invocation and Ritual Dance of the Young Pumpkin," from 1967's *Absolutely Free*, contains elements of Holst's "Jupiter" from *The Planets* suite. In addition, in "Drowning Witch," from 1982's *Ship Arriving Too Late to Save a Drowning Witch*, Zappa quotes the once-controversial rhythmic stabs so central to Stravinsky's pagan-ritual-sacrifice-inspired *The Rite of Spring*. The propulsive thrusts begin at approximately 1:45 as the words "ritual sacrifice" are sung. In an interesting twist, canned guffaws, generated by a laughing box, appearing at approximately 2:22, closely resemble those heard at the conclusion of King Crimson's "Easy Money" from 1973's *Larks' Tongues in Aspic*. The maniacal cackling is sped up and repeated in the album's closer, "Larks' Tongues in Aspic II," a song that also contains what may be a direct quote from Stravinsky's *The Rite of Spring*. (Years later Crimson added two sequels to the existing "Larks'" compositions, including ". . . Part III," found on the 1984 studio album *Three of a Perfect Pair*, and ". . . Part IV," which appears on the three-CD live compilation *Heavy ConstruKction*, the studio album *The ConstruKction of Light*, both released in the year 2000, and 2003's *Happy With What You Have to Be Happy With*.)
3. The keyboardist/bandleader Manfred Mann was fond of putting instrumental excursions on his pop-prog Earth Band outings, including tracks such as "Cloudy Eyes" from *Messin'*, "Wind" and "Sad Joy," which contains some vocalizations, from *Glorified Magnified*, and "Sky High" from 1974's *The Good Earth*.

Chapter 13. Prog Gets Punk'd: What Caused the Decline of the Genre?

1. It seems to have been reported in a couple slightly different ways: one is that Henry Cow broke the contract with Virgin and secondly, and alternatively, that the band's contract was up and wasn't renewed.

   "[Virgin] ignored us, except to make [*In Praise of Learning*] after *Desperate Straights* [with German avant-garde band Slapp Happy], as specified in their contract," says Art Bears/Henry Cow drummer Chris Cutler.
2. *Rolling Stone* magazine, June 14, 2007, page 74.
3. How and why the musical genre called progressive rock originated could be the subject of an entire book, alone. Briefly: Initially, psychedelic rock, prog rock's immediate precursor, caused some mild confusion on the part of established record labels that were unsure of how to market this new, underground sound. This "turbulence" in the music industry, as author Edward Macan noted in his book *Rocking the Classics: English Progressive Rock and the Counterculture*, was one force that helped to till the fertile artistic and commercial ground in which progressive rock would flourish. (Pirate radio in the U.K. and the AOR format in the U.S. were other contributing factors.) In increasing numbers, the listening masses were looking for popular art with credibility and integrity. In addition, prog-rock artists' "anything goes as long as it works" mentality mirrored a broader acceptance of free love and experimentation with illicit substances and non-Western spirituality found within the wider social context of the late 1960s and 1970s.

Chapter 15. Yes, an Implosion? The Behind-the-Scenes Drama of a Rock Powerhouse

1. Rick Wakeman once explained that he was waiting for UFOs to reveal themselves to the world and that the summer of 1977 would be the year that extraterrestrial life made contact with Earthlings. This image, of a solitary figure waiting for a UFO, in the middle of the night, is straight out of a song called "Arriving UFO" that would appear on *Tormato*. It was Anderson who said that Rick sits on mountains in Switzerland, waiting for alien contact. Rick warned, however, that we might not be met with friendly little green men, à la the then-recently released movie *Close Encounters of the Third Kind*, but something akin to a *War of the Worlds* scenario. No word, as of this writing, on whether aliens actually *did* touch down on the mountains of Switzerland . . . or anywhere else for that matter. In addition, Glass Hammer's independently produced 2000 studio record, *Chronometree*, was allegedly about a friend of the band, named Tom, who thought he heard voices of aliens communicating with him through Yes' *Close to the Edge*. "Tom," like Wakeman, is lured into waiting for alien contact.

2. "Fly from Here" was performed live, but not included on Yes' 1980 studio album, *Drama*. The song would resurface, of course, some thirty years later on Yes' 2011 album of the same title, produced by Horn and featuring Downes on keys. It also appears on the 2005 boxed set *The Word Is Live*.

Chapter 17. Shock to the System: Henry Cow and Rock in Opposition

1. Magma has appeared at these so-called reunion festivals, but they are not generally considered part of the movement, but a separate subgenre—or genre—altogether, having founded what's considered Zeuhl.
2. Conventional wisdom says that Henry Cow took their name from composer Henry Cowell, but this theory has not always been supported by all members.
3. Debate has raged as to whether material appearing on Wyatt's 1974 prog-pop solo record, *Rock Bottom*, was inspired by his fall from a third-story window, paralyzing him for life. Wyatt, himself, has said that most of the music was already written before the accident.

Chapter 20. Any Colour You Like: Tull, Eddie Jobson, and the Mysterious *Pink Album*

1. In the wake of the 1970s Tull lineup splintering, former Tull keyboardist John Evan and David Palmer formed the band Tallis to develop their classical-rock ideas. Years later, Palmer would undergo a gender change operation and change her name to Dee. "When I was born I had to have surgical procedures, because I had 'indeterminate genitalia,'" Palmer said to the author. "To make such a change, as I have, you can't do it unless it's something coming wholly [from] inside of you. I'm comfortable in my own skin and still beside me is David Palmer, you know?"
2. Tull was certainly changing its image. Kevin Sutter, former senior director of rock and alternative album promotions at Chrysalis, remembers the night Tull won the Grammy. "Between Ian and I, we never thought he should have been nominated for a heavy metal Grammy," says Sutter. "When Lita Ford announced that Tull had won, and Metallica didn't, everyone thought the fix was in. It wasn't. All the people voting were showing their affection for Jethro Tull. I will never forget watching the Grammys the night they announced that Jethro Tull had won. I jumped up and I called Ian [Anderson] at home. It was probably two or three in the morning [in the U.K.] and [Ian's] first words to me were, 'Were you there?' I said, 'No, Ian. [Chrysalis] didn't want me to go, because they didn't think you were going to win.' He was very upset, because, to his credit, he saw the shitstorm that was going to happen as a result of winning the award."

Chapter 23. ELP's *Black Moon* Rising: Romantic Warriors in Enemy Territory

1. Emerson's demos were originally released on the Kevin Gilbert–produced 1995 compilation album *Changing States*, through Griffin. It appeared, again, in 2003 on Amp Records and was reissued, once more, in 2014 via Esoteric Recordings.

Chapter 26. It's Worth Repeating: Minimalism, Steve Reich, and Radiohead

1. Eno was also heavily influenced by English composer Gavin Bryars' 1971 loop-based piece "Jesus' Blood Never Failed Me Yet." Organized around a spiritual sung by an unidentified homeless man, it caught Eno's ear, and the future ambient sound pioneer signed Bryars to his Obscure label. Eno released a recording of the piece, along with "The Sinking of the Titanic" on the 1975 album *The Sinking of the Titanic*.
2. Of course, Frippertronics doesn't just refer to a looping process. Frippertronics is only one part of a larger philosophy that sought to describe a human being's interface with a machine. Fripp, during his sabbatical in the mid-1970s, wanted to discern how he could be a musician and a human being simultaneously. His "Applied Frippertronics" is Fripp's alternative to the use of synthesizer and traditional orchestration, as heard on Fripp's 1979 solo album, *Exposure*.

Selected Bibliography

Books

Ammer, Christine. *The HarperCollins Dictionary of Music.* Second Edition. New York: Harper Perennial, 1987.

Ashe, Geoffrey. *The Glastonbury Tor Maze.* Glastonbury, Somerset, England: Gothic Image Publications, 2001.

Ashe, Geoffrey, Leslie Alcock, C. A. Ralegh Radford, and Philip Rahtz. *The Quest for Arthur's Britain.* Reprint. Chicago: Academy Chicago Publishers, 1987.

Briggs, John. *Fractals: The Patterns of Chaos: Discovering a New Aesthetic of Art, Science, and Nature.* New York: Touchstone/Simon & Schuster, 1992.

Brockett, Oscar G. *History of the Theatre.* Third Edition. Boston: Allyn and Bacon, 1977.

Bruford, Bill. *When in Doubt, Roll!: Transcriptions of Bruford's Greatest Performances, with Bill's Personal Commentary and Suggested Exercises.* Transcriptions by Michael Bettine. Cedar Grove, NJ: Modern Drummer Publications, 1988.

Classical Music. John Burrows (ed.) with Charles Wiffen. New York: Metro Books/Sterling Publishing, 2010.

De Givry, Grillot. *Witchcraft, Magic & Alchemy.* Translated by J. Courtenay Locke. New York: Dover, 1971.

De Ville, Nick. *Album: Classic Sleeve Design.* London: Octopus Publishing, 2005.

Dean, Roger. *Views.* Petaluma, CA: Pomegranate Artbooks, 1975.

Doniger, Wendy. *The Hindus: An Alternative History.* New York: Penguin Books, 2009.

Drum Techniques of Rush. Transcriptions by Bill Wheeler. Secaucus, NJ: Warner Bros. Publications/Core Music Publishing, 1985.

Gallant, David. *Asia: Heat of the Moment.* New York: Asia Music Limited/Original Asia, 2007.

Gallo, Armando. *Genesis: I Know What I Like.* London: Omnibus Press, 1987.

Genesis Anthology. New York: Warner Bros. Publications, unknown date.

Goulding, Phil G. *Classical Music: The 50 Greatest Composers and Their 1,000 Greatest Works.* New York: Fawcett Books, 1992.

Hammill, Peter. *Killers, Angels, Refugees.* London: Charisma Books, 1974

Hedges, Dan. *Yes: The Authorized Biography.* London: Sidgwick & Jackson, 1981.

Hofstadter, Douglas R. *Gödel, Escher, Bach: An Eternal Golden Braid.* New York: Basic Books/Perseus Books, 1999.

Holm-Hudson, Kevin. *Genesis and The Lamb Lies Down on Broadway.* Surrey, England: Ashgate Publishing, 2008.

Jung, Carl G. (ed.). *Man and His Symbols*. New York: Dell, 17th printing, 1978.

Jung, Carl G. *Memories, Dreams, Reflections*. Revised Edition, recorded and edited by Aniela Jaffé and translated by Richard and Clara Winston. New York: Vintage Books/Random House, 1989.

Kirkpatrick, Rob. *Magic in the Night: The Words and Music of Bruce Springsteen*. New York: St. Martin's Griffin, 2009.

Lilly, John C., M.D. *Center of the Cyclone: Looking into Inner Space*. Berkeley, CA: Ronin Publishing, 1972.

Livgren, Kerry and Kenneth Boa. *Seeds of Change: The Spiritual Quest of Kerry Livgren*. Milton Keynes, England: Word Publishing, 1991.

MacDonald, George. *Lilith*. New York: Ballantine Books, second printing, 1973.

Manning, Toby. *The Rough Guide to Pink Floyd*. London: Penguin Books, 2006.

Matthews, W. H. *Mazes & Labyrinths: Their History & Development*. New York: Dover, 1970.

Merriam-Webster's Collegiate Dictionary, Tenth Edition. Edited by Frederick C. Mish. Springfield, MA: Merriam-Webster, 1993.

Moore, Allan. *Aqualung*. New York: Continuum, 2004.

Morse, Tim. *Yesstories: Yes in Their Own Words*. New York: St. Martin's Griffin, 1996.

Nef, Karl. *An Outline of the History of Music*. Third printing, translated by Carl F. Pfatteicher. New York: Columbia University Press, 1939.

Nietzsche, Friedrich. *Thus Spoke Zarathustra*. Translation by Clancy Martin. New York: Barnes & Noble Classics, 2005.

Ortenberg, Veronica. *In Search of the Holy Grail*. London: Hambledon Continuum, 2007.

Rees, David. *Minstrels in the Gallery: A History of Jethro Tull*. Wembley, Middlesex, England: Firefly Publishing, 1998.

Russell, Ken. *A British Picture: An Autobiography*. London: Southbank Publishing, 2008 (revised).

Sandbrook, Dominic. *State of Emergency: The Way We Were: Britain, 1970–1974*. London: Penguin Books, 2010.

The Song of Roland. Mineola, NY: Dover, 2002.

Stanley Alder, Vera. *The Initiation of the World*. York Beach, ME: Samuel Weiser, 2000.

Tolinski, Brad (ed.). *Guitar World Presents: Van Halen: 40 Years of the Great American Rock Band*. NewBay Media/Time Inc., 2012.

Warwick, Neil, Jon Kutner, and Tony Brown. *The Complete Book of the British Charts*. Third Edition. London: Omnibus Press, 2004.

Whitburn, Joel. *The Billboard Book of Top 40 Hits*. New York: Billboard Books, 1989.

Wilcken, Hugo. *Low*. New York: Continuum, 2005.

Yogananda, Paramahansa. *Autobiography of a Yogi*. Los Angeles: Self-Realization Fellowship, 2002.

Magazines

Barnes, Ken. "Two from U.K.: Shaky and Fair." Rolling Stone, April 25, 1974.

Birnbaum, Larry. "Record Reviews: Billy Cobham: *Magic.*" *Downbeat*, December 1, 1977.

Bloom, Michael. "Records: Genesis: . . . *And Then There Were Three.*" *Crawdaddy!*, July 1978.

Cohen, Scott. "The *Circus* Magazine Interview: Peter Gabriel Ponders Cartoons, Costumes and the Myths of Genesis." *Circus*, December 1974.

Cohen, Scott. "Uriah Heep's John Wetton: From Mental to Metal." *Circus Raves*, November 1975.

Costa, Jean-Charles. "Reviews: Jethro Tull: *Minstrel in the Gallery.*" *Rolling Stone*, November 6, 1975.

Crescenti, Peter. "Guitar Synthesizer: $7,000 Is Cheap." *Circus*, September 1975.

Crescenti, Peter. "Nektar, Synergy Recycle Together." *Circus*, July 6, 1976.

Crescenti, Peter. "The Sunhillow Saga: Jon Anderson Delivers Fourth Yes Solo Album." *Circus*, October 26, 1976.

Crescenti, Peter. "Uriah Heep Gets a Buzz." *Circus*, July 6, 1976.

Crowe, Cameron. "Journey to the Center of the Stage." *Rolling Stone*, January 30, 1975.

Crowe, Cameron. "Yes Soars Back to Earth with 'Tales from the Topographic Ocean.'" *Circus*, March 1974.

Dalton, John. "Steve Hackett." *Guitar: The Magazine for All Guitarists*, August 1979.

Demorest, Steve. "Ian Anderson's Pearls of Wisdom." *Circus*, April 14, 1977.

"ELP Gets 5th Platinum Disk." *Cash Box*, September 7, 1974.

Farber, Jim. "The Emerson, Lake and Palmer Tapes, Part 3: Keith Emerson." *Circus*, September 8, 1977.

Farber, Jim. "Yes Is Going for the Big One: Wakeman Rejoins Former Partners for Mammoth US Tour." *Circus*, September 8, 1977.

Farnam, Michael. "Letters: From Genesis to Veneration." *Crawdaddy!*, September 1978.

Fricke, David. "Peter Gabriel: The Ethnic Shocks the Electronic." *Musician*, January 1983.

Frith, Simon. "Ian Anderson: Portrait of the Artist as a Young Squire." *Creem*, June 1978.

Goldstein, Toby. "From Genesis to Revolution: Steve Hackett Tells All." *Creem*, July 1978.

Gross, Michael. "Genesis: A Dose of the Surreal." *Circus*, February 1974.

Hull, Robert. "Jethro Tull: *Heavy Horses.*" *Creem*, July 1978.

Hull, Robert. "Rick Wakeman: *Criminal Record.*" *Creem*, March 1978.

Hutchinson, John. "Peter Gabriel: From Brideshead to Shrunken Heads." *Musician*, July 1986.

"International: The Battle of Britain, 1974." *Newsweek*, February 11, 1974.

Johnson, Rick. "Records: Genesis: . . . *And Then There Were Three.*" *Creem*, July 1978.

Kelleher, Ed. "Record Reviews: Emerson, Lake & Palmer: *Pictures at an Exhibition.*" *Circus*, April 1972.

Kenton, Gary. "Robert Fripp: *Exposure.*" *Creem*, September 1979.

Marshall, Wolf. "Allan Holdsworth: The Early Years." *Guitar for the Practicing Musician*, March 1989.

Miller, Jim. "Reviews: Jethro Tull: *War Child.*" *Rolling Stone*, December 19, 1974.

Miller, William F. "Phil Collins: Drummer to the Core!" *Modern Drummer*, March 1997.

Nelson, Paul. "Pinups: Why the Ramones Are Great (I Think)." *Circus*, July 6, 1976.

Nicolson, Kris. "Rock Down to Earth: The Trend Is to Cleaner, Tighter, More Musical Stage Shows." *Circus*, May 26, 1977.

O'Connor, Jim. "ELP Split for Solo Exploits." *Circus*, November 1974.

Parker, Kathryn. "Starcastle: The Band That Plays Together." *Circus*, May 26, 1977.

Pilgrims: Peter Hammill and VDGG Magazine #5, Sheffield, England, 1989.

Pond, Steve. "Peter Gabriel Hits the Big Time." *Rolling Stone*, January 29, 1987.

Proops, Tony. "Anderson's Fairy Tales: The Rocker Who Wouldn't Roll with the Times." *Circus*, August 10, 1976.

Robbins, Ira. "The New Wave Washes Out." *Trouser Press*, October 1977.

"Rock 'n' Roll News." *Creem*, July 1978.

Rose, Frank. "Rick Wakeman—The King of the Klassics Jousts with 'King Arthur.'" *Circus*, July 1975.

Rosen, Steve. "From England's Genesis, Here's Steve Hackett." *Guitar Player*, October 1976.

Saccone, Teri. "Manu Katche." *Modern Drummer*, August 1991.

Schact, Janis. "Emerson, Lake and Palmer: The Dagger Does More Than You Think." *Circus*, March 1972.

Silverton, Pete. "The Stranglers: Do the Pose." *Trouser Press*, October 1977.

Smith-Park, Paul. "Emerson Hopes to Break Banco." *Circus*, January 1973.

Swenson, John. Longplayers: "Yes: *Tormato*" record review. *Circus*, November 7, 1978.

Tan, Anne, and Howard Bloom. "Yes: Weaving the Fragile Web." *Circus*, March 1972.

"Trower and Fripp to Tango?" *Circus*, November 1974.

Walls, Richard C. "Records: Stanley Clarke: School Days." *Creem*, December 1976.

Walls, Richard C. "Review: Tony Williams: *The Joy of Flying* (Columbia Records)." *Creem*, September 1979.

Walters, Charley. "USA: King Crimson." *Rolling Stone*, July 31, 1975.

Welch, Chris. "Jethro Tull: *A Passion Play.* Tull: Enough Is Enough." *Melody Maker*, July 21, 1973.

Young, Charles M. "Emerson, Lake & Palmer Go for Broke." *Rolling Stone*, July 14, 1977.

Zakarin, Marc. "Rock Imports Crusade." *Rock Scene*, July 1976.

Newspapers

Alterman, Loraine. "Jethro Tull—Or Jethro Dull?" New York Times, August 19, 1973.

Associated Press. "Frank Zappa, 52, Wrote Musical Satire." *Albany Times Union*, December 6, 1993.

Bird, Peter. "Obituary: Don Allum." *Independent* (UK), December 5, 1992.

Blair, W. Granger. "Britain to Outlaw Pirate Radio Stations." *New York Times*, July 29, 1966.

Boehm, Mike. "Pop Beat: A Prog-Rock Renaissance?" *Los Angeles Times*, November 3, 1994.

Christgau, Robert. "Among Comebacks None Beat Nash's for Weirdness." *Newsday*, November 26, 1972.

Christgau, Robert. "No, No, No, No, No, No." *Newsday*, February 15, 1974.

Christgau, Robert. "Records: Waxing Prosaic." *Newsday*, August 4, 1972.

Dove, Ian. "Genesis of Britain Daring at Academy." *New York Times*, December 8, 1974.

Emerson, Ken. "Rock: U.K., British Band." *New York Times*, March 26, 1979.

Feron, James. "British Pirate Radio Stations Thrive." *New York Times*, January 3, 1965.

Ferretti, Fred. "FM Radio Grows Up to Have Its Own Convention." *New York Times*, April 2, 1970.

Fielder, Hugh. "Genesis: Track by Track." *Sounds*, April 1, 1978.

Flood, Mike. "Softs Ban in Italy." *Sounds*, May 31, 1975.

Gent, George. "Jimi Hendrix, Rock Star, Is Dead in London at 27." *New York Times*, September 19, 1970.

Goldstein, Richard. "Freedom Can Be Costly." *New York Times*, February 4, 1968.

Gould, Jack. "Radio: British Commercial Broadcasters Are at Sea." *New York Times*, March 25, 1966.

Harrington, Richard. "One Giant Step for Pink Floyd; 20 Years Ago, 'Dark Side of the Moon' Began Its Cosmic Trip." *Washington Post*, April 28, 1993.

Heckman, Don. "Melodrama Marks Rock by Emerson, Lake & Palmer." *New York Times*, November 27, 1971.

Holden, Stephen. "Recent Releases of Video Cassettes: Asia in Asia." *New York Times*. July 15, 1984.

Holden, Stephen. "Rock: Asia, a 'Supergroup,' Mixing Art and Hard Rock Styles." *New York Times*, May 6, 1982.

Jahn, Mike. "British Band Makes Debut at Fillmore." *New York Times*, May 2, 1971.

Jenkins, Mark. "Two-Thirds ELP, Two-Thirds Sad: 3." *Washington Post*, April 8, 1988.

"John Sebastian, Jethro Tull, at Fillmore East." *New Amsterdam News*, May 23, 1970.

"Last Pirate Radio Continues to Defy New British Law." *New York Times*, August 17, 1967.

"Lizard: King Crimson." *Evening Standard*, December 12, 1970.

Marsh, Dave. "Jethro's Snob-Rock." *Newsday*, August 29, 1973.

Marsh, Dave. "Music: Mushy Blues." *New York Times*, October 29, 1973.

Mayer, Ira. "From Kongos to ELP." *New York Times*, Feb. 20, 1972.

McGregor, Craig. "Zapparap on the Zappaplan." *New York Times*, November 8, 1970.

O'Hearn, Bradford. "The Coming of the Coliseum." *Newsday*, February 10, 1972.

Palmer, Robert. "Emerson, Lake and Palmer Go Classical." *New York Times*, July 8, 1977.

Peacock, Steve. "Robert Wyatt Backs Away from a 'Strange Alien World.'" *Sounds*, May 31, 1975.

Roberts, John Storm. "Progressive Rock's Classic Synthesizers." *Newsday*, July 3, 1977.

Robins, Wayne. "English Rock Invades Anew." *Newsday*, June 21, 1977.

Rockwell, John. "Emerson, Lake and Palmer + 60 = Rock." *New York Times*, July 9, 1977.

Rockwell, John. "Pitching Tent in 2 Culture Camps." *New York Times*, February 21, 1975.

Rockwell, John. "Renaissance and Sea Level Give a Well-Blended Concert of Rock." *New York Times*, February 21, 1977.

Rockwell, John. "The Sex Pistols—A Fired-Up Rock Band." *New York Times*, August 7, 1977.

Smith, David Hugh. "Record Guide: Asia." *Christian Science Monitor*, December 9, 1982.

Sullivan, Jim. "Kansas Keeps to Familiar Turf; Kansas in Concert with Molly Hatchet at Boston Garden Monday Night." *Boston Globe*, November 11, 1980.

Liner Notes

Gottlieb, Doug & Glenn. "That '70s Show: Madison Square Garden, 1978." Yes: *The Word Is Live* (Rhino/Elektra/Atco, 2005, R2 78234).

Hensley, Ken. Uriah Heep: *Look at Yourself* (Mercury Records/PolyGram, 1971, 814 180-2).

Reich, Steve. *Drumming* (Elektra/Nonesuch CD, 1987, 9 79170-3).

DVDs and Videos

El Topo, directed by Alejandro Jodorowsky (1970). VHS video date unknown.

Emerson, Lake & Palmer: Pictures at an Exhibition, Collectors Edition (DVD & CD). D2 Vision, Limited/Favourite TV, 2001.

Emerson, Lake & Palmer: Welcome Back. Beckmann Communications/Livezone. Chatsworth, CA: MMI Image Entertainment, 1992.

Yessongs: The 1973 Concert Video of the Original Yes (VHS). VidAmerica, 1984.

Other Documents and Sources

Anderson Bruford Wakeman Howe official tour program, 1989.
Asia tour program, 1983.
BBC Radio, World Service: "The Jethro Tull Story; Part 3: *Thick as a Brick* to *Passion Play*" (March 1979).
Emerson, Lake & Palmer tour program, 1977.
Jethro Tull tour program, 1974.
Yes North American tour program, 1984.

Websites and Web Pages

Bernstein, Leonard. "Young People's Concert: Berlioz Takes a Trip." Script of original broadcast from May 25, 1969. Leonard Bernstein Office official website. www.leonardbernstein.com/ypc_script_berlioz_takes_a_trip.htm
Mayo Clinic. "Dissociative Disorders." March 6, 2014. Mayo Clinic website. www.mayoclinic.org/diseases-conditions/dissociative-disorders/basics/definition/con-20031012
The Olivier Messiaen Page. www.oliviermessiaen.org/messiaen2index.htm
Reich, Steve. Composer's Notes on *Music for 18 Musicians*. Boosey & Hawkes website. www.boosey.com/pages/cr/catalogue/cat_detail.asp?musicid=548
"Rick Wakeman's *Criminal Record*." Rick Wakeman's Place, Discography. www.rwcc.com/title_detail.asp?int_titleID=7
Sex Pistols Official website. www.sexpistolsofficial.com
Sounes, Howard. "She'd had 20 lovers in two years. Now Linda was out to snare Paul McCartney—no matter who stood in her way." *Mail Online*, August 16, 2010. www.dailymail.co.uk/tvshowbiz/article-1303363/Paul-McCartneys-turbulent-love-life-Linda-snare-Beatle–matter-stood-way.html
"The Story Behind the Song: Lili Marlene." *Telegraph*, October 11, 2008. www.telegraph.co.uk/culture/music/3561946/The-story-behind-the-song-Lili-Marlene.html
The Tolkien Music List. www.tolkien-music.com
Wright, Jeb. "Interview: Rick Wakeman of Yes." Classic Rock Revisited, May 2002. web.archive.org/web/20041119185049/http://www.classicrockrevisited.com/interviews02/Rick+Wakeman.htm

Index

THE FAQ SERIES

Armageddon Films FAQ
by Dale Sherman
Applause Books
978-1-61713-119-6............ $24.99

Lucille Ball FAQ
*by James Sheridan
and Barry Monush*
Applause Books
978-1-61774-082-4...........$19.99

The Beach Boys FAQ
by Jon Stebbins
Backbeat Books
978-0-87930-987-9.......$22.99

Black Sabbath FAQ
by Martin Popoff
Backbeat Books
978-0-87930-957-2 ....$19.99

Johnny Cash FAQ
by C. Eric Banister
Backbeat Books
978-1-4803-8540-5 ..... $24.99

Eric Clapton FAQ
by David Bowling
Backbeat Books
978-1-61713-454-8...........$22.99

Doctor Who FAQ
by Dave Thompson
Applause Books
978-1-55783-854-4........$22.99

The Doors FAQ
by Rich Weidman
Backbeat Books
978-1-61713-017-5............ $24.99

Fab Four FAQ
*by Stuart Shea and
Robert Rodriguez*
Hal Leonard Books
978-1-4234-2138-2...........$19.99

Fab Four FAQ 2.0
by Robert Rodriguez
Hal Leonard Books
978-0-87930-968-8.......$19.99

Film Noir FAQ
by David J. Hogan
Applause Books
978-1-55783-855-1...........$22.99

The Grateful Dead FAQ
by Tony Sclafani
Backbeat Books
978-1-61713-086-1........... $24.99

Jimi Hendrix FAQ
by Gary J. Jucha
Backbeat Books
978-1-61713-095-3...........$22.99

Horror Films FAQ
by John Kenneth Muir
Applause Books
978-1-55783-950-3........$22.99

James Bond FAQ
by Tom DeMichael
Applause Books
978-1-55783-856-8........$22.99

Stephen King Films FAQ
by Scott Von Doviak
Applause Books
978-1-4803-5551-4 .... $24.99

KISS FAQ
by Dale Sherman
Backbeat Books
978-1-61713-091-5............$22.99

Led Zeppelin FAQ
by George Case
Backbeat Books
978-1-61713-025-0............$19.99

Modern Sci-Fi Films FAQ
by Tom DeMichael
Applause Books
978-1-4803-5061-8........ $24.99

Nirvana FAQ
by John D. Luerssen
Backbeat Books
978-1-61713-450-0 .... $24.99

Pink Floyd FAQ
by Stuart Shea
Backbeat Books
978-0-87930-950-3 ....$19.99

Elvis Films FAQ
by Paul Simpson
Applause Books
978-1-55783-858-2......... $24.99

Elvis Music FAQ
by Mike Eder
Backbeat Books
978-1-61713-049-6 .... $24.99

Prog Rock FAQ
by Will Romano
Backbeat Books
978-1-61713-587-3 .... $24.99

Rush FAQ
by Max Mobley
Backbeat Books
978-1-61713-451-7 .... $24.99

Saturday Night Live FAQ
by Stephen Tropiano
Applause Books
978-1-55783-951-0 .... $24.99

Sherlock Holmes FAQ
by Dave Thompson
Applause Books
978-1-4803-3149-5 .... $24.99

South Park FAQ
by Dave Thompson
Applause Books
978-1-4803-5064-9 ...... $24.99

Bruce Springsteen FAQ
by John D. Luerssen
Backbeat Books
978-1-61713-093-9...........$22.99

Star Trek FAQ
(Unofficial and Unauthorized)
by Mark Clark
Applause Books
978-1-55783-792-9...........$19.99

Star Trek FAQ 2.0
(Unofficial and Unauthorized)
by Mark Clark
Applause Books
978-1-55783-793-6...........$22.99

Three Stooges FAQ
by David J. Hogan
Applause Books
978-1-55783-788-2...........$22.99

U2 FAQ
by John D. Luerssen
Backbeat Books
978-0-87930-997-8........$19.99

The Who FAQ
by Mike Segretto
Backbeat Books
978-1-4803-6103-4........ $24.99

The Wizard of Oz FAQ
by David J. Hogan
Applause Books
978-1-4803-5062-5....... $24.99

Neil Young FAQ
by Glen Boyd
Backbeat Books
978-1-61713-037-3.............$19.99

Prices, contents, and availability
subject to change without notice.

HAL•LEONARD®
PERFORMING ARTS
PUBLISHING GROUP

FAQ.halleonardbooks.com